Lingering Shadows

A C. G. JUNG FOUNDATION BOOK

The C. G. Jung Foundation for Analytical Psychology is dedicated to helping men and women grow in conscious awareness of the psychological realities in themselves and society, find healing and meaning in their lives and greater depth in their relationships, and live in response to their discovered sense of purpose. It welcomes the public to attend its lectures, seminars, films, symposia, and workshops and offers a wide selection of books for sale through its bookstore. The Foundation also publishes *Quadrant,* a semiannual journal, and books on Analytical Psychology and related subjects. For information about Foundation programs or membership, please write to the C. G. Jung Foundation, 28 East 39th Street, New York, NY 10016.

LINGERING SHADOWS

Jungians, Freudians, and Anti-Semitism

Edited by
Aryeh Maidenbaum
and Stephen A. Martin

SHAMBHALA
Boston & London
1991

Shambhala Publications, Inc.
Horticultural Hall
300 Massachusetts Avenue
Boston, Massachusetts 02115

Shambhala Publications, Inc.
Random Century House
20 Vauxhall Bridge Road
London SW1V 2SA

9 8 7 6 5 4 3 2 1

First Edition

Printed in the United States of America on acid-free paper
Designed by Diane Levy
Distributed in the United States by Random House, Inc.,
in Canada by Random House of Canada Ltd., and
in the United Kingdom by the Random Century Group

Library of Congress Cataloging-in-Publication Data

Lingering shadows: Jungians, Freudians, and anti-semitism / edited by
   Aryeh Maidenbaum and Stephen A. Martin.—1st ed.
      p.   cm.
   "A C. G. Jung Foundation book."
   Includes bibliographical references.
   ISBN 0-87773-600-6 (alk. paper)
      1. Jung, C. G. (Carl Gustav), 1875–1961—Views on Jews.
   2. Judaism and psychoanalysis—History   3. Antisemitism—
   History—20th Century.   4. Psychoanalysis—History.
   I. Maidenbaum, Aryeh.   II. Martin, Stephen A., 1952–   .
   I. BF109.J8L56   1991   90-53383
   150.19′54—dc20   CIP

Contents

Part Three • WORKSHOP ON JUNG
AND ANTI-SEMITISM
Eleventh International Congress of the IAAP
(Paris, 1989)

Contents

Preface

The seed for this book was planted in Jerusalem, germinated in Zurich, and blossomed in New York. Some fifteen years ago, while applying for a postdoctoral grant from the Hebrew University to study at the C. G. Jung Institute in Switzerland, I was unexpectedly confronted with what I have now come to understand is the shadowy specter of Jung's "Jewish connection." Basically, I was told that Jung was an anti-Semite at best and in fact quite possibly a Nazi sympathizer if not an active party member.

At the time, I was in analysis with Rivkah Schaerf Kluger, who then lived in Haifa, Israel. Dr. Kluger, a widely respected scholar and author, had been a student and analysand of Jung himself. Through her testimony, and the corroboration of other professors at the Hebrew University who had known Jung, I was able to rebut these accusations and convince both myself and university officials that the charges were unjust. I was ultimately granted the award and spent the next three years studying at the C. G. Jung Institute of Zurich.

Nevertheless, during my years of study and training, I began reading some of Jung's statements and became increasingly uncomfortable with my own ignorance of the topic. Moreover, Jung's public and private comments left me feeling that there was more to this topic than meets the eye. Realizing that the help I'd received personally from my Jungian analysis with Rivkah, combined with a passionate desire to train as a Jungian analyst, had propelled me to plow ahead as if caught in an archetypal force, I resolved to continue researching this topic until I felt satisfied I had all the facts straight. A fellow student and friend, Stephen Martin, shared my concern and curiosity, and we spent many an hour in Zurich discussing various aspects of Jung's work, his personal life history, and his attitudes toward and involvements with Jews during the 1930s and later. Helpful to us was the contact we had with individuals who had known Jung personally as well as the published and archival material available in Zurich.

Over the course of time, both Dr. Martin and I completed our studies, returned to the United States, established analytical practices, and became actively involved at the C. G. Jung Foundation of New York. What struck us both was that the subject of Jung and anti-Semitism kept cropping up over and over. We found, for example, that many of our non-Jungian professional colleagues who knew little or nothing about Jung and his work cited as a reason (thereby dismissing his unique contributions) the charge that he was a Nazi or an anti-Semite. Among the public at large, especially the academic world, many found their genuine interest in Jung's psychology and ideas threatened by accusations revolving around Jung's alleged anti-Semitism.

Over the years, Dr. Martin and I came to realize that while rebuttals have been written by Jungians themselves addressing this issue, there has been no systematic effort to examine it in an objective, scholarly, and balanced manner. The literature on this topic ranges from idolatry to witch hunting, from those who felt Jung could do no wrong to others who blatantly condemned him without familiarizing themselves with the factual material.

Dr. Martin and I spent several years organizing and gathering material for a conference that was held in the spring of 1989 on this topic. Our intent was to examine as much of the relevant data as was available and invite serious academicians as well as Jungian and non-Jungian analysts to objectively discuss the issue and its implications. The ultimate aim was to publish this resource book, encompassing all of Jung's pertinent statements on the topic and including several of the earlier pieces and the best of the conference material. We are pleased and gratified, both personally and on behalf of the conference sponsors, that we were able to accomplish this task. Moreover, as an added and unexpected bonus, we are most heartened that as a result of the interest generated by the

New York conference, the International Association for Analytical Psychology added a special workshop on this topic at its August 1989 conference in Paris. Presentations at that workshop are included in this volume. In addition, a bibliographical essay has been contributed by Jay Sherry to help direct serious students of the topic to all significant published material on this issue.

The New York conference, of which this book is a direct outgrowth, was cosponsored by the New School for Social Research, the Union of American Hebrew Congregations, the Post-Graduate Center for Mental Health, and the C. G. Jung Foundation for Analytical Psychology of New York. I believe it is to the credit of all these organizations that the conference was held and conducted on a highly professional, academically sound level. The Board of the Jung Foundation, especially, is to be commended for its courage in facing this provocative question head on. The Board members were not only confident in Jung's unquestionably close personal connections with many of his leading Jewish students, but were also truly understanding that it was time for the important message inherent in Jung's psychology and ideas to stop being obscured by the controversy surrounding his life history. In this regard, we ourselves are convinced that Jung would have been the first to acknowledge that the message is more important than the messenger.

In examining the subject of both Jung's psychology and his life, the title *Lingering Shadows* seemed to leap out at us. There is apparently an inherently shadowy, perhaps unconscious area where many Jungians and Freudians meet in resisting further exploration of this topic. In Jungian terms we might say that the collective shadow of Jung's followers lay in zealously protecting the man and his public image for fear of uncovering some faults. Alternatively, it has become clear to us over the years that to this day the Freudian shadow, if you will, consists in keeping the emphasis on Jung the man while just as zealously resisting the importance of his psychology and ideas. Thus, unfortunately, in academic and analytical institutions around the country, it is remarkable how little attention is given to Jung's contributions to the field of depth psychology. Literally thousands of Ph.D.'s in psychology, M.S.W.'s, psychiatrists, and others in the helping professions receive their degrees each year with little or no knowledge of Jung's psychology and ideas.

It is Dr. Martin's and my hope that with the publication of *Lingering Shadows*, the public at large—lay and professional—will come to understand that Jung's approach to the psyche is the real underlying, neglected issue. That Jung as a man had his strengths and weaknesses, his light and shadow, is a fact he himself would have been the first to admit. Jung often pointed out that great lights have great shadows. Carl Gustav Jung, being one the most important figures in the development of the field of psychology, had both. In the end, when one goes to the trouble of sifting out all the material at hand, one comes to realize that he was neither guilty of most of the accusations hurled at him nor wholly innocent of prejudice, especially so in the early stages of his career. We trust and hope that this book will contribute to the important task at hand, that of lifting Jung's important message from the shadowy place to which it has been relegated and casting light on the many insights he has given us into the human psyche.

Aryeh Maidenbaum, Ph.D.

Acknowledgments

First and foremost, we thank the Board of Trustees of the C. G. Jung Foundation of New York for having the courage and wisdom to cosponsor and be a part of such a study. Thanks also to Dr. Jeffrey Satinover, Chairman and President of the Foundation, who not only stood behind the concept of open and honest scholarly study engendered by the conference, but who ultimately served as a superb moderator as well. At times, between conception and birth, the project faced the dangers of potentially negative publicity, but to the credit of the Foundation's Board, support for the academic integrity of the topic never wavered.

Along the way, many were helpful, and we thank them all. Several individuals, however, gave unstintingly of their time, energy, and enthusiasms, and we would like to particularly thank them. Dr. Michael Adams, Associate Provost of the New School for Social Research, and Jay Sherry, a diligent psychohistorian, both were truly generous with their time and always made themselves available for consultation. The "Significant Words and Events" they compiled for conference attendees, included in this book, has proven to be a unique contribution and time saver for those delving more deeply into this topic. Additionally, we are confident that the bibliographic essay compiled by Jay Sherry will prove to be an invaluable research tool and time-saving piece of scholarship for future students of the subject. Both Jay Sherry and Michael Adams deserve special commendation and thanks.

The "Lingering Shadows" conference could not have taken place without the assistance of Robert Hinshaw, who helped arrange interviews with several of Jung's colleagues and students, representing the last of the generation of people who knew Jung personally. Dr. Hinshaw's help was indispensable.

One man in particular who believed in us and enthusiastically supported the project both materially and spiritually was Dr. Maury P. Leibovitz. Without his initial help and contribution, this book would never have come into being. Successful businessman, psychologist, and friend, he was uncompromising and steadfast in his belief that, come what may, the search for an honest evaluation and discussion needed to be honored.

Finally, the real down-to-earth task of logistical planning and copy editing fell on the shoulders of Kendra Crossen, the excellent, resourceful editor assigned by Shambhala Publications to help us. Kendra was assisted in her work by A. Vernon Woodworth, whom we would like to thank as well. Nevertheless, the bulk of responsibility did fall on Kendra, and we are grateful to her for her patience with us as well as her insights, guidance, keen editorial eye, and sharp pencil.

Aryeh Maidenbaum and Stephen A. Martin

Introduction

Stephen A. Martin

The varied contents of this volume reflect the complexity of the question at hand. Debating whether C. G. Jung and his theory were anti-Semitic requires a flexible and many-sided approach because history is far from linear, and the antecedents of historical events are often not easily charted. On the contrary, it is usually only in hindsight that facts seem to line up logically or rationally. What we call history is really an active and ongoing process of distillation, a continuous moment that precipitates out of the swirl of events, personalities, and social and political conditions that can never be completely accounted for or fixed. We who are in the helping professions and who deal with the histories of our patients know the truth of this observation. History, therefore, is an approximate endeavor, at best relatively truthful. It is always open to refinement through the introduction of new data, new hypotheses, and new points of view. And it must be constantly reevaluated as we learn to eliminate misinformation, biased speculation, and outright propaganda.

This perspective helps us to appreciate the many viewpoints expressed in this anthology. Many of the essays originated from the 1989 conference "Lingering Shadows: Jungians, Freudians, and Anti-Semitism," hosted jointly by the C. G. Jung Foundation for Analytical Psychology in New York, the Postgraduate Center for Mental Health, and the Union of American Hebrew Congregations, and held at the New School for Social Research in New York City. The purpose of the conference was to examine, challenge, and put to rest some of the most persistent misinformation about Jung's attitudes toward Jews and about his professional and so-called political activities during the years preceding World War II, and to introduce new evidence, some of it not particularly flattering to Jung, about what seemed to be happening at that important time. In addition, we felt that since Jung placed so high a value on consciousness, the conference ought to raise questions about his own consciousness of his shadow involvement in relation to Nazism, totalitarianism, and the real or imagined differences between "Jewish psychology" and that of any other group or people. Most of all, we felt that this important dialogue had to take place because, through almost the eighty years since the breakup of the relationship between Freud and Jung, the charge of Jung's anti-Semitism has stood in the way of a creative reconciliation between the two great schools of depth psychology. It seemed imperative that we, the Jungians, should inaugurate the dialogue and initiate the rapprochement, because to look into the darkness, personal or collective, was, in Jung's mind, the cornerstone of a psychologically authentic and ethical life.

In addition to papers related to the conference, we are bringing together old and new scholarship in an effort to provide a source-book for the reader on the subject of Jung and anti-Semitism. Previously published papers, like those of Ernest Harms and James Kirsch, have been hard to find. Others are being made available to a wide readership for the first time, such as those presented at the eleventh conference of the International Association for Analytical Psychology in Paris in 1989. To fully appreciate the territory covered by these essays, it is helpful to be aware of three broad subject areas. The first pertains to the personal and professional relationship between C. G. Jung and Sigmund Freud, which, though lasting only eight years, was instrumental in crafting two profoundly original approaches to the psyche. The termination of their relationship also gave rise to the first accusation of anti-Semitism against Jung. The second domain has to do with Jung's professional activities and personal attitudes from his break with Freud in 1913 up to the onset of World War II. The third subject area is more speculative, circumambulating the possible conscious and unconscious motivations that moved Jung to behave as he did and speculating about the psychological and social conditions that influenced him. Most of the essays incorporate elements of all three of these subject areas. By keeping these three in mind while reading, and through a process of careful consideration and reflection, the reader may become the fourth and all-inclusive perspective that weaves a meaningful whole from what came before.

The early years of this century were legend-making times. New ground was being broken in every field, and creative personalities were redefining reality at every turn. Nowhere was the power of this fruitful time more obvious than in the field of depth psychology. As an assistant under the guidance of Eugen Bleuler at the Burghölzli, the cantonal psychiatric hospital in Zurich, Jung was one of the leaders of a growing Swiss cadre of professionals interested in psychoanalysis. He had read Freud's *Interpretation of Dreams* several times and had incorporated Freud's ideas about repression into his own research. Thus, by the time Jung first contacted Freud by sending him an inscribed copy of his *Studies in Word Association* around the end of 1905, he was well acquainted with Freud's work. The personal and professional relationship between the two men blossomed after this initial exchange, as is well documented.[1] Here I wish to focus on just a few aspects of their collaboration, for the purpose of navigating the treacherous waters of accusation and counteraccusation.

Freud was drawn to Jung because of the younger man's keen and inquiring mind and his understanding of psychoanalysis—and because he was not Jewish. On a number of occasions Freud commented that by enlisting Jung, the son of a Swiss Reformed pastor, psychoanalysis would escape the danger of becoming a "Jewish national affair."[2] Moreover, both men were drawn passionately into what appears to have been a father-son relationship that was characterized by massive projection and the potential for both creative partnership and destructive competition and enmity.[3]

Freud and Jung were collaborators of the closest kind. Exchanging hundreds of letters and many visits, they also shared the limelight internationally, traveling together to the United States in 1909 to advance the standing of psychoanalysis. Freud supported Jung's presidency of the International Psychoanalytical Association and the editorship of the *Jahrbücher für psychoanalytische und psychopathologische Forschungen,* and he regularly looked forward to Jung's contributions to the growing field. Jung, for his part, viewed Freud with great esteem as "the first man of real importance" in the field of depth psychology.[4]

Despite this seeming compatability, there was much that separated the two men from the start.[5] They disagreed on the value of the occult in psychological life: Freud saw occultism as regressive and dangerous, while Jung was strongly drawn to the psychological mysteries that it might contain. Of greater importance, however, was their difference over the role of sexuality in psychic functioning. At first cautiously then more openly, Jung expressed doubt about Freud's theory of the libido and his insistence on the primacy of the sexual drive. Jung envisioned libido as a more generic life urge that appears not only in sexuality but finds legitimate, primary expression in creative, intellectual, and spiritual activities as well.

On a more personal level, Jung had obvious difficulty acceding to Freud's paternal authority. Having been a rebellious son who at an early age saw through his own father's doubts about his religious beliefs, Jung had trouble acquiescing to his role as "adopted son" and "heir" to Freud and the expectations that he would follow in his mentor-father's footsteps.[6] Clearly both men were locked in a dialogue of projection; neither was to blame for the situation, nor was one more misguided than the other. As we have learned, complexes occur in an interpersonal field: when activated, they draw the individuals inexorably into this field, distorting perception and understanding with strong primitive emotions and all manner of unconscious material. Despite the psychological understanding of these two remarkable men, their respective needs and complexes contaminated the relationship and set the stage for its most painful demise.

The climax of the drama was precipitated by Jung's publication of *Wandlungen und Symbole der Libido* in 1912, a work that openly challenged Freud's theory of the child's incestuous desire for the parent of the opposite sex. Jung felt that such longings were symbolic expressions of psychic energy and not to be taken literally. In fact, the publication of this work merely tipped the scales of an already changing relationship between Freud and Jung. Skirmishes had been increasing around the issues of sexuality and of Freud's authority, particularly between the Vienna and Zurich camps of the psychoanalytic community. As Jung's relationship with Freud grew more problematic, and Jung grew uncomfortable with the role of "crown prince" and heir,[7] the delicate balance of forces in the world of psychoanalysis began to fall apart, culminating in the final severance of their personal and professional connections in 1913.

It is out of this tumultuous ending of their relationship that the first published accusations of anti-Semitism were leveled at Jung. Although as early as 1908 Ernest Jones, a close colleague of Freud's and his biographer, seemed to have detected anti-Semitism in Jung, this feeling was held in check.[8] Undoubtedly, the very nature of Freud's reliance on Jung's being Christian (thus staving off the accusation that psychoanalysis was an exclusively Jewish science) constellated the potential for anti-Semitism by this very strategy directly and dramatically; but so long as a working relationship existed in the psychoanalytic community, there was no overt discord. However, by the time Jung withdrew from Freud and others in the psychoanalytic community, the accusation of anti-Semitism spread with alarming rapidity, like a malignancy that could no longer be policed by a healthy immune system. Whether it was Freud's reference to "the brutal sanctimonious Jung," in a letter to Karl Abraham in 1914[9] or his private accusations of Jung's anti-Semitism in a letter to James Putnam in 1915,[10] nowhere was his condemnation more fateful than when he wrote in his "Outline to a History of Psychoanalysis" (1914) that Jung was unable to remain faithful to psychoanalysis because of "certain racial prejudices."[11] Coming from the pen of the master himself in a seemingly official document, this damning, retributive, and, for Freud, clearly face-saving statement began a historical controversy that has simmered and frequently boiled over, with disastrous results, since that time.

Following the end of his relationship with Freud, Jung retreated for some time into a period of introversion, a time of personal and professional crisis and reevaluation that culminated in 1921 with the publication of *Psychological Types,* a work that Jung felt addressed the differences between himself, Freud, and Freud's other apostate son, Alfred Adler.[12] Freud was extremely prolific during that time as well, producing some of his most important theoretical papers. There seemed little of substance to fuel the issue of anti-Semitism between 1915 and the early 1920s. Jung, however, was clearly attempting to process and defend himself against the accusation of anti-Semitism while at the same time differentiating himself from the "Jewish doctrines" of psychoanalysis. As early as 1917 he was drawing distinctions between a Jewish and a Germanic psychology. The Jewish psyche, he believed, though extremely sophisticated and rich, was not in touch with the "power of the chthonic depths,"[13] whereas the Germanic psyche was so deeply enmeshed in this primeval reality as to be almost "barbarian," a quality he described as both a "dangerous peculiarity" and a potentially "valuable . . . asset."[14] Some ten years later, in 1928, he challenged the lingering charge of anti-Semitism directly by stating that all races, although having a common collective point of origin, differentiate and develop specific essential characteristics and that none of these characteristics is generally valid for all the other groups. The perception and recognition of these differences, he said, did not equal anti-Semitism. Despite the logic of these arguments, one can sense between the lines of Jung's theorizing a continuing struggle with the legacy of his involvement in the psychoanalytic movement. It is likely that his comments arose out of more than theoretical issues—that in fact they were expressions of Jung's negative feelings toward Freud and evidence of the projections that persisted in Jung (and in Freud as well) as a result of their traumatic parting of the ways.

By the beginning of the 1930s, the stage was set for extraordinary developments with regard to the allegations of Jung's anti-Semitism. The success of Hitler and the Nazi party and the full-scale persecution of Jews and other "undesirables" in Germany were becoming horrific facts of life. Out of this overheating container erupted a critical turn of events in 1933. Responding to a "frenzied" call from his colleagues, Jung assumed the presidency of the General Medical Society for Psychotherapy from the German psychiatrist Ernst Kretschmer.[15] It is well substantiated that Jung purposefully and rapidly sought to reconstitute the Society as an international body by 1934 in an effort to stave off German demands to exclude certain colleagues, notably Jewish ones, from membership.[16] According to Geoffrey Cocks, Jung wanted to enable these excluded colleagues to join as "extraordinary members" beyond the veto power of the large and "newly aggressive" German society headed by Matthias Heinrich Goering, a cousin of the Nazi party leader Hermann Goering. At the same time, Jung became the nominal editor of the society's journal, the *Zentralblatt für Psychotherapie,* which had been published in Germany. It was in this publication, in late 1933, that a manifesto appeared by Matthias Goering—with the consent of Jung, who had thought that it was to be published only in a special German edition—which called for a rallying by professional colleagues to the racial colors of Nazi Germany.[17] To compound matters, appearing in this same issue of the journal was Jung's essay "On the State of Psychotherapy Today," in which he starkly reiterated the differences between German and Jewish psychologies that he had posited some years earlier. In addition, his article compared Jews unfavorably to "nomads" and women, and criticized Freud and Adler for stressing pathology while failing to appreciate the creative aspects of psychological life. This essay was ill-timed, easily misunderstandable, and—coupled with Goering's piece—certain to put Jung in the worst possible light. And indeed it became the principal theoretical document that Jung's accusers offered as a demonstration of his anti-Semitism.

Jung's writings of the 1930s and '40s display a consistency of theme and thrust. He returns again and again to the supposition that there are definite, obvious differences in the psychologies of "races" and "nations" that must be acknowledged and understood. Jung also criticizes Freud's denial of his spiritual roots and the embeddedness of psychoanalysis in a "materialistic" and "rationalistic" framework. Jung takes pains to distinguish between "culture" and "cultural form," trying to make clear that although the Jews have an ancient culture, their lack of a homeland has worked against the evolution of a "cultural form." In Hitler, Jung saw a leader "possessed" by archetypal energies that symbolized the profound "inferiority complex" of the German people and the compensatory drive toward superiority at any cost, one who personified their collective shadow: that is, their unacknowledged and uncontrolled unconscious motivations and their blindly nationalistic longings. By way of a "mass psychosis," Jung felt, Hitler was able to subvert German consciousness to the negative and evil potential of these unconscious forces and lead it to inevitable catastrophe. His reflections on Germany and Hitler characterized Jung's frequent attempts to apply the principles of individual psychology to the understanding of nations, national character, and political action, thereby viewing Germany, for instance, as if it were a patient and he the doctor. He frequently bridled at the fact that his criticisms of Freud and psychoanalysis were immediately perceived as anti-Semitic. He would write often that he was no anti-Semite and that his sole aim was to explore and illuminate the complexities of the human psyche. Finally, in several instances, he admitted that he had been wrong to believe that the arousal of unconscious forces in Germany might bring about positive results in the form of a genuine psychocultural and spiritual transformation.

Historical realities are referred to again and again in this anthology, as if the writers hope that by restating the facts enough times, they can dispel the extraordinary misinterpretations generated by the activities and writings of Jung that I have touched upon. As soon after the war as 1946, Ernest Harms, in an article reprinted here, laid out the facts unequivocally but, oddly enough, to little avail. Aniela Jaffé, one of Jung's closest colleagues and a Jew to whom Jung gave personal, financial, and emotional help during the difficult war years,[18] restated them again in the late 1960s and '70s, but failed to stem the distortions and misconstruals. As recently as 1982, James Kirsch, one of the best-known German Jewish analysts who worked and communicated with Jung during these critical years, presented the details again, this time in response to a diatribe against Jung in a Jewish publication. I hope that the publication of some of these papers, along with others of more recent and revealing scholarship, will promote a more balanced assessment of Jung in the light of documented evidence.

More problematic is the question of Jung's motivations, both conscious and unconscious, and the way they influence the allegation of his anti-Semitism. While some writers flatly deny this charge and others forthrightly affirm it, most feel that Jung temporarily lost his perspective, fell prey to unintegrated shadow feelings, and acted them out. The most obvious reason for Jung's lapse is, as I have indicated, his unresolved feelings about Freud, the father figure, mentor, and friend by whom Jung felt painfully disappointed and betrayed. Some have speculated that something more than astute theoretical observation lay behind Jung's sharp criticism of Freudian psychology for its tendency to impose itself on other "psychologies": out of his resistance to being personally "imposed upon" by Freud's expectations and demands, Jung may have unconsciously sought to do damage to his mentor. In reaction to these demands, or by way of compensation, Jung might have fallen into an unconscious identification with events in Germany, and perhaps even with the power of Hitler. Caught in this inflation and unconscious power drive, Jung may very well have taken the opportunity during the 1930s, when Freud and psychoanalysis were being hounded, to promote his own psychology and himself with such ambitious concerns as "diagnosing dictators," becoming a psychologist of nations, and attempting, with good but perhaps overstated intent, to help rescue the field of psychotherapy from the fires of totalitarianism.

Alongside his possible opportunism was Jung's fascination with the archetypal images of Wotan, the "inspired leader," and the alchemical figure of Mercurius. Jung was beguiled by the events in Germany and the way in which the forces of the irrational, the heroic, and the instinctive were taking over and leading a civilized people. It was as if his observations about the archetypal Germanic "blond beast" of 1918 were coming true, or as if his own observations of renewal from the depths of the unconscious at the hands of an inspired leader were being enacted and confirmed on a national scale.[19] How could this renewal from the depths not fascinate a psychological explorer of Jung's vision or, more personally, a man who himself sought guidance with regard to his desire for leadership in his profession and who must have identified with the archetypal image of the formerly misunderstood yet inspired leader? And how could he help getting caught in the duplicity of the situation? Here, as Jay Sherry points out, one thinks of Mercurius duplex, the presiding spirit of alchemy, a duplicitous archetypal permutation of Wotan who dupes those in whom he manifests by causing them to see only half of a very complex and dangerous state of affairs.

Whatever the reasons for Jung's attitudes and actions, he displayed, in the midst of a dangerous and frightening time, a regrettable lack of sensitivity toward the plight of the Jews and a lack of awareness of the political and personal consequences of his written and spoken words. There is no doubt that he wished to help friends, patients, and colleagues who were suffering from the madness infecting the European continent. But in dramatically human fashion he proved himself vulnerable to the insidious effects of the very forces he was seeking to make sensible, and to the accumulated and unprocessed depths of his own past as a rebellious Swiss pastor's son and the fallen heir to a "Jewish science."

Perhaps Jung personally experienced some redemption for this lack and loss when, after a heart attack in 1944, he had a series of visions of a distinctly Jewish nature. In them he saw himself attended to by an "old Jewish nurse" and nurtured on "ritually prepared kosher food," and was privileged to be present at the kabbalistic marriage of Malchuth and Tifereth.[20] Also, in his forceful *Answer to Job* of 1952, in which he wrestles with the problem of a Jewish God who seems capricious and unresponsive to the undeserved suffering of his loyal servant, Job, and in his later studies of Kabbalah, Jung may have discovered what was missing in his encounter with Freud: connection to a Judaism that was connected to its original spiritual roots and that could truly "feed" him in a way that he was so painfully denied by the empty religiosity of his natural father. Perhaps in this profound near-death encounter with the imagery of the mystical tradition of Judaism, Jung experienced a healing, a bringing together of his Christian worldview with the hidden spring that fed Freud's, and to which he was undoubtedly deeply attracted from the start. It is sad that the two men did not accomplish the same conjunction on a personal level and thus lay to rest the divisiveness that has for so many years fueled the accusation of anti-Semitism.

In view of Jung's belief that a psychological system is a "subjective confession" of its founder, an important question raised by this anthology is whether shortsightedness or failing on the part of Jung invalidates the psychology that he created. When he was attacking psychoanalysis, Jung referred often to the idea that Freud's Jewishness rendered him unable to appreciate the "chthnoic" dimension of the Germanic psyche. Would it not be equally true to say that Jungian psychology would be comparably blinded or constrained? Were we to evaluate Jungian psychology as primarily a reflection of its creator in the context of the disturbing question of Jung's possible anti-Semitism, could it not be judged a psychology of elitism or racism? Or, insofar as Jung seemed fascinated by the unconscious power of the German psyche, could his psychology not be judged as one that is too susceptible to intoxication with the irrational at the terrible expense of the rational? The answer to this basic question, both for psychoanalysis and for Jungian psychology, must be an unequivocal no. To hold a creation accountable for the flaws of its creator would leave us with little if any greatness or breadth in our culture. For the sake of comparison, it would invalidate the extraordinary vision of Van Gogh's art because of his mental illness, or the beauty of Ezra Pound's poetry because of his fascist beliefs. Jung himself must have recognized this when, as late as 1953, in a response to questions from the *New York Times*, he was prepared to credit "Freud's contributions to our knowledge of the psyche" as being of the "greatest importance" without any reference to his misgivings about Freud the man or how his psychology betrays his personal limitations.[21] Yet at the same time there is truth to the notion that the creator's personality informs and conditions what he observes, describes, and analyzes. As Goethe said, "we see what we know"; so must Jung's complexes have affected the development of his psychology. Therefore, as some of the contributors to this book point out, Jungian psychology must be extremely sensitive to such tendencies to value the transpersonal over the quotidian and thus miss the "real" in favor of the "symbolic," or to "analyze" nations, peoples, races when trying to discern what is specific about how they have embodied aspects of the archetypal or universal and risk falling into dangerous stereotyping and possibly even more dangerous scapegoating.

To encounter and integrate the shadow is one of the great tasks of individuation. That does not mean the rejection of what is found but rather the painful acceptance of its role in the making of consciousness. It is painful for us as Jungians to look squarely at the questions raised in this anthology, to see displayed so blatantly how our standard bearer's own shadow distorted his judgment and perception. But as Jung's psychology is a psychology of consciousness, by confronting his personal flaws and opening ourselves and the system to the same hard, tireless scrutiny, we do the work of consciousness-making. In so doing, we go beyond personal vendettas of the past and the battlegrounds of intellectual giants, to arrive at the creative present, that moment in which we can, for ourselves and for the future, make history anew.

Notes

1. See *The Freud/Jung Letters;* Peter Gay, *Sigmund Freud: A Life for Our Time* (New York: W. W. Norton, 1988); C. G. Jung, *Memories, Dreams, Reflections;* and Gerhard Wehr, *Jung: A Biography* (Boston & London: Shambhala Publications, 1987).

2. Sigmund Freud and Karl Abraham, *A Psycho-Analytic Dialogue: The Letters of Sigmund Freud and Karl Abraham 1907–1926,* p. 34.

3. Alexander Irving, "The Freud/Jung Relationship: The Other Side of Oedipus and Countertransference," *American Psychologist,* Spring 1982, pp. 1009–1018; Gay. *Sigmund Freud,* pp. 200–202.

4. Jung, *Memories, Dreams, Reflections,* p. 149.

5. Liliane Frey-Rohn, *From Freud to Jung: A Comparative Study of the Psychology of the Unconscious* (Boston & London: Shambala Publications, 1990).

6. Jung, *Memories, Dreams, Reflections,* pp. 52ff.; Murray Stein, "The Significance of Jung's Father in His Destiny as a Therapist of Christianity," *Quadrant,* Spring 1985, pp. 23–33; cf. note 3.

7. Letters from Freud to Jung, April 16, 1909, and October 15, 1908. *Freud/ Jung Letters*, pp. 218 and 172; Gay, *Sigmund Freud*, p. 198.

8. Ernest Jones, quote in Ronald W. Clark, *Freud: The Man and the Cause* (New York: Random House, 1980), pp. 249–250.

9. Freud and Abraham, *A Psycho-Analytic Dialogue*, p. 186.

10. Clark, *Sigmund Freud*, p. 333.

11. Sigmund Freud, "Outline to a History of Psychoanalysis," *Standard Edition*, 14, p. 43.

12. Jung, *Memories, Dreams, Reflections*, pp. 207–208; Henri Ellenberger. *The Discovery of the Unconscious* (New York: Basic Books, 1970), pp. 670–674.

13. C. G. Jung, "The Role of the Unconscious" (1918), CW 10, para. 19.

14. Ibid., para. 20.

15. C. G. Jung, "A Rejoinder to Dr. Bally" (1934), CW 10, para. 1016. It is worth noting that Kretschmer apparently did not resign this post because of his uncompromising rejection of Nazism, as is commonly believed. In fact, he continued his work quietly in Germany throughout the war years and as late as 1944 published an article on "the relevance of his theory of constitutional types to increasing war production," as noted by Geoffrey Cocks.

16. Geoffrey Cocks. *Psychotherapy in the Third Reich*, pp. 110, 127–128; Aniela Jaffé, "C. G. Jung and National Socialism," in *From the Life and Work of C. G. Jung*, pp. 78–102.

17. Cocks, *Psychotherapy in the Third Reich*, pp. 131–132; C. A. Meier, personal communication.

18. Aniela Jaffé, personal communication.

19. C. G. Jung, "The Role of the Unconscious," (1917) CW 10, para. 17.

20. Jung, *Memories, Dreams, Reflections*, pp. 293–294.

21. C. G. Jung, "Answers to Questions on Freud" (1953), CW 18, para. 1069.

Part One

HISTORICAL OVERVIEW

Carl Gustav Jung:
Defender of Freud
and the Jews

Ernest Harms

Ernest Harms was a child psychotherapist who studied for a time with Freud and later with Jung, with whom he was closely associated for many years. He was not, however, a formal adherent of either the Freudian or the Jungian school.

This article was originally published—with the subtitle "A Chapter of European Psychiatric History under the Nazi Yoke"—in the April 1946 issue of the *Psychiatric Quarterly*. Harms was the first to address the allegations against Jung in a historical manner, and his article remains a primary source of information on the subject.

He begins by recounting the development of the relationship between Freud and Jung and the reasons for its termination. He also discusses relevant events in the history of psychoanalysis, including Jung's controversial role in the International Society for Psychotherapy during the 1930s. His extended quotation from Jung's 1934 article "The Present State of Psychotherapy" was the first time that an English-speaking audience had an opportunity to read the article. By consistently presenting Jung's words and actions in a sympathetic light, Harms builds a strong case for his claim that the allegations of anti-Semitism and pro-Nazi sympathy leveled against Jung are largely the result of distortions, misinformation, and outright error.

During recent months a wave of misinformation concerning certain periods in the early development of modern analytical psychiatry and psychology has swept through professional periodicals and popular informative literature. Since these publications have received a great deal of attention in professional circles, it seems important to correct the information which they conveyed. This present article is intended to be a historical report based upon published material available in the libraries of the United States, with the exception of some quotations from personal letters by Carl Gustav Jung. The authors of the misstatements this paper aims to refute will not be mentioned here, although their assertions will be included in this presentation.

This report concerns mainly the Swiss psychiatrist Carl Gustav Jung, whose role in the development of modern psychiatry is generally recognized as highly important—even if one notes that dogmatic and fanatical representatives of other schools have repeatedly attempted to minimize his importance. Academic recognition does not always constitute the perfect criterion for scientific achievement, but it may be emphasized that Jung has received more honor in this country than any other non-American psychiatrist, including Sigmund Freud. Although most of the attacks upon Jung's name have come from fanatic followers of Freud, a correct evaluation of Jung's role in the development of psychoanalysis is of greater importance for an objective understanding of the history of the "psychoanalytic movement" than that of any other person. This is particularly true if the historic perspective is continued beyond the point where Freud closed his own chronicle, that is, up to the years when psychotherapy was threatened in Europe by the outbreak of the Nazi movement, or until about 1935.

It seems important to emphasize, as part of the introduction to this report, that its author is not a member of the association of the pupils of C. G. Jung, nor has Dr. Jung himself been consulted in regard to the presentation of the historic facts attempted here. The author has undertaken this writing on his personal initiative, because he believes that it is important for American psychotherapists to have objective information concerning certain momentous developments in their science.

CARL GUSTAV JUNG
AND SIGMUND FREUD

It has been repeatedly asserted that Jung started out as a disciple of Sigmund Freud and subsequently became a traitor to his master. Freud himself—in his brief "History of the Psychoanalytic Movement," which he wrote shortly after the separation between himself and the Zürich psychiatrists Bleuler and Jung, and which he doubtless undertook as a justification to his more faithful pupils and himself of the break with the Swiss—wrote a significant objective report of the beginning of their relationship. We learn that Jung belonged to the Zürich school of psychiatry and that the first contact with Freud had been made by the head of the school, Eugen Bleuler, during 1907; that it was Jung's invitation which brought together Zürich and Vienna to the first Psychoanalytic Congress in Salzburg (1908); and that Freud and Bleuler joined as editors* *(Herausgeber)* of the *Jahrbücher für Psychoanalytische und Psychopathologische Forschungen,* for which Jung took over the task of managing editor *(Schriftleiter)* in 1909. Freud also emphasizes the importance of the work Jung had already done before he came in touch with him. Very correctly, he points out that it was the problem of the "complex-theory" which offered Jung the point of contact with him. Their break and the controversy in which Freud presents a highly subjective personal opinion in reference to the early history of his movement will be discussed later.

Jung's own writings mirror authentically and unambiguously how he stood and how he developed in regard to Freud. His first larger publication is a monograph of 122 pages, *Zur Psychologie und Pathologie sogenannter occulter Phaenomene,* which he used as required publication for his qualification as *Privatdozent* (free

---

*The translator of the Modern Library edition of Freud's work, Dr. A. A. Brill makes the mistake of saying on page 947, "published by Bleuler and Freud and edited by Jung." Bleuler and Freud signed as *Herausgeber* and Jung as *Schriftleiter. Herausgeber* means editor and *Schriftleiter* must be translated as managing editor.

lecturer) at the University of Zürich. Here we see him struggle
with the same problem which every sincere research worker at that
time tried to solve: the problem of hysteria. We see him, together
with Freud and his contemporaries of that period, as a student of
the French school of psychiatry of Binet, Janet, and Charcot. He
tried to reach understanding of such abnormal psychological factors as the so-called occult experiences through their parallel to
similar experiences expressed by the mentally ill. We find him
twice in one sentence mentioning Freud, whose *Studien über
Hysterie* (published together with Breuer) and *Die Traumdeutung*
seemed to have attracted him considerably. This was in 1902.

We have already learned from Freud himself that Jung belonged
to a certain school of abnormal psychology known widely as the
Zürich School. Eugen Bleuler, known for his famous textbook of
psychiatry and his research in the field of schizophrenia, was the
head of this school. Jung was a senior member of the group.
Together with another member, Riklin, he was occupied in an
intensive research into associations, which under the title of "Diag-
nostische Associations Studien," appeared in the *Journal für Psychologie und Neurologie* in successive volumes from No. 3 to No.
9. Later, this became the basis for the entire school of associative
criminological testing, and Jung must be considered the founder
of this method. Before the first of these diagnostic studies appeared, Bleuler wrote an introduction in which he emphasized that
this work continued the tradition of the research of Wundt,
Kraepelin, and Aschaffenburg. A search was in progress for the
unveiling of "non-conscious" elements, pointing in the same direction in which Freud was advancing, but using other means, that of
the association experiment. The meeting of the Zürich and Freudian groups was the meeting of searchers for the same goal who
hoped to use techniques in common, since they had a common
aim. However, as they became acquainted with each other, they
not only discovered that their views on techniques did not coincide,
but that their aims did not either. Therefore, after a short union,
they resumed divergent paths. This was the nature of the relationship between Freud and Jung as the present writer believes it
appears to the objective observer.

In the many years during which Jung worked on the diagnostic association studies, he was deeply interested in Freud; and this is impressively stated in practically every study. It was always one subject which interested Jung in connection with Freud. He hoped that Freud's method would solve this problem into which he felt the associative diagnosis did not lead deeply enough: the problem of hysteria and of the complexes. We find this stated in the section of the diagnostic association studies devoted to dream and hysteric symptoms (*J. f. Psychologie u. Neurologie*, Vol. 8, 1906) in the following passage: "If one desires information about the more intimate experience, e.g., the complex, in a case of hysteria one is forced to reach it by a detour. Freud has converted this detour into a method: This is psychoanalysis." Surely one of the simplest and at the same time most impressive descriptions of the essential contents of psychoanalysis. However, when Jung in the same year presented a review of Freud's theory of hysteria before a professional congress (reprinted in *Monatsschrift für Psychiatrie und Neurologie*, Vol. 23, 1908), he expressed the fact very clearly that he was not a completely uncritical adherent of Freud's views. "Freud has never developed a complete theory of hysteria," he says, "but has merely attempted from time to time to formulate the theoretical results of his experience. However, what Freud has formulated theoretically must be acknowledged as a working hypothesis which adapts itself everywhere to experience. Therefore we cannot speak of a comprehensive theory of hysteria by Freud at the present moment, but of a variety of experiences which show certain common traits." The year before, Jung had published his important book, *The Psychology of Dementia Praecox*, which was, again, chiefly a contribution in the field of research of his own Zürich School, and which, he emphasized, was based upon his diagnostic association studies. In its introduction, we find a very clear statement of his attitude toward Freud. We read, "My readings brought Freud to my attention. It so happened that I first read the 'Interpretation of Dreams' but I have also studied the rest of his writings. I can assure everyone that at first I naturally made to myself all the objections which have been made against Freud in the literature. However, I said to myself, that only those could

refute Freud who have applied the psychoanalytical method extensively and who have searched as Freud searches.

"Justice toward Freud does not imply, as many fear, an uncon-
ditioned surrender to a dogmatic concept; one can very well
preserve an independent judgment. If, for instance, I agree to
Freud's theory of the complex mechanism, of the dream, and of
hysteria, this by no means implies that I acknowledge the exclusive
role which Freud evidently attributes to the juvenile sexual trauma;
just as I do not place sexuality in general so predominantly in the
foreground, or even ascribe to it the psychological universality
which Freud seems to postulate for it, impressed by the powerful
role which sexuality evidently plays in the psyche. As regards
Freud's therapy, it is at best one amongst other possible procedures
and probably does not always fulfill the theoretical expectations."
Here then, we see, a definite line was drawn, before the actual
cooperation began, between acknowledgement and rejection of
Freud's major concepts.

Wherever we investigate Jung's later writings, we shall find no
change in his standpoint toward Freud as just outlined. Since many
attempts have been made to use an alleged negative attitude of
Jung toward Freud as an argument, let us quote a few sentences
from Jung's address before the meeting of the International Association of Psychotherapists at Bad Nauheim in 1934, a meeting
which will interest us still more later on, for, at this time, German
Nazism raged against the Jews and, among them, particularly
against Freud. Before a German assembly in a German town, Jung
said, "Without the existence of the complexes the unconscious
would be—as it was for Wundt—nothing but the residue of
obscure representations. Through his investigations of these dark
areas Freud became the discoverer of the psychological unconscious. . . . As a logical outcome, the first medical theory of the
unconscious was the theory of repression postulated by Freud,
which was based upon purely empirical presuppositions, without
taking into account the philosophical works concerning the unconscious by Leibniz, Kant, Schelling and Carus, up to Eduard von
Hartmann." After this period of over 25 years, Jung therefore gave
to Freud the same acknowledgement as he had done on the eve of

his cooperation with "the psychoanalytic master from Vienna." In 1929, Jung wrote a short article which is reprinted in his American book *Modern Man in Search of a Soul,* on "The Freud-Jung Contrast." At the end he says: "The contrast between Freud and myself goes back to essential differences in our basic assumptions." And these basic assumptions as they are enumerated in this article are exactly the same as those expressed in the excerpt already quoted from the introduction to his *Psychology of Dementia Praecox,* written in 1906.

Let us now follow the history of scientific and personal relationships. In his *Psychology of Dementia Praecox,* Jung, in 1907, had offered a very positive contribution to the concept of schizophrenia which was one of the scientific concerns of the Zürich group, especially of its leader, Bleuler. It was Jung himself who, at the Salzburg meeting in 1908, had suggested the cooperation of his group with the group of Freud. In 1909, Jung took up the task of acting as managing editor of the *Jahrbücher für Psychoanalytische und Psychopathologische Forschungen,* for which Bleuler and Freud signed as editors, thus confirming the definite union of their two groups. In the first volume, one finds Freud publishing his famous treatise on infantile sexuality. To this, Jung adds, "Die Bedeutung des Vaters für das Schicksal des Einzelnen" which was followed in the next volume by his paper "Über Konflikte der kindlichen Seele." If we compare the relationship between Jung's schizophrenia study and Bleuler's work on this problem on the one hand, with the relationship, on the other hand, between Freud's writings on juvenile problems and these two contributions by Jung on the same subject, we discover the two attitudes are diametrically opposed. The relationship with Bleuler is characterized by an affirmative elaboration and an addition; whereas, in regard to Freud, Jung introduces a differing and critical viewpoint. Nobody could consider these first real contributions to the joint work of the two groups as the work of a follower and pupil of Freud. We also know that in other ways the cooperation between the groups was not too smooth. Bleuler had been severely attacked in academic circles for his association with a man like Freud, who was considered a scientific outlaw. Bleuler responded with several articles, reaffirming his acknowledgement of Freud and of psycho-analysis. The most impressive of these appeared in the second volume of the *Jahrbücher für Psychoanalytische und Psychopath-ologische Forschungen*. Whoever reads this paper today will feel that Bleuler never had arrived at a deeper or comprehensive inner relationship to Freud's conceptions; conversely, his own ideas on autism, which occupied him at that time and of which the most important appeared in the same periodical, never had any acknowl-edgement in the more intimate circle around Freud. The discrep-ancy between Jung and the entire Zürich conceptions on the one side and Freud on the other appears even more markedly in the largest literary contribution which Jung made during the coopera-tion of the two groups—in the subsequent two volumes of the *Jahrbücher*. This contribution contained his ideas on the libido concept of Freud, and was later published (1912) in one volume under the title *Wandlungen und Symbole der Libido*. We are told that Freud seriously opposed the publication of these studies as a separate monograph of the *Jahrbücher*. As is well known, the concept of the libido, to which he had given a very clear and precisely formulated description in his *Drei Abhandlungen*, was for Freud a most fundamental one. Jung has reprinted in his American book *Psychology of the Unconscious* (1937) the most essential part of his *Psychologie der Dementia Praecox*. From this, we learn how he attempted to transform the Freudian concept according to his own thinking and that of the Zürich School. We read on page 144 of *Psychology of the Unconscious:* "For a long time the theory of libido seemed to me inapplicable for dementia praecox. With increasing experience in analytical work, however, I became aware of a gradual change in my conception of libido. In place of the descriptive definition of the 'Three Contributions' [Freud's *Drei Abhandlungen*] there gradually grew up a genetic definition of the libido, which rendered it possible for me to replace the expression 'psychic energy' by the term 'libido.' " And in continuation of this different concept Jung developed a theory of the libido which is completely at variance with that of Freud. In view of this fact, it is not surprising that on the first excuse, a break occurred in their personal relations.

In 1909, Freud and Jung, together with a number of international authorities in psychology, psychiatry and education, had been invited by Stanley Hall to celebrate the twentieth anniversary of Clark University by a series of lectures and by receiving honorary degrees. We are told that during the long sea voyage, when Freud and Jung had ample time to discuss and to work out problems of psychoanalysis in personal discussion, the differences of scientific opinion and of basic philosophical concepts became glaringly evident; and a break almost occurred at the time. In the *History of the Psychoanalytic Movement,* Freud relates, however, that it took three more years before the final break at a meeting in Munich in the fall of 1913. According to Freud's account, Jung presided in an "unamiable and incorrect fashion" and "accepted the presidency of the International Psychoanalytic Association again, although two-fifths of the members present refused him support." And Freud adds, "We took leave of one another without feeling the need to meet again." To the present writer, it would seem that Jung's consent to continue as the president of the international association expressed his desire to uphold and save the relationship and the collaboration; while Freud, angry and disappointed that events did not develop according to his wishes, pushed toward the break. Consequently, we witness in the same year—after the publication of five volumes—the resignation of Bleuler and Jung from the editorship and managing editorship of the *Jahrbücher.* From the fact that his note of resignation motivates it with "personal reasons," one can infer that it was Freud's personal attitude which forced the resignation, and that both sides would have been willing to continue if objective reason had been the main consideration. With the next volume, the *Jahrbücher* ceased to appear, thus ending the literary expression of this short collaboration of the Vienna and the Zürich groups.

Freud spoke harsh words about Jung in his *History of the Psychoanalytic Movement,* from which we quote here: "Jung, by his modification of psychoanalysis, has furnished us a counterpart of Lichtenberg's famous knife. He has changed the hilt and has inserted a new blade into it, and because the same trademark is engraved upon it, we are required to regard the instrument as the former one." We find similar expressions wherever Freud comes to speak about Jung, often indeed in an unjust manner. He had expected a pupil who completely accepted his theories. Jung, on his side, never desired, or committed himself to, such a complex allegiance, and he maintained a more objective and unbroken acknowledgment to Freud. He has never spoken of Freud in such impassioned negative terms as the latter did about Jung. In the controversy over the psychoanalysis of Freud and his own—which he termed "analytical psychology"—he always tried to keep the debate on the level of a scientific discussion or of an explanatory description. He always acknowledged Freud's basic importance and historic role. No one could express this more valiantly than did Jung in his speech on Freud on the occasion of the aforementioned Nauheim meeting after the Nazi purge. This speech is indeed, the present writer thinks, the expression of one of the most knightly and courageous attitudes in the records of present-day science.

MAJOR TRENDS IN DEVELOPMENT AND ORGANIZATION OF CONTINENTAL PSYCHOTHERAPY DURING THE FIRST THIRTY YEARS OF THIS CENTURY

During the twentieth century psychiatry and psychotherapy have just begun to outgrow their children's shoes. Previously, no definite line or pattern had been discernible in the development of "scientific help to the sick soul." During the last two decades of the past century, the most advanced and intensive work of this kind had been done in France, and no one who was interested in the advances in the field could fail to study the results obtained by the "doctors of the mind" of Nancy and Paris. This work earned for itself a certain international reputation, but no national or international organization was connected with it. There were intelligent and successful workers elsewhere, too, who even created scientific schools for themselves such as Lombroso in Italy, Bleuler in

Zürich, or Kraepelin in Münich. With the start of the new century a fundamental change occurred. A strong demand arose for organization in psychotherapy. We must emphasize that it was around Freud and his psychoanalytical teaching that the first real international organization grew. Soon after the International Psychoanalytical Association had been started, the students around Alfred Adler—who, like Jung, had, for a short while, attempted an association with Freud—organized themselves into a similar group, which after some changes became the international "individual psychological" association. Not long after Jung had left the post of an alienist in the Zürich Psychiatric State Hospital, the Burghölzli, students from all over the globe congregated around him and founded a similar international organization. This was rather a new pattern in psychotherapeutic work. Of course the old academic neurological and psychiatric medical associations existed; but they had no specific aims to differentiate them from any other academic association, whether made up of philosophers or entomologists. Naturally, these psycotherapeutic international groupings, each around its own teacher, comprised only a small proportion of the entire professional group of psychiatrists, which has been rapidly growing since the end of the past century. Among the latter, a good many were interested in one or the other of these three organized schools without feeling inclined to commit themselves to any one of them. There were also several rather distinguished teachers in psychotherapy who had their own theories and concepts and were unwilling to associate themselves with any group with a one-man leadership. There were Dubois and Forel, for instance, in Switzerland; Steckel in Vienna; Van der Horst and Bowman in Holland; Joergensen, Bjerre, Gadelius and Voght in Scandinavia; and there were a number of Germans like J. H. Schulz, Ernst Kretschmer, Arthur Kronfeld, and, especially, Robert Sommer. In the wider circle of academic workers in abnormal psychology, Sommer had a role similar to that of Adolf Meyer here in America. Although he had never written a large textbook defining his own basic psychiatric or psychotherapeutic concepts, he wrote a great number of shorter papers and booklets which contained communications which aroused the greatest attention and discussion. He had a great many independent pupils and a still greater number of friends. No professional worker, including Freud himself, exercised a greater influence in middle European psychiatric circles than did Robert Sommer.

Perhaps as a result of the organization of the pupils of the three individualistic leaders, perhaps because it was the trend of the time, an impulse arose in the middle of the 1920's to organize the independent workers in an association on an international level. During 1926 and 1927, discussions were held which centered around Robert Sommer, and, in 1928, an Allgemeine Ärztliche Gesellschaft für Psychotherapie [General Medical Society for Psychotherapy] was founded with Robert Sommer as president. This society created as its organ an *Allgemeine ärtzliche Zeitschrift für Psychotherapie und psychische Hygiene,* of which Sommer was the editor (*Herausgeber*), while Wladimir Eliasberg and Rudolf Allers were nominated managing editors. After a further year and a half, that is, at the beginning of the third year of the new organization, the title of the publication was changed and Dr. Eliasberg's connection as managing editor ended. Sommer was then joined by Ernst Kretschmer as editor. Arthur Kronfeld and J. H. Schulz were appointed managing editors, together with Allers, who was taken over as review editor. The new journal, under the title of *Zentralblatt für Psychotherapie,* grew rapidly until it became the most widely read and most progressive psychotherapeutic periodical in Europe. Hand in hand with the growth of the journal, the society rapidly became an acknowledged group which drew membership from all the countries of middle and northern Europe. A number of the more independent members of Freud's and Adler's societies also joined the Allgemeine Ärztliche Gesellschaft. Freud and Adler themselves appear never to have belonged to it. Jung must have been a member, since he is reported to have been vice-president (2. *Vorsitzender*) in 1933. Considerable interest in Jung evidently existed among the members of the society, since, in 1932, one of Jung's pupils reported on one of the series of seminar lectures which Jung gave for the members of his own organization.

Jung had come to hold a central position in mid-European

psychotherapy when, in 1933, the Nazi purge destroyed much of the collaboration which in manifold ways had been built up during the previous twenty years. The first effect was the elimination, as a result of Nazi anti-Semitism, of the work done by Jewish scientists. The organizations of Freud's as well as Adler's pupils were dissolved, and their members were expelled from the German national sphere. At the same time all Jewish members of the staff of the *Zentralblatt* had to resign. One should note here that it had been due mainly to Arthur Kronfeld's effort that the *Zentralblatt* had grown to a periodical of such extensive influence. At the same time, Rudolf Allers, who belonged to an extremely religious Roman Catholic group, also resigned from the editorial board. All Jewish members of the Allgemeine Ärztliche Gesellschaft für Psychotherapie were dismissed from the organization. Many inaccurate and untruthful statements have been made about the events of these fateful months. They convey a distorted and misleading picture. I am basing this report strictly upon the information provided by the *Zentralblatt,* of which the complete set of issues is available in the Library of the New York Academy of Medicine.

As mentioned before, the Allgemeine Ärztliche Gesellschaft existed as an international organization in which psychotherapists from all countries, from Czechoslovakia to Holland and Belgium, and from Norway to Hungary, were united. Nazism never would permit such an organization to continue, since all international relations were ordered to be severed. The only possibility of organization under the Nazi rule was to found in every country a national Ärztliche Gesellschaft; and permission was obtained for these individual national societies to cooperate—not in an "international" but, according to a newly created German term, in an *übernationale Gesellschaft* which can best be translated as "supernational society." This actually meant an association of the various societies. If this was to survive, then any trouble with the Nazi authorities had to be avoided. Ernst Kretschmer, who had been the last president of the former international society for the year 1932–1933, resigned. Those who were blinded and embittered by their hatred of the National Socialist excesses, in reviewing the events have deeply resented the fact that at this point the aged director of a mental hospital of the Ruhr district, Dr. M. H. Goering, should have been elected president of the German psychotherapeutic society. He had never played any significant role in this field but had derived his prestige only from being a relative of Hermann Goering. It is evident from the report on the events as given in No. 3 (December, 1933) of Vol. 6 of the *Zentralblatt*, page 142, that it was a matter of expediency to make Dr. Goering the "Führer" of German psychotherapy as a person capable of maintaining contact with the Nazi government.

Carl Gustav Jung never has been a member of the German "Nazified" Allgemeine Ärztliche Gesellschaft für Psychotherapie. Under the new set-up, he had become a member of the Swiss Allgemeine Ärztliche Gesellschaft, which was organized as a national group like the Dutch and the Scandinavian psychotherapists. However, as we read on the same page of the *Zentralblatt* from which we quoted before, Dr. Jung, who had been the vice-president of the former international society from 1932 to 1933, was asked to become the president of the association of national societies— the Überstaatliche Ärztliche Gesellschaft für Psychotherapie, which had taken the place of the international society. The report, which was written by the secretary of the German society, says: "On account of his acceptance of the presidency on June 21st, 1933, we owe to Dr. C. G. Jung the survival of our scientific society and of the *Zentralblatt*." Because of the great decrease in membership it would have been impossible for the relatively small German group to support the *Zentralblatt*, of which Jung at the same time assumed the editorship. Again, it must be emphasized that the choice of a non-German, a member of the Swiss people, who at that time were already extremely anti-Nazi, was motivated by the desire to prevent the whole psychotherapeutic society from falling under the influence of National Socialism. Here again, all subsequent reports regarding the attempts to Nazify psychotherapeutic work in Europe are completely false and misleading. At the first meeting of the new association of national therapeutic societies, which occurred in May, 1934, the report of which can be found in No. 3 (1934), Vol. 7, of the *Zentralblatt*, page 130, Jung himself told of the difficulties which arose in Switzerland when, upon request of the "German society" he agreed to take over the presidency of the *überstaatlichen* society. He had accepted it at a personal sacrifice which he had been willing to make. But before we continue the report of the history of this period, we consider it necessary to insert some more general statements concerning Jung's fundamental opinions and concepts, which should contribute toward a better understanding of his actions and of the origins of certain misstatements which have been circulated in regard to those actions.

JUNG, NAZISM
AND ANTI-SEMITISM

The most severe and at the same time the most unjust accusation ever levelled at Jung is that he had a share in the horrors of anti-Semitism which have swept across the civilized world. This accusation originates in a sentence which Freud wrote in the already mentioned *History of the Psychoanalytic Movement,* from which we have already quoted. "He [Jung] also seemed prepared to enter into friendly relations with me, and to give up, for my sake, certain race prejudices which he had so far permitted himself to indulge." I have read through all of Jung's writings prior to the date of Freud's statement and instead of discovering any statement which might be interpreted as anti-Semitic, I have found no allusions to any Jewish factors and no derogatory remarks regarding other "racial" groups. In this statement, Freud has revealed the Achilles heel of his character-structure, a vulnerable spot of a dangerous nature.

Jung always had and still has today a considerable number of Jewish pupils. Not long before the anti-Semitic wave in Europe rose to its National Socialist height, he said in a lecture to the Swiss Protestant clergymen (reprinted in the American volume *Modern Man in Search of a Soul,* page 264 ff.): "I have treated many hundreds of patients, the larger number being Protestants, a smaller number Jews, and not more than five or six believing Catholics." No convinced anti-Semite would write such a sentence.

In his attitude regarding racial and collective problems, Jung has

been tragically misinterpreted, because his basic concepts, govern-
ing his motivations, have been misunderstood. No one who has
accused Jung of Fascist tendencies and of anti-Semitism has
grapsed what he said and meant. These persons have not confronted themselves with the same demand Jung made of himself when he encountered Freud, "to search as Freud searched."
Only he who fully understands Jung would have the right to contradict him.

Jung's psychology is a differential, comparative psychology, a
verstehende Psychologie in German, an expression which is difficult to translate. Jung is interested in the differentiation of structural and functional manifestations of the psyche and their causa-
tion. This has made him the exponent of psychotypology, which
has won him his fame. However, his differential viewpoint does
not stop at character and personality differentiation but does go
on to typological expressions as they appear in a social, cultural
and, finally, anthropological, psychological aspect. Jung is striving
to find clear and understandable descriptions of the differences of
national groups, of religious groups and of cultural groups. He
considers these differences to be the expressions of the various
human families on this earth. He is not a believer in the exclusively
physical differentiation of man, or the purely biological reality of
man; humanity's religions and all cultural expressions are as real
for him as are our eyes or any part of our physical anatomies. He
therefore asks himself about the *how* and *why* of each specific
form and content of these cultural realities. Jung believes that the
collective powers which make up our social and cultural life are
much stronger than many of the attitudes which express the
individual configuration. He sees these collective patterns survive,
even though the individual may perish, and he sees these super-
individual patterns inherited as psychological traits, just as we
observe in ourselves inherited similarities from the physiognomies
of our parents or grandparents. Jung has acquired a deep knowledge of the various types of this collective language, which assumes
its own shape in symbolic and formal expressions. He has set for
himself as the major therapeutic task that of assisting the individual
to achieve a positive relationship with these collective forces,

which, he holds, have a basic tendency to overpower the individual existence. Many of these conflicts exist on a subconscious level or in the realm of our irrational and emotional lives. The one effective means for their control is to lift them to the level of conscious experience. This does not mean rationalization, but rather awareness of their existence and of their symbolic manifestations.

To raise to a conscious level all discussions which are kindled by collective and individual emotional tensions such as, for instance, hate between racial or other human groups, would form the only basis for overcoming them or for paving the way toward a positive mutual understanding. Finally, there is still another postulate: The competent worker in the field of psychotherapy does not regard any life situation with either dogma or hypothesis but accepts it as it presents itself when help is desired or administered, making the best use of the prevailing circumstances and preventing their deterioration. The foregoing brief summary of some concepts of Jung is intended to assist in understanding the events which are to be described in the chronicle of 1933 and 1934, especially 1934.

Let us first consider these events by using the material which has formed the basis of the accusations concerning Jung's alleged Fascistic and anti-Semitic attitude. These quotations deserve a thorough discussion and need to be put in the right light. Finally, excerpts from a letter written by Jung to a Jewish friend in the spring of 1934 will be presented to demonstrate clearly his personal interpretation of the occurrences of those tragic months.

One recalls that the Allgemeine Ärztliche Gesellschaft and the *Zentralblatt* were founded because a large number of psychotherapists did not wish to be members of any of the psychiatric groups headed by one leader, but preferred a general organization. When, in 1933, Jung was asked to help save this international group and its journal by becoming president of the international association of national psychotherapeutic societies, the request came at a moment when it would have been senseless to launch an intensive attack upon anti-Semitism. During the preceding period, psychotherapy had become largely identified by the lay public with Freudianism, which was now being denounced by the Nazi propagandists as a prototype of Jewish psychology. In the true interest of the Jews, it would have been unwise to make a frontal attack against the German psyche, which was seething with hatred. To achieve any positive result, it was imperative to approach the question rationally and carefully.

How did Jung attempt to solve this obviously explosive problem? When taking over the editorship of the *Zentralblatt* he wrote a one-page announcement in which he said: "Although psychotherapy as a science has nothing to do with politics, fate has ordained that I take over the editorship of the *Zentralblatt* at a moment which is characterized by a confusion of theories and standpoints in psychotherapy not unlike that which has hitherto prevailed in politics. One-sided viewpoints, which cannot be brought to agreement, have gained too great an influence not only on specific medical concepts but also on the psychological opinions of many educated laymen. The ensuing contradictions were still further increased when my completely different conceptions became known; and this, to such a degree, that the phrase 'confusion of the minds' seems to be the only applicable one. It will therefore be the most distinguished task of the *Zentralblatt* to create a general attitude which will do justice to the basic facts of the human psyche to a higher degree than has hitherto prevailed, by means of an impartial appreciation of all objective contributions. The factually existing differences between the Germanic and Jewish psychologies should no longer remain blurred—to present them clearly is an aim from which science can but derive benefit. There exists in psychology, more than in any other science, a kind of 'personal denominator,' the disregard of which falsifies the results of practice and theory. I wish to state emphatically that this does not imply a depreciation of the Semitic psychology, just as a discussion of the distinctive psychology of the Far Eastern peoples does not imply a depreciation of the Chinese."

By attempting to raise the emotions underlying anti-Semitism to a higher level, Jung tried to give to the psychotherapeutic groups the basis of an existence despite the fanaticism of the Nazis. We know that he succeeded at least in the first rounds of the fight. His demand for an acknowledgment of all factual contributions to psychotherapy, in which he himself, as has already been mentioned, undertook the defense of Freud, subsequently aroused considerable antagonism on the part of National Socialism; and this finally forced Jung to give up his efforts.

Unfortunately, Jung's first attempts were as violently misunderstood by the Jewish side as they were by his personal enemies who used his statements against him. A Jewish periodical in Switzerland accused him of identifying the Jews with Mongolian hordes. The intolerance expressed in such a distortion is the equivalent of the intolerance of the anti-Semitic standpoint. Neither of these hostile viewpoints recognizes the higher objectivity which characterizes Jung's own viewpoints and action. Jung has been a great admirer of Chinese religion and culture as proved by his editorship of, and commentaries on, the *Tibetan Book of the Dead* and the *Secret of the Golden Flower.*

But a second step remained to be taken. This step was to make the psychotherapist aware of the subconscious and collective-psychological background of National Socialism and to try to understand the role of anti-Semitism as a powerful weapon in its hands. Jung has not explicitly stated the following maxim; but it speaks through each of his lines: If you want to render help under such threatening conditions, you must first understand their cause. In the next issue of the *Zentralblatt* (Vol. 7, Nos. 1 and 2), he wrote a long paper entitled: "Zur gegenwärtigen Lage der Psychotherapie" (On the Present Situation of Psychotherapy), from which we quote here in careful translation the pages which have been widely circulated in misleading abbreviations and translations, and from which extracts have been pieced together in a fashion which distorts their meaning. In the first seven pages Jung discusses mainly Freud's and Adler's concepts of psychotherapy, maintaining that they have developed therapeutic techniques which could be used in a routine manner, but not a therapeutic concept which would take care of the sick person as a total personality, and, at the same time emphasize the responsibility of the therapist, whose own attitude and background—in short, whose own personality—represent integral elements in his task of helping. Jung says:

> All these reflections lead us back to the attitude of the physician and to the need of a critique of the subjective promises. A

Weltanschauung must not be uncritically applied to the concept
of the neuroses, as happens for instance in the case of the
Freudian concept of the unconscious or its materialistic prejudice
in regard to the religious function of the soul. The psychotherapist
should no longer indulge in the delusion that the treatment of the
neuroses demands nothing more than the knowledge of a technique; he needs to understand very clearly that the psychological
treatment of a patient constitutes a relationship which involves
the physician as much as the patient. True psychological treatment can only be individual, therefore, even the best technique
possesses only relative value. Greater significance accrues to the
physician's own general attitude, of which he himself must be
sufficiently aware not to destroy the particular values—whatever
they may consist of—in the patient entrusted to his care. If Alfred
Adler should request an analytic treatment from his old teacher
Freud, Freud would have to accommodate himself to seeing
Adler's special psychology and even acknowledge its collective
right of existence. For there are countless persons who have the
psychology of the frustrated son. If, on the other hand, I were to
analyze Freud, I would be doing him a great and irreparable
wrong if I did not take fully into account the historic reality of
the nursery, the importance of the emotional entanglements
within the family chronicle, the bitterness and seriousness of
early acquired resentments and their compensatory concomitants
of (unfortunately) unfulfillable wish fantasies, and if I did not
accept their existence as an accomplished fact. Freud would
certainly not be satisfied if I were to tell him that resentments are
nothing but a "substitute" (*Ersatz*) for neglecting to love one's
neighbor, or something of the sort. True as this statement may
be in other cases, it would be inaccurate here, even if I should
succeed in convincing Freud of the truth of my idea. Doubtless,
Freud means what he says, therefore he must be accepted as the
person who says such things. Only then is his individual case
accepted, and, with him, are recognized those others whose
psychology is similarly constituted. Now, insofar as one can
hardly assume that Freud and Adler are universally valid representatives of European humanity, there exists for myself the
immediate hope that I, too, possess a specific psychology and
with me all those who similarly cannot subscribe to the primacy
of infantile-perverse wish fantasies or to that of the urge to

power. It is self-evident that this must not be a matter of naive self-deception, but rather an opportunity for critical self-observation in the light of these negative psychologies which no psychotherapist should forgo. Freud and Adler have seen very clearly the shadow which accompanies everyone. The Jews have this peculiarity in common with women: Being physically the weaker they have to aim at the chinks in their opponent's armor, and since this technique has been enforced upon them during a history of many centuries, the Jews themselves are best covered at the spots where others are most vulnerable. In consequence of their more than twice as ancient culture they are vastly more conscious of human weaknesses and inferiorities and therefore much less vulnerable in this respect than we are ourselves. They also owe to the experience of ancient culture the ability to live consciously in benevolent, friendly and tolerant neighborhood with their own defects (*Untugenden*), while we are still too young to have no illusions about ourselves. Moreover we have been called upon by fate still to create culture (for we are in need of it) to which end so-called illusions in the shape of one-sided ideals, convictions, plans, etc., are essential. The Jew as a member of a race whose culture is about 3,000 years old, like the educated Chinese, is psychologically conscious in wider areas than we are. Consequently it is less dangerous, generally speaking, for the Jew to devaluate his unconscious. The Aryan unconscious, on the other hand, contains tensions and creative germs of an as yet unfulfilled future which one may not devaluate as nursery romanticism without endangering the soul. The still young Germanic peoples are entirely able to produce new forms of culture, and this future still lies in the darkness of the unconscious of each individual, as a germ laden with energy, capable of a mighty blaze. The Jew, as relatively a nomad, never has produced and presumably never will produce a culture of his own, since all his instincts and gifts require a more or less civilized host-people for their development. Therefore the Jewish race as a whole has, according to my experience, an unconscious which can only conditionally be compared to the Aryan. Aside from certain creative individuals, the average Jew is already much too conscious and differentiated to be pregnant with the tensions of the unborn future. The Aryan unconscious has a higher potential than the Jewish; that is the advantage and the disadvantage of a youthfulness not yet fully

estranged from barbarism. In my opinion, it has been a great
mistake of all previous medical psychology to apply Jewish
categories, which are not even binding for all Jews, indiscriminately to Christian Germans or Slavs. In so doing, medical
psychology has declared the most precious secret of the Germanic
peoples—the creatively prophetic depths of soul—to be childishly
banal morass, while for decades my warning voice has been
suspected of anti-Semitism. The source of this suspicion is Freud.
He did not know the Germanic soul any more than did all his
Germanic imitators. Has the might apparition of National Socialism, which the whole world watches with astonished eyes, taught
them something better? Where was the unheard-of tension and
energy when there was as yet no National Socialism? It lay hidden
in the Germanic soul, in that profound depth which is everything
else except the garbage bin of unreliable childish wishes and
unresolved family resentments. A movement which seizes a whole
people has ripened in every individual, too. It is for this reason
that I say that the Germanic unconscious contains tensions and
possibilities which medical psychology must consider in its evaluation of the unconscious. It does not deal with neuroses but
with human beings, and it is truly the fortunate privilege of a
medical psychology that not only is it permitted to *treat the
whole person;* it even needs to do so. Therefore its framework
must be widened to reveal to the eye of the physician not only the
diseased aberrations of a disturbed psychological development,
but also the constructive and creatively active forces of the soul,
not only an obscure section but the significant whole.

Neurosis, namely, is by no means something merely negative,
it is also positive. Only a soulless rationalism could overlook,
and has overlooked, this fact, supported by the narrowness of a
merely material *Weltanschauung*. In reality, the neurosis contains
the patient's soul, or at least an essential part of it, and if,
according to rationalistic intention, the neurosis could be ex-
tracted like a diseased tooth, the patient would have gained
nothing but would have lost something very essential, namely, as
much as a thinker who has lost doubt about his conclusions, or
a moral man who has lost his temptations, or a brave man who
has lost his fear. To lose a neurosis means to become unsubstan-
tial, indeed life loses its point and so its meaning. It would be no
cure but an amputation; and it is a deceptive consolation if

thereupon "psychoanalysis" assures us that nothing has been lost except the infantile paradise with its (perverse) wish-chimeras. One has lost much more, for in reality there is embedded in the neurosis a piece of still undeveloped personality, without which the human being is condemned to resignation, bitterness and other antagonisms to life. The psychology of neuroses which sees only the negative, empties out the baby with the bath, in that it neglects the meaning and value of the "infantile," i.e., the creative fantasy. Often the efforts of this psychology consist essentially in an attempt to find out how one could explain—anything at all— downward, and actually there is nothing incapable of an obscene caricature. This possibility never proves, however, that the symptom or symbol explained in this way actually has this meaning, it only proves the dirty adolescent fantasy of the interpreter.

I cannot avoid mentioning how often it happens that otherwise serious physicians, in complete disregard of all the fundamental tenets of scientific conscience, explain psychological material by means of subjective conjectures—conjectures of which one can really make nothing, except that they are attempts to find that particular obscene witticism through which the material under investigation could be in some way related to an anal, urethral or other sexual abnormality. The poison of a devaluating interpretation has infiltrated the very marrow of these people, so that they can no longer think at all except in the infantile perverse jargon of certain cases of neuroses which are characterized by the special features of Freudian psychology. It is really too grotesque that the physician himself falls into that way of thinking which he rightly objects to as infantile in others, and therefore would like to cure. It is certainly much easier to make conjectures over the heads of other people than to discover what the patient's empirical material means in itself. After all, one must assume that the patient comes to the doctor to free himself of his pathological modes of thought and of approach and, therefore, one might well assume—as is moreover the case in all modern medicine—that in the syndrome itself are also contained the healing tendencies of the diseased system. But if the physician's thoughts overtly or silently are as negative and devaluating as the patient's, and are equally desirous of pulling everything and anything into the infantile-perverse morass of an obscene wit-psychology, one must not be surprised if the latter's soul becomes a barren waste and he compensates for this barrenness by an incurable intellectualism.

No one with any objectivity can maintain that we are here confronted with a document of anti-Semitic character or one which registers consent to, or admiration of National Socialism. In the accusations made against Jung the following expression in particular has been used as a weapon of attack: "the mighty apparition of national socialism which the whole world watches with astonished eyes," or, in the original German: "*die gewaltige Erscheinung des Nationalsozialismus, auf den die ganze Welt mit erstaunten Augen blickt.*" There are two points in this sentence which need to be interpreted in their original meaning. The first is that the word *gewaltig* has a somewhat different connotation in Swiss usage than it has in German. Jung has frequently used the word—we would like to refer the reader to a context already presented in these pages, where he speaks of the *gewaltige* (powerful) role which sexuality plays in the human psyche. In the German language, as it is understood by those who have exploited this sentence, one would hardly place sexuality and a political uprising on the same level. The Swiss dialectic version of German uses the word in a more dynamic sense and with greater frequency to describe an impressive event.* The second point concerns the expression "with astonished eyes." Those who interpret these words as admiration of Nazism are motivated by the undercurrent of their own negative emotions, the projection of which makes them incapable of evaluating fairly any objective statement, which they can only perceive as an emotionally loaded one in a positive or a negative sense. Anyone among us today, opening an illustrated magazine of 1934 showing the massing of regiments and their flags on an occasion such as a Nürnberg meeting, must agree that this was an astonishing display, unexpected in its forcefulness,

---

*For analogy, consider such differences in British English and American English as the usages of "bloody" and "bitch"; or note that a British (or German) "billion" is a thousand times the size of an American "billion." One might also recall the colloquial American—particularly adolescent American—habit of applying "terrific" to anything from a new movie star to a thunderstorm.

especially to those who spent their lives at a distance of several hundred miles. One can be astonished by certain phenomena without sympathizing with them; and one can be deeply disturbed by them and yet prefer not to express one's own negative feelings—in order to preserve one's own plans for helping others against new outbreaks of violence. One must remember what position Jung occupied at that time, when he had to write for and to keep alive a publication printed for German doctors in Germany itself. Fanatics may often look upon cleverness with suspicion, but the question is whether this cleverness achieves the positive help for which it aims. Not one action can be found which could be interpreted in any way as showing that Jung had any part in National Socialist acts and plans, either in Switzerland or in Germany. On the other hand, we have positive proof of the opposite, particularly where he opposed the anti-Semitism and the plans for anti-Semitic action made by the Nazis.

There is one point which must still be reported here in detail. From the days when Jewish psychiatrists in Germany were disqualified, Jung made every attempt to help them, as he fought against anti-Semitism in general whenever it was possible to do so without endangering his own moves to help. Anyone who, like this present author, has tried to learn from Dr. Jung must have been struck by the fine distinctions expressed through his actions and in the restraint imposed upon the spoken word.

We have already reported Jung's fine and gallant attitude during the first meeting of the international association of the national groups of psychotherapists in Bad Nauheim in central Germany in May, 1934, when he chose as the topic of his address the "Theory of Complexes," in which he paid homage to Freud, who was then the target of Nazi hatred. I recall how, on the following day, the German press raged against Jung and carefully registered the number of times on which Jung had pronounced the hated name of Freud. There would certainly have been no reason to expose one's self in this manner during these weeks of the most fanatical outburst of anti-Semitism if one had wished to ingratiate himself with the National Socialist regime and its leaders.

During those same weeks, Jung undertook something which he

would not have been able to do openly without destroying its success. He had caused a kind of amendment to be added to the rules of the international association of the national groups of psychotherapists. This amendment was not communicated in an official manner through the *Zentralblatt* but was circulated quietly alongside one issue of the journal. The communication reads:

> During the last Congress of the Überstaatliche Allgemeine Ärztliche Gesellschaft für Psychotherapie it was decided, to constitute the society in the form of national groups. Consequently, national groups have now been founded or are in process of formation in the various countries which were represented at the Congress [Denmark, Germany, Holland, Sweden and Switzerland]. The conditions of membership in these national groups vary according to local by-laws. On account of the political circumstances in various regions, and because of the lack of national groups in certain countries, making it impossible for individuals to join their respective groups, it has been decided that membership in any national group is on a purely voluntary basis, in other words individual membership can be achieved directly in the Überstaatliche Allgemeine Ärztliche Gesellshaft für Psychotherapie without the intermediary of a national group. The Überstaatliche Gesellschaft is politically and confessionally neutral. Those wishing to become members in it are asked to communicate with the office of the secretary general of the Überstaatliche Gesellshaft represented by Dr. W. Cimbal in Altona, or with the business manager of the president, Dr. C. A. Meier, Burghölzli, Zürich. The organ of the society is the *Zentralblatt für Psychotherapie*. . . . We therefore politely invite you to join the Überstaatliche Allgemeine Ärztliche Gesellschaft für Psychotherapie.

> *Zürich-Küsnacht*   Dr. C. G. Jung.

What Jung had done here was actually to find means of reviving under the nose of the Nazis the old "international society" by making it possible for anyone to become a member of the international association. At the same time something else was achieved, of which no mention was made, but which I, living at that time in Europe, knew was the main reason for this arrangement. This is corroborated by Jung's own report in the letter which will be reprinted later in this paper. German Jewish psychotherapists, who were not allowed to join the German or any other national organization, were thus enabled to become members of the supernational association. One more deduction can be made from this announcement. The de-nationalized psychotherapists wishing to join the international group could make their application through the business manager of the German "Nazified" group. If this group was willing to lend its services against the Nazi Order, then the entire psychotherapeutic association, including the German national group, must have been strongly anti-Nazi. This was actually so, as I can assert from personal knowledge of the circumstances. Jung did not "play along with the Nazis," as has more than once been charged; instead, he fought in a clever way, and the only possible way, against them, adjusting himself to the given conditions so he could extend his help.

Here is another refutation of the charge of anti-Semitism against Jung: The first book he published after the Nazi rise is his volume *Wirklichkeit der Seele*. The book has 409 pages. Of these, 50 are given over to a long study by a Jewish pupil of Dr. Jung, Hugo Rosenthal, entitled "Der Typengegensatz in der jüdischen Religions-geschichte" (The Typological Opposites in the History of the Jewish Religion). Certainly this also was not an action which could have been intended to win him sympathy and friendship from the Nazis, and it was not meant to do so. Its meaning will become clear from the letter, which will be reprinted.

Of course, persons with hate-inflated emotions may accept the presentation given here and yet may find the proof inadequate. However, the presentation here is made for sound and humanly adjusted minds and not for psychopathological personalities.

It now remains to follow the events which led to Dr. Jung's eventual resignation from cooperation with the Überstaatliche Gesellschaft and consequently from any contact with the then-existing German organizations.

To give a reasonable start to the collaboration within the framework of national groups, set up by stipulation of the Nazi government, a first series of issues of the *Zentralblatt* was planned and executed, each issue undertaken by one of the national groups. The first one was a German issue, followed by Swiss, Dutch and Scandinavian numbers. Soon, however, regular publications became the rule once more.

Considerable distrust on the part of German officialdom appears to have existed concerning the psychotherapeutic organization, distrust which, however, did not find sufficient grounds for interfering with its existence. However, a year later, we see Dr. Goering appearing as co-editor with Dr. Jung, while Dr. Cimbal retired in favor of a man who seems to have appeared more trustworthy to the Nazi authorities. This was in 1936. A neurologist and psychiatrist about whose political attitudes I have been unable to obtain sure information, Dr. von Weizsaecker, was added to the editorial board. This arrangement, however, only lasted for two more years. From 1937 onward, Jung's name was retained only more or less *pro forma* as a co-editor of the *Zentralblatt*.

Following, is the letter written by Jung during May of the fateful year, 1934, to a Jewish pupil and friend who at that time still lived on the other side of the Atlantic but who is now a practicing medical psychotherapist in this country. The recipient of this long letter has kindly agreed to have it reprinted in part. All and any passages of a personal nature have been omitted as well as those not essential to the task which this reprinting serves. Because the wording of such pronouncements is of basic importance, it is first reproduced in German, with an English translation appended.

> . . . Es scheinen ja amüsante Gerüchte über mich ausgestreut zu werden. Die einzige Tatsächlichkeit, die hinter all diesem blöden Geschwätz liegt, ist, dass ich als Ehrenvorsitzender der Internationalen Gesellschaft für Psychotherapie diese nicht im Stiche lassen konnte, im Moment als Kretschmer zurücktrat. Ich bin von den deutschen Aertzten dringend ersucht worden, diese Stellung beizubehalten und habe in der Folge das getan, was jeder an meiner Stelle getan hätte, mämlich meine Pflicht gegenüber dem Internationalen Verein. Diese bestand wesentlich darin, die Rahmenorganisation zu halten und die deutche in diese Organisation

einzugliedern. Dies ist nun im letzen Nauheimer Kongress gelungen, und es ist auch die erfreuliche Tatsache zu verzeichnen, dass auf meinen Vorschlag ein besonderer Paragraph angenommen wurde, der es nun den deutschen jüdischen Aertzten ermöglicht, als Einzelmitglieder dem internationalen Verband beizutreten. Damit sind sie vollberechtigte Mitglieder geworden.

Auf die übrigen Gerüchte brauche ich wohl kaum einzugehen. Es ist eine glatte Lüge zu behaupten ich hätte gesagt, die Juden seien in der Analyse unehrlich. Die Leute müssen mich doch für reichlich dumm halten, wenn sie meinen, dass ich so etwas idiotisches behaupten könne. Ebenso habe ich weder im Rundfunk noch sonst irgenwie Hitler angesprochen oder irgend etwas in politischer Hinsicht gesagt.

Was nun meine Ansicht ambetrifft, dass die Juden voraussichtlich keine eigene Kulturform erzeugen, so beruht diese Ansicht, I. auf historischen Tatsachen, 2. auf der anderen Tatsache, dass die eigentliche kulturelle Leistung des Juden sich am deutlichsten entfaltet innerhalb einer Wirtskultur, wo der Jude sehr oft zum eigentlichen Kulturträger wird, oder zu deren Promotor. Diese Aufgabe ist so eigenartig und anspruchsvoll, dass man kaum absehen könnte. Da nun in Palästina tatsächlich sehr eingenartige Verhältnisse vorliegen, so habe ich ein vorsichtiges "voraussichtlich" in meinen Satz eingeführt. Ich möchte keineswegs die Möglichkeit bestreiten, dass dort etwas eigenartiges ensteht, aber ich weiss es bis jetzt noch nicht. Ich kann schlechterdings in dieser Ansicht nichts antisemitisches entdecken. . . .

. . . Der jüdische Christuscomplex ist eine sehr beachtenswerte Angelegenheit. Wie Sie wissen, stimme ich Ihnen in dieser Hinischt durchaus zu. Die Existenz dieses Complexes bedingt eine etwas hysterisierte allegemeine Geisteshaltung, die mir besonders jetzt bei der gegenwärtigen antichristlichen Hetze gegen mich, deutlich geworden ist. Die blosse Tatsache, dass ich von einer Differenz zwischen jüdischer und christlicher Psychologie spreche, genügt schon, um jeden das Vorurteil vorbringen zu lassen, ich sei ein "Antisemit." Oder wie "z. B. das Schweizerische Israelitische Wochenblatt" meint: mit meiner Behauptung, dass ich ebensowenig ein Antisemit wie ein Antichinese sei, wolle ich die Juden einer mongolischen Horde vergleichen. Diese Empfindlichkeit ist einfach krankhaft und macht jede Diskussion beinahe unmöglich. Schon Freud hat mich, wie Sie wissen, des Antisemitismus angeklagt, weil ich seinen seelenlosen Materialismus nicht billigen konnte. Mit dieser Bereitwilligkeit überall Antisemitismus zu wittern, beschwört der Jude direkt Antisemitismus herauf. Ich sehe nicht ein, warum der Jude nicht ebensogut wie ein sogennanter Christ annehmen kann, man kritisiert ihn persoenlich, wenn man eine Meinung über ihm hat. Warum muss denn immer gleich angenommen werden, dass man das jüdische Volk damit verdammen wolle? Der Einzelne ist doch tot zu machen. Ich bin mit meinen jüdischen Patienten oder Kollegen in der grossen Mehrzahl der Fälle sehr gut ausgekommen. Dass ich an Einzelnen Kritik üben musste, das kommt auch bei anderen Leuten vor, wird aber vom diesen nicht darauf bezogen, dass sie Engländer, Amerikaner oder Franzosen seien. Allerdings gibt es da eine Ausnahme, die ich erwähnen will, das sind die Deutschen. Es ist mir naemlich mehr als einmal passiert, dass wenn ich einen einzelnen Deutschen kritisierte, er flugs auf die Idee verfiel, ich ein Deutschenhasser. Es ist aber zu billig, wenn man seine eigene Minderwertigkeit hinter einen politischen Vorurteil verbergen will. . . .

. . . Sie wissen doch zur Genüge, wie sehr ich den Menschen als Persönlichkeit nehme und mich bestrebe, ihn aus seinen Kollektivbedingungen herauszuheben und zu einem Individuum zu machen. Es ist ja, wie Sie ebenfalls wissen, nur möglich, wenn er seine Besonderheit, die ihm durch das Schicksal aufgenötight ist, erkennt. Keiner der ein Jude ist, kann zum Menschen werden, ohne dass er weiss, dass er ein Jude ist, denn das ist die Basis von der er ein höheres Menschentum erreichen kann. Das gilt für alle Nationen und Rassen. Der Nationalismus, so unsympathisch er auch ist, ist darum eine *Conditio sine qua non,* nur darf der Einzelne nicht darin stecken bleiben. Aber als Massenpartikel soll er sich auch nicht darüber erheben. Als Mensch bin ich ein Europaeer, als Massenatom bin ich ein schweizertischer Spiessbürger, wohnhaft Seestrasse 228 Küsnacht bei Zürich. . . .

Zum Schluss möchte ich Ihnen noch mitteilen, dass mein neues Buch "Wirklichkeit der Seele" erschienen ist, worin ich einen jüdischen Autor über alttestamentliche Psychologie aufgenommen habe, um die Nationalsozialisten zu ärgern, und alle diejenigen Juden, die mich als Antisemiten verschrieen haben. Das Nächste was jetzt erfunden werden wird, ist, dass ich an einer kompletten Standpunktslosigkeit leide und weder ein Antisemit bin noch ein Nazi. Wir leben in einer Zeit, die von Narrheit überströmt. "*Quem Deus vult perdere primus dementat.*"

Mit den besten Grüssen, Ihr

C. G. Jung,
et semper idem.

The Translation

. . . It appears that amusing rumors are being spread about me. The only unquestionable fact which lies behind all this stupid gossip is that having been elected honorary chairman (*Ehrenvorsitzender*) of the International Society for Psychotherapy, I could not desert the society at the moment when Kretschmer resigned. I have been urgently requested by the German physicians to retain this position and have consequently done what anyone else would have done in my situation, namely, my duty toward the International Society. This consisted in the main in preserving the (*Rahmenorganisation*) supernational society and in affiliating to it the German society. This was accomplished at the last Nauheim congress. We can also register the satisfying fact that at my suggestion a special paragraph has been adopted to the effect that German Jewish physicians can individually join the international organization. They have thus become full members with equal rights.

I need hardly mention the other rumors. It is a downright lie to quote me as having said that Jews are dishonest in analysis. Anyone who believes that I could say anything so idiotic must think me extraordinarily stupid. Neither have I addressed Hitler over the radio or in any other manner, nor have I expressed anything in regard to politics. In regard to my opinion that the Jews probably do not create their own forms of culture, this opinion rests upon (1) historical facts, (2) the fact that the specific cultural contribution of the Jew achieves its clearest results within the circle of a host-culture, where the Jew frequently becomes the very carrier of this culture, or its promoter. This task is in itself so specific and so demanding that it is hardly to be conceived that any individual Jewish culture could arise alongside it. Since Palestine actually presents very peculiar conditions [the recipient of this letter was at that time living in Palestine], I have cautiously inserted the word "probably" (*voraussichtlich*) in my sentence. I would in no wise deny the possibility that something specific is being created there, but so far I do not know it. I cannot discover anything anti-Semitic in this opinion. . . .

. . . The Jewish Christ-complex is a very remarkable affair. As you know I completely agree with you in this respect. The existence of this complex makes for a somewhat hystericized general attitude of mind (*Geisteshaltung*) which has become especially clear to me in the course of the present anti-Christian attacks upon myself. The mere fact that I speak of a difference between Jewish and Christian psychology suffices to allow anyone to voice the prejudice that I am an anti-Semite. Or, in the opinion of the Swiss Israelitic Weekly, my assertion that I am as little an anti-Semite as an anti-Chinese proves my intention to compare the Jews with a Mongolian horde. This hypersensitivity is simply pathological and makes every discussion almost impossible. As you know, Freud previously accused me of anti-Semitism because I could not countenance his soulless materialism. The Jew truly solicits anti-Semitism with his readiness to scent out anti-Semitism everywhere. I cannot see why the Jew, like any so-called Christian, is incapable of assuming that he is being personally criticized when one has an opinion about him. Why must it always be assumed that one wants to condemn the Jewish people? Surely the individual is not the people? I regard this as an inadmissible manner of silencing one's adversary. In the great majority of cases, I have got along very well with my Jewish patients and colleagues. It happens in the cases of other people, too, that I have to criticize the individual; but they do not ascribe it to the fact that they are English, American or French. However, there does exist one exception worth mentioning in this respect, and that is the German. It has happened to me more than once that when I criticized a German he immediately concluded that I am a hater of Germans. It is really too cheap to try to hide one's own inferiority behind a political prejudice. . . .

. . . You know well enough to what extent I approach the human being as a personality and how I endeavor to lift him out of his collective conditioning and to make him into an individual. This, as you know, is only possible if he acknowledges his peculiar features (*Besonderheit*) which have been forced upon him by fate. No one who is a Jew can become a human being without knowing that he is a Jew, since this is the basis from which he must reach out toward a higher humanity (*Menschentum*). This holds good for all nations and races. Nationalism is therefore a *sine qua non*—no matter how objectionable it may appear—but the individual must not remain stuck in it. On the other hand, insofar as he is a particle of the mass of the people he must not elevate himself above it either. As a human individual I am a European, as an atom of the masses I am a Swiss bourgeois, domiciled at 228 Seestrasse, Küsnacht near Zürich. . . .

Finally I want to inform you that my new book, *Wirklichkeit der Seele,* has appeared. I have included in it a Jewish author [writing] on the "Psychology of the Old Testament" in order to annoy the Nazis and all those Jews who have decried me as an anti-Semite. The next thing they are now going to invent about me is that I suffer from a complete absence of convictions and that I am neither an anti-Semite nor a Nazi. We happen to live in a period which overflows with lunacy. "*Quen deus perdere vult primum dementat.*"

With kindest regards,
Yours,

C. G. Jung,
et semper idem.

Carl Gustav Jung
and the Jews:
The Real Story

James Kirsch

James Kirsch, M.D., studied with Jung in 1929 and remained in frequent contact with him until Jung's death in 1961. He practiced psychiatry in Berlin from 1926 to 1933. After Hitler came to power, Dr. Kirsch left Germany and went to Palestine. He lived in London for several years before finally settling in Los Angeles in 1940. He was one of the founders of the C. G. Jung Institute in Zurich, the Analytical Psychology Club in Berlin, and the Analytical Psychology Club of Los Angeles.

In this article, first published in 1982 in the *Journal of Psychology and Judaism,* Dr. Kirsch draws upon his extensive personal and professional relationship with Jung and his review of the historical material to refute specific allegations made by Robert Haymond in the same issue of the journal. While the article makes many of the same points that Harms did in his article thirty-six years earlier, Kirsch does recognize Jung's insensitive timing in his publication of assertions about Jewish psychology during the 1930s. He also acknowledges the question-able nature of these assertions, and regrets that Jung's misunderstanding of Jewish culture, psychology, and religion have caused so much pain and contro-versy. Nevertheless, like so many of Jung's Jewish colleagues and followers, Kirsch maintains that he never witnessed any evidence of anti-Semitism in Jung's personal relationships. He contends that Jung grappled with his misconceptions, acknowledged his errors to several Jewish colleagues, and eventually resolved his "Jewish complex" through the cathartic writing of *Answer to Job.*

I

There is no doubt that the Swiss psychologist Carl Gustav Jung, who died in 1961, was one of the greatest psychologists of the twentieth century. He is usually mentioned in connection with two other German-speaking physicians who made significant contributions to the science of psychology and the art and practice of psychotherapy—Sigmund Freud and Alfred Adler. The two were Jews, while Jung, as the son of a Swiss Reformed minister, was naturally brought up as a Christian. Both Adler and Jung at first worked closely with Freud, the pioneer and founder of psychoanalysis, but later left him for different reasons and at different times. When Jung broke away from Freud, the accusation that he was anti-Semitic was flung at him, and coming at the time that anti-Semitism became the avowed tool of the German government and the justification for the vicious and inhuman destruction of European Jewry, the accusation against Jung assumed enormous proportions. Many Jews and some others considered him a theoretical and practical partner with the Nazis. Now, some twenty years after Jung's death, Robert Haymond has renewed these attacks on Jung by writing, from a psycho-social point of view, a paper entitled "On Carl Gustav Jung: Psycho-social Basis of Morality During the Nazi Era" (1982). I am very grateful to Dr. Reuven Bulka for allowing me to respond to this article and to say how I, as a Jew who was a student and friend of Jung from 1928 on through the Nazi era until his death in June 1961, view this controversial question.

II

In the Summer 1979 issue of the *Journal of Psychology and Judaism* Robert Haymond published "Roots in the Shtetl: Modern Western Thought and the Case of Sigmund Freud." It is meritorious to investigate the genius of Sigmund Freud, the discoverer of the unconscious as a clinical fact and the pioneer of modern psychology, from a sociological point of view; naturally we expect the author to have adequate knowledge of the most important facts in regard to his subject. However, we find a most astonishing statement in this essay:

> Ironically, the use of free-association, called by Freud word-association, and credited by him as being one of the main contributions to the psychoanalytic method, was created, not by him, but by the pastor's son, Carl Jung, of the Swiss School. (p. 245)

Does the author really not know the difference between the method of free association and the word-association experiment? The word-association experiment was invented by Wilhelm Wundt and used by Jung, though for a different purpose. The result of Jung's experimental work with Wundt's association test led to his discovery of the so-called *gefühlsbetonter Komplex* (autonomous feeling-tone complex).

In "On the History of the Psychoanalytic Movement," quoted by Haymond (Freud, 1914/1957), Freud justly claims the invention of the method of free association for himself (p. 28). Actually, free associations are the backbone of psychoanalysis and were used by Freud many years before he met Jung. The formulation of this method was one of the great achievements of Freud's scientific life.

Robert Haymond's preoccupation with Freud as a social phenomenon made it probable that he would turn his attention to Freud's disciple, friend, and later antagonist, C. G. Jung, and would write about him from a psycho-social point of view. His article contains misstatements of facts and deserves correction, clarification, and rebuttal from the Jewish point of view.

Haymond's article starts with a misstatement. He claims that Professor Kretschmer was a Jew, and, several pages later, he comes back to this statement and makes a good deal out of it as ammunition against Jung.

I had met Professor Kretschmer, myself, at one of the International Congresses of Psychotherapy and knew that Professor Kretschmer was not a Jew. To be absolutely sure of this fact, I asked my friend Dr. Hans Dieckmann of Berlin to inquire from Professor Kretschmer's son whether or not Kretschmer was a Jew. Dr. Dieckmann, in a letter of February 1, 1980, wrote me:

Though it was known to me that Professor Ernst Kretschmer was no Jew, I still did some more inquiries. He certainly was an opponent of the Nazi regime and has maintained himself only on the basis of his prominent position during the Nazi time. I also have telephoned his son, Professor Wolfgang Kretschmer in Tübingen, and he has assured me that neither his father nor anybody else in his whole family has been Jewish. You have the right to raise an objection to the essay you mentioned and to correct this fact.

Ellenberger, who also discusses the election of Jung for the presidency of the Allgemeine Gesellschaft für Psychotherapie in 1933, writes:

If Jung really had taken over Kretschmer's post in the German Association, as Jones erroneously contends, it is obvious that Kretschmer would have mentioned the fact in his autobiography. However, Kretschmer does not say anything of the kind and he gives a very sympathetic picture of Jung. (Ellenberger, 1970, p. 740)

Robert Haymond's first paragraph contains an altogether simplified and, therefore, misleading description of how and why Jung accepted the presidency of the International (soon to be called "Supranational") General Medical Society for Psychotherapy and its publication, *Zentralblatt*. Kretschmer resigned for political reasons. He just did not agree with the Nazis and felt, like other members of the Society, that only a non-German could deal successfully with the new Nazi government. Haymond says that Jung *automatically* assumed the position, while Barbara Hannah, whom he quotes extensively, describes Jung's conflicts about accepting the presidency and mentions the fact that "leading members of the Society pressed Jung—fervently—to take the chair" (Hannah, 1976, p. 228). Haymond himself quotes Jung's answer to a critic (from "A Rejoinder to Dr. Bally," published under the title "Zeitgenössisches"):

A moral conflict arose for me as it would for any decent man in this situation. Should I, as a prudent neutral, withdraw into security this side of the frontier and wash my hands in innocence, or should I—as I was well aware—risk my skin and expose myself to the inevitable misunderstandings which no one escapes who, from higher necessity, has to make a pact with the existing political powers in Germany? (Jung, 1934a/1964, pp. 535–536)

The election and the presidency by Jung in the thirties has been described and evaluated by several writers. Professor Ernst Simon, of Jerusalem, in an article published in the *Mitteilungsblatt* (a small Israeli weekly) around the time of Jung's centennial, called Jung's acceptance of the presidency "the blackest spot in Jung's career." To which I responded, "It is an exceedingly white spot." For Robert Haymond it is a question of "condemning or exonerating" (p. 82). To do this one has to "examine the sociohistorical context" (p. 81) and "understand the social tensions which fostered particular attitudes" (p. 82). He gives, then, a fair description of the "German unification program," the *Gleichschaltung*, and its effects on Jewish scholars in Germany (pp. 82–83).

Aniela Jaffé describes the situation most vividly in the following words:

> When the Nazis seized power (1933) Professor Ernst Kretschmer, president of the General Medical Society for Psychotherapy (Allgemeine Ärztliche Gesellschaft für Psychotherapie), resigned. As with all scientific societies that were located in Germany, the *Gleichschaltung* of the "General Society" seemed only a matter of time. At this critical moment (June 1933), and at the urgent request of its leading members, Jung, then honorary vice-president, accepted the presidency in the hope of being able to avert the worst. In acceding to his colleagues' request, Jung was in an altogether different situation from Kretschmer: as a Swiss he could accept the presidency without being bound by the Nazi ideology. Unlike Kretschmer, neither his intellectual nor his political freedom was at stake. (Jaffe, 1971, pp. 78–79)

Even Haymond has to admit that "to this end [to salvage the continuing work of the whole association] he made it possible for his German-Jewish colleagues to become members of the German contingent. We would call them members-at-large" (p.83). In fact, as Aniela Jaffé writes in her essay:

within a matter of months he had used his freedom as a Swiss to redraft the statutes of the Society so as to make it formally and effectively international in character . . . and German-Jewish psychotherapists could and did immediately become individual members of the International Society. Jung's amendment of the statutes gave de facto existence to the International General Medical Society for Psychotherapy which was composed of different national groups. (pp. 79–80)

Professor C. A. Meier wrote to me in a letter of February 28, 1980:

> There never were two editions of the *Zentralblatt*. As Secretary-General of the Society, however, I carried into effect the publishing of articles of Jewish colleagues during the Nazi time. I also had either to correct again and again insulting and faulty reviews of Jewish books and articles or to suppress them. This was all comparatively easy because I had a free hand until the end. Officially, Jung was in it until the end, but from the beginning had left everything to me. In the latter years a German co-editor was imposed upon me. This was Curtius, but he as well never did anything.

I can do no better than quote, with her express permission, from Aniela Jaffé's chapter "C. G. Jung and National Socialism" in her book *From the Life and Work of C. G. Jung:*

> The *Zentralblatt für Psychotherapie,* which had been published in Germany since the inception of the original Society, was thereupon taken over as the organ of the International Society, whose headquarters were in Zürich, with Jung as editor. The following event put Jung into a very awkward situation: it had earlier been planned that Professor Göring would bring out a "Sonderheft der deutschen Gesellschaft," as a special German supplement to the *Zentralblatt,* for exclusive circulation in Germany. It was to contain a signed declaration by Professor Göring obliging the members of the German Society to adopt Hitler's political and ideological principles. Whether through negligence or by mistake (or, one asks retrospectively, by design,) Göring's manifesto appeared not only in the supplement *Deutsche Seelen-*

heilkunde (Leipzig, 1934), but in slightly different form, also in the current December 1933 issue of the *Zentralblatt*—without Jung's having been apprised of this fact. An issue appearing under his name as editor and carrying the Nazi manifesto was a grave embarrassment to him. In the eyes of the world it was even worse: the Swiss psychiatrist, Dr. Gustav Bally, launched a sharp attack on Jung in the *Neue Zürcher Zeitung* (27 February 1934) and therewith the discussion began. (1971, p. 79)

Aniela Jaffé continues:

> One may have honest doubts as to whether Jung acted correctly in sitting down at a table with German doctors at that time of terror, even if he did so under the auspices of an international society. On the other hand, there was no other conceivable way in which his German-Jewish colleagues might have been helped. We shall see that in due course Jung took vigorous steps in this direction. If we wish to form, so far as we can, an objective judgment, we must raise a question of principle which even today, thirty years after the event, has not received a definitive answer: Should the outlawing of an incriminated nation, and its spiritual isolation, be considered a necessary consequence of its crimes, or should one strive with as much right for spiritual and cultural collaboration in the interests of "coexistence"? Jung opted for collaboration with the doctors and psychotherapists of Nazi Germany and thus exposed himself to the judgment of his contemporaries and of posterity.
>
> In his "Rejoinder to Dr. Bally," which, like Bally's attack, still makes instructive reading today, Jung set forth the personal reasons that led him to his decision: before everything else he was concerned to keep the young science of psychotherapy alive, which "at a single stroke of the pen in high places" could have been swept under the table in Germany. For its sake he was willing to risk his person and his name. He was out to help suffering humanity, regardless of nationality and differences of political sentiment. The core of his defense is contained in the following words, which sum up his attitude at that time: "The doctor who, in wartime, gives his help to the wounded of the other side will surely not be held a traitor to his country."
>
> To judge of the difficulties faced by a scientific society during

the years of the Nazi revolution one may take for comparison the fate of the Freud group of the Psychoanalytic Society in Nazi Germany. Paul Eitingon, the Jewish-Polish member of its executive committee, was replaced by the German "Aryan" Felix Boehm, and Freud declared himself in agreement with Eitingon's resignation. In the same fateful year (1933), the Jewish members "voluntarily" seceded in order to "preserve the integrity of psychoanalysis in Nazi Germany." Lewis Mumford seized on these facts—they are reported in Ernest Jones' biography of Freud—and compared them with Jung's all-too-tolerant attitude and his cooperation with the "Nazi-controlled German psychological society," calling it "a hardly less reprehensible Freudian parallel."

But expressly in this connection it should be noted that one of Jung's first official acts as president of the International Society was the implementation of a statutory provision which worked in favor of his Jewish colleagues in Germany. At the Congress of the International Society at Bad Nauheim in May 1934, Jung stipulated that the German-Jewish doctors who had been ejected or excluded from the German section could individually become members of the International Society with equal rights, thus preserving their professional and social status. Even though this measure later proved ineffective in the face of the Nazi terror, it was nevertheless Jung's intention to come directly to the aid of his Jewish colleagues in Germany in the teeth of the anti-Semitic restrictions promulgated by the Nazi regime. His stipulation that the Society be "neutral as to politics and creed" affirmed its complete independence of the German section.

After the Bad Nauheim Congress and at Jung's special request his assistant, Dr. C. A. Meier of Zürich, secretary general of the International Society, . . . was appointed managing editor of the *Zentralblatt*. Later, in 1936, when Professor Göring became co-editor of the *Zentralblatt*—a fact which is often mentioned as weighing heavily against Jung—it was due to Jung and Meier that the *Zentralblatt* was not "conformed," and it continued to publish unbiased reviews of books by Jewish authors, as well as contributions by foreign writers such as H. G. Baynes, Esther Harding, and C. Baudouin. In 1938 the last congress of the International Society took place under Jung's presidency at Oxford. On this occasion the University of Oxford conferred upon

him the degree of *Doctor honoris causa.* Jung's Presidential
Address dealt with the points common to the different schools of
psychotherapy; his aim was to give psychotherapy, on this common basis, "a well-merited place among the other branches of
medical science." (1971, pp. 80–83)

III

I also wish to point to an article which examined C. G. Jung's
actions, not his writings, during the Nazi period in the light of
Jung's later statements that the only motivation for his actions
during that time was to preserve psychotherapy in Germany as
much and as long as possible. The conclusion which the author
arrives at is that all of Jung's actions could be understood to be in
complete agreement with such intentions (Cocks, 1979). I will not
repeat here all the evidence this article communicates but will
direct the attention of all fair-minded readers to this article. I,
myself, and my former wife were very much helped by Jung during
the Nazi time.

It is also worth mentioning a note I received from Dr. med.
H. K. Fierz which contained a copy of the minutes of the charter
meeting of the Supranational General Medical Society of May 12,
1934. He introduces them with the following chronological remarks:

> When, because of the taking over of the Government by the Nazis
> (*Machtergreifung*), Kretschmer resigned the Presidency of the
> Society, C. G. Jung as Vice-President arranged a 7th Congress of
> the Society in Bad Nauheim. Since he was a foreigner in Germany
> he had here a freer hand than Kretschmer. At this congress he
> with others founded the Supranational Society. By this the Gen-
> eral Society . . . was "degraded" to be nothing more than the
> German national group, and it could be arranged from foreign
> countries that "non-aryans" could without any difficulty be
> admitted to participate in the congress. They could also become
> individual members of the Supranational Society. (Personal com-
> munication, February 8, 1980)

I sent a copy of the minutes of the meeting in which Jung accepted the presidency to Dr. Bulka, the editor of this journal, with further documents.

Haymond says that with Jung accepting the presidency of the International General Society for Psychotherapy "commenced a most problematical controversy, which, almost fifty years later, still has not been satisfactorily resolved" (p. 81). The facts have become fully known since that time, and have been presented here as fully as space permitted. What remains to date are rumors and repetitions of the same accusations which circulated around these events of fifty years ago. It is quite possible today (in 1982) to form a clear opinion about Jung's attitude as president of the Supranational Society and his actions during the Nazi period.

All these rumors have been going around essentially in Jewish circles and especially among some psychoanalysts of the Freudian school. The facts have been explained before to a large extent, especially by Ernest Harms (1946) and also by Aniela Jaffé.

I had known Jung personally from 1928 until the time of his death. I had seen him frequently before the Second World War and many times afterward; I had talked to him quite often about the Jewish question and never found any kind of anti-Semitism in him. I say without hesitation that Jung was the only man who, in his personal relations with me, never expressed any kind of anti-Semitism, though he had quite a number of mistaken notions about the Jews in our early conversations between 1929 and 1931. The reason for this was that Jung knew himself very well—he knew his "shadow," a term he coined for an important archetype and which refers to all that a human individual does not want to know about himself. He also knew how common it is to project the shadow onto other people. He knew, also, that the national shadow is usually projected upon another nation: the Germans projected their shadow upon the Jews. Jung, himself, was very much aware of both his personal shadow as well as his Swiss shadow.

He has written about different nations and cultures, several times specifically about the German people, with regard to whom he expressed himself much more sharply and with much stronger language than he ever did with regard to the Jews. But there is hardly a German today who would call Jung anti-German.

Jung has often been accused of being anti-Semitic. Actually, the flood of rumors about Jung being anti-Semitic started with Freud's statement, quoted in *On the History of the Psychoanalytic Movement,* that Jung could not "rid himself of certain racial prejudices."

I once asked Jung what caused Freud to make such a statement about him, and he told me that he had once told Freud a certain dream (Jung and Freud analyzed each other's dreams whenever there was an opportunity to do so) in which there appeared some members of Freud's circle. Freud had pressed him to give more and more associations, and Jung had given him a long series of free associations. Finally Freud said, "Oh, you mean '*meine Judenbengel,*' " or some such derogatory term, to which Jung then said, "Yes." So this is the only basis that Freud had in the course of their friendship to think of Jung as being anti-Semitic.

The sensitivity to anti-Semitism of Jews is well described by Ernest Jones in his *The Life and Work of Sigmund Freud:*

> I became, of course, aware, somewhat to my astonishment, of how extraordinarily suspicious Jews could be of the faintest sign of anti-Semitism and of how many remarks or actions could be interpreted in that sense. The members most sensitive were Ferenczi and Sachs; Abraham and Rank were less so. Freud himself was pretty sensitive in this respect. (1955, p. 163)

In all my many conversations with Jung, I never found the slightest reason to assume that Jung was anti-Semitic or held negative prejudices or biases against the Jews.

Without presenting any evidence, Haymond goes even further. He claims that in the home of Carl Gustav Jung there was an anti-Semitic atmosphere. I, personally, never found evidence of Jung's home showing any kind of anti-Semitism. To me, it appears most improbable that the Reverend Paul Jung, who was an outstanding Hebraist, had any anti-Semitic feelings or nurtured them in his home.

Haymond again brings no evidence for the strong assertion that Jung "with his Fundamentalist (*sic*) upbringing had internalized this cultural baggage (the Jew as Christ denier and Christ killer!) as a child" (p. xx). Paul Jung was a Swiss-Reformed minister, not an American Fundamentalist. It is astonishing that a scientist can make such a statement without even the slightest hint of evidence.

It is true that Jung never justified a particular political mode (for example, the National Socialist). He tried to explain the psychological forces which made such an outburst of emotions possible. The breakthrough of the collective unconscious and its destructive political effects were poignantly described by him as the return of the old Germanic god, Wotan. "Wotan" was a psychological force, a collective complex dormant in the German psyche. Therefore, Jung characterized the whole situation in Germany as a collective psychosis. Are we not afraid that this kind of collective psychosis could repeat itself, even on a grander scale, and possibly destroy all life, on our planet? Would it not be better if as many of us as possible understood the human psyche deeply and would be aware of the terrible dangers which such irrational outbursts of the human psyche bring for the whole of mankind?

IV

Some of the things which Jung published during the Nazi era had to be understood as anti-Semitic. I quote from Aniela Jaffé:

> . . . in his writings at that period, Jung expressed views on the Jewish character and on Judaism which were false and gave offense. Above all, his assertion that "the Jew, who is something of a nomad, has never yet created a cultural form of his own . . . since all his instincts and talents require a more or less civilized nation to act as a host for their development" has aroused much ill-feeling. Statements like this sprang from lack of comprehension of Judaism and Jewish culture which is scarcely intelligible today, though it was widespread then. Thus even Freud, the Jew, could assert in 1908: "We Jews have an easier time [than Jung], having no mystical element." Freud knew so little of Judaism that he was totally unaware of the rich mysticism of the cabala and the mystic wisdom of Hasidism. A general interest in Judaism, particularly among non-Jews, was initiated—strangely enough—

during the Hitler era and became still stronger with the founding of the state of Israel. From then on the works of Martin Buber, Gershom Scholem, Franz Rosenzweig, and many others have become known to a wider public. They helped to deepen a general knowledge of Judaism and Jewish culture or to explain them for the first time.

For all the justified accusations leveled at Jung and for all our sense of disappointment, we should not forget that when he spoke of the difference of Jewish psychology he did not, like the Nazis, imply any "depreciation" of it. This is quite apparent from an unprejudiced reading of his formulations, but is frequently over-looked. Certainly Jung did not make it easy for his readers to see into his mind. When he wrote that the subjective premise, or the "personal equation" of the Jew implied "no depreciation of Semitic psychology, any more than it is a depreciation of the Chinese to speak of the peculiar psychology of the Oriental," this could easily be misunderstood by anyone who did not know Jung. Jung took it for granted that his readers were aware of his veneration for the Chinese mind and Chinese culture. Thus his comparison had just the opposite effect to the one intended: it aroused resentment and correspondingly distorted reactions, and soon one was reading in the press that Jung had compared Jews to a Mongolian horde! (1971, pp. 85–86)

Aniela Jaffé asked the question,

What was his attitude towards National Socialism as a political movement? Some of his observations from the years 1933–34 lead one to conclude that he set his hopes on a fruitful develop-ment in Germany, and that he was willing to give National Socialism a chance in its early days. That the "Aryan" uncon-scious contains creative tensions and "seeds of a future yet to be born" was the psychological foundation of his hopes. Only this deceptive hope that something positive might emerge from the chaos can explain Jung's attitude. Later he admitted this himself. In his "Epilogue to Essays on Contemporary Events" (1946) he wrote: "When Hitler seized power it became quite evident to me that a mass psychosis was boiling up in Germany. But I could not help telling myself that this was after all Germany, a civilized European nation with a sense of morality and discipline. Hence the ultimate outcome of this unmistakable mass movement still seemed to me uncertain, just as the figure of the Führer at first struck me as being merely ambivalent. . . . Like many of my contemporaries, I had my doubts." (Jaffe, 1971, pp. 89–90)

In a conversation I had with Jung in Berlin in May of 1933, I found that in contrast to me, he had some hopes that there would be a positive outcome of this Nazi movement. He could not accept my utterly pessimistic view and my decision to leave Germany as soon as possible. The first time I saw Jung after the war in July of 1947, the first thing that Jung did was to remember this conversation and to apologize to me and to apologize for some things he had written at that time. I regret very much that this apology was made only to me personally but was never put in public writings, so that one could see how Jung's opinions in regard to Jews changed between 1934 and 1947. Some people, disappointed by Jung's attitude, expected a public statement about his mistakes and some kind of clarification. He felt that his article "After the Catastrophe" (1945/1967) was sufficient to state his position. It would, indeed, be a grave falsification of the facts to speak of Jung's guilt for having identified with the Nazi ideology. At no time was there any such identification, even though in the beginning he was fascinated by the formidable phenomenon of National Socialism. Psychologically, it was a mass psychosis; it represented an outburst of the collective unconscious. As with his patients, Jung counted on the healing and creative forces inherent in the human psyche to do their work. He felt justified in this attitude because, as he says, the contents of the collective unconscious are, themselves, ambivalent.

Aniela Jaffé quotes, then, from Jung, and then observes:

> The driving forces of a psychological mass movement are essentially archetypal. Every archetype contains the lowest and the highest, evil and good, and is therefore capable of producing diametrically opposite results. Hence it is impossible to make out at the start whether it will prove to be positive or negative.
>
> In spite of his psychological knowledge Jung remained optimistic, which proves once again the truism that a great scientist is not necessarily a good politician! (1971, p. 90)

One of the great difficulties that Haymond has is this misunderstanding of the way Jung sees the psyche, especially the functions of the archetype. An archetype is a psychic structure which exists in every human being. By its very nature it is indefinite, it has no definable borders. Therefore, the same archetype can make its appearance in many different inner subjective or outer objective situations. That is why Jung was able to enumerate a number of different collective events, like wars and revolutions of different historical times, as constellated by the same archetype. To Haymond this seems total nonsense. His misunderstanding is used as an argument against Jung. But facts are facts, and psychological facts are as real (*wirklich*) as other natural facts.

I cannot quote everything that Aniela Jaffé wrote in her article on Jung and National Socialism, although it would be the best rebuttal one could give to Haymond's article. I therefore have to quote again at some length from her.

> After the fearful abysses of the Nazi regime had become known, Jung revised his hopeful and expectant attitude and was pitiless in his public criticism. In these later pronouncements on Germany there may also be heard the disappointment of a man who realized just how much he had jeopardized his reputation when he staked his personality, his work, his energy, and his hopes on collaboration with doctors and psychotherapists in Nazi Germany. It is true that this comes out most clearly in his essay "After the Catastrophe," which he wrote when the gruesome drama was over. But already in 1936, in his essay on "Wotan," he had branded Nazism as a manifestation of the typical "furor Teutonicus," which he saw personified in Wotan the storm-god. (1971, p. 91)

It is really amazing that Haymond, who has read this article, could never grasp the sharp sarcasm and criticism that this article had about the German people.

Aniela Jaffé continues:

> I hope I have made it clear that despite his mistakes Jung was neither a Nazi nor an anti-Semite. This charge has already been rebutted on several occasions in the press, with supporting doc-

umentation. Nevertheless the legend of Jung's Nazi sympathies persists, and even today, thirty years afterwards, it is still held against him with undiminished virulence. Hence, besides setting forth the facts of the case we must raise the no less important question of the psychological reasons for the persistence of these attacks. An inquiry into the unconscious psychic background is thus unavoidable. . . . One of the deepest roots probably lies in the relationship between Freud and Jung, which still exerts a peculiar fascination on people living today, and by no means only on psychologists of the Freudian or Jungian persuasion. The relationship between the two researchers was problematical from the start, and it ended tragically in mutual resentment which has never quite died out. Ultimately it was fruitful for both men and enriched them. In their friendship and separation, so spotlighted by the world, it was not only two great personalities that confronted one another in scientific and man-to-man discussion, not only the old master and the young disciple, but, above all, the Jew and the gentile. All this lent particular weight to their encounter and it explains the emotionality in evaluating it, the violence of the arguments pro and con. (1971, pp. 92–93)

Let me comment on some misunderstandings which appear in Haymond's article. Jungian archetypes lack historicity, he says. They do, of course. Per se, they are psychic structures, patterns of behavior totally ahistoric. Only when they are activated are they the moving forces in the fate of an individual. Due to their collective nature, they are, under certain conditions, also the moving forces in the fate of nations. When external conditions like an economic depression exert social pressures, they come to the fore and become the moving historical forces. Jung saw their increasing activity in the German psyche long before others did. He raised his voice in 1918 for the first time and several times later. Instead of listening to his warning voice, he was interpreted as being identified with these forces or supporting them. Haymond himself confuses Jung with the subject about which he was writing. In so doing he traps himself hopelessly when he accuses Jung in such manner. To quote Haymond, "This closed world view characterizes the limitations of Jung's conception of cultural archetypes" (p. 106). He refers his readers to page 182 of the Wotan article. On this page Jung quotes from Nietzsche's *Zarathustra* at great length and also from some of his poems, in order to characterize the returning "god" Wotan in the German psyche. Paragraph 375 begins, "The German youths who celebrated the solstice with sheep sacrifices were not the first to hear a rustling in the primeval forest of the unconscious" (1936/1964). It appears that Haymond sets up a straw man, then shoots at him. Jung obviously had a clear insight into the developments of the collective German psyche. That he could write so clearly about the German psyche is the strongest evidence that he was not identified with the Germans and that he had the widest open world-view. His insights were truly *prophetic!*

In my opinion and that of a steadily growing number of people, it is Jung's great merit to have discovered and described the unconscious in a very different and much more comprehensive manner than the great pioneer, Freud. The resistance and hostility against Jung, his methods, discoveries and ideas have not so much to do with his person as such, as with the fact that Jung exposed himself to the depths of the unconscious and by that became something like an archetype himself, a kind of modern medicine man. Such a confrontation of consciousness with the unconscious is always dangerous. It can, in some human beings, create a psychosis. Therefore, people fear and avoid it, if possible. However, the prophets, mystics, Kabbalists, and Zadikim suffered such a confrontation with what we now call by the scientific name "unconscious." Jewish culture is based on a continuing intercourse and discourse with the unconscious. Actually, the Maggid of Mezeritsch, Dov Ber of Mezeritsch, was the first to call it "the unconscious" (*Kadmut ha'sechel*) (Hurwitz, 1952).

The great contribution of the Jewish people in the Bible, Palace mysticism, Kabbalah, and Hasidism arose out of the continuing intercourse with the numinous experiences of what is implied in the term "collective unconscious." Freud discovered the unconscious again, this time as a practical clinical fact and as a source of healing of illness. He rejected the introverted religious and transcendental understanding which had ruled supreme for most of Jewish history in regard to the collective unconscious. Now it had to be a non-Jew who rediscovered the fascinosum of eternal images, found it to be the most important part of the human psyche, and described his discoveries in numerous smaller and greater publications. Jung gave different names to this layer of the human psyche—"the world of eternal images," "the objective psyche," "the non-ego"—but he preferred the scientific name "collective unconscious." At first he called particular contents of the unconscious "dominants of the unconscious," later, "archetypes."

Haymond again misunderstands Jung's term "archetypes" and therefore uses it incorrectly when he speaks, for example, of "Hebrew 'archetypes.' " There are psychic structures common to all humankind, archetypes which played a particular role in the history of the Jewish spirit. It is an annoying habit of Haymond to quote Jung with no particular chronological order as if Jung had been the same man all his life and always had the same ideas and attitudes. The outstanding fact about Jung is that he continually changed, that his unceasing confrontation with the collective unconscious produced a continuing transformation of his individuality. His ideas changed, sometimes radically. They assumed greater and greater depth the older he became. With it he also acquired new fields of knowledge. When I first met Jung, I found that he did not know much about Jewish psychology. Freud was actually the only Jew he had known intimately. But later on his ideas about Jews and Judaism changed profoundly.

He, for example, read the whole of the Cabala Denudata, 3,000 pages in Latin, besides many other Jewish source books. From then on until his last great book, *Mysterium Coniunctionis* (1955–1956/1970), he demonstrated great knowledge and understanding of Jewish authors. For example, he quotes with deep appreciation from the Shiur-Koma, from the Zohar. He knew Lurianic Kabbalah very well and emphasized in his writings the basic similarity of alchemical concepts with the Kabbalistic symbols. In our frequent conversations about Jewish psychology, he once went even so far as to say that in his opinion "due to the millennia of relationship to the Transcendental, the Jews are the kings of the spirit."

In our long history, we Jews have been an essentially introverted-intuitive people, deeply involved in many aspects of the collective unconscious, and have expressed them, for example, in the Bible, the Sefer Bahir, the Zohar and many other books. With our entrance into the European culture and especially our participation in the American way of life, we have turned away from the great treasures of our past.

Understandably, we do not want to be reminded by a non-Jew of this aspect of our great history and the contributions we have made to the development of consciousness of humankind. It is this aspect of our modern national psychology that arouses our friendly as well as our hostile interest in Jung.

VI

These general remarks are necessary in order to understand the hostility of so many Jews to Jung. The facts on which this anti-Jung feeling is based are few. Around them a host of half-truths, lies and rumors have been assembled. This whole complex is psychologically very similar to the negative feelings, affects, and hatred called anti-Semitism, to which we have been exposed during our history and still are, exactly for the same reason: our contact with the archetypes.

After separating from Freud, Jung did not know which way to go. He underwent a great psychological change. It took him years to arrive at his own new conceptions. One cannot say that he, on turning away from Freud, "founded" a method of psychological analysis which he termed analytical psychology. Any reader of Jung's book *Memories, Dreams, Reflections* (1961) is aware that from the beginning Jung had certain different opinions from Freud on sex and the causes of neuroses. Only gradually, through the encounter with the unconscious and many clinical experiences with his patients, did new ideas and approaches develop in Jung. However, he never formulated theories or dogmas. His writings have more the quality of discoveries. It was in agreement with Freud that he never applied the term "psychoanalysis" to his most unmethodical method of thinking. Therefore he called his school, which was no school, *Komplexe Psychologie,* or more often,

"Analytical Psychology." He wanted to keep the psychologist's thinking as open and undogmatic as possible. It was only in 1947, when Jung was seventy-two years old, that he agreed to the founding of an institute which would bear his name. Its original purpose was research and acquisition of new knowledge on the basis of his discoveries.

Jung always expressed his opinions as a psychiatrist, as a medical psychologist. When he spoke in an article about the German guilt after the catastrophe, he used many pages to explain that he did not mean moral guilt or legal guilt. He emphasized that he was speaking as a psychologist about a psychological condition which existed in Germany at that time and which he had already described in an article in 1918.

He had diagnosed a *psychological disassociation* in the German unconscious which made the phenomenon of Hitler possible. He also described Hitler, whom he must have seen somewhere, although I do not know where, as a *Popanz,* something like a "mere dummy." It was a great puzzle for him how this kind of a fool and psychopath could become the leader of the German people and could exert such a magical effect on the German nation—just such an effect as only a medicine man exerts on a primitive society.

Haymond claims, also, that he will clarify the psychological motives, including the most hidden ones, which caused Jung to act as he did. By this, then, he arrives at the conclusion that Jung acted out of an unconscious power drive. The fact is, however, that Jung did not have such a power drive. For example, as mentioned before, he did not want to organize his disciples in the way Freud did, because such an organization would create a hierarchical structure and would unavoidably open the way for all kinds of power plays.

The whole intention of his psychotherapy was to make people as free and independent of their analyst as possible.

By his far-reaching integration of the collective unconscious, Jung was the very kind of personality who radiated enormous powers, but he certainly was not a man who had ego-power motives. His ego dissolved and acted only as a representative of the self. As Erich Neumann said, he had become a new species of human being.

It was a most astounding experience to spend time with Jung because he was the one human being I know in whom conscious and unconscious were one. In conversations with Jung, one became aware of the uninterrupted creativity of this man. The power of such a personality can hardly be imagined. One has to forgive Haymond for seeing Jung only as if he had remained the small, ego-driven, but unusually intelligent man he was at the time of his friendship with Freud (Jones, 1955, p. 85).

Haymond can be assured that Jung showed deep interest and concern about the incredible economic depression. Of course he did. I remember his anger and upset especially when Switzerland devalued the franc in 1935. But he did not write about it because it was not his business as a psychiatrist. He suffered psychically very much during both world wars, as can easily be seen from his book *Memories, Dreams, Reflections* (1961) and from many letters, of which some important ones have now been published. His profound interest in the collective unconscious implies that "he ascribes significance to the social and economic context." But he did it in a different manner than Haymond; he always paid attention to the aspect sociologists tend to neglect, the psychological one.

I believe it was in 1947 that Winston Churchill visited Switzerland as an honored guest of the Bundesrat (the seven heads of the confederate government of Switzerland). During the official banquet, Jung was seated beside the guest of honor. Jung tried to talk of psychology, but did not get any response from Churchill. So Jung changed the subject to politics. That set Churchill on fire. Jung showed that he was quite familiar with international politics, and they talked vivaciously about that for hours.

If one does not understand a certain subject, one is always inclined to call it "mystical." That happened even to Freud. It is no surprise that Haymond calls Jung's explanation of mass psychology "a quasi mystical psychological reductionism" (p. 87). "The peasant wars, the Anabaptists, French revolution, etc." are, of course, quite different historical events, but they have something in common. In each case the conscious dominant decayed and an irruption of chaos followed. In each case a different dominant of consciousness decayed. Jung just described a definite psychological mechanism, the decay of a dominant of consciousness and its catastrophic results. Since we are in a similar political situation, we had better pay attention to Jung's psychological comments. The Nazi time and World War II should have taught us that we also can be overcome by chaos, because our conscious dominant is also decaying.

Jung was such a great personality and had such a vast knowledge that one unconsciously expects of Jung that he should have known everything and written about everything. He had no such delusions of grandeur. He wrote about history and social conditions from the psychological point of view. His book *Aion* (1951/1964) is a classic, describing the development and differentiation of the archetype of the Self in the last 1,900 years, from Gnosis to modern science, but does not tell about historical events, mass movements, wars, emperors, in a factual sense. He could safely leave this task to historians and sociologists. He did *his* work and did it very well. Of course, he knew Marx.

To speak of Jung as sharing "the common weaknesses of most intellectuals, heirs as they were to an ivory-tower tradition" (p. 88), is particularly surprising when Haymond quotes Ellenberger's *The Discovery of the Unconscious* (1970, pp. 664–666). Ellenberger tells of the "Zofingia," a Swiss student society. Quoting Albert Oeri, he mentions that Jung participated actively in the discussions mainly "when the topic was on matters of philosophy, psychology or occultism" (p. 665). What is so bad about Jung being affected by occult influences? It certainly indicates the opposite of the "ivory-tower tradition."

To call Jung "a staunch and committed Swiss bourgeois" (p. 88) and to claim that he preferred "order or stasis" is somewhat funny to anybody who has known him. In his own environment he always preferred conflict to constant harmony. In his own psyche he suffered deep conflicts and experienced the mandala as a union of opposites and a symbol of order, but not of stasis. He went on to new and deeper conflicts which brought further changes in his personality. It was only at the very end of his life, a few days before his death, that the unconscious through two dreams told him that he had achieved totality. His life was the opposite of stasis.

VII

There is, of course, a great difference in the psychological typology of Jung and Haymond. The fact that Jung and Haymond are such different types explains why it is difficult for Haymond to empathize and understand the introvert-intuitive attitude of Jung. It is out of this psychological type difference that Haymond arrives at such a total misunderstanding of Jung.

And Haymond approaches the border of ridiculousness when he derides Jung for having lived in Switzerland in a comfortable home when millions of people in Europe were suffering and dying. Where else should he have lived but in his house, which he had designed and built in 1905? After all, he was a Swiss and not a German, and it happened that Hitler did not attack Switzerland for very good reasons. Twice he had prepared everything for such an attack. Jung was on the list and would have been the first to be killed by Hitler's minions.

I have looked through all of Jung's collected works in German and found the word *Volk* quite rarely, always in the sense of a people, a nation, never in a sense which would connect it with Volksgeist or Volks-psychology. In respect to Wilhelm Wundt's "Volks"-psychology, it must be stated that such a form of nationalism never developed in Switzerland. On the contrary, Switzerland was the model for other countries as a state in which people speaking four different languages lived peacefully together.

I visited Switzerland for the first time in 1929 and can attest to the difference of atmosphere when I crossed the frontier into Switzerland. Jung was far too much of a genuine Swiss democrat to feel and act like so many German intellectuals.

I am sorry that Haymond does not realize Jung's irony when he describes the "Nazi euphoria" in his "Wotan" article. As a psychiatrist he had seen and written up many case histories of psychotics, but this does not mean that he himself was a psychotic. In the same way, he did not identify with the Nazis or their psychology when he wrote about them. If a scientist writes something about the peculiar behavior of a certain bacterium, does this mean that he behaves like this bacterium? The world would have done much better if it had listened to Jung's psychiatric diagnosis of the German condition and its psychological roots. At least Allen Dulles, the head of the American Secret Service, the OSS, regularly consulted Jung during World War II about Nazi psychology and especially about Hitler.

It is a peculiar, to say the least, and unfriendly method of Haymond to smear Jung by association with statements and attitudes of other men, always Germans, with whom Jung had nothing in common and whose minds functioned in a totally different way than his. Haymond mentions Richard Strauss' narrow attitude, his egocentric and limited character, as if it had any similarity with Jung's mind. He tries to throw aspersions on Jung by putting statements Jung made, as a psychiatrist, about the Nazis, beside some of Hitler's sentences, though he adds that these statements had nothing to do with the vulgar Volks-psychology of Hitler's *Mein Kampf*. What else should Jung's content (the description of Nazi psychology!) be but neutral? It was not Jung who glorified primeval forces, but the Nazis. Jung just described most aptly the Nazi psychology.

Could Haymond not see the irony with which Jung speaks of himself when he calls himself a Swiss bourgeois in a letter to me? In one of his letters he mentions that he is a *Sanitätshauptmann* (something like Colonel in the Medical Corps of the Swiss Army), but this fact is not his only qualification. He knew much better than Haymond what he was. He wrote extensively about self-knowledge and knew that he was something quite different besides having the appearance of a Swiss bourgeois. He was attacked and accused because he was something very great and important and because he gave voice to the archetypes. His book *Memories, Dreams, Reflections* (1961) is not an autobiography, but a record of his psychological development, of his individuation. The time to write a biography of Jung has evidently not yet come and will have to be left to another generation. It will then be shown that not only did Jung vote in all elections which took place in his canton, but he also had a great interest in international politics. But as a psychologist he commented on them from the viewpoint of his own psychological discoveries.

If one takes this into consideration, one appreciates why he writes in the prologue of *Memories, Dreams, Reflections:*

> In the end the only events in my life worth telling are those when the imperishable world irrupted into this transitory one. That is why I speak chiefly of inner experiences, amongst which I include my dreams and visions. These form the *prima materia* of my scientific work. They were the fiery magma out of which the stone that had to be worked was crystallized. (1961, p. 4)

Robert Haymond's understanding of Jung's experience of the "imperishable world" is so minimal that his statement of "where Jung's psychology is lacking" is missing the essence of Jung's originality and immense creativity. How can I convey to Haymond what the "imperishable world" is? Can I ask him to read Rabbi Nachman of Bratzlav's stories and conceive what made this Zadik tell those *Sippurei Ma'assiyoth?* He is in the same place as Freud was when he declared the collective unconscious *"die Schlammflut des Okkultismus"* (the mud floor of occultism).

To quote Franz Schoenberner is utterly irrelevant because he lived in New York during the war and had no direct knowledge of Jung's writings or activities. He simply repeated rumors. There were many people who believed vicious rumors about Jung, such as that he was a Nazi-collaborator. Secondhand or third-hand rumors are no evidence. It is amazing that a scientist like Haymond would quote them almost forty years later.

It is true that Jung never wrote about those Germans who actively resisted the Nazis. It is also true that he never wrote about Germans who submitted to the Nazis. He did not write about any individual Germans. He wrote about a collective illness. He pointed out that there were always individuals who were not infected by the general illness of the German people.

When Jung wrote about the Germanic mentality, he stated that

> [Freud and Adler] are thoroughly unsatisfying to the Germanic mentality; we still have a genuine barbarian in us who is not to

be trifled with, and whose manifestation is no comfort for us and not a pleasant way of passing the time. (1918/1964, p. 14)

But he did not refer to "the barbarian in us" as a compliment. It was a fact which he discovered and suffered in his own psychology, as can be seen in his dream of "his house," reported in *Memories, Dreams, Reflections* (1961, pp. 158–159). The entire sentence is certainly not in good taste and quite out of place at the time it was written. Unfortunately, it was to be misunderstood as anti-Semitic.

There never was a shift of his identification to this Swiss background. He always felt to be Swiss and acted as one. He identified his unconscious with the *Germanic* psyche, but never with the German psyche and its illness—the dissociation, the lack of a genuine feeling function in the German psyche.

It is repeatedly mentioned by Jung's detractors that his own race-cum-cultural theories might have had a terrible effect on the German people. I agree that these theories were mistaken and should never have been published during the terror-regime of the Nazis, but I never found any evidence that in fact they did such damage. I fully understand that under the terrible prevailing circumstances one could see these mistaken ideas as an expression of anti-Semitism. I fully agree with what Aniela Jaffé wrote about this severe mistake of Jung, but I could forgive him not only because he apologized to me, but because I could see that he had grown out of that frame of mind, and also because I knew to what great extent he had become conscious of his own Jewish psychology, although he had no Jewish ancestors. (See *Answer to Job* [1952/1970]; *Mysterium Coniunctionis* [1955–1956/1970], pp. 411–414, 429–430.) He shows a deep understanding of the psychological causes of anti-Semitism (*Mysterium Coniunctionis* [1955–1956/1970], p. 452). If Rabbi Leo Baeck, a leader of German Jews during the Nazi time and a survivor of the concentration camp, found it in his heart to forgive Jung and be his personal, revered houseguest, it should be possible for all Jews to forgive him and start reading his books. We will then discover how much his approach and his concepts will help to retrieve many treasures of the great Jewish past. Jung's teaching of the collective unconscious and its archetypes will give a new dimension in the understanding of the Bible, the Zohar, and many other great books.

To compare the case of the famous psychologist, Erich Haensch, with Jung's attitude during the Nazi period is simply another attempt to picture Jung as a Nazi or Nazi sympathizer by associating him with a German who obviously was or became an out-and-out Nazi. Jung's mind was galaxies distant from Erich Haensch's.

On page 92 Haymond states that "Jung maintained that nothing could be done about the political situation, that one had to play ball with the National Socialists." As reference he gives "Jung 1934a article on page 539." I could not find anything of the sort on this page nor anywhere in this article, "A Rejoinder to Dr. Bally." What Jung talks about is that "medicine has nothing to do with politics—I only wish it had! and therefore should be practised for the good of suffering humanity under all governments." It is on this page that one finds the classic sentence: "The doctor who, in wartime, gives his help to the wounded of the other side will surely not be held a traitor to his country." Maybe Haymond misunderstood the first sentence of the next paragraph (1023): "There is no sense in us doctors facing the National Socialist regime as if we were a party."

The historian Roepke, whom Robert Haymond quotes (p. 93), is mistaken when he says that "the Nazis courted him." I can speak from my own experience. During his stay in Berlin in May 1933, Jung was invited to see Dr. Goebbels, the infamous minister of propaganda. Jung went and the following conversation occurred:

Goebbels: You wanted to see me, Dr. Jung.
Jung: No. You wanted to see me.
Goebbels: No. You wanted to see me.

Jung turned around and left Goebbels' office—and vomited!!! From there he came to my house for lunch where my wife had prepared an ocean fish. He ate with excellent appetite! This was the end of the "courting" of Jung by the Nazis.

It was recognized very early in Jung's life that he had an extraordinary mind. The students in his school, the Basel Gymnasium, knew this. Later, the members of the Zofingia, a scientific fraternity at the University of Basel, were very well aware of his great intellect, as were, last but not least, the circle of Freud's friends and disciples in Vienna. Is it really difficult for Haymond to understand that Jung was an extraordinary man with outstanding gifts? That by 1933 his colleagues had accepted him as the foremost psychologist and psychiatrist besides Freud, and that this was the main reason, and not some power complex, which motivated the members of the board quite naturally to choose him as president of the International General Medical Society for Psychotherapy?

Haymond's statement that "Jung did not create a close circle of unflinching followers as was the alarming case with Freud (Wittels)" proves that Jung was not on an "ego trip," as the modern jargon would have it, but that the author of such books as *Psychological Types* (1921/1976) and *Two Essays on Analytical Psychology* (1917, 1926, 1943 & 1928/1972) was worthy and had the prestige to be the president of the said International Society.

It is at this point in his article (p. 94) that Robert Haymond returns to the error in fact that Kretschmer was a Jew and quickly adds a second one. Rudolf Allers, who as Ernest Harms says on page 12 (not 210 as mistakenly cited by Haymond), "belonged to an extremely religious Roman Catholic group," was in fact racially a Jew. This was the reason he had to resign (see letter of Jung to Rudolf Allers of November 23, 1933 [Adler & Jaffé, 1973, vol. 1, pp. 131–132]). "Not out of voluntary conviction!" But Haymond takes this as another opportunity to throw another perfectly groundless accusation at Jung. "Circumspect in what he uttered, there was no outcry at the injustice done to Kretschmer and no further public statement." (p. 94).

As said before, I never had the impression that Jung was anti-Semitic or that he, in any way, shared the collective prejudices and the more or less open feelings of a "metaphysical" hatred against the Jews. The fact is that he chose Aniela Jaffé, a Jewish refugee from Germany, as his secretary and eventual co-worker, and

Gerhard Adler, Ph.D., another Jewish refugee from Germany, as confidant and editor of his collected works. This should be enough evidence that he was no anti-Semite in the usual collective meaning of the word. However, I have to agree with Robert Haymond in this one respect: that some of his statements in his newspaper article, "A Rejoinder to Dr. Bally," were ill-conceived and could and had to be understood as expressions of anti-Semitism. To insist in 1934 that the Jewish question had to be brought up and publicly discussed when the Nazi terror was sweeping through Germany and Jews were tortured and killed only because they were Jews was a serious blunder, a sign of naiveté and uncon- sciousness. "I have tabled the Jewish question. This I did deliber- ately. . . . The Jewish problem is a regular complex, a festering wound, and no responsible doctor could bring himself to apply methods of medical hush-hush in this matter" (Jung, 1934a/1964, p. 539). One cannot acquit Jung of having made a terrible mistake by pronouncing such ideas at such a time. These unfortunate statements are the reason that his accusers continue until today to blame him, declare him an anti-Semite, and question "the ethics of a therapeutic man" (Karrier, 1976):

> The still youthful Germanic peoples are fully capable of creating new cultural forms that still lie dormant in the darkness of the unconscious of every individual—seeds bursting with energy and capable of mighty expansion. The Jew, who is something of a nomad, has never yet created a cultural form of his own and as far as we can see never will, since all his instincts and talents require a more or less civilized nation to act as host for their development. (Jung, 1934b/1964, pp. 165–166)

One can blame Jung for ignorance of what was going on in Germany, one can speak of his naiveté and excuse it with the fact that in 1933 and 1934 few foreigners knew the true barbaric situation of Germany, and of the concentration camps in particu- lar. The depth of the abyss of brutality into which the cultured German nation had fallen was inconceivable for Jung in 1933 and somewhat later. He simply did not believe me when I tried to tell him some of the facts in May of 1933. He still hoped that the Nazi terror would be over in six weeks or, latest, in six months.

It was at this time, also, that Jung picked up the idea of a difference between *Kultur* and *Kulturform*, culture and cultural form, and therefore could make statements like: "The Jews, like the cultured Chinese, have a wider area of psychological consciousness to their development" (Jung, 1934b/1964, p. 166).

Haymond mentions Aniela Jaffé as a critic and defender of Jung and Clarence Karrier as a critic, a man who did not know Jung personally. It is worthwhile to quote Aniela Jaffé again, because she was a Jewish refugee from Germany:

> Criticism of Jung's attitude during the years 1933–34 is justified by the facts, as is evident from the account I have given. But it lends itself to counter-criticism when it gets overheated, is exaggerated and one-sided, and when it glosses over or denies everything positive and falsifies the facts. This kind of criticism is just as untenable as the opposite approach which turns a blind eye to Jung's mistakes during those years or considers them mere trifles. (1971, p. 92)

As Jung's secretary, Jaffé was also the collaborator on his book *Memories, Dreams, Reflections*. Being so close to Jung and his work, she has, in my opinion, written a fair and objective description of Jung's conduct during the Nazi time.

Another point that Haymond makes is that Jung never mentioned the two great Jewish sages who were contemporaries of Jesus and had formative influence on the life and culture of the Jewish people in exile. It is true that Jung never mentioned Hillel or Shammai. He never posited a "singular Jewish tradition," (*sic!*) simply for the reason that he was mainly interested in the unconscious and its differentiation as it expressed itself in the development of Jewish mysticism.

Haymond's statements about the economic catastrophe of 1929 and its effect on the German people are correct as far as they go, but omit the psychological aspects for at least 1,900 years, if not longer. What about Haman? Or Tacitus' exclamation of the Foetor Judaicus?

How can Haymond assert that Jung did not like Jews, that he had a negative attitude to Jews, when he has read the Freud/Jung correspondence and discovers how much love and friendship existed between the two men in the first years of their close relationship; when a number of Jews like Erich Neumann (by the way, he never was a professor in Tel Aviv—another misstatement) and Gerhard Adler were his devoted students for many years, or that Aniela Jaffé was his personal secretary during the last six years of his life? It is a rather distorted view if one speaks of Jung's scientizing, psychologizing and theorizing. E. Glover, Haymond's reference for this conception, was an outstanding Freudian analyst in London, England. As such, it was only natural that he pronounced such views. But today it is realized more and more, in Europe as well as in the United States, Canada and some Latin American countries, that Jung's ideas and discoveries of how the human mind functions were far ahead of his time. They gain more and more acceptance today.

To comment more on the Freud/Jung relationship would go far beyond the purpose of this article. It is far too complex a subject, but I can assert that though the Jewish question played an important role in it, it had nothing to do with any vulgar or political anti-Semitism nor with the atmosphere in the home of the Reverend Paul Jung.

Jolande Jacobi's answer to Albert Parelhoff did of course not hit the point. In the first place, Jung's article as an answer to Dr. Bally was not anti-Semitic. Secondly, I never saw this article listed anywhere as one of Jung's achievements. Nevertheless, Frau Dr. Jolande Jacobi's answer was quite remarkable because she was a convert to Catholicism. It must have been an unusual situation for her to confess that she was a Jewess, and even publicly!

After throwing quite a number of big rocks at Jung such as "Volksgeist," and anti-Semitism in his parental home, Haymond suddenly tones down his attack and discovers nothing more than a "conflictedness in Jung's personality towards Jews." Who does not have that? And which Jew is free from such a conflictedness towards his own people? Or was Goethe free from such a conflictedness against his own Germans? It is nothing new that Freud

considered Jung his "enemy." Even Freudian analysts have been
aware of paranoic trends in Freud's personality. It is possible, but
there is no evidence, that he read Jung's publications in the thirties.
To understand Freud's hostility against Jung, one need only go to
Freud's often quoted article on the "History of the Psychoanalytic
Movement," where Freud speaks of "racial" prejudices of Jung. In
my conversations with Jung which sometimes touched on the
subject of Freud, he always spoke of Freud with warmth. Even in
his later years, he was puzzled by Freud's theories and tried to
understand them. He wondered whether there were any Hasidic
influences on Freud. I do not think they existed.

The next accusation of Haymond against Jung is utterly baseless.
Jung never wrote "drafts which served Nazi propaganda." Or does
Haymond refer to the articles which Jung wrote in the thirtes,
which, to my knowledge, never served Nazi propaganda? Can
Haymond refer to a single pamphlet, article or book in which
Jung's statements were used as propaganda material against Jews
and had an effect, at least in academic circles?

I am grateful to Haymond for quoting Jung from another article,
"A Review of the Complex Theory," written in the same year,
1934, in which he, Jung, fairly and objectively acknowledges
Freud's originality and praises him as a "theoretician," obviously
including himself as one of the theoreticians after (or before?) he
talked so strongly against theories and techniques in psychology:

> Ich bin kein ausgeklügelt Buch.
> Ich bin ein Mensch mit seinem Widerspruch.

> I am no sophisticated book.
> I am a man with his contradiction. (Meyer, 1872, p. 41)

In regard to the contradiction in Jung, I would not draw the
same conclusion which Haymond did. For one thing, in all his
criticism of Freud's theories he never spoke "demeaningly" of
Freud; for another, the inference that somebody "personally respects people who are Jews, but not if they symbolize the aggregate
(the Jewish race!)" is often true. It is a sign that a certain collective
content is projected on a group of people. It characterizes an

undifferentiated state of consciousness. But I agree, however, with Haymond that in this case, in 1934, Jung did not have "sufficiently broad self-understanding," but he gained it in later years, actually to such a degree that a highly respected analyst like Dr. Edward Edinger considers Jung's *Answer to Job* (1952/1970) a new dispensation!

If someone makes such a demand as "sufficiently broad self-understanding" on a psychologist, one is entitled to ask how broad is this author's self-understanding? The serious shortcomings which this author sees in Jung—abstracted intellectualism, psychological reductionism—in my opinion did not exist in Jung, not an ounce of it. He had a great and sharp mind; no doubt, Freud and Freud's circle admired it, but it was the opposite of "abstracted intellectualism." Jung had an original, seminal mind; the eighteen volumes of his *Collected Works* prove it as well as that many of the terms he introduced have become quite popular, like extraversion, introversion, complex, collective unconscious, individuation, et al. How can one speak of Jung's psychological reductionism if all his books describe and emphasize the cosmic nature of the human soul?

Haymond says Jung's "high flown speech, the vapid 'pardon me,' cannot be condoned in the light of the desperate seriousness of the social reality of those times" (pp. 104–105). Here is raised a serious ethical and religious problem: Is there any condition which we human beings cannot condone in another human being? "To me belongs vengeance and recompense," said the Lord in Deuteronomy (32:35), not to human beings.

Like Aniela Jaffé, Rabbi Leo Baeck, Erich Neumann and other Jews, I can find it in my heart to forgive Jung and to thank him for what he did for Jews like me during the Nazi time and for the great new knowledge which became a luminous key for my self-understanding as a Jew.

The annoying habit of Haymond to muddle Jung's ages is no more apparent than when he quotes the Jung of 1909, when he was an outspoken and probably the most visible Freudian, just after condemning him for two articles he wrote in 1934. So much had happened in Jung's life in those twenty-five years! The confrontation with the unconscious, books like *Psychological Types, Two Essays on Analytical Psychology,* and many similar articles all testify to Jung's continuing change as a human being. He, himself, was the best example of the transforming power of a conscious confrontation with the collective unconscious, of the process of individuation.

As an outspoken extravert, Haymond would not understand Jung's profound introversion, his concepts, his values and his scientific interests. Contrary to Haymond's statements, Jung took full responsibility for the social consequences of his teachings. He "slipped" that one time, as he ruefully admitted to Rabbi Leo Baeck. (See Scholem's letter to Aniela Jaffé, in *From the Life and Work of C. G. Jung,* 1971, pp. 97–98.)

Robert Haymond's calling Jung "a modern Christian prophet obliquely upbraiding the Jews for not accepting the Christ" (p. 105) by quoting something Jung had written in 1909 and to which he had added another remark about the Jewish prophets in 1927, borders on the ridiculous. Jung treated patients from all races of mankind and from most religions of the world. He travelled to Africa and visited the Pueblo Indians of Taos, New Mexico, for the purpose of studying their religious concepts and myths in the context of their psychology. In his psychotherapeutic work, he always paid great attention to the traditions of his patients and felt that healing could only occur if the patient could reconnect with the tradition of his ancestors. I tried to show the particular role the Christ complex played in the unconscious of Jews by analyzing the "Christ" dream of an Orthodox rabbi, R. Hile Wechsler, published in a brochure in 1881, when Jung was six years old (Kirsch, 1973). Jung himself corrected his own one-sided statements in his *Answer to Job,* which he wrote at a mature age in 1951! He never "upbraided" the Jews for not accepting the Christ. He expressed himself very clearly about the "Christ" complex in Jews in a letter to me (Adler & Jaffé, 1973, vol. 2, p. 154) which begins: "I scarcely think that the Jews have to accept the Christ symbol. They need only understand its meaning." The last thing he ever wanted to do was to create a new religion, Germanic or otherwise.

XI

In conclusion, it must be said that Robert Haymond's psychosocial method is rather unsatisfactory and misleading for describing an individual. Jung himself used the example of 1,000 rocks in a riverbed. It is assumed that the average size of the rock is three centimeters. Then it may be found that not one of them is actually three centimeters. In the same way, it is impossible to judge the quality and ethics of an individual by associating statements and behaviors of his with those of many others. This is particularly true of an individual such as Jung, the man who discovered and extensively described the process of individuation, the process of becoming an individual.

Furthermore, Haymond has a number of facts wrong (Kretschmer, Allers, Volksgeist et al.). He does not distinguish between the atmosphere and political conditions in Germany and those in Switzerland, between the presidency of the Supranational General Society for Psychotherapy and that of the German Division, between the terms "German" and "Germanic" and other minor matters.

In order to judge Jung as an individual, one has to examine his deeds and his writings. In regard to his deeds, I can only refer to the relevant portions of the articles of Ernest Harms and Aniela Jaffé and to the article in *Spring* (Cocks, 1977) which concludes that Jung accomplished what he set out to do, i.e., the protection of the young science of psychotherapy to the largest possible degree. In regard to his writings, it is obvious that he made a grave mistake in publishing his opinions on Freud and Adler as well as on Jews in general during the Nazi time and especially in the *Zentralblatt,* which mostly circulated in Nazi Germany at that time. As Aniela Jaffé writes, in this respect the medical discretion enjoined upon every physician would have been the order of the day (1971). If one reads this controversial article today—*sine ira et sine studio*—one finds a sharp and correct criticism of any psychotherapy which is reduced to nothing but technique or a sum of techniques. The situation in the broad field of psychotherapy has not changed significantly since 1934.

One could, perhaps, summarize the situation in this way. C. G. Jung tried consciously and intentionally to help Jews from the beginning of the Nazi time, but unconsciously an unresolved "Jewish" complex persisted in him. It was activated in him through his personal relationship with Sigmund Freud, at first in a positive and enthusiastic transference on him. Later, after his break with his great teacher and friend, critical and negative feelings came up in him, feelings which extended to the collective, to Jews in general. He finally and completely resolved this archetypal complex in his book *Answer to Job*. In it he described Job's encounter with the biblical image of God and indirectly his own *Auseinandersetzung* (encounter and clarification). By writing it he liberated himself from any trace of anti-Semitism.

It appears to me that the only fair way of dealing with the controversial question of Jung's so-called anti-Semitism is to state the facts as they are and to examine Jung's personal psychology, for which he left us ample material in his books and letters.

References

Adler, G., & Jaffé, A. *C. G. Jung letters* (2 vols.). Princeton: Princeton University Press, 1973.

Cocks, G. C. G. Jung and German psychotherapy, 1933–1940: A research note. *Spring*, 1979, 221–227.

Dieckmann, H. Personal communication, February 1, 1980.

Ellenberger, H. *The discovery of the unconscious: The history and evolution of dynamic psychiatry*. New York: Basic Books, 1970.

Fierz, H. Personal communiation, February 8, 1980.

Freud, S. On the history of the psychoanalytic movement. In James Strachey (ed. & trans.), *Standard Edition of the Complete Psychological Works of Sigmund Freud* (vol. 14.). London: Hogarth, 1957. (Originally published, 1914.)

Hannah, B. *Jung, his life and work: A biographical memoir*. New York: Putnam, 1976.

Harms, E. Carl Gustav Jung—Defender of Freud and the Jews. *Psychiatric Quarterly*, 1946.

Haymond, R. Roots in the shtetl: Modern western thought and the case of Sigmund Freud. *Journal of Psychology and Judaism*, Summer 1979, 3,(4), 235–267.

———. On Carl Gustav Jung: Psycho-social basis of morality during the Nazi era. *Journal of Psychology and Judaism*, Spring/Summer 1982 6(2), 81–112.

The Holy Scriptures (2 vols.). Philadelphia: Jewish Publication Society, 1917.

Hurwitz, S. *Zeitlose Dokumente der Seele*. Zurich: Rascher, 1952.

Jaffé, A. *From the life and work of C. G. Jung*. (R. Hull, trans.). New York: Harper & Row, 1971.

Jones, E. *Sigmund Freud: Life and work* (vol. 2). London: Hogarth, 1955.

Jung, C. G. Two essays on analytical psychology. In H. Read, M. Fordham & G. Adler (eds.), *The collected works of C. G. Jung* (vol. 7). Princeton: Princeton University Press, 1972. (Originally published, 1917, 1926, 1943 & 1928.)

———. The role of the unconscious. In H. Read, M. Fordham & G. Adler (eds.), *The collected works of C. G. Jung* (vol. 10). Princeton: Princeton University Press, 1964. (Originally published, 1918.)

———. *Psychological types*. Princeton: Princeton University Press, 1976. (Originally published, 1921.)

———. A rejoinder to Dr. Bally. In H. Read, M. Fordham & G. Adler (eds.), *The, collected works of C. G. Jung* (vol. 10). Princeton: Princeton University Press, 1964. (Originally published, 1934.) (a)

———. The state of psychotherapy today. In H. Read, M. Fordham & G. Adler (eds.), *The collected works of C. G. Jung* (vol. 10). Princeton: Princeton University Press, 1964. (Originally published, 1934.) (b)

———. A review of the complex theory. In H. Read, M. Fordham & G. Adler (eds.), *The collected works of C. G. Jung* (vol. 8). Princeton: Princeton University Press, 1969. (Originally published, 1934.)

———. Wotan. In H. Read, M. Fordham & G. Adler (eds.), *The collected works of C. G. Jung* (vol. 10). Princeton: Princeton University Press, 1964. (Originally published, 1936.)

———. After the catastrophe. In H. Read, M. Fordham & G. Adler (eds.), *The collected works of C. G. Jung* (vol 10). Princeton: Princeton University Press, 1964. (Originally published, 1945.)

———. Aion: Researches into the phenomenology of the self. In H. Read, M. Fordham & G. Adler (eds.), *The collected works of C. G. Jung* (vol. 9). Princeton: Princeton University Press, 1964. (Originally published, 1951.)

———. Answer to Job. In H. Read, M. Fordham & G. Adler (eds.), *The collected works of C. G. Jung* (vol. 11). Princeton: Princeton University Press, 1970. (Originally published, 1952.)

———. Mysterium coniunctionis. In H. Read, M. Fordham & G. Adler (eds.), *The collected works of C. G. Jung* (vol. 14). Princeton: Princeton University Press, 1970. (Originally published, 1955–56.)

———. *Memories, dreams, reflections*. (A. Jaffé, ed., and R. & C. Winston, trans.). New York: Random House, 1961.

Karrier, C. The ethics of a therapeutic man. In G. Dren and L. Rappoport (eds.), *Varieties of psychohistory*. New York: Springer, 1976.

Kirsch, J. *The reluctant prophet*. Los Angeles: Sherbourne Press, 1973.

Meier, C. A. Personal communication, February 28, 1980.

Meyer, C. F. *Homo sum*. Leipzig, 1872.

Roepke, W. *The solution of the German problem*. New York: Putnam, 1946.

Jung's "Mana Personality" and the Nazi Era

Richard Stein

Richard H. Stein, M.D., is a Jungian analyst with a private practice in San Francisco. He is on the teaching faculty of the C. G. Jung Institute of San Francisco and is assistant Clinical Professor at the University of California at San Francisco.

Dr. Stein reviews here the history of Jung's actions and comments in regard to Judaism and National Socialism. He contends that Jung became identified with the image of the "mana personality," a condition that led to an inflation and infatuation with the power and vitality of the Third Reich. He sees Jung's attitude toward Jews as a manifestation of his father complex, acted out both in his personal relationship to Freud and in his attitude toward the God-image of the Hebrew Bible. Stein is responding here specifically to James Kirsch when he challenges the suggestion that writing *Answer to Job* magically resolved all questions about Jung's father complex and his ambivalence toward Jews.

The question of C. G. Jung's alleged anti-Semitism has been coming up both within professional Jungian circles and in the public press with increasing regularity. This issue is important not just for a historical understanding of Jung's personal life or biases, nor for the much-needed healing of the rift between Freudian and Jungian analysts, but also because it raises deep questions about Jung's fundamental understanding and treatment of the individual. All geniuses have their shadows, but the implications of alleged anti-Semitism in Jung have more disturbing resonances than the shortcomings of other great men, like Shakespeare or Eliot, who have been known to hold such prejudice. Jung's psychology has a central premise of resolving the shadow problem, both personal and cultural, as far as possible. In trying to establish a spiritually progressive psychology with a moral basis broader than that of Christianity and deeper than rational humanism, Jung entered, by necessity, a realm of subjectivity fraught with danger.[1] His flirtation with the devil was, like Faust's, a close call with the possible loss of soul. At stake for analytical psychology is the underlying belief that Jung had achieved the kind of personality integration he proposed.

Everyone has a shadow, which includes racial prejudice to one degree or another. As Polly Young-Eisendrath has pointed out, "defensive moves to contain the Good in subjectivity while projecting the Bad in objectivity,"[2] which are used in early childhood to establish the boundary between self and other, are similar to the dynamics of racial prejudice. The nature of the resulting shadow projection is influenced by cultural as well as family dynamics. Given the inevitability that any person will have a cultural (as well as a personal) shadow, I wish neither to exonerate nor to condemn Jung, but to try to make understandable in the psychological terms of his own theory what he did and why the question is still so vividly with us.

Jung grew up in the late nineteenth century in a small Swiss village. Deeply contained in a Protestant culture, he had little contact with Catholics or Jews. As he reports in *Memories, Dreams, Reflections,* he mistook a darkly robed Jesuit for the devil when he was a small boy. He had little knowledge of Jewish culture, and I think it is safe to assume that as an unknown quantity, the Jew was a shadow carrier in Jung's environment. As James Kirsch reports, Jung's first association with anyone Jewish was his relationship with Freud.[3]

Jung had an enormous father problem, due in part to the fact that an early separation from his mother had forced him to turn to his father for the nurturance she might have provided. He was left with a mistrust of women and of the word *love,* as he reports in *Memories, Dreams, Reflections.* This early loss of the maternal seems to have intensified the natural splitting of the masculine archetype, which he projected onto his father, who died when Jung was only twenty years old. His early dream of the underground phallus anticipates the problem as it arose later in personal relationships (including that with Freud) and his struggle with the Judeo-Christian Godhead (see *Answer to Job*). The dream ends with his mother's voice warning him, "That is the man-eater." But the young boy was not sure whether "that" referred only to the underground phallus or to the Jesus of his father's church—an enormous split between instinct and spirit was already at work. For better or worse, Jung's reliance on his father left him open to the cultural and spiritual winds of his time. In later life, he approached psychological questions with a religious passion that his father lacked in his role as a pastor.

Jung's childhood dreams and metaphysical questioning point in a very different direction than his father's Swiss Protestantism, which he consciously rejected by the time he was in college. Jung met Freud (who was culturally but not religiously Jewish) for the first time on March 3, 1907, and from the beginning a strong father transference was constellated. In 1909 Jung published a paper entitled "The Significance of the Father in the Destiny of the Individual," which I mention here for two reasons. First, his own encounter with Freud seems to bear out the title; and second, it shows how far beyond his personal development Jung's intuitive mind could leap: his father projection onto Freud was to have enormous consequences for the remainder of his life. In the preface to the second edition of this paper, in 1949, Jung alludes to the changes in his understanding of the father problem since his discovery of the archetypes. Later I shall explore James Kirsch's discussion of the archetypal nature of Jung's transference to Freud and how it was expressed specifically at the level of the cultural unconscious, as defined by Joseph Henderson.[4]

Jung had a deep need for the worldliness and maturity that he saw in Freud, but the transference was complicated by homosexual and religious elements that made Jung feel uneasy. In a letter to Freud dated October 28, 1907, Jung wrote that "my veneration of you has something of the character of a 'religious crush.' Though it does not really bother me, I still feel it is disgusting and ridiculous because of its undeniable erotic undertone . . . as a boy I was the victim of a sexual assault by a man I once worshipped. . . ."⁵ And on November 8, 1907, he wrote: "My old religiosity had secretly found in you a compensating factor which I had to come to terms with eventually, and I was able to do so only by telling you about it."⁶

We hear no more from Jung about the childhood sexual assault or its effect on the transference, but he could hardly have come to terms with his religious feelings by this simple confession. His experience of his "old religiosity" in the transference seems to anticipate the deeper archetypal and cultural dimensions of Jung's feelings about his father, whose Christian faith had failed him. The transference of this problem to Freud was the beginning of Jung's adult encounter with the Judeo-Christian Godhead, but at this early date Jung was adopting, perhaps even mimicking, Freud's rationalistic stance, which would later have to yield to deeper experience. For his part, Freud was immediately concerned about the religious nature of the transference, but he had neither the insight nor the theory to handle it, and responded, "I shall do my best to show you that I am unfit to be an object of worship."⁷ Both men had rejected the religions of their family backgrounds in favor of a scientific attitude, and in these early years of psychoanalysis neither had a psychological understanding of the enormous questions involved. From a modern Jungian perspective, we could say that Freud did not know the nature of the archetypal transference and the spiritual questions it involves.

In a further attempt to find the proper fit, Jung asked Freud "to let me enjoy your friendship not as one between equals but as that of father and son. This distance appears to me fitting and natural. Moreover, it alone, so it seems to me, strikes a note that would prevent misunderstandings and enable two hard-headed people to exist alongside one another in an easy and unrestrained relationship."⁸

Jung sidestepped the religious question as well, and despite the very real differences of opinion about analytic theory and technique, the two men developed a very close and intimate connection. Eventually Freud chose Jung as his heir to lead the psychoanalytic movement, and Jung became the first president of the International Psychoanalytic Association (1910–14). This was not only because of Jung's keen and energetic mind, nor for the empirical evidence he had provided for the existence of the unconscious in the word-association experiments. Freud thought that because Jung was not Jewish, as were so many of the other early analysts, he could make psychoanalysis more acceptable to a larger public. On August 13, 1908, Freud wrote to Jung: "With your strong and independent character, with your Germanic blood which enables you to command the sympathies of the public more readily than I, you seem better fitted than anyone else I know to carry out this mission."[9] One can imagine Jung's ambivalent feelings about being used in such a way, and Freud's open preference for Jung intensified the feelings of envy among Freud's other followers.

The first reference in the literature to Jung's alleged anti-Semitism was made after the two men bitterly parted. In *The History of the Psychoanalytic Movement* (1914), Freud wrote that Jung had certain "racial prejudices." He apparently referred to Jung's associations to a dream, in which he admitted being uncomfortable with Freud's Viennese circle, which was predominantly Jewish. Freud was quite sensitive to anti-Semitism and was acutely aware of the tenuous assimilation of German Jewry, which had been violently attacked by such fanatical movements as that of Adolph Stoecker in 1879. But given the sibling nature of the transferences among Freud's analysands, there was also the question of Jung's awkward position in the group, which contributed to his feelings.

Though the break between Jung and Freud was seemingly over theoretical issues (the conception of libido and the theory of archetypes), it is evident that there was much more to it, both personally and culturally. Freud did not deny that myth played a role in the unconscious, but given his personal history, the nature of his own neurosis, and his commitment to a biological drive theory, the only myth he could accept was that of Oedipus. Jung's natural psychic abilities, along with his early maternal deprivation (in later psychoanalytic terms, a pre-Oedipal wound), led him on an inner journey resembling a shamanic descent more than the culturally later patriarchal encounter of King Oedipus. Jung's dream of the several-storied house, which was his first inkling of the collective unconscious, ends with his descent below the basement into a cave with two disintegrating skulls.[10] To Jung, this dream meant a cultural layering of the psyche, while to Freud it indicated Jung's Oedipal wish to kill him. These skulls may also be seen as symbols of the earliest known initiation rites of hunting cultures, in which the bone represents the seed of life. Jung's early psychic wound was also his entrée into developmentally earlier and culturally deeper levels of the unconscious than were known to Freud.

Freud could not understand Jung's "pre-Oedipal need," and his ambitious plans for him must have been wounding to Jung, at least unconsciously. I can imagine that Jung experienced Freud as the kind of parent, described by Heinz Kohut in *The Analysis of Self,* who narcissistically wounds his child by using the child's very real gifts for his own aggrandizement. To preserve his integrity, Jung had to break away and follow his own line of inquiry, which meant publishing *Wandlungen und Symbole;* this precipitated Freud's rejection of him and the painful, angry rupture of their relationship. The final chapter of Jung's book, entitled "The Sacrifice," seems to anticipate the loss of his close relationship with Freud as a prerequisite to achieving his own original contribution. As a German Swiss, Jung had been greatly influenced by Eduard von Hartmann, Goethe, Kant, Schopenhauer, and of course Nietzsche. His cultural affinities were German, and his mature development lay outside the sphere of Freud's theory, which he later criticized (quite likely with some resentment) as "Jewish psychology." But the narcissistic wound from his father transference to Freud, including personal, cultural, and archetypal elements, was left unresolved. Perhaps it was impossible for two such different men to work out the transference and countertransference dynamics of such a multifaceted, worldly, and analytically uncontained relationship, but the loss of this opportunity left Jung professionally isolated and personally devastated.

The abrupt ending of such a powerful transference relationship has enormous consequences. As we know, Jung went through a major psychological regression and became severely depressed from 1913 until 1919. Bereft of a father substitute, he was driven into the depths of his mother problem, but with the help of Toni Wolff, he had the strength and discipline to return with a new understanding of the archetypal dimension of the psyche. This process, which can be seen in retrospect as the hero's "night sea journey," also resembles the descent of the shaman into the underworld. Like many other great men, Jung followed the pattern of "withdrawal and return" described by Arnold Toynbee, and this time in his life was deeply formative in his creation of a unique psychological theory.

In the 1920s Jung developed a professional life that flourished independently of Freud, and he attracted a formidable circle of analysands and students. He resisted, however, the idea of leading a psychological movement for many years. The Psychological Club flourished in Zurich throughout the 1920s and 1930s, but it was not until 1948 that a training institute was formed. One can only speculate what role the unresolved father issue played in Jung's uneasiness with becoming the leader of a psychological organization. But it was during the early 1930s that Jung began to write and speak about various cultural issues, artistic trends, and historical developments in the light of his archetypal theory, which had already proved its value in individual depth analysis.[11]

Having freed himself from the mother problem, Jung encountered his ambivalence to the feminine at a new level. As with the 1909 essay on the significance of the father, his personal and theoretical development were intertwined. The theoretical formulation of the anima, or "soul image," developed out of his intimate and collaborative relationship with Toni Wolff, but Jung's own anima split would have to be lived fully in the triangle with her and his wife, Emma, to be integrated. To what extent this living arrangement was in reaction to Jung's unresolved transference to Freud is open to question, but it seems significant that the next archetypal figure that he formulated is connected to the father imago. In a major revision (1926) of *Two Essays on Analytical*

Psychology, first published in 1916–18, he includes a discussion
of other archetypal personifications emerging from the deep unconscious. Following the "conquest of the anima as an autonomous complex," there is the incorporation of her "mana" by the
ego.

> Well then: who is it that has integrated the anima? Obviously the
> ego consciousness, and therefore the ego has taken over the mana.
> Thus the ego becomes a mana-personality. But the mana-person-
> ality is a dominant of the collective unconscious, the well-known
> archetype of the mighty man in the form of hero, chief, magician,
> medicine-man, saint, the ruler of men and spirits, the friend of
> God.[12]

Jung warns of inflation, describing how such a personality is now
possessed by the figure of the magician (or Great Mother in the
case of woman) after mastering the anima (or animus) complex.
He questions the authenticity of the mana role:

> But why does not this importance, the mana, work on others?
> That would be the essential criterion! It does not work because
> one has not in fact become important, but has merely become
> adulterated with an archetype, another unconscious figure. Hence
> we must conclude that the ego never conquered the anima at all.
> . . . All that has happened is a new adulteration, this time with a
> figure of the same sex corresponding to the father-imago, and
> possessed of even greater power.[13]

In the following sentence, he makes an unequivocal identification of the mana personality with the Great Father: "Thus he
becomes a superman, superior to all powers, a demigod at the very
least. 'I and the Father are one'—this mighty avowal in its awful
ambiguity is born of just such a psychological moment."[14] In this
crucial passage, which is the only place where he discussed such an
important archetype, I believe, Jung defined a process that he had
yet to complete in his own development. His unresolved transference to Freud had fallen back into the objective psyche, leaving him
to complete the remainder of the work on his father complex by
himself. It seems to me that the mana personality represents an

aspect of the archetypal father problem, which must be integrated by certain men who have had to "return to the mother" to heal an early wound. The shaman is probably the most ancient cultural expression of the mana-personality, and it is this figure that plays such an important role in Jung's psyche. The mana figure would be less an issue for a more ego-intact person whose development can follow the lines of Freud's Oedipus complex, but the two are not mutually exclusive, and Jung's attitudes and actions in the Nazi era can certainly be seen to contain elements of both.

Throughout the 1930s Jung was preoccupied with this archetype as it appeared in German culture, which he discussed at length in *Nietzsche's Zarathustra* (1988; edited from seminars that took place from May 1934 to February 1939). It is also in this decade of the dictators that the rise of the Nazi movement, with its threat to psychoanalysis in Germany, along with Jung's actions and untimely comments about Jewish psychology, Wotan, and Hitler, created the controversy with which we still live today. I will leave the question of Jung's psychological development for the moment, to give a brief description of the issues in this controversy.

A comprehensive account of Jung's efforts to save the profession of psychotherapy in the early 1930s is given by Ernest Harms in his 1946 essay "Carl Gustav Jung: Defender of Freud and the Jews," reprinted in this volume. Harms, a Jewish child analyst who practiced in America, knew both Freud and Jung, but was not affiliated with either school. He writes:

> Jung had come to hold a central position in mid-European psychotherapy when, in 1933, the Nazi purge destroyed much of the collaboration which in manifold ways had been built up during the previous twenty years. The first effect was the elimination, as a result of Nazi anti-Semitism, of the work done by Jewish scientists. The organizations of Freud's as well as Adler's pupils were dissolved, and their members expelled from the German national sphere. At the same time all Jewish members of the staff of the *Zentralblatt* had to resign.

The *Zentralblatt* was the main German-language psychotherapy journal in Europe, published by the Allgemeine Ärztliche Gesellschaft (General Medical Society), an international organization based in Germany, to which psychotherapists from all countries and theoretical persuasions could belong. In 1933 Ernst Kretschmer resigned as president of the Society in protest against the Nazis' policies. Harms describes how this organization had little chance of survival under the new German government, since psychotherapy was identified with Freudianism, which the Nazis were denouncing as the prototype of Jewish psychology. While a direct attack on the Nazi propaganda might have precipitated a more severe repression, one possible solution lay in the formation of national organizations that would be free of Nazi control and that could join together to form a "supranational" society. Freud's fears that psychoanalysis would be endangered if it were seen as a "Jewish science" were becoming a reality.

The membership felt that a non-German would be less vulnerable to political pressures by the Nazis, and asked Jung, who had previously been a vice-president of the international organization (1930–33), to become president. (It is ironic that Freud had wanted Jung to lead psychoanalysis partly because he was not Jewish; here he is asked to lead psychotherapy because he is not German. In both cases, being an outsider was seen as an asset.) It was the presidency of the new General Medical Society for Psychotherapy that Jung accepted in 1934, and in 1935 he founded the Swiss society. He was never a member of the German national society, which was then under Nazi control and headed by Dr. M. H. Goering, a relative of Hermann Goering.

When taking over the editorship of the *Zentralblatt,* Jung wrote a one-page announcement comparing the confusion of standpoints in therapy to the current political conflict. Harms quotes Jung as follows: "The factually existing differences between the Germanic and Jewish psychologies should no longer remain blurred—to present them clearly is an aim from which science can but derive benefit." This seemingly scientific proposal could not be taken as politically neutral, given the climate, and many Jews, including members of Jung's own school, were dismayed and angered. Jung responded to criticism that he was anti-Semitic by writing that he

was pursuing scientific questions and that the charge had originated with Freud near the end of their relationship.

One of Jung's earliest maneuvers in the organization was to
amend the bylaws, allowing German Jewish psychotherapists to
apply to the General Medical Society without having to be members of the German society, from which they had been banned by
Nazi decree. This was not reported in the *Zentralblatt* but was
quietly circulated alongside one issue of the journal. Whatever mix
of personal ambition and altruistic service we might imagine,
Harms concludes that Jung's conscious motives in this matter were
honorable; and the testimonies of close Jewish colleagues support
the argument that Jung was not anti-Semitic in his personal
dealings with people.

Jung's writings, personal correspondence, and public interviews
are more difficult to defend. He made statements about "Jewish
psychology" referring to the typical characteristics of a Jewish
person, but he also used the phrase to describe the psychological
theories of Freud and Adler. Although some of the controversial
passages have been taken out of context or mistranslated, there are
published papers from the early 1930s that include references to
the Jews' physical weakness, their inability to create their own
culture form, and their nomadic nature, which seem to play into
the Nazis' hands.[15] But Jung also made positive statements about
the high degree of civilization of such an ancient culture, its greater
acquaintance with the shadow, and its contribution to the development of its host cultures.

Speaking in Berlin at the 1933 Congress, Jung was emphatic in
his praise of Freud's contribution, which provoked the anger of
the Nazis. Yet in a radio interview of May 26, 1933, Jung agreed
with Weizsacker that the effects of "Jewish psychology" (meaning
the theories of Freud and Adler) were "corrosive" to the German
psyche, which Jung believed saw the beauty of the whole of life,
not the dissected parts.[16] The word "corrosive" had already become
part of the Nazi propaganda, and as part of the well-known
persecution of the German Jews, the books of Freud and his
followers had been publicly burned just two weeks earlier. In the

interview, Jung went on to characterize the Jewish theorists as "hostile to life"—a phrase that more accurately described the Nazi repression, which he seemed tacitly to condone. He also spoke of the need for the leader to follow his own inner voice if he is to lead the people, and referred to a recent comment by the Führer in seemingly appreciative tones.

What seems problematic even to Jung's most staunch supporters is the naiveté with which he wrote and spoke of these issues at a time (1932–38) when the Nazis were already virulently attacking the Jews. James Kirsch expressed his fear of the Nazis in 1933, but Jung reassured him that it would blow over in a short time. When they met again after the war, in 1947, Jung was quick to apologize for the mistake, but the apology was not made public by Kirsch until recently. Not only did he make disparaging statements about Jews, but it is evident that Jung was overly optimistic about the possible contribution of the National Socialist movement and the effect of the Germanic storm god Wotan, which he considered to be the ambivalent archetype behind it.

To explain the paradox presented by Jung's writings and behavior, we have to look to his *unconscious* motives and personal psychology. It is in this regard that I would like to come back to his father complex and the unresolved transference to Freud.

There are passages in Jung's writings from as early as 1918 (*Psychological Types*) that demonstrate his awareness of what he called the "barbarian element" in the not-fully-Christianized German psyche and the dangerous projection of this shadow on the Jews. Why, then, did he seem to lose sight of this awareness in the early days of the Nazi movement? During the 1930s, as Jung began to write and speak of cultural issues, he wrote a number of less inflammatory essays, such as his dismissive reviews of Picasso and Joyce's *Ulysses* (both in 1932) and "The Complications of American Psychology" (1930), which still provoke controversy. Jung's attitude toward modern art may be traced in part to his ambivalent relationship to the "Salome" anima figure,[17] but I believe his disturbing political actions can be linked directly to an unconscious identification with the archetype of the mana personality and its cultural expression, the shaman.

After the long period of intense introversion it seems that Jung's psychic energy underwent an enantiodromia, turning from the deep interiority of archetypal experience toward social and political life on a scale beyond his expertise. He saw the upheaval in Germany partly as a conflict between the senex attitude of the older generation and the puer enthusiasm of the Hitler youth.[18] His feeling for Wotan, which James Kirsch tells us was such a positive experience for Jung,[19] provides a metaphoric image of the psychic renewal Jung himself must have been feeling by way of identification with the upsurge of this youthful masculine energy in Germany:

> . . . we are driven to conclude that Wotan must, in time, reveal not only the restless, violent, stormy side of his character, but also his ecstatic and mantic qualities—a very different aspect of his nature. If this conclusion is correct, National Socialism would not be the last word. Things must be concealed in the background which we cannot imagine at present, but we may expect them to appear in the course of the next few years or decades.[20]

Jung had gone deeply into the underworld in his "night sea journey" following the break with Freud, but he had not completed the shamanic initiation that would include an ascent to heaven to experience the "ecstatic and mantic" qualities he attributed to the positive side of Wotan. His essay on Wotan ends in a poetic crescendo from the *Voluspo:* "After the wolf do wild men follow. . . ."

Jung's fascination with this wildness in the German psyche is evident two years later in a 1938 interview with H. R. Knickerbocker, in which he analyzes Hitler as a mystic and a medicine man, with little personality of his own but the ability to give voice to the hidden thoughts and wishes of the German people:

> There is no question but that Hitler belongs in the category of the truly mystic medicine man. As somebody commented about him at the last Nurnberg party congress, since the time of Mohammed nothing like it has been seen in the world.[21]

When Knickerbocker questions what Jung means by "Hitler's magic," Jung responds by explaining the working of subliminal impressions on the unconscious mind:

> . . . you would be surprised if I should tell you all that I have already learned unconsciously about you in this short space of time.
>
> Now, the secret of Hitler's power . . . is twofold: first, that his unconscious has exceptional access to his consciousness, and second, that he allows himself to be moved by it. He is like a man who listens intently to a stream or suggestions in a whispered voice from a mysterious source and then *acts upon them*. In our case, even if occasionally our unconscious does reach us through dreams, we have too much rationality . . . to obey it. This is doubtless the case with Chamberlain, but Hitler listens and obeys. The true leader is always led.[22]

Jung implies a similarity between his own perceptiveness, based on the method of listening to the unconscious, and Hitler's magic. Throughout the interview, which occurred just weeks before *Kristallnacht*, Jung seems more impressed with Hitler's ability to perceive and take advantage of power situations than he is with the political or human consequences. His admiration for the goose step; his unbridled affection for Mussolini's "bodily energy," originality, and good taste; and his tolerant attitude toward the more moderate form of anti-Semitism in Italy show a Jung at play with the triumph of his ideas (over whom?). "Now, as I observed Mussolini watching the first goose step he had ever seen, I could see him enjoying it with the zest of a small boy at a circus."[23] Given the tone of the whole interview, I cannot help but wonder if Jung is projecting his own unconscious grandiosity.

After a diagnosis of Stalin's personal ambition and power drive, Jung turns to the German problem again and changes the subject to therapy: "It is for this, then, that I propose a therapy. . . . the only way to save Democracy in the West . . . is not to try to stop Hitler. . . . Let him go to Russia. That is the logical *cure* for Hitler. . . . Nobody has ever bitten into Russia without regretting it. . . . It wouldn't matter to Russia if somebody took a bite. . . ."[24] It is striking how Jung, responding to recognition by a famous journalist, presents this commonly held view as his own therapeutic prescription for a frightened world.

I am not suggesting that Jung was consciously seeking political power, but I do believe that his inner development, his worldly success along with an earlier denial of leadership strivings, and his unresolved transference feelings to Freud synchronistically combined with the drama of European history to thrust him into a dangerous inflation. Despite his psychological sophistication, Jung seems to have harbored commonly held prejudices, not only about the Jews but about other groups, including the Russians and Slavs.

Jung had a very telling dream that occurred shortly after the Hitler-Stalin nonaggression pact was signed on August 23, 1939; that event, which seemed to eliminate the possibility of Jung's "cure" for Hitler, was terribly upsetting to him, and Jung rightly feared that Hitler would turn his expansionism to the West. In the dream, which Jung related to Esther Harding after the war, he was in a castle made of dynamite. Dr. Harding writes:

> Hitler came in and was treated as divine. Hitler stood on a mound as for a review. C. G. was placed on a corresponding mound. Then the parade ground began to fill with buffalo or yak steers, which crowded into the enclosed space from one end. The herd was filled with nervous tension and moved about restlessly. Then he saw that one cow was alone, apparently sick. Hitler was concerned about the cow and asked C. G. what he thought of it. C. G. said, "It is obviously very sick." At this point, Cossacks rode in and began to drive the herd off. He awoke and felt, "It is all right."[25]

Jung's interpretation was purely objective, seeing Hitler as "an intrument of divine forces, as Judas, or, still better, as the Antichrist." The herds are the primitive masculine forces in the German unconscious, like the masculine Nazi ideology disturbed by too prolonged and extreme a separation from feminine values. The cow represents the sick feminine element, and the Cossacks refer to Russia, which Jung considered "more barbaric than Germany, but . . . of sounder instinct" and which he believed "would . . . cause the overthrow of Germany."[26]

As Jay Sherry points out, "Jung's interpretation is both incomplete and unsatisfactory . . . turning the dream into another example of his prescience regarding historical developments in Europe."[27] Jung obviously ignores the subjective meaning of the dream, namely that his own psyche is dangerously explosive. The unconscious deification of and identification with Hitler are clear; not just the German soul but Jung's anima, too, is sick from a hypertrophy of the masculine. He is full of power and animosity toward his former colleagues, the Jewish psychoanalysts, which he projects onto the Russians as a deeply primitive aggressiveness.

In a world stunned by the accord between archenemies, Jung feared being "swallowed up," yet he awakens with a reassuring "It's all right." What followed during the war was obviously not "all right," but might that felt sense of the dream not refer to the internal "overthrow" of what Hitler represents within Jung? If Jung intuitively knew the rightness of this, he certainly had no idea on a feeling level what personal suffering it would involve for him.[28] The other possibility for his relief is more simple: denial.

Many of Jung's political views, including his Chamberlain-like attitude toward Hitler and his deep fear of Russia, were common in Europe at that time. The Princeton historian Arno J. Mayer argues that we must remove our cold-war blinders to understand the events leading up to the Holocaust.[29] In addition to the ancient history of the persecution of the Jews, there are twentieth-century class and national conflicts contributing to that horror. Mayer sees the period from the Russian Revolution to the end of World War II as a "second Thirty Years' War" and believes that the convergence of anti-Bolshevism and anti-Semitism in the frightened middle and upper classes reached a climax in the "interconnection of anticommunism and anti-Semitism in the Nazi ideology and project."[30] Fascism was no less "collective" or harmful to the individual than communism, yet Jung repeatedly attacked Russia without considering his own blindness about Germany and Italy. It was only after the war that Jung returned to these questions in an introverted, thoughtful way.[31] Acknowledging how "churned up" he still was at that time, he wrote:

I had not realized how much I myself was affected. There are others, I am sure, who will share this feeling with me. This inner identity of *participation mystique* with the events in Germany has caused me to experience afresh how painfully wide is the concept of *collective guilt*. So when I approach this problem it is certainly not with any feelings of cold-blooded superiority, but rather with an avowed sense of inferiority.[32]

He goes on to analyze the pathological hysteria that gripped the German psyche, adding that any German who denies his share of the blame "merely compounds his collective guilt by the sin of unconsciousness."[33] He reiterates his earlier view that the Germanic unconscious has a great polarization of the opposites, which is its source of creative tension but which, as in the individual hysteric, can lead to a dissociation. One such pair of opposites would be the sense of superiority over other groups with an underlying feeling of inferiority about oneself, which gets projected onto the scapegoat:

Inferiority feelings are usually a sign of inferior feeling—which is not just a play on words. All the intellectual and technological achievements in the world cannot make up for inferiority in the matter of feeling. The pseudo-scientific race-theories with which it was dolled up did not make the extermination of the Jews any more acceptable.[34]

Jung's creative genius functioned very much in keeping with his description of the Germanic character. As in "Wotan," his intuitive ability took off in a dangerous direction, leaving behind his feeling function and social consciousness. Even here, in "After the Catastrophe," this is his only reference to the genocide. If one reads the entire essay, it is evident that "the catastrophe" refers to the spiritual downfall of Germany and not to the grim fate of European Jewry. As deeply as Jung was concerned with these issues, I am aware of no place in his writings where he takes up the question of the Holocaust in depth.

Jung's fascination with Wotan, his early ambivalence about Hitler, his deep interest in Nietzsche (including the fear that he might end up like him), and his relative blindness to the dangers of Germany's anti-Semitism were all an outgrowth of his own renewed struggle to integrate the father complex at a cultural and archetypal level, as he had not been able to do it in his personal, transference relationship with Freud.

In the "Epilogue to 'Essays on Contemporary Events,' " also published in 1946, Jung writes:

> When Hitler seized power it became quite evident to me that a mass psychosis was boiling up in Germany. But I could not help telling myself that this was after all Germany, a civilized European nation with a sense of morality and discipline. Hence the ultimate outcome of the unmistakable mass movement still seemed to me uncertain, just as the figure of the Führer at first struck me as being merely ambivalent.[35]

> As a psychiatrist, accustomed to dealing with patients who are in danger of being overwhelmed by unconscious contents, I knew that it is of the utmost importance, *from the therapeutic point of view, to strengthen as far as possible their conscious position and powers of understanding so that something is there to intercept and integrate the contents that are breaking through into consciousness.* These contents are not necessarily destructive in themselves, but are ambivalent, and it depends on the constitution of the intercepting consciousness whether they will turn out as a curse or a blessing.[36]

> It is part of the doctor's professional equipment to be able *to summon up a certain amount of optimism* even in the most unlikely circumstances . . . *it should not be forgotten that Germany, up to the National Socialist era, was one of the most differentiated and highly civilized countries on earth, besides being for us Swiss a spiritual background to which we were bound by ties of blood, language, and friendship.*[37]

And in discussing his insistence that all Germans, whether conscious participants in Nazism or not, accept their guilt, he continues:

> In saying this it is not my intention to accuse or condemn. I am obliged to mention it only because my diagnosis has been

doubted. A medical diagnosis is not an accusation, and an illness
is not a disgrace but a misfortune. As early as 1936 I pleaded for
compassion in judging the German mentality. Even now, I adopt
the standpoint of the therapist.[38]

Aside from glossing over terrible wars in Germany's prior
history, these passages are remarkable for Jung's confusion of
roles. As in "Diagnosing the Dictators," he talks of Germany as
though it were his patient with an ego consciousness that had
submitted itself to him for treatment. His comments about the
attitude of the doctor and therapist are part of the deep wisdom
he has left us in our work as individual healers, but the application
of these attitudes to an entire nation reaches far beyond the role of
even a shaman, whose domain might rightfully include the collective soul of his tribe. Here, Jung seems identified with the mana
personality resulting from an inflation of the very real shamanic
aspect of his own psyche. Unconsciously, I believe, the metaphor
of therapist to a nation was part of Jung's felt need to heal his
"father culture," and his unconscious shadow projection on Freud
(as religious skeptic?) prevented him from seeing the potential
harm to the Jewish people.

After the war broke out, Jung condemned the Nazi regime at a
time when Germany seemed poised to invade Switzerland, but his
unconscious identification with the mana figure, which he had
recognized in Hitler, prevented him from seeing the political reality
in time to prevent serious emotional harm to others as well as
damage to his own reputation. Perhaps his illness and depression
in the 1940s were an inevitable part of the ensuing deflation.

A change in his attitude toward Jewish culture seems to have
emerged from the deepest unconscious and is evident in the near-
death visions Jung had after his heart attack in 1944. He experienced his nurse as "an old Jewish woman . . . preparing ritual
kosher dishes for me." A series of beatific coniunctio images
occurred as he lingered between this world and the next; the first
of these was "the wedding of Tifereth and Malchuth," an image
from the Kabbalah in Jewish mysticism.[39] I will return to Jung's
developing interest in the Kabbalah later on.

In reviewing this material, I realized how difficult it is to see the problem without subjective bias even fifty years after the events. I do not believe that Jung was a conscious anti-Semite, but I do think that his "inner identity . . . with the events in Germany" obscured his feeling function and social attitude, leading him to destructive actions. Until very recently, the evidence of any overtly anti-Semitic statement was lacking.

Aniela Jaffé, James Kirsch, and others have referred to comments about Jewish psychology made by Jung in the 1930s as misconceptions that he later corrected. I think that questions such as "Was Jung anti-Semitic?" and "How much so?" or "In what way?" might have gone on endlessly, each accusation provoking a new round of defense, were it not for the frank discussion of the topic by James Kirsch following the publication of a letter from Jung to his former asisstant, W. M. Kranefeldt. Kirsch reproduces the available portion of this letter, written by Jung on February 9, 1934, at about the same time that "The State of Psychotherapy Today" was published in the *Zentralblatt*.

> As is known, one cannot do anything against stupidity; but in this instance, the Arian (*sic*) people can point out that with Freud and Adler specifically Jewish points of view were publicly preached, and, as can be proven likewise, points of view that have an essentially corrosive character. If the proclamation of this Jewish gospel is agreeable to the government, then so be it. Otherwise, there is also the possibility that this would not be agreeable to the government.[40]

Of this passage, Kirsch says:

> The letter is really quite devastating. It is written by Jung to a former assistant who had, at least psychologically, become a Nazi. Jung somehow got into a mood which gave free rein to his negative feelings about Freud and he propounded untenable opinions such as calling Freud's and Adler's viewpoints "typically Jewish"; that is, he made the same generalizations which anti-Semites make in regard to Jews.[41]

Jung and Kranefeldt had shared strong negative feelings about Freud, and both considered his therapeutic ideas "corrosive" to the psyche.⁴² The Nazis were using this same word (*zersetzend*) to describe the purported effect of Jews on the Aryan society. Kirsch continues:

> What Jung said in 1934 has to be seen as political, whether written in a letter or published in an article. . . . Statements by Jung carried great weight, and these, in particular, coming from the healer, were seen as poison.⁴³

In a letter to Aniela Jaffé, Gershom Scholem tells of a meeting between Jung and Rabbi Leo Baeck, in which Jung admitted, "I slipped up." (There is no reference to this comment by Jung or Baeck anywhere else.) Kirsch quotes other letters by Jung to support his contention that Jung was not consciously anti-Semitic but had "slipped" into an unconscious complex, a complex that included archetypal as well as personal elements. Kirsch recounts a comment reportedly made by Hitler, that it was a time of battle between Yahweh and Wotan, and then continues:

> In addition to Jung's projection of the personal father on Freud, there was also in those years the tremendous unconscious archetypal content of Yahweh and Wotan in their transference relationship. The Wotan aspect comes out very clearly in Jung's article called "Wotan" and the Yahweh aspect, of course, in *Answer to Job*.⁴⁴

It is in the writing of *Answer to Job* (1952) that Kirsch finds Jung's redemption. The book was written, during an illness, with such passionate intensity that Jung completed the essential part of it in two weeks. Kirsch points to a resolution of Jung's transference to Freud at an archetypal level.

> In this book, Jung gives us nothing less than the history of a divine image in Western man's soul and man's changing and developing consciousness in his confrontation with the image of Yahweh. *Answer to Job* is, after all, the experience of the living God, not only as it happened to the Jewish people in the aion of Aries . . . but also as it happened for Western culture as a whole in the appearance of the specifically differentiated image of

Yahweh's son. It is Jung's own, direct, and immediate experience
of Yahweh that he puts down in *Answer to Job*.[45]

Kirsch's personal feeling for Jung is quite clear:

> To my mind, Jung is the only man who, though he gave into
> feelings and opinions of anti-Semitism for a short period, solved
> the problem of his unconscious anti-Semitism. He had a genuine
> and conscious collision with the living archetype and worked it
> out of his system by writing *Answer to Job*. . . . Jung was the
> only non-Jew I have ever known who, in my opinion, truly
> overcame the last trace of anti-Semitism. To the extent that the
> living image of God is not integrated, especially among Jews,
> there exists the black ghost of anti-Semitism. It is for the same
> reason that so many Jews are so sensitive to the smallest sign of
> anti-Semitism in non-Jews.[46]

I accept Dr. Kirsch's testimony that Jung had finally freed
himself from the archetypal source of his "unconscious anti-
Semitism," but in addition, the confrontation with Yahweh
brought to a climax his identification with the mana personality
("the ruler of men and spirits, the friend of God"). One source of
this inflation must surely have been Jung's experience and formulation of the God-image or Self, which he initially assumed was a
God of goodness. It was only in confronting his own dark rage at
Yahweh after the war that Jung fully experienced God as other.
Although Jung did not address the Holocaust directly as a historical event, it seems that his psyche forced him to wrestle with the
religious issues it raises at a deeply mythological level. But the
question remains whether he resolved the shadow projection at the
level of the cultural unconscious.

The work of Jewish analysts following Jung, such as Rivka
Kluger, Erich Neumann, James Kirsch, and others, has opened up
a new relationship to the Jewish tradition for many Jews attracted
to Jung's ideas. In a letter to Kirsch dated February 16, 1954,
Jung's thoughts and feelings about Jewish psychology have an
entirely different tone than what he wrote in the 1930s:

> The Jew has roughly the same moral development behind him as
> the Christian European, consequently he has the same problem.

A Jew can recognize the *self* in that hostile pair of brothers, Christ and Satan, as well as I can or perhaps even better, and with it the incarnation of Yahweh's assimilation to man. Naturally the status of man is profoundly altered because of this.

The Jew has the advantage of having long since anticipated the development of consciousness in his own spiritual history. By this I mean the Lurianic stage of the Kabbalah, the breaking of the vessels and man's help in restoring them. Here the thought emerges for the first time that man must help God to repair the damage wrought by the Creation. For the first time man's cosmic responsibility is acknowledged. Naturally, it is a question of the self and not the ego, although the latter will be deeply affected.[47]

And Jung wrote to the Reverend Evans on the following day, February 17:

In a tract of the Lurianic Kaballah, the remarkable idea is developed that man is destined to become God's helper in the attempt to restore the vessels which were broken when God thought to create the world. Only a few weeks ago, I came across this impressive doctrine which gives meaning to man's status exalted by the incarnation.[48]

Whether or not one agrees with Jung's analysis of the problems of the modern Jew, his ideas are informed and his expression respectful. By recognizing the wisdom of the Kabbalah, especially in reference to the integration of the shadow side of God represented by "shards," he came to understand Judaism's importance as an ongoing religious tradition and not just as an antecedent of Christianity. It seems fitting that the doctrine of the shards helped Jung to understand the archetypal shadow problem, which he had to confront to free himself of his own prejudice. In the long run his "*participation mystique* with the events in Germany" may have been, like Mephistopheles in Goethe's *Faust*, "that power of evil which eventually does good."

Dr. Kirsch seems to have experienced a true feeling of reconciliation with Jung, but if Jung's writing of *Answer to Job* resolved the problem at its archetypal source, why did he not make amends with a wider public and recant his mistakes more openly than the anecdotal apologies to Kirsch and Rabbi Baeck? If in *Job* he metaphorically had helped "God to repair the damage wrought by the Creation," could he not make ordinary, human reparation as well? Was he too ashamed to express his remorse, or did he fail to understand and feel the import of his actions? Whichever is true, I suspect that the accusation of anti-Semitism had become an ongoing narcissistic wound that made it all the more difficult for him to apologize publicly. Perhaps a similar feeling of shame has kept Jung's followers from openly discussing these issues until very recently, when his ideas have gained wider acceptance.

There are other points on which I question Dr. Kirsch. His observation that Jews who have not integrated the "living image of God" are more sensitive to anti-Semitism may be true for many areligious Jews (including Freud), but I cannot accept such a psychological statement in reference to Holocaust survivors and their families. These are individuals for whom notions such as "hypersensitivity to anti-Semitism" become meaningless. I also question how many people are called, and have the psychic capacity, to integrate "the living God." Kirsch's assumption of such a theistic psychology confuses Jung's personal religious experience with his psychological theory. There are other spiritual paths leading to the Self and other cultural attitudes than the religious which lead to individuation.

Finally, I think that there are numerous gradations of trauma between surviving the Holocaust and a schoolyard fistfight. "Hypersensitivity" to anti-Semitism (as well as to being accused of it) may derive from outer experience, so the archetypal questions must be understood in the light of the personal life. A Jew who has suffered from severe racism, especially in childhood, may be less equipped or less willing to make the eloquent distinction between conscious anti-Semitism and slipping into an unconscious complex. And if he is psychologically minded, he may know only too well the cumulative effect in the collective psyche of many such unconscious projections.

Anti-Semitism is one of the numerous forms of racism that results from such splitting and shadow projection. Jung was a great man with a large impact on life, but also a man with a problematic shadow. I have tried to show that the aspect of his shadow that he expressed in the 1930s had cultural (as distinct from religious) sources as well as the previously explored personal and archetypal sources. His early narcissistic wounding predisposed him to a cultural regression to the most ancient of initiation rites, that of shamanic cultures. It is in Jung's writings on the "mana-personality," whose cultural prototype is the shaman, that he reveals the source of his unconscious fascination with National Socialism, Wotan, and finally Hitler, in whom he saw a similar, though totally unpsychological, shamanic temperament at work. It seems to me that Jung's residual anger at Freud is less central than his unconscious identification with the mana figure in his apparent anti-Semitism. Joseph Henderson has pointed out that a neglected aspect of the personal shadow may fall back into the collective unconscious and, as the archetypal shadow, become the container for the Self, including in its constellation an array of synchronistic phenomena.[49] Elements of Jung's personal shadow from his unresolved transference to Freud fell back into the collective unconscious and brought him perilously close to the archetypal shadow. His wish to heal the father culture of Germany came together with historical events in Europe as he attempted to save and lead the science of psychotherapy in the 1930s; but his failure to save the German psyche forced him to deal with the central religious problem of his life—the light and dark sides of God.

Jung's struggles have given us great insight, but they should also make us cautious about too broad an application of archetypal views. We must recognize our limits in analyzing the very collective which Jungian theory so often demeans and open ourselves to the input of colleagues in related social sciences. There is a complement to his identification with the mana-personality in our tendency to project that archetype onto him. To those who idealize him, he is the great healer or prophet who can do no wrong. But the negative face of the mana personality is the evil witch doctor or black magician, which is the projection of those who villify him as a Nazi collaborator. By responding to the baser attacks on Jung with a denial of the problem, we may perpetuate this split projection. Just as it is erroneous to make Jung a symbol of the evil we have come to equate with anti-Semitism, it would be equally naive to project the resolution of our own racism onto his later religious development. If we are to deepen our self-knowledge, we must use his phenomenological method and not identify with his personality, and in doing so each of us must take responsibility for the personal shadow.

Notes

1. See *Answer to Job* for references to a "differential moral valuation" and a "morality of evil," *Collected Works* 11, pars. 696, 742.

2. Polly Young-Eisendrath, "The Absence of Black Americans as Jungian Analysts," *Quadrant* 20, no. 2 (1987): 42.

3. James Kirsch, "Jung's Transference on Freud: The Jewish Element," *American Imago* 41, no. 1 (Spring 1984): 63–84.

4. Joseph Henderson, "The Cultural Unconscious" (1987), in *Shadow and Self* (Wilmette, Ill.: Chiron Publications, 1990).

5. *The Freud-Jung Letters*, p. 95.

6. Ibid., p. 97.

7. Ibid., p. 98.

8. Ibid., p. 122.

9. Ibid., p. 168.

10. C. G. Jung, *Memories, Dreams, Reflections*, ed. Aniela Jaffé, trans. Richard and Clara Winston (New York: Vintage Books, 1965), pp. 158–159.

11. See the index of *CW* 10.

12. *CW* 7, par. 377.

13. Ibid., par. 380.

14. Ibid.

15. Jung, "The State of Psychotherapy Today," *CW* 10, esp. pars. 353–356.

16. See Matthias von der Tann, "A Jungian Perspective on the Berlin Institute for Psychotherapy: A Basis for Mourning," *San Francisco Jung Institute Library Journal* 8, no. 4 (1989).

17. See Russell Lockhart, *Psyche Speaks* (Wilmette, Ill.: Chiron Publications, 1987), pp. 66–72.

18. Arvid Erlenmeyer et al., "Destructiveness in the Tension between Myth and History," *The Archetype of the Shadow in a Split World*, Proceedings of the Tenth International Congress for Analytical Psychology, Berlin, 1986.

19. Kirsch, "Jung's Transference on Freud."

20. Jung, "Wotan" (1936), CW 10, par. 399.

21. "Diagnosing the Dictators," in *C. G. Jung Speaking,* p. 117.

22. Ibid., p. 119.

23. Ibid., p. 127.

24. Ibid., pp. 132–133.

25. Ibid., p. 181.

26. Ibid., pp. 181–182.

27. Jay Sherry, "Jung, the Jews, and Hitler," *Spring* (1986), p. 171.

28. John Beebe, personal communication.

29. Arno J. Mayer, *Why Did the Heavens Not Darken?* (New York: Pantheon Books, 1989).

30. See V. R. Berghahn, "The Twisted Road to Auschwitz," *New York Times Book Review,* February 19, 1989.

31. Jung, "After the Catastrophe" (1945). CW 10, par. 402.

32. *CW* 10, par. 402.

33. Ibid., par. 404.

34. Ibid., par. 416.

35. Ibid., par. 472.

36. Ibid., par. 473. Emphasis added.

37. Ibid., par. 474. Emphasis added.

38. Ibid., par. 484.

39. *MDR,* p. 294.

40. Kirsch, "Jung's Transference on Frued," p. 71.

41. Ibid., p. 72.

42. Weizsacker interview, May 26, 1933.

43. Ibid.

44. Ibid., p. 74.

45. Ibid., p. 80.

46. Ibid., p. 77.

47. C. G. *Jung, Letters,* vol. 2, p. 155. On the breaking if the vessels, Gershom Scholem, in *Major Trends in Jewish Mysticism* (p. 267), writes: "The 'shards' . . . form the counterpole of the ten sephiroth, which are the ten stages in the revelation of God's creative power. The shards, representing the forces of evil and darkness, were originally mixed with the light of the sephiroth. The Zohar describes evil as the by-product of the life process of the sephiroth. Therefore, the sephiroth had to be cleaned of the evil admixture of the shards (for creation to manifest). The elimination of the shards took place in what is described in the cabalistic writings—particularly of Luria and his school—

as the 'breaking of the vessels.' Through this the powers of evil assumed a separate and real existence."

48. *Letters*, p. 157.
49. Henderson, *Shadow and Self*, pp. 65–66.

The Case of Jung's Alleged Anti-Semitism

Jay Sherry

Jay Sherry received a master's degree in psychology from the New School for Social Research in New York and has studied at the C. G. Jung Institute in Zurich. Currently a social studies teacher in New York, he has taught at the C. G. Jung Foundation for Analytical Psychology and at New York University. His articles have appeared in *Spring, Quadrant, Harvest,* and the *San Francisco Jung Institute Library Journal.*

This essay explores aspects of Jung's comments about Jewish psychology, National Socialism, and Hitler that have been the focus of controversy. Sherry makes a case for understanding these comments in terms of Jung's relationship with Freud and the bitter termination of that relationship. He analyzes a dream of Jung's and Jung's heart attack of 1944 in terms of an impaired relation to his feeling function. He sees Jung's inability to realize the inappropriate nature of his ideas and remarks about Jewish psychology, National Socialism, and Hitler as stemming from this impairment. Sherry concludes by criticizing Jung for failing to take a strong stand on "the major political-moral crisis of our time."

The dual charges of anti-Semitism and pro-Nazism have been leveled against Jung for many years, casting a dark shadow over his reputation. We wonder how a man dedicated to self-understanding could be charged with such a prejudice. Much of what has been written about his alleged anti-Semitism has, unfortunately, been based on misinformation, quotes taken out of context, projection, or evasion.

Jung is frequently criticized for assuming the presidency of a psychotherapeutic association in the 1930s. One example appears in a recent biography of Otto Rank, in which we learn that "the Berlin stronghold of psychoanalysis [was] dissolved, to be replaced by Aryan psychiatrists led by Jung."[1] This damning statement misrepresents the facts and creates the impression that Jung was the czar of Nazi psychiatry. He was not. The charge is based not on accurate historical research but on a projection: that is, on the image of "Jung the heretic," the crown prince of psychoanalysis who became the black prince of mysticism and anti-Semitism.

Jung's defenders, on the other hand, after pointing out that a significant number of his closest followers were Jewish, do admit that he "slipped up." They attribute this to bad timing and political naiveté. Such explanations are unsatisfactory because, besides being evasive, they are unpsychological. Those who do try to offer psychological explanations invoke Jung's concept of the shadow, but they rarely use this approach to analyze the specific personal and cultural factors that influenced his behavior.

My aim is to briefly review Jung's relationship with Freud as a necessary background to the subject and then to give an accurate account of Jung's involvement in the General Medical Society for Psychotherapy and his views on events in Germany in the 1930s. Attention to historical detail is absolutely necessary but not sufficient to understand why Jung said the things he did. He continually emphasized that psychology is a "subjective confession," so we must also consider relevant unconscious material as a basis for a psychological interpretation and a moral response.

All commentators agree that what Jung said about Jews must be understood in the context of his relationsip with Freud. The two men met in 1907 and initiated an intimate personal and professional relationship. Concerned about the future of psychoanalysis, Freud cultivated Jung, who, as a Gentile and a psychiatrist at Switzerland's leading mental hospital, seemed perfectly suited to champion psychoanalysis.

Their correspondence is filled with discussions of many topics: personal feelings, theoretical formulations, psychoanalytic politics and publications, and family matters (one constant was Freud's chiding Jung for not writing more frequently). The year 1912 was pivotal in their relationship. Jung was in the process of writing *Wandlungen und Symbole der Libido* (now known in English as *Symbols of Transformation*) and was apprehensive about Freud's reaction to his new understanding of the libido. His fears seemed to be confirmed by Freud's cool response to Jung's Fordham lectures in which he distanced himself from key tenets of Freud's sexual theory. In the process of declaring his intellectual independence, Jung felt it necessary to quote Nietzsche's Zarathustra: "One repays a teacher badly if one remains only a pupil."² His sensitivity was manifested in his reaction to what he called Freud's "Kreuzlingen gesture," an apparent slight that he felt was further evidence of Freud's displeasure. (This involved an incident in which Freud apparently visited Switzerland without notifying Jung in time to allow for a rendezvous. Jung later acknowledged that he was at fault in the matter.) This topic dominated his letters until the air was cleared at a meeting in September in Munich at which Jung admitted making a mistake. His letters of December are increasingly emotional. On December 3 he cautioned Freud to take his bit of neurosis seriously: "I have suffered from this bit in my dealings with you, though you haven't seen it and didn't understand me properly when I tried to make my position clear."³ After Freud brought a slip of the pen to his attention, Jung's conflicted feelings burst out in his letter of December 18: "I would, however, point out that your technique of treating your pupils like patients is a *blunder* . . . so long as you hand out this stuff I don't give a damn for my symptomatic actions; they shrink to nothing in comparison with the formidable beam in my brother Freud's eye. I am not in the least neurotic. . . . If ever you should rid yourself of your complexes and stop playing the father to your sons and instead of aiming continually at their weak spots took a good look at your own for a change, then I will mend my ways. . . ."⁴ This last sentence contains in embryo the critique of psychoanalysis that Jung would later make in his notorious 1934 article "The State of Psychotherapy Today." Freud phlegmatically replied that "none of us need feel ashamed of his own bit of neurosis. But one who while behaving abnormally keeps shouting that he is normal gives ground for the suspicion that he lacks insight into his illness. Accordingly, I propose that we abandon our personal relations entirely."⁵ In 1914 he published *On the History of the Psychoanalytic Movement*, in which he said of Jung, "he seemed to give up certain racial prejudices which he had previously permitted himself."⁶ This is terribly important: the founder of psychoanalysis has here, in its official history, branded Jung an anti-Semite, a judgment that would henceforth be accepted as fact. No researchers have, however, found any hard evidence of anti-Semitism on Jung's part during his association with Freud. Jung felt unjustly maligned and as a result harbored a resentment toward Freud that lasted throughout his life.⁷

Freud discussed the cultural and religious differences between the Vienna and Zurich groups with Karl Abraham, who had studied under Jung and early on expressed his suspicions about his former chief. Freud wrote to him, "you are closer to my intellectual constitution because of racial kinship, while he [Jung] as a Christian and a pastor's son finds his way to me against great inner resistances. His association with us is the more valuable for that. I nearly said that it was only by his appearance on the scene that psychoanalysis escaped the danger of becoming a Jewish national affair."⁸ After the break with Jung, Freud wrote that the publication of his book *Totem and Taboo* "will cut [us] off cleanly from all Aryan religiousness."⁹ By labeling Jung an anti-Semite, Freud played to the longstanding jealousies of his Viennese followers, who resented Jung's privileged position as Freud's heir apparent.

Jung subsequently developed his theory of psychological types, partly as a way of understanding his differences with Freud and Adler. In time he came to consider the role of cultural differences in distinguishing his theory from Freud's. In 1918 he explained Freud's and Adler's tendency to reductionism as a result of their being Jews. He noted that "these specifically Jewish doctrines are throroughly unsatisfying to the Germanic mentality."¹⁰

In the late 1920s Jung became involved in the General Medical Society for Psychotherapy, a predominantely German organization founded to promote the use of psychotherapy by doctors. He was named vice-president in 1930 and was prevailed upon to assume the presidency when Ernst Kretschmer resigned in April 1933. Many members of the Society hoped that his reputation and Swiss citizenship would help maintain the society's independent status in the wake of the Nazi takeover. He began to reorganize the society as the International General Medical Society for Psychotherapy, and this change was approved at the Bad Neuheim Congress in May 1934. The new society was composed of national groups from Germany, Denmark, Holland, and Switzerland. The German group was by far the largest and was headed by Martin Goering, a cousin of the Reichsmarschall. To avoid their domination, voting was limited to no more than 40 percent of any one national group. Significantly, individual membership was arranged for those colleagues barred from the German group—namely, its Jewish members.

The common misunderstanding is that Jung was the president of a Nazified German organization (in fact, he actively promoted the formation of new groups in Sweden and England). This error is due mainly to developments in the society's journal. Although the society's headquarters were in Switzerland during Jung's term as president, the journal continued to be published in Germany. It had been agreed that a special edition would be published for distribution only within Germany, since all organizations there had to conform to Nazi ideology. Owing to Nazi political pressure the international edition of December 1933 appeared with a manifesto that said, in part, "the society expects all members who work as writers or speakers to work through Adolf Hitler's *Mein Kampf* with all scientific effort and accept it as a basis." Although the manifesto had Goering's byline and referred explicitly to the German rather than to the International Society, the damage to Jung's reputation was done. It was compounded by a passage in Jung's inaugural editorial that said, "The differences which actually exist between Germanic and Jewish psychology and which have long been known to every intelligent person are no longer to be glossed over. . . . I should like to state expressly that this implies no depreciation of Semitic psychology."[11]

These words were immediately challenged by the psychiatrist

Gustav Bally in the *Neue Züricher Zeitung,* prompting Jung's "Rejoinder to Bally." In it he explained his reasons for involving himself in the society, saying that preserving psychotherapy in Germany was worth risking his reputation for. Doctors "must learn to adapt themselves. To protest is ridiculous—how to protest against an avalanche?"[12] He addressed the fact that he had raised the Jewish question: "This I did deliberately. My esteemed critic appears to have forgotten that the first rule of psychotherapy is to talk in the greatest detail about all the things that are the most ticklish and dangerous, and the most misunderstood. The Jewish problem is a regular complex, a festering wound, and no responsible doctor could bring himself to apply methods of medical hush-hush in this matter."[13] He concluded in his defense, "But my public will object, why raise the Jewish problem today of all days and in Germany of all places? . . . I did not speak of it only since the revolution; I have been officially campaigning for criticism of subjective psychological premises as a necessary reform in psychology ever since 1913. This has nothing to do with the form of the German state. If I am to be exploited for political ends, there's nothing I can do to stop it."[14]

Shortly afterward Jung published his article "The State of Psychotherapy Today" in the society's journal and went from the frying pan into the fire. The article was intended as a critique of psychoanalysis, which Jung faulted for its overreliance on technique, its dogmatic emphasis on infantile experiences and the sense of superiority it conveyed on the analyst (echoing his letter of December 18, 1912, Jung said that Freud's ideas had exerted influence "largely on the easy opportunity they afford of touching the other fellow on his sore spot, of deflating him and hoisting oneself into a superior position. What a blessed relief it is when one can say in a tight corner, 'That's nothing but resistance,' or no longer takes one's opponent's arguments seriously. . .)."[15]

Jung felt that it was important to recognize the "personal equation" in psychology and to articulate the subjective premises that qualify each theory. This became his point of departure for his controversial remarks about Freud and Jews. He saw Freud and Adler as exponents of leveling psychologies that did not do justice to the complexities of the human psyche. Jung further felt that there were fundamental psychological differences between Jews and Germans (as well as between other groups) that had to be taken into account when analyzing members of each group.

His analysis of the Jewish psyche is not wholly negative, asserting that the Jew has a wider area of psychological consciousness than the German, but it is nevertheless based in great part on stereotypes. One is the image of "the Jew as nomad." This widespread image depicted Jews as city-dwellers alienated from the soil, the soul-renewing womb of nature, and it appears to have informed Jung's contention that the Jews had not created a cultural form but required a host nation for their development. Another stereotype is found in his statement that "The Jews . . . have to aim at the chinks in the armour of their adversary. . . ."[16] This comment reverberates with significance both personal and cultural. Personally, it reiterates the sense of woundedness we have seen in Jung's comments regarding Freud and psychoanalysis. Culturally, it evokes the "stab in the back" fantasy that pervaded Germany after 1918 and was so successfully exploited by Hitler, which, in turn, evoked the murder of Siegfried by the treacherous Hagen.

The bitter tone and unfair characterization of psychoanalysis continued when Jung declared that it had been "a grave error in medical psychology up till now to apply Jewish categories—which are not even binding on all Jews—indiscriminately to Germanic and Slavic Christendom."[17] Throughout the article he berates psychoanalysis for its fixation with obscene material, saying that "to suspect . . . natural wholesomeness of unnatural obscenities is not only sinfully stupid but positively criminal."[18]

It is clear that Jung was here giving vent to long-smoldering resentments toward Freud in the guise of a scientific typology that, unfortunately, relied on cultural stereotypes rather than empathic insights. Although Jung claimed that he had assumed the presidency for altruistic reasons, we must also consider the role of his power complex. After a twenty-year hiatus Jung was again president of an international organization and had a journal as a forum for his ideas. He was also undoubtedly flattered by the positive treatment that he received from other members of the group.

All this was happening, of course, while Hitler was consolidating his power over Germany. Jung was initially impressed by the spirit of nationalism alive there, which he saw as a constructive force. After the war he wrote, "Our judgment would certainly be different had our information stopped short at 1933 or 1934. At that time, in Germany as well as in Italy, there were not a few things that appeared plausible and seemed to speak in favor of the regime . . . after the stagnation and decay of the postwar years, the refreshing wind that blew through the two countries was a tempting sign of hope."[19]

In June 1933 Jung was in Berlin to give a dream seminar and while there gave a radio interview. To a series of leading questions he offered a series of compromising answers. Asked about the role of psychology in the collective movement, he said, "Only the self-development of the individual . . . can produce consciously responsible spokesmen and leaders of the collective movement. As Hitler said recently, the leader must have the courage to go his own way. . . ." Later in that interview he returned to this theme: "It is perfectly natural that a leader should stand at the head of an elite, which in earlier centuries was formed by the nobility. The nobility believe by the law of nature in the blood and exclusiveness of the race. Western Europe doesn't understand the specific psychic emergency of the young German nation because it does not find itself in the same situation either historically or psychologically."[20]

In 1936 he published his article "Wotan," in which he analyzed the effect of that archetype on Germany. After discussing the stormy side of this god, he predicted that in time the divinatory side would also be revealed, and he seemed to be invoking this side by opening the article with a prophecy by Nostradamus and closing it with a cryptic reference to Wotan consulting the head of Mimir. Still, he was beginning to take a more critical view of Germany. "The impressive thing about the German phenomenon is that one man, who is obviously 'possessed,' has infected a whole nation to such an extent that everything is set in motion and has started rolling on its course toward perdition."[21]

Part of Jung's fascination with events in Germany was due to his conviction that his theory of archetypes was better able to explain what was going on there than any alternative theory ("I venture the heretical suggestion that the unfathomable depths of Wotan's character explain more of Nationalism Socialism than all three reasonable factors [economic, political, and psychological] put together").[22] It is in this light that the widely quoted (and misinterpreted) passage from his 1934 article makes sense: "Has the formidable phenomenon of National Socialism, on which the whole world gazes with astonished eyes, taught them [Freud and his followers] better? Where was that unparalleled tension and energy while as yet no National Socialism existed? Deep in the Germanic psyche, in a pit that is anything but a garbage-bin of unrealizable infantile wishes and unresolved family resentments."[23] Jung intended this as a vindication of his theory, not of Hitler's program.

In the late 1930s Jung gave a number of interviews in which he discussed current events. The most lengthy was the one he gave to the American journalist H. R. Knickerbocker. In it he described Hitler as a mystic medicine man, "the mirror of every German's unconscious, but of course he mirrors nothing from a non-German. He is the loudspeaker which magnifies the inaudible whispers of the German soul until they can be heard by the German's unconscious ear. . . . He is the first man to tell every German what he has been thinking and feeling all along in his unconscious about German fate, especially since the defeat in the World War, and the characteristic which colors every German soul is the typically German inferiority complex—the complex of the younger brother, of the one who is always a bit late to the feast. Hitler's power is not political, it is magic. . . ." "He himself has referred to his Voice. His voice is nothing other than his unconscious into which the German people have projected their own selves, that is, the unconscious of 78 million Germans. That is what makes him powerful."[24]

Jung was a conservative, upper-class Swiss and felt that the best thing to do vis-à-vis Germany was to follow the "give it a chance" policy exemplified by the British prime minister Neville Chamberlain. Jung told Knickerbocker, "The only way to save Democracy in the West—and by the West I mean America too—is not to try to stop Hitler . . . you can only hope to influence the direction of his expansion. . . . Let him go to Russia. That is the logical *cure* for Hitler. . . . Nobody has ever bitten into Russia without regretting it. . . . It wouldn't matter to Russia if somebody took a bite. . . ."[25]

This callous indulgence in Realpolitik created a reaction in his unconscious which was expressed in a dream he had shortly after Hitler and Stalin signed their nonaggression pact in August 1939. The dream exists in two versions, one by Esther Harding, the other by E. A. Bennet. I will first give the version and interpretation recorded by Harding, my interpretation, the Bennet version, and then a comparison of the two.

> He found himself in a castle, all the walls and buildings of which were made of trinitrotoluene (dynamite). Hitler came in and was treated as divine. Hitler stood on a mound as for a review. C. G. was placed on a corresponding mound. Then the parade ground began to fill with buffalo or yak steers, which crowded into the enclosed space from one end. The herd was filled with nervous tension and moved about restlessly. Then he saw one cow was alone, apparently sick. Hitler was concerned about this cow and asked C. G. what he thought of it. C. G. Jung said, "It is obviously sick." At this point, Cossacks rode in at the back and began to drive the herd off. He awoke and felt "It is all right."

Jung's interpretation:

> Hitler was treated as *divine*. Consequently, he felt, we had to view him like that, that Hitler is not to be taken primarily as a human man, but as an instrument of "divine" forces, as Judas, or still better as the Anti-Christ must be. That the castle was built of trinitrotoluene meant that it would blow up and be destroyed because of its explosive quality. The herds are the instincts, the primitive, pre-human forces let loose in the German unconscious. They are not even domesticated cattle, but buffalo or yaks, very primitive indeed. They are all male, as in the Nazi ideology: all the values of relationship, of the person or individual, are completely repressed; the feminine is sick unto death, and so we get a sick cow. Hitler turns to C. G. for advice, but he limits his comment to the diagnosis "the cow is very sick". At this, as

though the recognition of the ailment released something, the Cossacks burst in. Even before that, the herd had been disturbed and nervous, as indeed the male animal is if separated too long or too completely from its complement, the female. The Cossacks are, of course, Russians. From what C. G. said, he deduced that Russia—more barbaric than Germany, but also more directly primitive, and therefore of sounder instinct—would break in and cause the overthrow of Germany.[26]

His interpretation is both incomplete and unsatisfactory. One of Jung's great contributions to dream interpretation is his distinction between objective and subjective interpretation. An objective interpretation relates dream figures to actual persons in the dreamer's life; a subjective one takes the figures as personifications of different aspects of the dreamer's personality. Although both are important, Jungian dream analysis tends to emphasize subjective interpretation. In this one Jung is exclusively objective, turning the dream into another example of his prescience regarding historical developments in Europe (reminiscent of his pre–World War I vision of a European bloodbath). We must consider a subjective interpretation to reach a deeper understanding of Jung's unconscious situation.

"In Hitler, every German should have seen his own shadow, his own worst danger . . ."[27] In the dream Jung is on intimate terms with the shadow and is partly identified with it (raised up on a similar mound).

The personality is often symbolized by a house. That it is here a castle relates to Jung's medieval interests. Ominously, it is constructed of dynamite. We usually associate castles with security for those inside; here its explosive nature would pose the greatest danger to those within. Into this explosive psychic space crowds the herd, the instincts. They are in a state of disharmony.

We must connect the dream image of the Cossacks with Jung's conscious attitude. He had a low opinion of the Russians ("More barbaric than Germany"; "the Slav mujiks, the poor white trash of Europe").[28] He had recently advocated a German invasion of Russia, so the appearance of the Cossacks forebodes revenge, not liberation. The dream took place at a time of great anxiety when

Jung said that the Swiss feared being "swallowed up"—a reversal of his comment that "it wouldn't matter to Russia if somebody took a bite."

Now the Bennet version:

> He was in a vast field with, in the distance, buildings like barracks. The place was filled with hordes of buffalos (i.e., Germans). He was on a mound, and Hitler was on another mound. He felt that as long as he fixed his gaze on Hitler all would be well. Then he saw a cloud of dust in the distance, and horsemen-Cossacks rounding up the buffalos and driving them out of the field. Then he woke and was glad, for he knew that Germany would be beaten by Russia. This, he said, was a collective dream, and very important.[29]

There are two significant differences between the two versions. The dynamite castle in the Harding version becomes a field in the Bennet. Also, the sick cow is missing in the Bennet version. The reason for these discrepancies most likely stems from the fact that Jung gave more details to Harding, an old friend, and an edited version to Bennet, a recent acquaintance. What two images did he choose to exclude? The dynamite castle (explosiveness) and the sick cow (sickness). The key to the dream is Jung's diagnosis of the cow. He calls this the culmination—the point at which something happens that determines the outcome of the dream. The scene is dominated by a herd of steers that Jung associated with the overly masculine Nazi ideology. The solitary cow is sick. This deeply divine image connects us with the nurturing mother who gives life-promoting milk. What has made the feminine in Jung so isolated and sick? I think it was his fascination with the archetypal forces alive in Germany and his bitterness toward his old psychoanalytic colleagues that caused him to lose touch with the feeling level of what was happening.

In 1944 Jung broke his foot and then suffered a heart attack, an event that likely had an important symbolic dimension. While in the hospital he experienced a series of visions that he described in his autobiography.[30] At his evening meal he saw his nurse as an old Jewish woman who was serving him kosher food. This is an important development: the feminine has been transformed from a sick cow into a maternal figure who nourished him with the food of a people whom he had not sufficiently appreciated. This was followed by a series of visions of the sacred marriage in which he was Rabbi Simon ben Jochai. He is now identifying with a Jew, joining the feminine in wholeness and reconnecting himself with that universal humanity at the heart of the collective unconscious.

That he had still not consciously worked through this problem can be seen in his postwar article "After the Catastrophe." There he said that the doctor's and psychologist's "relationship to the world involves them and all their affects, otherwise their relationship would be incomplete. That being so, I found myself faced with the task of steering my ship between Scylla and Charybdis, and—as is usual on such a voyage—stopping my ears to one side of my being and lashing the other to the mast. I must confess that no article has ever given me so much trouble, from a moral as well as a human point of view."[31] Besides being the closest Jung ever came to making a public admission that he had made a mistake, this passage contains a slip within his classical allusion. Jung confuses Odysseus' encounter with Scylla and Charybdis with the hero's preceding encounter with the sirens. This slip can be taken as a complex indicator pointing to an area of unconscious vulnerability. Who were the sirens and why were they forgotten? They were the beautiful sea nymphs whose beguiling songs lured sailors to their deaths, negative anima figures whose voices gave them power. A series of associations from Jung's writings will lead to the conclusion that Hitler was at the root of the slip. In his various analyses of the German dictator, Jung emphasized the power of his Voice, compared him to the Sybil and Delphic oracle,[32] and observed that as a result of an anima possession he was destructive.[33] Jung stopped his ears to the friends and critics who tried to bring to his attention the anti-Semitic nature of some of his remarks. Like Odysseus, he thought he could listen to the siren-Hitler's voice and not be affected.

In spite of some often brilliant analyses, what was missing from Jung's prewar viewpoint? Like the majority of the people of the time, Jung failed on a feeling level to appreciate the depth of *evil* incarnated in Hitler and his movement. The political and medical neutrality that Jung claimed for himself was accompanied by a *moral* neutrality as well, which helps explain the ambiguous tone of his contemporary comments. In "After the Catastrophe" he continued his lifelong involvement with Faust, of whom he wrote, "We never get the impression that he has real insight or suffers genuine remorse. His avowed and unavowed worship of success stands in the way of any moral reflection throughout, obscuring the ethical conflict, so that Faust's moral personality remains misty."[34]

Admitting to a participation mystique with events in Germany, Jung was affected by Wotan. Wotan is associated with Hermes, or Mercurius, the alchemical figure who came to occupy a central place in Jung's imagination. He wrote in his article "The Spirit Mercurius" (first presented at the 1942 Eranos conference): "Mercurius, following the tradition of Hermes, is many-sided, changeable, and deceitful. Dorn speaks of 'that inconstant Mercurius,' and another calls him *versipellis* (changing his skin, shifty). He is *duplex* and his main characteristic is duplicity."[35] Critics have noted the shifts in Jung's pre- and postwar comments, and there is truth in this criticism. His remarks could also vary with his audience. To a Jewish writer he wrote in 1934, "Your criticism of my lack of knowledge in things Jewish is quite justified. I don't know Hebrew."[36] Three years later, to the Nazi head of the German Faith Movement, he wrote, "I myself have treated very many Jews and know their psychology in its deepest recesses, so that I can recognize the relation of their psychology to their religion. . . ."[37] In 1936 Jung was in the United States to be honored at Harvard's trecentenary. Before his return to Europe, he gave an interview to the *New York Times* in which he said about Roosevelt, "I am convinced that here is a strong man, a man who is really great."[38] In London two weeks later he said, "Make no mistake, he [Roosevelt] is a force—a man of superior and impenetrable mind, but perfectly ruthless, a highly versatile mind which you cannot foresee. He has the most amazing power complex, the Mussolini substance, the stuff of a dictator absolutely."[39]

A final example of the shifts in Jung can be seen in his relationship to Britain's two prime ministers of the time, Chamberlain and Churchill. We have already seen that Jung identified with Chamberlain's "give it a chance" policy, which is now considered the epitome of spineless appeasement. After the war Jung met Churchill at two public receptions and told his students that during the war he dreamed of Churchill whenever he was passing through Switzerland on his way to a secret conference.[40] I believe that this synchronistic connection served a compensatory function: namely, it was a case of unconscious heroic identification compensating for a conscious attitude of compromise.

Returning to Jung's slip, we must remember that Odysseus did not survive the perils of Scylla and Charybdis by sailing a middle course; rather, he had to make a choice and so chose to sail past Scylla and lose six men rather than risk losing his ship and all his crew to Charybdis. Opting for the middle course of neutrality, Jung failed to make a similar heroic-moral choice in response to the major political-moral crisis of our time.

Notes

1. E. James Lieberman, *Acts of Will* (New York: Free Press, 1985), p. 326.
2. *The Freud/Jung Letters,* p. 491 (March 3, 1912).
3. Ibid., p. 525.
4. Ibid., p. 534–535.
5. Ibid., p. 539 (January 3, 1913).
6. Frued, *On the History of the Psychoanalytic Movement* (New York: W. W. Norton and Co., 1967), p. 43.
7. C. G. Jung, *Letters,* vol. 1, pp. 167–68, (June 19, 1934).
8. *A Psycho-Analytic Dialogue: The Letters of Sigmund Freud and Karl Abraham, 1907–1926,* letter of December 26, 1908.
9. Ibid., (May 13, 1913).
10. C. G. Jung, *CW* 10, para. 19.
11. *CW* 10, para. 1014.
12. Ibid., para. 1020.
13. Ibid., para. 1024.
14. Ibid., para. 1034.

15. Ibid., para. 347.

16. Ibid., para. 353.

17. Ibid., para. 354.

18. Ibid., para. 357.

19. CW 10, para. 420.

20. C. G. *Jung Speaking*, pp. 64, 65–66.

21. CW 10, para. 388.

22. Ibid., para. 385.

23. Ibid., para. 354.

24. C. G. *Jung Speaking*, pp. 118, 119–120.

25. Ibid., pp. 132–133.

26. Ibid., pp. 181–182.

27. CW 10, para. 455.

28. C. G. *Jung Speaking*, p. 123.

29. E. A. Bennet, *Meetings with Jung, 1946–61* (Zurich: Daimon Verlag, 1985), p. 14.

30. C. G. Jung, *Memories, Dreams, Reflections*, p. 294.

31. CW 10, para. 402.

32. C. G. *Jung Speaking*, p. 93.

33. Ibid., p. 140.

34. CW 10, para. 203.

35. CW 13, para. 267.

36. Jung, *Letters*, vol. 1, p. 154 (March 26, 1934).

37. Ibid., p. 233 (June 7, 1937).

38. C. G. *Jung Speaking*, p. 88.

39. Ibid., p. 93.

40. Ibid., p. 183; Hannah, *Jung, His Life and Work*, p. 293; van der Post, *Jung and The Story of Our Time*, p. 199.

Part Two

LINGERING SHADOWS

An International Conference
New York, 1989

The Cultural Foundations
of Racial Religion
and Anti-Semitism

Arthur H. Williamson

Arthur Williamson is a historian specializing in the cultural history of early modern Europe. He has written extensively about concepts of sacred time and the creation of secular modes of discourse. The author of *Scottish National Consciousness in the Age of James VI: Apocalypse, Union, and the Shaping of Scottish Public Culture,* he is currently working on a book entitled *Scots, Jews, and Indians: The British Imperial Impulse and the Discourse of Cultural Difference.* Dr. Williamson is Dean of Graduate Studies at California State University, Sacramento.

In this essay, Dr. Williamson explores the origins of modern anti-Semitism and philo-Semitism in fifteenth-century Spain and sixteenth-century England, particularly in relation to the intellectual developments that led to the Enlightenment and to the modern world. He argues that philo-Semitism and anti-Semitism, tolerance and intolerance, derive from common conceptual structures and have a surprisingly intertwined cultural history. His essay suggests that modern anti-Semitic vocabularies can only be fully comprehended within such contexts. He proposes that this approach will prove useful in reassessing the intellectual experience of the twentieth century and thus the place of Freud and Jung within both its triumphs and its catastrophes.

All the heresies in Germany, France, and Spain have been sown by the descendants of Jews.   —Philip II, 1556

. . . a little Jewish blood is enough to destroy the world.
                    —Francisco de Torrejoncillo, 1623

Quit your selves therefore like men and be valiant (o ye Jewish people), you must one daye enter combat and fight a battel, and that a terrible one as ever there was anywhere, as is clearly foretold in Daniel 12.1. And yet be not afraid, neither let your hearts faile you for feare; you are surely to get the victorye and to attaine ever lasting joye. . . .   —Thomas Brightman, c. 1600[1]

In 1992 Spain will commemorate one of the most decisive dates in Western history: the discovery of the Americas and, simultaneously, the destruction of one of the West's most creative cultures. The González government is expected to express regret for the latter, and the ancient synagogue of Gerona (Girona) is being restored for the occasion. The commemoration will give rise to a great deal of reflection about anti-Semitism in European history, and this is only appropriate. After all, 1492 led to events of enormous significance in the formation of modern anti-Semitism— events vastly more influential than Luther or the German Reformation. For, unlike sixteenth-century Germany, sixteenth-century Spain integrated the diabolized Jew of the later Middle Ages into a new racialized theory of separation. This development marks a major transition from the medieval world. Equally important, it invites scholars of anti-Semitism to approach their subject from a broad contextual and cultural perspective rather than from the narrower "line of development" focus that too often has been adopted.

   This essay undertakes an overview of the rise of modern European anti-Semitism. It seeks to locate this phenomenon within more basic intellectual structures than is commonly done and suggests that Europe's most creative and most destructive impulses derive from common sources and even intertwine with one another. This approach will prove useful in assessing the intellectual experience of the twentieth century and thus the place of Freud

and Jung within its catastrophes no less than within its achievements.

THE APOCALYPTIC ROOTS OF
EARLY MODERN PHILO-SEMITISM
AND ANTI-SEMITISM

Few cultures have more profoundly shaped modern civilization
and the contours of its politics than have the Hispanic and the
Anglophone. Both cultures took shape during the upheavals of the
sixteenth century. Both came to see themselves as playing a unique
role in human destiny, in the historical redemption, and in the
final triumph of the true faith. Both were exercised by ancient
Christian traditions about the prophesied role of the Jews, whose
conversion could be seen as a central element within this entire
apocalyptic process. Both would experience a severe crisis about
the meaning of community, and both would find the Jews an
important element in the resolution of their problems of political
and spiritual identity. Yet, despite such striking similarities, the
conclusions these societies reached appear polar opposites. The
one led, with some ambiguity, to philo-Semitism and eventually to
the cultural foundations of toleration, the other to anti-Semitism
and to the creation of racial religion.

Massive Jewish conversions to Christianity—largely forced and
on an unprecedented scale—occurred in late medieval Spain. Ostensibly this event should have reinforced the much repeated notion
of the Spanish nation as the heir of the children of Israel in
receiving the "grace of election." Thus, the visible triumph of
Christianity over Judaism, a crucial event in the culmination of
human history, had occurred under the aegis of the Spanish crown.
Simultaneously, imperial Spain was visibly disseminating Christianity to the ends of the earth, and the gathering in of the Gentile
nations was an event of no less significance to the prophesied latter
days than the calling of the Jews. And yet exaltation intermingled
with the deepest anxiety. If Spain found itself realizing the final
acts of the sacred drama, that moment also involved enormous

danger, for the nation was locked in a final struggle with heresy both at home and abroad. Did not secret Jews occupy positions of power everywhere within the realm and, most alarmingly, within the Church? Was not Europe itself aflame with Luther's heresies? A politico-spiritual crisis accompanied Spain's greatest victories, for the "New Christians"—the Marranos, the swine—endangered the country's cultural and spiritual integrity, an integrity that increasingly seemed a precondition for its messianic mission. The preoccupation with blood, one of the most pronounced traits of Spanish society in the sixteenth century, issued in the notorious regulations of *pureza de sangre* or *limpiezas de sangre*. The problem of Spanish cultural diversity and heterodoxy would resolve itself through this category, and indeed confessional categories led into it and were ultimately supplanted by it. In the view of one of the most authoritative students of the period,

> It is no coincidence that the rise of tribunal to impose religious orthodoxy [the Inquisition] was accompanied by the growth of certain practices designed to secure racial purity, for religious and racial deviation were easily equated in the popular mind. Indeed, alongside the obsessive concern with the purity of the faith there flourished a no less obsessive concern with purity of the blood; both obsessions were at their most violent in the middle decades of the sixteenth century; both employed the same techniques of informing and delation; and both had the effect of narrowing the extraordinarily wide range of Spanish life, and of forcing a rich and vital society into a straight-jacket of conformity.[2]

A certification from the Inquisition testifying to the purity of his blood was required of any individual who sought appointment to government municipal office, a religious or military order, the faculty of the universities, and nearly any position of social significance. "Clean" blood became the determinant of one's good name.[3] More than a century after the diaspora of Hispanic Jewry and the destruction of its ancient culture, Spanish writers could still proclaim:

> Who can deny that in the descendants of the Jews there persists and endures the evil inclination of their ancient ingratitude and lack of understanding, just as in Negroes [there persists] the inseparability of their blackness. For if the latter should unite themselves a thousand times with white women, the children are born the dark color of the father. Similarly, it is not enough for the Jew to be three parts aristocrat or Old Christian, for one family-line [i.e., Jewish ancestor] alone defiles and corrupts him.[4]

"Pure" blood, "clean" blood, became the criterion of community, of civic capacity, and ultimately of survival. Such categories translated readily into the circumstances of the New World, where the authorities sought to introduce certifications of "whiteness."[5]

Today we tend to forget that Spain was by far the greatest power in sixteenth- and early seventeenth-century Europe. Its spectacular successes are breathtaking even now. As a result, we also tend to ignore its enormous and enduring impact on the values and perceptions of the modern world. Indeed, the Marranos themselves, as Yosef Kaplan and others have shown, would adopt the attitudes and preoccupations with blood of their persecutors and torturers—with what may turn out to have been disastrous consequences for secular European culture. Even so, the Elizabethan conquerors of Ireland had studied the experience and apologias of the Spanish conquistadores.[6] Still, British apocalypticism, if anything more intense than the Hispanic variety, pointed in a startlingly different direction. Unlike Spain and Portugal, England and Scotland never experienced a forced and thus "failed" conversion, and the prospect of active Jewish participation within the dynamic of world salvation has persisted in the Anglophone world from the sixteenth century—in some form even into our own times.

By the 1580s visions of an "elect" England whose history comprised the core of the sacred drama or of a covenanted Scoto-Britain as the harbinger of world reformation deeply informed British Protestantism. In one of its more bizarre forms an Essex minister proclaimed during that decade that the persecuted English puritans were "the very Jews of nature" and sought to lead them off to Palestine, where they would await the millennium at the turn of the century. British Israelitism, Christadelphianism, and the like find their roots securely in the Reformation. During that extraordinary decade remarkably large numbers of Englishmen came to adopt less radical but no less compelling Jewish formulations of their society and its purposes.

If Englishmen and Scots were successors to the Jews, they nevertheless also expected to be their future partners as well. The Jews, it seemed, had a powerful and vitally important role to play in the great events of the latter days and thereby in precipitating the millennium or the second coming. British destiny and Jewish destiny seemed to join in prophetic events of utterly cosmic significance. Patriotism and philo-Semitism therefore came to bear a curious symbiosis for many English-speakers, and it is by no means fortuitous that in this decade the puritan opposition introduced the neologism *patriot* into the English vocabulary. This line of thinking saw fruition at the end of the century in the writings of the great English philo-Semites, Hugh Broughton and Thomas Brightman.[7]

No Elizabethan more thoroughly and explicitly developed the notion that English experience lay at the heart of the historical redemption than did Brightman. No Elizabethan ever articulated a more or even comparably profound affection for "our brethren, the Jews," nor had as high expectations of their direct political role in the final triumph of righteousness and justice. If the English nation had been elected to lead the world into its final era and thereby redeem the promise of ancient Israel, modern Jewry did not become irrelevant as a result. Quite the contrary, they continued as God's people with a special destiny, independent of but comparable to that of the Christian elect. If the Jews had experienced cruelty in the past, they could look forward to the greatest kindness, for the Gentiles "will empty all the power they have to encrease, advance, and extoll them." To be sure, Brightman expected the Jews to convert to Christianity. The sixteenth century simply could not visualize final and fraternal coexistence outside a comprehensive structure of religious truth. But the Jewish national identity would continue. Indeed, the new Jewish Christians would destroy the Ottoman Empire and its allies (Gog and Magog). A great Jewish state would emerge in Palestine, and the

Jewish Christian church, based in Jerusalem, would become the center of a reformed Christian world. In that restored age the Jews would emerge no less as great teachers than as great warriors. Daniel had indicated that the Jews would once again "teach and turne others to righteousness." So renewed and so restored, they would again enter the Temple, and their "dignity and honour" would be utterly glorious, "as if he [God] had created all things new again." In a way unparalleled elsewhere, the new Jerusalem in the Middle East promised to complete the Reformation, to realize the fullest articulation of Christian truth, and provide a beacon to the world.

> . . . as it seemeth, the church of the Jews is to be at length more abundantly filled with the gifts of the Holy Ghost than this of ours that be gentiles. (Exod. 25:31)

Indeed, Christian shortcomings would find their correction in the Jewish city John of Patmos beheld in Revelation 21:2.

> But this Jerusalem of ours which is deformed and with many errours and contentions, will make this of the Jews that shalbe most pure, to appear as if it were a new one altogether.

Accordingly, Brightman spoke expectantly of walking "in the light of the church of the Jews."

One of the finer intellectual products of Elizabethan puritanism, Brightman came to exercise a profound influence on British thought that even today has yet to be fully recognized. British Protestants of a great many persuasions found his vision compelling, and his influence would reach its apogee during the English Revolution of the mid-seventeenth century. Such thinking received further reinforcement from still other sources early in that century with such writers as James Maxwell and Sir William Alexander. Both enthusiasts for the new Britain that appeared to be forming immediately after 1603, they celebrated a messianic British Empire, an empire and age in which the Jews seemed curiously relevant. Like many Britons and surprisingly large numbers of continental Protestants as well, Maxwell saw King James I as the

successor and heir to Constantine the Great and the Roman
Empire. As such, Maxwell insisted, the British would overthrow
the Ottomans and reestablish themselves (and the Jews) in the
Middle East. In verse too precious to pass over, Maxwell would
present the most extraordinary picture of King James, receiving
the acclaim of the Jews gathered in Jerusalem—while representing
Christ in the fullest conceivable sense.

> O happy sight to see Great Britaines King
> One day descending from Mount Olivet!
> O happy song, to heare the Hebrewes sing!
> For joy of heart James to congratulate:
> Blest be the king that comes in Jesus name
> To christen Jewes and crowne Jerusalem.

Maxwell probably numbers among the earliest to suggest that the
restoration of the Jews would prove one of the great tasks of the
British Empire. This expectation turned out to have a very long
life indeed. Herein surely lie the intellectual roots of the Balfour
Declaration.

Not all agreed. Not all were confident either of the moment or
of its putative implications. Fear of apocalypticism within early
modern British political culture linked readily with hostility toward Judaism and toward philo-Semitic expectations about the
Jews. By the 1620s the issue of the Jews became a flash point
between radical and conservative Protestantisms. Conservative
Protestant thinkers who sought rapproachement with Catholicism
often drew on the biblical criticism of the Laudian Henry Ham-
mond or on continental scholars like Hugo Grotius, and their
conclusions worked to the decided disadvantage of the Jews. Few
Jews would convert in the latter days. The wrath of God would
fall upon them—along with the great Jewish Antichrist which
Catholic and now conservative Protestant theorists expected to
arise at the end of human history. The Jews' "carnal" understanding of faith and scripture and its prophecies closely paralleled that
of the "frenzied" enthusiasts. Generally speaking, the more deeply
apocalyptic an individual's perspective, the more likely he would
possess philo-Semitic attitudes. In contrast, the more deeply "An-

glo-Catholic" an individual, then the more he would be suspicious of apocalypticism and the more anti-Semitic would be his commitments. It may well emerge that there exists an anti-Semitic intellectual tradition in Britain running from William Laud to T. S. Eliot.

The English Revolution led to agitation for the readmission of the Jews to England, to Menasseh Ben Israel's mission to Oliver Cromwell, and to the inconclusive Whitehall Conference. Some of the most significant minds of the age—Robert Boyle, Thomas Hobbes, James Harrington—found themselves exercised by the role of the Jews in the latter days. If almost everyone but the most radical spoke in terms of conversion, a surprising number appeared to feel that in its final and true articulation Christianity would be informed by Jewish wisdom and piety, a perception Brightman himself had at times seemed to intimate. Moreover, a deepening sense of time and historical process could push the moment of merger—however conceived—further and further toward the horizon. At some point there would emerge a final, shared truth, but for the immediate future the pursuit of its complex strategies required the insight of various learned traditions. Not surprisingly, those who sought the readmission of the Jews—however conversionist their vision—were also overwhelmingly those who proposed toleration in ways we could begin to recognize as modern.

The British peoples' fascination with Jews grew directly out of their understanding of their community and its apocalyptic meanings. In this respect they were utterly similar to their Hispanic rivals. But if each culture's sense of apocalyptic destiny and mission derived from strikingly common origins, the conclusions they drew could hardly have contrasted more sharply. If the Hispanic world feared a Jewish presence, the Anglophone world came to fear its absence. If Spaniards were anguished at the thought that they might be Jewish, Englishmen became increasingly concerned that they might not be.

The creation of modern attitudes toward Judaism, toward race, and toward toleration—like the creation of modern culture itself—does not thus derive from easily identified polarities nor from categories we could recognize as obviously either good or bad. The

fundamentally religious dynamics of secularization and modernization generated both from common materials. Philo-Semitism
and anti-Semitism, pluralism and racism, achievement and horror
turn out closer than we could have at first imagined. Examining an
allied topic, Heiko Oberman has rightly noticed that the world
which created our own held assumptions, made associations, and
acted through intellectual dynamics strikingly different from
ours—and that it is a world to which we can only be admitted as
foreigners. As we will see, that remains the case even on the very
edge of modernity with the rise of Enlightenment thought.

Viewed in this way Martin Luther assumes a new complexion.
His Judaphobia and his intense apocalypticism never merged with
one another. However virulent his late anti-Jewish tracts—and his
anti-Judaism was visibly less virulent than that of his great Catholic opponent, Johannes Eck—his attitudes toward the Jews turn
out to be far less consequential than those of later reformers and
contemporaneous counter-reformers. Vastly important as he was
for the creation of the modern world, his views here did not launch
discernible new directions. If our own times and times near our
own have sought and found support for modern politico-racial
anti-Semitism in his writings, the cultural impulses that engendered the search find their most significant origins elsewhere.[8] We
will need to locate the cultural foundations of racial religion and
anti-Semitism within the far broader vocabularies of social context
and political legitimation. The traditional view of a linear development running from Luther to Hitler simply will not do. If we
truly wish to penetrate our present dilemma, we will need to do
far more and confront the painfully interwoven problematics that
have made us what we are.

THE AMBIVALENT ROAD
BEYOND THE JUDEO-CHRISTIAN
WORLDVIEW

Apocalyptic philo-Semitism persisted throughout the age of reason
and well beyond. In a surprising number of eighteenth-century

contexts it created a bridge—and one of decisive importance—between the historical redemption and the rights of man. The abbé Henri Gregoire led the struggle for Jewish emancipation in France at the time of the Revolution and proved one of the more articulate opponents of racism generally. A millenarian, Gregoire is the direct heir of an at times bizzare Jansenist apocalyptic spiritualism with powerful philo-Semitic expectations.[9] Such well-known English radicals of the late eighteenth century as Joseph Priestley and Richard Price were among many who saw the American and French revolutions as the realization of Judeo-Christian prophecy and the advent of the millennium. Implacably hostile to slavery and anti-Semitism, the faith triumphant would issue in a world of democratic republics where all men, at once saints and citizens, would find their redemption.[10] Above all, it would be Anglophone America where radical Protestant apocalyptic traditions assumed a bewildering variety of shapes, perhaps most interestingly in that odd commonwealth of Rhode Island which eventually brought together Quakers, Freemasons, and Jews.[11] The intellectual successors of Brightman most often found themselves in North America, where the Jews seemed to require no special "emancipation." Although, then as now, anti-Semitism would be very much a part of American society, it never acquired the intensity and systemic formulation of its continental counterparts, and of all the Anglophone societies, only the culture of Irish Catholicism has sustained a mass fascist movement in our time.

But if apocalyptic expectations remained enduringly significant in the eighteenth century, they were by no means as mainstream or as compelling as they had previously been—not even in America. The values of the French and American Revolutions, indeed liberal values generally, did not arise exclusively from such expectations, but from the already secularized or semi-secularized environment of the Enlightenment. Richard Popkin and others have shown the strikingly racist attitudes of such central Enlightenment figures as Locke, Hume, Voltaire, and Kant.[12] Focusing exclusively on French Enlightenment attitudes toward the Jews, Arthur Hertzberg's observations of two decades ago have yet to be challenged.

> Modern, secular anti-Semitism was fashioned not as a reaction
> to the Enlightenment and the Revolution, but within the Enlight-
> enment and Revolution themselves. Some of the greatest of the
> founders of the liberal era modernized and secularized anti-
> Semitism too.[13]

For Hertzberg, the great figures of the French Enlightenment—and
signally Voltaire—undertook to discredit the particularist revelation of the Christian world by displaying the poverty of its Jewish
base. In the process Voltaire resurrected the pagan Judaphobia of
classical antiquity, which would become the foundation for modern, secular anti-Semitism. The French Revolution, like all revolutions, sought to create "new men," to turn subjects into citizens,
to make Frenchmen of peasants. But could the originators of the
spirit that had so maimed the Western experience be expected to
make the transition? As in the questions of race, the answers were
ambiguous and troubling.

The post-Judeo-Christian world therefore possessed considerable ambivalence about what are often regarded as its most characteristic and attractive assertions. The sources of this ambivalence
are many and often complex. They range from the limitations of
the eighteenth-century vocabularies for articulating qualitative cultural difference and for imagining qualitative social change—to
what in the cases of Hume and Voltaire verges on intellectual
dishonesty.

There is perhaps no better illustration of the close association of
such ostensibly contradictory ideas than the attitudes of the Portuguese Jews of Amsterdam and those of no less a figure than
Baruch de Spinoza. Yosef Kaplan has shown persuasively that the
Amsterdam community was heavily influenced by Spanish political
thought, which it much admired, and, amazingly enough, exiled
Portuguese Jews fully endorsed their former realm's methods for
ensuring orthodoxy and repressing sacrilege (though of course not
their application). Deeply concerned with defining community
identity, the Amsterdam Jews consciously followed the pattern of
their persecutors and supplanted confessional categories with
those of blood, lineage, and honor. Departing from the practices
of medieval Judaism, the community stressed its identity as a

nation (*naçao*) rather than a spiritual entity, one whose people were fundamentally different from the Gentiles. To accept Judaism as a religion did not thereby enable one to belong to the body of the nation.[14]

Few individuals are more associated with the rejection of revelation, with the emergence of biblical criticism, with the creation of a secular system of ethics, and with the creation of a secular culture generally than is Spinoza. His links with the early Enlightenment—especially with the English Deists and ultimately with Voltaire—are profound and only now being fully explored. His intellectual roots within Iberian traditions are also just now being recognized. Most important, however, his critique of Jewish practice in the name of universal reason was utterly devastating and would deeply inform the age whose foundations he helped so much to lay. Not only were the claims of this obscure desert tribe preposterous, their laws were utterly willful and thoroughly nasty by any standard of human decency. The outstanding authority today on early modern European Judaism, Jonathan Israel, has been less reluctant than earlier scholars to recognize the connection between Spinoza and modern anti-Semitism: "Spinoza's biting scorn for the observations and ceremonies of Judaism which, as he saw it, had 'emasculated the minds of the Jews,' helped stoke up the deep-seated animosity towards Judaism which eventually pervaded almost the entire output of the European Enlightenment."

> Some of the later philosophes, such as Voltaire, may have been given to personal anti-Semitism, but, fundamentally, animosity towards Jewish tradition was ingrained in the ideology of philosophic deism from the outset. Spinoza, who, in his anti-Judaism, as in much else, was a true precursor of the Enlightenment, believed that the Jews' adherence to the Mosaic Law had blocked and imprisoned their minds. And it was so of the Spinozists generally.[15]

Such a context would not require the Iberian preoccupation with blood and race for the task of creating an enlightened Jewry to appear formidable indeed—and perhaps impossible. And what might this non-Jewish Jew—seen within these matrices, the Jew who ceased being a Jew—actually look like? Would he profess a species of reformed Judaism as proposed in that huge, remarkable, and deeply puzzling work, *The Turkish Spy*? Would he proclaim an original, uncorrupted Judaism whose rationalist deist tenets outran the wisdom of the Persian and Chinese sages?[16] No such option would seize the eighteenth-century imagination. No alternative emerged to the Spinozist problematic in which the secular, universalist claims for human capacity became inextricably entangled with Judaphobia. Within this context, Voltaire's attitudes toward the Jews—utterly unsavory and enormously influential as they were—nevertheless become better comprehensible as symptom more than cause.

The eighteenth-century European social imagination's absorption with universal categories and its inability to visualize radical cultural relativity sealed the predicament. Without a social science sophisticated enough to conceptualize different cultures within their own assumptions and vocabularies, it is hard to see how a fully satisfactory resolution might have been reached. As things stood, the eighteenth century offered at the popular level little more than a secularized version of attitudes common in the sixteenth century. As the "dead" law stood opposed to the "living" and "quickening" spirit, as empty works deflected men from saving faith, as human traditions over time perverted God's revealed and universal truth made accessible through His Word, so the sixteenth-century Jew easily became metaphor and type for all that was truly wrong. As vain ceremonies and vicious laws invented and manipulated by priestcraft had disfigured the European experience and obscured universal reason, so too the eighteenth-century Jew found himself at the heart of the problem. In both centuries "the Jew" as metaphor slid easily into "the Jews" as people.

THE AGONY OF THE MODERN AGE

With the French and American Revolutions and through the first three quarters of the nineteenth century, Jews in Europe gradually acquired the civil liberties associated with citizenship. To be sure, anti-Jewish prejudice in all its religious and secular forms remained largely unfaded, but legal restrictions were slowly eliminated, and their disappearance appeared to promise a better age. As with slavery, legal unfreedom declined throughout the world, even if the attitudes that underwrote it retained currency and power.

And then something happened. The term *anti-Semitism* first appeared in Germany during the 1870s to identify something new, a type of hostility to Jews that claimed to be based on new intellectual foundations and new perceptions of social reality. This new Judaphobia, anti-Semitism, took overt political forms and entered social discourse with great authority and respectability. It could claim support from the new ideology of science. It spoke to social life and daily intercourse as well as to larger concerns of community with what seemed unprecedented cogency. With the violence of World War I and its aftermath, anti-Semitism turned increasingly murderous and ultimately genocidal.

The rise of political anti-Semitism has been seen as the result of many factors: as part of a general decline of liberal values, a coarsening of life linked with the obsessions of the new imperialism, an outgrowth of the new political biology called social Darwinism, a manifestation of the *völkisch* thought that had derived from Romanticism, and a consequence of the revitalized racisms of the late nineteenth century, among many other evident associations.

Socially, anti-Semitism has been seen as a continental reaction to industrialization and modernization, which seemed disrupting to traditional piety and traditional social ties. It has been linked to the emergence of mass society and large-scale political movements which translated traditional hatreds and wide-ranging fears into effective social action. Anti-Semitism filled the churches even if it could not restore the grip of old-fashioned religion and the worldview that had so long given religious authorities their power. It generated religious revival in fin-de-siècle Vienna without creating new piety or new religious sensibilities. More than that, it created solidarity and political cohesion among radically different social groups with strikingly different agendas. The Viennese Christian

Social movement provides a good example, although there exist many others. The movement attracted property owners, school-teachers, middle- and lower-ranking government officials, artisans, merchants, shopkeepers, and a number of intensely anti-Semitic Roman Catholic clerics. The Christian Socials would dominate Viennese politics in the decades prior to the war, destroying the much more upper-class Liberal party and liberal Vienna in the process. Anti-Semitism proved useful to such a wide coalition with many ostensibly conflicting objectives. The tension between those who sought to protect property rights and those who sought some form of redistribution appeared to resolve itself through anti-Semitic preoccupations. At issue was Jewish property and the resulting Jewish "domination," rather than the more direct if painful issues of class and social justice. Race in this context emerges as a semi-religious notion designed to discover and artic-ulate "soul" and thereby define society in ways that "transcend" politics, class antagonisms, and industrialization. Similarly, oppo-sition to the corrupting West—and, above all, to Britain—with its "soulless" industrial culture, easily translated into opposition to those grasping aliens at home who also seemed to lack "soul."[17]

The rise of the socialist left did not deflect Christian Social anti-Semitism, but gave it still further voices. The propertyless working class were also outsiders, "guests" of an imagined, homogeneous "burghertum," and the association of "Red" with "Jew" came easily enough. Anti-Semitism lessened the persuasiveness of social-ism's moral intensity, while it emphasized the fundamentally alien character of the industrial worker.[18] This was the Vienna that taught politics to the young Adolf Hitler, where his bitter objec-tions to socialist internationalism transformed into an unrelenting, politicized Jew-hatred. Hitler's discovery of the basic character of "the Jewish dogma of Marxism" seemed to him to be one of his most significant insights, and the struggle against "Judaeobolshev-ism" comprised one of his movement's most central purposes.[19]

Perhaps one of the most striking aspects of this whole phenom-enon has been the persuasiveness of anti-Semitism to modern intellectual elites. Traditionalist thinkers—outstandingly French Catholics—identified that complex tissue of thought we now call "modernism" with its Jewish exponents and thereupon with the Jews generally. Modernism, with its antihistorical orientation, its insistence upon discontinuities, its focus upon the fragmented, its moral ambiguities, its displacement of the "real" and opaque, all articulated and "caused" the disruption of the community as traditionally imagined. Modernism appeared to discount national experience, delegitimize patriotism, dissolve social ties, reject dominant philosophic and religious truths. And all of this seemed distinctly Jewish.

Yet, ironically, modernism itself developed an anti-Semitic strain, one associated in the Anglophone context with such figures as Ezra Pound, T. S. Eliot, Evelyn Waugh, and Wyndham Lewis. Judaism of course embodied a highly historical traditionalism, made strikingly visible through the large-scale westward migration of often poor Ashkenazic Jews. More important, the emancipation of the Jews had resulted from the culture of nineteenth-century liberalism. Precisely that culture was now being rejected, and that rejection might easily extend to one of its more visible creations, the modern Jew. Such a figure would become emblematic—ultimately to the point of caricature—of the inauthenticity, cultural exhaustion, and spiritual poverty of contemporary life.

Both modernism and antimodernism contributed materially to anti-Semitism.[20] Their matrices are crucial in shaping the attitudes of early twentieth-century intellectuals toward Jews. Like earlier anti-Semitic vocabularies, our century's can only be fully comprehended within the age's intellectual and cultural configurations.

Only from such a perspective will this century's radical political transitions—as from the Weimar republic to the Third Reich—and the stark juxtaposition of striking creativity and still more stunning destructiveness become intelligible. The enthusiastic acceptance of racial anti-Semitism and its politics by so many fine minds has understandably drawn a great deal of comment.[21] The passive, accepting, "apolitical," and thus legitimating response has done so as well. In addition, the organization of intellect, its structural problems, the professions' fears for their identity, integrity, and social place are of manifest importance. But the vocabularies of anti-Semitism have long been suffused within the intellectual textures of modern culture, and neither functional analyses of it nor analyses based on simple lines of development will ultimately prove satisfactory.[22] From their beginnings in the late fifteenth century—whether apocalyptic anti-Semitism and the advent of modern racism or apocalyptic philo-Semitism and the advent of modern toleration, whether the anti-Semitic critique of the past or the philo-Semitic promise for the future, whether the anti-Semitic horror at cultural fragmentation or the philo-Semitic exhilaration of a world rising on new foundations—the ambiguous dynamics within modern Western thinking have continuously associated its best with its worst. In the end nothing will assure the humanity and decency of our most significant thought but ourselves.

Notes

1. J. H. Elliott, *Imperial Spain, 1469–1716* (New York, 1963), p. 219; Henry Kamen, *Inquisition and Society in Spain in the Sixteenth and Seventeenth Centuries* (Bloomington, 1985), p. 120; Jerome Friedman, "Jewish Conversion, the Spanish Pure Blood Laws and Reformation: A Revisionist View of Racial and Religious Antisemitism," *The Sixteenth Century Journal* 28.1:17; A. H. Williamson, "Latter-day Judah, Latter-day Israel: The Millennium, the Jews, and the British Future," *Chiliasmus in Deutschland und England im 17. Jahrhundert* (Göttingen, 1988), p. 149.

2. Elliott, *Imperial Spain*, p. 217.

3. Yosef Kaplan, "Political Concepts in the World of the Portuguese Jews of Amsterdam during the Seventeenth Century: The Problem of Exclusion and the Boundaries of Self-Identity," in *The World of Menasseh Ben Israel*, ed. Yosef Kaplan, Henry Méchoulan, and Richard H. Popkin (Leiden, 1989), esp. pp. 52–53; For the comments in this paragraph I am much indebted to Dr. Kaplan and to Richard H. Popkin, "The Philosophical Bases of Modern Racism," in *The High Road to Pyrrhonism*, ed. Richard A. Watson and James E. Force (San Diego, 1980) pp. 79–80. Kamen, *Inquisition and Society in Spain*, p. 122: "Genealogy became a social weapon, and in a society where the genealogical proof was a passport to employment in Church and State, it may be safely said that racialism had been erected into the system of government." The power of racism, the extent to which it penetrated the textures of the Hispanic cultures, and its persistence are truly extraordinary. The limpieza requirement for State office would only be rescinded in 1865. The gradual slackening in the number of *autos de fe* during the later eighteenth century resulted not from any growth in tolerance, but simply from the utter extirpation of nonconformity. At the popular level there

emerged a remarkably powerful iconography of infamy, which made use of the penitential sackcloth (*sanbenito*) as a species of inverse relic explicitly designed to translate religious categories into racial ones."

4. Friedman, "Jewish Conversion," pp. 16–17. The contrast with Luther is vital. Heiko Oberman's comments on Luther's views throughout his career are worth noting here: "Luther does not see 'race' when he looks at the Jews, nor are baptized and unbaptized Jews for Luther the exponents of an ethnic, racial unit. Baptized Jews belong unqualifiedly to the people of God, just as do baptized Germans, the gentiles." *The Roots of Anti-Semitism in the Age of the Renaissance and Reformation* (Philadelphia, 1984), p. 102.

5. Popkin, "The Philosophical Bases of Modern Racism," p. 80.

6. Nicholas Canny, *The Conquest of Ireland: A Pattern Established, 1565–1576* (New York, 1976), pp. 66, 126, 133–4; Karl S. Bottigheimer, "Kingdom and Colony: Ireland in the Westward Enterprise, 1536–1660," in *The Westward Enterprise: English Activities in Ireland, the Atlantic, and America, 1480–1650*, ed. K. R. Andrews, N. P. Canny, and P. E. Hair (Detroit, 1974), p. 51; cf. Loren E. Pennington, "The Amerindian in English Promotional Literature," in *The Westward Enterprise*, pp. 175–94.

7. See Williamson, "Latter-Day Judah," for the material in this and the succeeding six paragraphs. Ironically, Britain inadvertently became a significant benefactor of the hunted and varied remnants of Spanish Jewry when its forces seized Gibraltar in 1704, enabling the creation by 1717 of what must have been the only legal synagogue on the peninsula (Kamen, p. 233). Perhaps it is only appropriate that the restoration of the first synagogue in Iberia should occur under the protection and authority of the British Empire.

8. Oberman, *The Roots of Anti-Semitism*, pp. 102, 117, and passim. R. Po-chia Hsia has recently argued in his study of the blood libel that the prime effect of Lutheranism was to "disenchant" and desacralize late medieval anti-Semitism. In some instances—notably that of Andreas Osiander—it led to philo-Semitism, but that was not typically the case. Still, in its struggle with the Religion of the Mass, the Religion of the Word found itself increasingly preoccupied with language rather than with nonverbal symbols like blood. *The Myth of Ritual Murder: Jews and Magic in Reformation Germany* (New Haven, 1988).

9. R. H. Popkin, "Mordecai Noah, the Abbé Gregoire, and the Paris Sanhedrin," *Modern Judaism* 2 (May 1982): 131–149; Arthur Hertzberg, *The French Enlightenment and the Jews*, pp. 258–267. Cf. David Bankier, "The 'Restoration of the Jews' in French Jansenism," in Shumel Almog et al., *Israel and the Nations* (Jerusalem, 1987), pp. 71–86.

10. Jack Fruchtman, Jr., *The Apocalyptic Politics of Richard Price and Joseph Priestley* (Philadelphia, 1983), and esp. Jan van den Berg, "Priestley, the Jews, and the Millennium," in *Scepticism, the Jews, and Millenarianism*, ed. David S. Katz and Johnathan I. Israel (Leiden, 1990), pp. 256–274.

11. David Katz, *Sabbath and Sectarianism in 17th Century England* (Leiden, 1988); Popkin, "Millenarianism in England, Holland, and America: Jewish-Christian Relations in Amsterdam, London, and Newport, Rhode Island," in *Philosophy, History, and Social Action*, ed. S. Hook, W. L. O'Neill, and R. O'Toole (n.p., 1988), p. 349–371. Cf. A. Hertzberg, "The New England Puritans and the Jews," *Israel and the Nations*, pp. 47–66.

12. Popkin, "The Philosophical Bases of Modern Racism" and "Hume's Racism," in *The High Road to Pyrrhonism*, pp. 79–102, 251–266; Popkin, "Hume's Racism Reconsidered," *The Journal*, 1(No. 1):61–71.

13. Hertzberg, *The French Enlightenment and the Jews*, p. 7.

14. Kaplan, "Political Concepts."

15. Jonathan I. Israel, *European Jewry in the Age of Mercantilism, 1550–1750* (Oxford, 1985), pp. 219, 232; Jacob Katz, *From Prejudice to Destruction: Anti-Semitism 1700–1933* (Cambridge, Mass., 1980), p. 67; cf. Hertzberg, *The French Enlightenment and the Jews*, pp. 37–40.

16. Popkin, "A Seventeenth Century Gentile Attempt to Convert the Jews to Reformed Judaism," in *Israel and the Nations*, pp. 25–45; Hertzberg, *The French Enlightenment and the Jews*, p. 43.

17. See, for example, A. D. Beyerchen's discussion of the Nobel laureat in physics Philipp Lenard: *Scientists under Hitler* (New Haven, 1977), pp. 79–85; cf. George Mosse, *Germans and Jews* (New York, 1970), chap. 1.

18. John Boyer, "Karl Lueger and the Viennese Jews," *Leo Baeck Institute Yearbook*, 26:125–141; Boyer, *Political Radicalism in Late Imperial Vienna* (Chicago, 1981).

19. Adolf Hitler, *Mein Kampf*; cf. Arno Mayer, *Why Did the Heavens Not Darken? The "Final Solution" in History* (New York, 1988).

20. Norman F. Cantor, *Twentieth-Century Culture: Modernism to Deconstruction* (New York, 1988).

21. See Beyerchen, *Scientists under Hitler*; Mosse, *Germans and Jews*; Richard Proctor, *Racial Hygiene* (Cambridge, Mass., 1987); Fritz Ringler, *The Decline of the German Mandarins* (Cambridge, Mass., 1969); Geoffrey Cocks, *Psychotherapy and the Third Reich* (Oxford, 1985); *The Persisting Question: Sociological Perspectives and Social Contexts of Modern Anti-Semitism* 1 (Hawthorne, New York, 1987), ed. Helen Fein.

22. See, for example, Richard L. Rubenstein, "Luther and the Roots of the Holocaust," in *Persistant Prejudice: Perspectives on Anti-Semitism* (Fairfax, Va., 1988), ed. H. Hirsch and J. D. Spiro, pp. 31–41. The exemplar of the traditional approach is Katz, *From Prejudice to Destruction*. Norman Cohn's well-known *The Pursuit of the Millennium* provides the outstanding example of the utter poverty of functional analyses which concern themselves with anti-Semitism and the apocalypse. Antique and medieval apocalypticism began as, and overwhelmingly continued to be, a court phenomenon

and only occasionally informed popular movements. The reductive equation that seeks to identify the thinking of Trotsky or Hitler with the thinking associated with popular revolts in the later Middle Ages will prove both politically reactionary and intellectually barren.

The Nazis
and C. G. Jung

Geoffrey Cocks

Geoffrey Cocks is Professor of History at Albion College in Michigan. He is the author of *Psychotherapy in the Third Reich: The Göring Institute* (1985) and co-editor of *Psycho/History: Readings in the Method of Psychology, Psychoanalysis and History* (1987) and *German Professions: 1800–1950* (1990).

While it is tempting to view history as a by-product of the ideas and actions of powerful and charismatic individuals, Cocks argues here that the historical context of Jung's attitudes must be fully understood before judgment is passed on his words and deeds. Jung's theories, he asserts, were somewhat amenable to certain tenets of the Nazi movement, including its anti-Semitism, and were thus not accorded the same discriminatory treatment as those of Freud. Although Jung was probably not displeased to have received this recognition, in no way did he seek it. Jung sought to use the influence accruing from this popularity to protect the psychotherapy movement in Germany and even to protect its Jewish practitioners. But, in the final analysis, Jung's involvement with psychotherapists in Germany between 1933 and 1940 also raises important questions of cultural prejudice as well as the social roles and moral duties of intellectuals and professionals.

In this essay I shall explore some of the historical context for Carl Jung's words and actions regarding Jews between 1933 and 1940. More specifically, my primary aim is to concentrate on events in Nazi Germany in order to complement the usual emphasis on Jung himself. This is why I have titled my paper "The Nazis and C. G.

Jung." The word order of the proper nouns is meant to carry the action from the Nazis to Jung. This is not, as will shortly become evident, an attempt to whitewash Jung or portray him as passive or victimized. It is to show both the compromising and extenuating complexities of this fateful era.

There is a tendency among psychoanalysts, and nonhistorians generally, to focus on individuals, especially on the "great" in history. This was especially true in a time, the first half of the twentieth century, when the world was seemingly dominated by larger-than-life figures, both benevolent and malevolent. Clearly, the significance of individuals, such as Freud or Jung—or Hitler— should not be underestimated, but too often forays into recent history by psychoanalysts in particular have slighted proper historical method and exhibited both an ahistorical concern with the anecdotal and, even more troublingly, the prejudgments that come with partisanship.

The latter problem is especially acute when it comes to debates between Jungians and Freudians, camps divided by deep philosophical differences, differences that became manifest in Europe during the period between the two world wars. Anti-Semitism of course bulked large in European life in those years and thus unavoidably played a role in the intramural clashes within the psychoanalytic movement. These general philosophical differences and the specific tradition of anti-Semitism also naturally played a part in the reception and use of Jung and Jungian psychology in Germany between 1933 and 1940.

First, I would like to offer a brief survey of Jung's involvement in German affairs during these years and the contemporary and subsequent reactions to it. I do this in order to highlight what I think are the major shortcomings on both sides of the debate about Jung's words and actions during the fascist era. This will also give me the opportunity to present some of my own views on this question.

On June 21, 1933, Jung took over the presidency of the General Medical Society for Psychotherapy from German psychiatrist Ernst Kretschmer. Kretschmer, no friend of the Nazis and an opponent of any psychotherapy or psychoanalysis independent of medical control, had resigned the office he had held since 1930 on April 6. On September 15 a German society was founded under the leadership of psychotherapist Matthias Heinrich Göring as part of what was to become an international society headed by Jung that was formally constituted in May of 1934. Jung had been vice-president of the old society, founded in 1926, since 1930. Thus it is not accurate to say, as Nathaniel Lehrman did in the spring of 1988 in a letter to the New York Times, that Jung and Göring presided jointly over the same organization. In the attempt to understand Jung's motives, historical accuracy is vital. That the intentions and attitudes of all concerned were overdetermined is exemplified by Kretschmer himself, who, contrary to the common implication of an uncomplicated rejection of the regime, went on to work quietly in Hitler's Germany, publishing as late as 1944 an article in the popular press on the relevance of his theory of constitutional types to increasing war production.[1]

As president of the International Society, Jung also became editor of the society's journal, the Zentralblatt für Psychotherapie, which was published in Germany by Hirzel Verlag of Leipzig. The journal, like the international society as a whole, was dominated by the large and newly aggressive German group that had formed the bulk and center of the old society. It was in this journal that Jung published his observations on the distinctions between German and Jewish psychology alongside calls by Göring to the Nazi colors. While Jung's words here betrayed habits of mind that I shall explore critically in a moment, Jung's opponents have often reduced these pronouncements to proof of unalloyed anti-Semitism and wholehearted collaboration with the Nazis. Such a view, however, ignores Jung's increasing disaffection toward the Nazis and his desire to protect psychotherapists in Germany from dangerous Nazi equations with so-called "Jewish" psychoanalysis. Any dissection of Jung's motives and actions, therefore, cannot be based simply on a recitation of his words in the Zentralblatt, as has most recently been attempted by Jeffrey Masson. By 1940, in any case, Jung had resigned as president of an international society rendered moribund by war and had likewise left the editorship of the journal to a now estranged Göring and his collaborators.

While Jung's critics must be more attentive to historical detail and to multiple and evolving motives on Jung's part, his defenders must be more candid about the disturbing ambiguities in his thought, especially with regard to Jews. As Paul Roazen has rightly observed, "just as Jung shared sexist prejudices toward women, it would not be surprising for him to have uncritically adopted many traditional stereotypes about Jews."[2] There have been two interrelated ways in which insufficiently critical admirers of Jung have attempted to render harmless his expressions of such views in connection with the Third Reich. The first is to quote Jung's postwar reflections on Nazism and to trace the growth of his doubts, beginning with his "Wotan" essay of 1936. The second, and less noted, means of rendering Jung's statements less ambiguous and questionable is through their alteration in translation.

For example, in his 1934 *Zentralblatt* essay, Jung twice uses the adjective *arisch* in discussing "Aryan" psychology. In the translation by R. F. C. Hull in the Bollingen Series of Jung's collected works, the German adjective *arisch* is capitalized and placed in quotation marks.[3] In the original, however, the word appears in the lower case and without quotation marks. The translator might argue that current usage demands the quotation marks or that they indicate what Jung really meant or would have said later on, but proper historical inquiry demands fidelity to the primary source. At the time, to be sure, the word "Aryan" was used often and without quotation marks. The word occurs regularly, for example, in Freud's correspondence, as Peter Gay has shown in his recent biography.[4] Of course, the important matter is what the word meant to its user, and in the case of Jung's *Collected Works* it seems likely that the editorial decision was designed to cosmeticize and thus alter the historical picture. The same is true of the translation of a footnote to a speech given by Jung in Vienna in November 1932 that was published in 1934 as part of a book entitled *Wirklichkeit der Seele*. The note is to the following text:

> . . . the great liberating ideas of world history have sprung from leading personalities and never from the inert mass. . . . The huzzahs of the Italian nation go forth to the personality of the

Duce, and the dirges of other nations lament the absence of strong leaders.[5]

The note itself in the original German reads: "*Seitdem dieser Satz geschrieben wurde, hat auch Deutschland seinen Führer gefunden.*"[6] The translation reads, incorrectly: "After this was written, Germany also turned to a Führer." The latter verb construction implies a neutrality or even a disparagement on Jung's part and a resignation or desperation on the part of the Germans not expressed by the original language. The translation should read: "Since this sentence was written, Germany too has found its leader." The Jungian cultural specificity of the possessive pronoun is missing in the Hull translation, as is the positive connotation of discovery in "has found" that corresponds to the endorsement of strong leaders found in the text, a theme to which Jung returned in a 1933 interview on Radio Berlin with German disciple Adolf von Weizsäcker.[7]

Jung, however, did not involve himself unilaterally in the domestic affairs of Nazi Germany. He was in fact sought out by psychotherapists there who felt that his association and endorsement would add luster to their bid for professional autonomy from the dominant nosological psychiatry and dissociate them from Freud in the eyes of the Nazi regime. The German Jungians in particular were eager to promote Jung for generally defensive as well as specifically partisan purposes. This was precisely the theme, for example, of an article concerning the work of a Jungian member of the so-called Göring Institute, Gustav Schmaltz, that appeared in the major Cologne newspaper in 1937.[8] So though Jung could hardly have been averse to the advancement of his school of thought at the expense of that of Freud, he was involved in a project that he could rightly claim served the survival of psychotherapy in general. Should he have anticipated the extent to which psychotherapy could contribute to the repressive aims of National Socialism? Since Jung in any event had little influence on the operations of the Göring Institute, that is a question I shall not pursue here. Rather, I will concentrate on the specific reception and use of Jungian psychology in Nazi Germany.

Jung's abiding emphasis on the unique collective experiences and memories of the world's cultures, nations, and races provided inspiration for various individuals and groups in Nazi Germany. While Freud and his theories were officially disapproved and thus, when used, were cloaked in Aesopian language, Jung's ideas were often evaluated positively in Nazi literature. One article in the journal *Rasse* in 1939 equated Jung's notion of the collective unconscious with the Nazi concept of heredity and race.[9] And this article was listed in the official Nazi party bibliography. This is not to say that in fact Jung's ideas and those of the Nazis were identical, only that such identifications could be and were effected. And while, as Robert Proctor has noted in his recent book on medicine in Nazi Germany, Jung never went on from differentiation to denigration in his cultural relativism, Nazi "racial anthropologists" and physicians sought to elucidate the pernicious peculiarities of "Jewish" science and culture.[10]

Göring and others had originally hoped to use Jung and his followers at the institute in Berlin, individuals such as G. R. Heyer, Wolfgang Kranefeldt, and Olga von König-Fachsenfeld, as a major resource for the construction of a non-Freudian "German psychotherapy." Although this fascistic spirit pervaded the institute, neither a "German psychotherapy" nor Jung's theories by themselves in fact played a predominant role in the psychotherapists' activities. The various practical demands assumed by the psychotherapists in applying and advertising their therapeutic expertise in the realms of German society, industry, and the military took precedence over the more abstract and less pragmatic characteristics of Jungian psychology. Still, such Jungian themes continued to be applied to the events and rigors of the time. In 1943, for example, the *Zentralblatt* published an article extolling the asserted healing power of the symbols of mother earth and father heaven from the ancient German religion of nature, powers supposedly helpful in strengthening the "feminine" sphere of the home as a refuge for the returning soldier.[11]

The regime itself displayed little scientific interest in Jung or his followers. It did, however, monitor their activities even outside of Germany. This is clear from the files of the former Reich Education

Ministry held by the Zentrales Staatsarchiv in Potsdam, Germany. From 1935 to 1939, various government agencies gathered information on the annual Eranos conferences at Ascona in Switzerland. In 1936 the Ministry refused to grant Germans permission to attend. The next year Göring arranged to have Eranos secretary Olga Fröbe-Kapteyn visit the Ministry to smooth the way for German participation. This intervention proved successful, but by 1938 the Nazi Auslands-Organisation was objecting that there were lots of Jews at the meetings, that some of the topics were "politically conflictual," and that in general the whole organization seemed "mysterious." To resolve such doubts, a Ministry official asked Göring to have a report prepared on that year's meeting. On August 23, 1938, Olga von König-Fachsenfeld duly reported that she had heard nothing political at the conference, that the Swiss in particular seemed to have gone out of their way not to criticize Germany, and that while there were a number of Jews in attendance, none was on the program. Permission was given for Germans to participate in 1939, and in December of that year the German consulate in Locarno commented that while the participants at the meeting were certainly "different," the conferences did not seem to serve the interests of foreign powers, Jews, or Masons and that therefore Germans should be allowed to attend. The only restriction was to be that they could not address sessions where Jews were present.[12]

By 1939 Jung, his ideas, and his followers were not an important issue for the Nazis. By that time as well, Jung and Göring were at odds over German domination of the international society, and Jung was now casting a critical eye over the Nazi phenomenon. The significance of Jung's attitudes, actions, and experiences during these years, I think, lies less in the question of any overt prejudices on his part than in the various suprapersonal dynamics his words and deeds engaged. Anti-Semitism was endemic in European society but particularly in the German lands where strong nationalism was aggravated by the proximity of the Slavic world and by the migration of *Ostjuden* into Germany and Austria. The traditional elites in Germany, for example, remained closed to Jews. As historian Fritz Stern has put it in describing the homogeneity of the officer corps, "In Germany there was no Dreyfus Affair because there was no Dreyfus."[13] The medical profession was particularly anti-Semitic owing to the pervasiveness of Social Darwinist, eugenic, and racist theorizing and, after 1918, as a result of economic pressures that increased jealousy and resentment of the many prominent and successful Jewish physicians in Berlin and other large cities. Thus the Nazis could appeal to doctors and other professionals on the basis of an interlocking grid of nationalism, self-interest, and anti-Semitism.

European anti-Semitism was not usually racist in the Nazi sense; rather the interwar fascist movement capitalized on a more general cultural movement against materialism that often caricatured Jews as lacking "spirituality." Historian George Mosse has shown how pervasive this caricature was, citing as one example the late-nineteenth-century Swiss historian Jacob Burckhardt, who, while not close to the nascent *völkisch* movement, fulminated against the decline of aesthetics and civilization as evidenced by the machinations, among others, of venal Jews.[14] Jung never expressed himself in this way but did share the widespread concern about the deterioration of spiritual values that, among other things, led him to see in the mass movements of the 1920s and 1930s elements of what he called liberation. This philosophical stance cultivated degrees of anti-Semitism inherited from the culture, the intensity of which varied with time and event. It must be said that Jung broke from these notions in a way that suggests a dialectic of prejudice and tolerance within him that was ultimately resolved in favor of the latter. This is not to agree, however, with the argument of Wolfgang Giegerich that all along Jung was purposefully engaging the shadow of racial prejudice in order to extirpate it.[15] Such a judgment naively ignores the plurality of motives and conditions present in any human action, a number of which we have explored in the case at hand. Such a rationalization also turns a blind eye to the negative effects of Jung's lack of vigorous early criticism of Hitler and the possible legitimacy for the regime created in the minds of many or some through Jung's association with it, whatever protective professional capacity he effected or intended.

Jung's philosophical outlook also proved to be problematic in a more general way. Although the Nazis exploited modern technical and material resources, including medicine and psychotherapy, they also built their power on yearnings for the mysterious and the transcendent. In so doing, they revealed the perils of fascination among intellectual luminaries who, more than anyone, must maintain a critical, rational, and ethical distance from destructive enthusiasms, recognizing the crucial difference between saying "This is amazing" and saying "This is wrong."

Notes

1. Ernst Kretschmer, "Konstitution und Leistung," *Westfälische Landeszeitung,* August 20, 1944; microcopy T78, roll 190, frames 1866–67, National Archives, Washington, D.C.

2. Paul Roazen, *Freud and His Followers,* p. 292.

3. C. G. Jung, "The State of Psychology Today," *CW* 10, pp. 165–166.

4. Peter Gay, *Freud: A Life for Our Times* (New York: Norton, 1988), pp. 205–239.

5. C. G. Jung, "The Development of Personality," *CW* 17, pp. 167–168.

6. C. G. Jung, "Vom Werden der Persönlichkeit," in idem, *Wirklichkeit der Seele* (Zurich: Rascher Verlag, 1934), p. 180n.

7. *C. G. Jung Speaking,* p. 65.

8. "Die Sprache des Unbewussten," *Kölnische Zeitung,* October 9, 1937; REM 2954; Zentrales Staatsarchiv, Potsdam. See also Paul Feldkeller, "Geist der Psychotherapie," *Deutsche Allgemeine Zeitung,* October 5, 1937; REM 2954.

9. Alfred A. Krauskopf, "Tiefenpsychologische Beiträge zur Rassenseelenforschung," *Rasse* 5 (1939): 362–368.

10. Robert Proctor, *Racial Hygiene* (Cambridge: Harvard University Press, 1988), pp. 162–163.

11. Frederik Adama van Scheltema, "Mutter Erde und Vater Himmel in der germanischen Naturreligion," *Zentralblatt für Psychotherapie* 14 (1943): 257–277.

12. REM 2797; Zentrales Staatsarchiv.

13. Fritz Stern, "The Burden of Success: Reflections on German Jewry," in idem, *Dreams and Delusions* (New York: Knopf, 1987), p. 108.

14. George Mosse, *Germans and Jews* (New York: Fertig, 1970), pp. 57–60.

15. Wolfgang Giegerich, "Postscript to Cocks," *Spring* 10 (1979): 228–231.

C. G. Jung's Analytical Psychology and the *Zeitgeist* of the First Half of the Twentieth Century

Hans Dieckmann

Dr. Med. Hans Dieckmann is a psychoanalyst and psychotherapist who lectures at the Berlin Institute for Psychotherapy. He is a founder and honorary president of the C. G. Jung Institute of Berlin, a former president of the International Association for Analytical Psychology, the patron of the C. G. Jung Institutes of Perth (Australia) and Capetown, and the author of a dozen books.

Dieckmann observes that Jung's psychological theories took shape during a period when worldviews were being radically altered. In the years following World War I, the old order was shattered and dictatorships sprang up all over Europe. Dieckmann sees the psychological projections upon charismatic leaders during that time as a collective defense against the burden of facing our destinies as individuals, an avoidance that led to the horrors of World War II and an eventual confrontation with the shadow side of science and technology. In reaction to this mass-minded era, Jung advocated a view of human nature based on the primary value of the individual. Dieckmann argues that this led to a sense of elitism among Jung and his followers and that prejudicial attitudes were an inevitable by-product of this elitist attitude.

I chose a rather general title for this paper on purpose, as innumerable statements and analyses have already been produced on C. G. Jung's personal attitude toward nationalism and anti-Semitism, so that any additional statement amounts to nothing more than a repetition. But I would like to draw attention to a recent objective-critical book written from rather a Marxist point of view by Tilman Evers.[1] Such a publication from the German-speaking world is especially interesting, as Jung was fiercely attacked there particularly after the war. I am firmly convinced that Jung was neither an anti-Semite nor a Nazi, as even his most violent critics concede today. Nevertheless, the question remains open why, particularly in the first years after Hitler's seizure of power, Jung became at least unconsciously infected by Nazi ideas and wrote that irresponsible message in the *Zentralblatt* in which he stressed a distinction between German and Jewish psychology. He took the same line in 1934 in his paper "On the Present Situation of Psychotherapy," in which where he even attributed a higher potential to the Aryan unconscious than to the Jewish and spoke in a more or less admiring manner of the "powerful phenomenon of National Socialism." It is well known that James Kirsch vehemently protested this article in his letters to Jung.[2] Jung's reply to the reproach was quite a lame excuse. There is even a passage in his writings—although we must admit that it is the only one—in a letter to Kranefeldt, in which Jung is openly anti-Semitic.[3] He writes that "with Freud and Adler specific Jewish points of view are preached publicly . . . which have an essentially subversive character."

It is certainly not enough simply to cite such "slips," as Jung himself called them after the war; we have also to ask how a convinced Swiss democrat and son of a Protestant minister who used copious material drawn from Jewish culture in his exploration of the collective unconscious, who worked with many Jewish scholars, and who counted many Jews among his own disciples—how he could succumb to such an infection. We have to ask Jung the very same question that we ask all our patients: "Where does it come from?" In my opinion, neither his personal conflict with Freud nor the anti-Semitism that existed at that time in Switzerland in a more or less latent manner offers a satisfying answer.

Jungians and analytical psychology have been time and again

reproached for fostering fascist ideology. This criticism especially comes from the leftist intellectuals. They say that analytical psychology follows the idealistic line of German philosophy and encourages elitist thinking—and, as a result, racial prejudices. If we take this reproach seriously, we have to admit that it has at least partial justification. There are passages in Jung's work that correspond to a dictatorial ideology: for example, when he speaks of the "leader principle," which he continued to emphasize even after the war, in his letter to UNESCO.[4] In this letter he describes his psychology as appropriate only for the cultivated strata of society. At the same time he stresses that it is the task of these strata to influence the ignorant masses in the right way. Indeed, that is not a very democratic psychology.

Although Jung's psychology is based on the tension between the opposites, as demonstrated in his conception of the archetypes, Jung was certainly closer to the ideas of Plato than to those of Aristotle; and he certainly preferred Albertus Magnus to Thomas Aquinas and Goethe to Newton in their well-known argument about the theory of color. The principle of individuation may appear to be inherently elitist—and indeed many Jungian analysts do see it that way, although strictly speaking, even a poorly developed tree (for example) is also individuated. Jung certainly had a special liking for the idealistic branch of philosophy, as is reflected by his work. But he also tried very hard to reconcile these ideas and connect them with the other side, the materialistic philosophy. His conception of typology is an excellent example of this. But here, too, an idealistic, elitist element creeps in, inasmuch as the introverted thinking type appears superior to the extraverted sensation type, who, according to Jung's description, would be best employed as a street sweeper.

Regarding the elitist element, we have to attribute it—not without justification—to Jung himself as a person. One should not ask a lighthouse to resemble a flashlight. But as regards his method of treatment and the concepts of the archetypes and the collective unconscious, I think that he was wrong in considering them to be applicable only to a determined circle of so-called cultivated people. According to my practical experience, analytical psychology can be applied successfully to patients from lower social strata, as I have shown with some case studies.[5]

No researcher, not even the greatest one, lives and structures his work independently from the *Zeitgeist* of the culture that surrounds him. This is why it is worth looking at the social-evolutionary development in which Jung was placed in the first half of this very agitated century. Norbert Elias has pointed out that in the course of the development of humankind, people tend to form larger and larger social units for the sake of survival.[6] Those units gradually consolidate, then disband after a while in order to turn into even bigger groupings. Prehistoric people before the Neolithic stage, who lived as hunters and gatherers in very small groups of fifty to one hundred persons at most, did not need to develop very much individuality. The invention of farming and stock breeding slowly brought about the formation first of tribes, then of city-states, and finally of the ancient empires. But one should not be too much impressed by the extension of these empires. Their population often was smaller than that of a modern city. In any case, these larger groups provoked the division of labor and consequently the promotion of greater individuality.

According to Spengler and Toynbee, all these cultures had a period of rise, a heyday, and a period of decline.[7] Spengler treats each culture, including our own, as a unified whole. That is, every culture starts its rise at point zero, and there is no connection to the preceding ones. Toynbee, however, supports the hypothesis of affiliation: that there are certain connections between the declining culture and the newly arising one. Some cultural possessions were taken over at any one time, which included a principle of development. According to Elias, who looks upon this process from the point of view of the social sciences, larger and larger centralized units developed, with the corresponding regressions and "phenomena of time lag." This is how France under Louis XIV became a centralized state with a strong hierarchy, and how, after 1871, the many small German duchies became the German empire (Second Reich). The single tribes or provinces increasingly lost the importance they had as apparent or real guarantee of security and survival of their population. Finally, the disruptions provoked by the two World Wars brought about the division of our globe into two large spheres of influence. If the unification of these two spheres ever occurred, it would mean a world state that comprehended the entire earth.

But what do these reflections have to do with our problem? Jung was younger than Freud by twenty years, and in 1914, at the onset of World War I—which was a deciding factor for the development of today's situation—he was at the beginning of his most productive period. After his intensely painful separation from Freud, which had occurred shortly before, he must have felt thrown back all the more on his own ideas and concepts. But those are never independent of the social trends of the time in which an individual lives and grows. The beginning of our century was a period of important change, a fact of which we are mostly not very much aware. Paradisiacal hopes had been pinned on the beginning of the industrial-technical era. Humankind expected finally to be able to master the dangers and uncertainties of the future. We were not only to be master of the earth and of the present, but, according to Kant/Laplace, we were to be able to predict the future in a verifiable manner.

All these theories broke down when quantum theory, the non-Euclidean geometries, and the theory of relativity were developed around the turn of the century. Planck still believed that his quantum theory could be replaced one day by a causal and objectively verifiable system, but modern physics passed over this belief and has been relativizing it more and more. It was a scientific world of radical change and doubt that Jung grew into, a world where the subjective factor began to play an increasingly important part. Jung could no longer remain in agreement with Freud, who wanted to objectify psychoanalysis in the science of the past century.

A second process has run parallel to the scientific revolution, and this brings us back to the process of the formation of large groups. The larger and more undifferentiated a group becomes, the fewer possibilities of identification it offers to the individual and the less it is able to furnish unconscious preconceptions as a basis for the individual's experience and behavior. This leads to isolation, loneliness, and an increasing compulsion to individuation. At the same time, a regressive longing is bound to develop, as a necessary compensatory countermovement. This longing leads back to small collectives, which alone are able to convey a feeling of safety.

After World War I, a phenomenon occurred all over Europe that I have never found described from this point of view. After the overthrow of most of the European monarchies and their nearly complete deprivation of power, dictatorships sprang up all over Europe in the years from 1919 on. In a surprisingly large number of countries, men from the most various social strata arose and seized power, partly by force, partly by democratic means, and set up dictatorships that suppressed every opposition. Great hopes and expectations were often pinned on these dictators by their peoples. There was Atatürk in Turkey, Salazar in Portugal, Stalin in Russia, Mussolini in Italy, Pilsudski in Poland, Mannerheim in Finland, Franco in Spain, Horthy in Hungary, and, as the diabolic culmination of this series, Hitler in Germany. (I would like to emphasize that certainly not all of them are to be judged negatively and that, for example, Atatürk's achievement for his country was surely outstanding.)

Analytically we might consider this phenomenon as the search for the Great Father, an archetypal figure that had until that time been represented by the king. Alternatively, we could also raise the question whether the phenomenon of dictatorships had anything to do with the increasingly strong tension between larger and larger masses and the isolated individual. The well-being and life of a nation-state and its people were no longer hoped for or expected from the king by the grace of God, but were determined by a single individual who came from the people itself. In a highly projective process, this individual was endowed with special qualities and talents, an unfortunate remnant of the cult of the genius that had marked the beginning of the nineteenth century. Thus the great individual acting for the whole of his people embodied the *principium individuationis* by taking upon himself the loneliness of the individual development out of the collective. The others, the people, were lowered to the level of "just following orders" and in doing so were freed from this loneliness, from the burden of making their own decisions, and from the responsibility that individuation demands. There is, of course, a fatal connection between, on the one side, the leader principle and, on the other, an increasing subjection and conformity of individuals. One cannot just leave individuation and decisions about one's own life up to somebody else. In this sense the Chinese proverb, often quoted by Jung, is right in saying that a great man is a misfortune for his people.

When today we look back to this time it appears as an inappropriate, dangerous, and destructive attempt—analytically as a defense mechanism—which led to the devastations of World War II. But perhaps it took the nightmare of the extermination camps to make man aware of the horrible shadow that he carries, in whose service science and technology still allow themselves to be used today.

Jung's very dubious statements may appear more comprehensible when we consider the massive tension that this process provokes between man as a collective being who, deep in his archaic unconscious, still lives in a horde, and the compulsion to individuate, which found its expression especially between these two wars. Yet we do not seem to have learned very much from this tension, considering the campaign of extermination that we are leading—unconsciously or only partially consciously—against our own planet.

The basic concept of analytical psychology developed by Jung is the concept of psychological individuation. It has to do with becoming an individual, a slow development of the individual psyche out of a collective basis, that is, the collective unconscious in connection with socialization. This process, as I have indicated, is not very compatible with the formation of groups, since it stresses the importance and the uniqueness of the individual.

We now have to raise the concluding question: What has all this to do with anti-Semitism? At first thought one might say: nothing! Hitler was the only one among the dictators I have mentioned who was expressly anti-Semitic; even Mussolini had to be forced by Hitler to join in the persecutions of the Jews. But we have to assume that dictators are especially predestined to need enemy images and to react to them with paranoid aggression.[8] Hitler presumably chose just this enemy image because of the prominent role that anti-Semitism had always played in the German-speaking countries. I think that neither Jung nor Freud was ever able to recover from the deep rift between them; and the flood starting from Germany was bound to touch on this deep wound in Jung's psyche. Just as Jung regarded himself as superior, the Aryans considered themselves an elite. The Jews, however, were the other elite of Central Europe. Psychologically seen, it is not surprising that they became the favorite enemy image, and it is rather astonishing that Jung, who was so deeply disappointed by Freud, did not get thoroughly infected by the rabble-rousing propaganda against the Jews. In addition, Jung was convinced of the prospective healing powers of the unconscious, and as an intellectual he was fascinated by the elemental energy of the primitive German barbarian. I think that taking into account a combination of genesis, social stratum, and trends of the *Zeitgeist* to which an individual is exposed helps us to understand such "slips" as those made by Jung. Those slips remain, nevertheless, a source of guilt that we Jungians are still confronted with, for one expects a lighthouse to illuminate a larger circumference than other, lesser lights. But one should also know, as the Chinese proverb states, that at the base of a lighthouse the shadow is particularly dark.

Notes

1. Tilman Evers, *Mythos und Emanzipation: Eine kritische Annäherung an C. G. Jung* (Hamburg: Junius Verlag, 1987).

2. Letters to Dr. James Kirsch, 26 May and 29 September 1934, in C. G. Jung, *Briefe*, vol. 1 (Olten: Walter Verlag, 1972).

3. Cited in J. Grunert, "Zur Geschichte der Psychoanalyse in München," *Psyche* 10 (1984): 865–905.

4. C. G. Jung, "Memorandum für die UNESCO" (1947/48), CW 18, paras. 1388–1402.

5. See Hans Dieckmann, "Über einige Beziehungen zwischen Traumserien und Verhaltensänderungen in einer Neurosenbehandlung," *Zeitschrift für Psy-*

chosomatische Medizin, October-December 1962, and *Methoden der analytischen Psychologie* (Olten: Walter Verlag, 1979).

6. Norbert Elias, *Die Gesellschaft der Individuation* (Frankfurt am Main: Suhrkamp Verlag, 1987).

7. See Oswald Spengler, *The Decline of the West* [1918/22], 2 vols. (New York: Alfred A. Knopf, 1945) and Arnold Toynbee, *A Study of History,* 10 vols. (New York: Oxford University Press, 1946–1957).

8. See Hans Dieckmann, "The Enemy Image," *Quadrant* 17, no. 2 (1984).

National Socialism, National Psychology, and Analytical Psychology

Andrew Samuels

Andrew Samuels is a training analyst of the Society of Analytical Psychology, London. His books include *Jung and the Post-Jungians* and *The Plural Psyche*. He also wrote the introduction to the 1989 edition of C. G. Jung's *Essays on Contemporary Events: Reflections on Nazi Germany*.

In this paper Samuels argues that Jung's attempt to develop a theory of national psychology led him inexorably into a conceptual framework that resembled Nazi anti-Semitic ideology. He suggests that Jung's leadership ambitions were greater than his followers acknowledge and that this was particularly evident during the 1930s. Samuels considers that, in order to renew itself, analytical psychology must resolve its mourning for Jung the man, in order fully to claim its autonomy. Theories of psychological difference, including national differences, are urgently needed in today's fragmenting world, and Samuels concludes that there is much to respect and value in Jung's efforts in this general area.

In this paper, I try to show that it was Jung's attempt to establish a psychology of nations that brought him into the same frame as Nazi anti-Semitic ideology. In addition, Jung was absorbed by the question of leadership. Exploring these ideas as thoroughly as possible leads to a reevaluation in positive terms of what Jung was trying to do. Moreover, such an exploration is itself a necessary act of reparation.

ON NOT ANALYZING JUNG

Some readers may be disappointed that I scarcely mention Jung's personal psychology or psychopathology—his father complex, the scars of the break with Freud, his shadow problems, his Swiss bourgeois mentality, and so forth. Nor do I give much space to the many personal testimonies that exist, intended to show that Jung cannot be regarded as anti-Semitic and, to the contrary, that he had a positive attitude to Jews and helped many Jews to achieve a relationship with their Jewishness for the first time.

For a while I worried that these omissions added up to a failure of feeling on my part. And even now I do not think that we should totally ignore Jung's experiences and experiences of Jung, forgetting that the simple answer may be the best one. Indeed, I will consider Jung the man as an example of a leader or potential leader. But gradually I have come to see that *the true failure of feeling is found when the personal dimension is given too much weight or used to close an awkward issue once and for all.* A similar point was made by Reuven Bulka, the editor of the *Journal of Psychology and Judaism*, in his introduction to the issue in which Robert Haymond's and James Kirsch's articles were published. Bulka wrote:

> Resolution of this conflict [about Jung, anti-Semitism, and the Nazis] is important, not only for the sake of historical record, or for the condemnation or exoneration of an individual. There are very crucial implications, which relate to the role and responsibility of the scientist, relative to political roles, and also the matter of Judaic scholars seriously studying the analytical psychology of Jung.[1]

I am sure I am not the only one to have mixed feelings about an analysis-at-a-distance of Jung's internal life (his dreams, for example) that does not observe the rule of professional confidentiality even to the slightest degree. The trouble with any psychological analysis of Jung the man is that its results can almost always be known in advance. Jung, by his own admission (regarding his Number One and Number Two personalities), was an extremely complex person who excited equally complex reactions. So, for me, analyzing Jung the man is not the best way to proceed.

WAS JUNG ANTI-SEMITIC?

It may seem strange that a Jewish Jungian analyst wants to write about Jung's anti-Semitism. I make no apology for doing this because I believe that the manifold strengths and subtleties of analytical psychology are being lost. Such loss results not only from the alleged Nazi collaboration and anti-Semitism (both of which Jung denied), but also from what can sometimes seem like an inability on the part of many Jungians to react to such charges in an intelligent, humane, and honest way. Thus, psychoanalysis and other intellectual disciplines are permitted to continue to ignore the pioneering nature of Jung's contributions and, hence, the work of post-Jungian analytical psychologists.

Is there something in the fundamental structure of Jung's thinking about the Jews, in its heart or essence, that made it inevitable that he could develop the degree of anti-Semitism that would seriously concern us, to the point of questioning the value of remaining declared analytical psychologists? When Jung writes about the Jews and Jewish psychology, is there something in his whole attitude that brings him into the same frame as the Nazis, even if he were shown not to have been an active Nazi collaborator? Is there something to worry about?

My brief answer is yes, and my hope is that by exploring the matter as deeply as I can, a kind of reparation will ensue. Then, as we shall see, there will be a base from which to explore the full potential of Jung's psychological thinking in the 1930s, and it becomes possible to revalue his entire project.

DEFENSES OF JUNG

Having reviewed the essential contents of the many attacks on Jung, I am stirred by the nature of the equally numerous defenses of Jung that have been put forward. I find myself reacting to the psychological similarity between the defenses and the attacks. Both

defenders and attackers of Jung are sitting in judgment on him.
Both are looking for a "final solution" to the Jung problem.
Between the cries of "Let's clear our man once and for all" and
"Let's finish the bastard off," there is a call for a middle way: to
carefully assess the competing claims of attackers and defenders
so as to reach an apparently balanced point of view. It is said that
the matter is too complicated to be settled decisively. Though it is
tempting to join in this Olympian arbitration between attack and
defense, that position can be seen as disengaged, morally supercil-
ious, politically evasive, pseudo-mature, and, in any case, as full
of certitude as overt attack or defense. The shadows surrounding
Jung are going to linger anyway, for they want us to pay psychological attention to them.

One common defense of Jung is that he was only expressing the
attitudes of his time. Many eminent men and women were guilty
of a kind of *trahison des clercs*. It is said that casual, social anti-
Semitism was apparently so normal and acceptable in Jung's
culture and time that remarks about the Jews, even when couched
in scientific language, did not seem outré. Jung, it is argued, was
just a typical, petit bourgeois, unthinking, small-minded Swiss
burgher. But this claim actually stimulates a search for evidence
that would contradict it and thus undermines the intention of
defending Jung. For it seems that there must have been other
attitudes available to Jung at the time, other choices that he could
have made, other viewpoints possible, particularly as he was not
under direct personal threat. Even in Germany there were *Juden-
freunde*, "friends of the Jews"—not just the anecdotal good Germans but people actually prosecuted in the courts by the Gestapo
for their attitudes and behavior. Then there were the *Rassenschan-
der*, "race defilers," who were imprisoned for doing what hundreds
and thousands had done quite legally before 1933, as the intermar-
riage statistics show. We know from a fascinating letter in the
London *Times* of November 13, 1988—from a typical *Times*
correspondent, an Anglican clergyman of the old school—that
problems faced by Jews were discussed in Germany in the late
1930s:

> Sir, Any suggestion that most British people at the time neither
> knew about nor would have cared about what the Nazis were
> doing to their Jews is wrong. I went in 1937 with a party of the
> Cambridge University Mummers to perform two English plays,
> by invitation of four German universities.
>
>   A major topic of conversation with our hosts, liberal ones and
> otherwise, was their treatment of the Jews. War between us was
> never mentioned. Such a possibility was not recognized in 1937.
> Jews was the topic. This I remember well after 51 years.

During this time, we find warning signals about the nature of
fascism being posted in the sociological works of Emile Durkheim
and Franz Boas. Closer to home, there were the public and private
admonitions of Jung by Gustav Bally and James Kirsch. And the
Dutch section of the International General Medical Society for
Psychotherapy refused to host its 1935 congress on political
grounds. Jung was critical of this decision because, he said, it
brought politics into science.

So as a result of the claim that the world displayed a universal
anti-Semitism in the 1920s and '30s, and that Jung and the others
were just part of that *Zeitgeist*, has been to constellate a counter-
claim, one that is potentially damaging to Jung. Other non-Jewish
analysts, who might also have been expected to reflect "ordinary"
anti-Semitism, felt the need to take action: D. W. Winnicott, for
instance, wrote the following letter to Mrs. Neville Chamberlain
in 1938 urging her to question her husband over his silence on the
subject of the Jews and Nazi persecution:

> Dear Mrs. Chamberlain,
>
>   . . . Why does the Prime Minister never mention the Jews? Does
> he secretly despise them? When in England we say WE, we include
> Jews who are people like ourselves. I am not asking him to be
> pro-Jew, but I want to know definitely whether he is or is not
> secretly anti-Jew . . . at present we seem to be secretly sharing
> Germany's anti-Jew insanity, and this is not where we want our
> leaders to lead us.[2]

As Jeffrey Masson (1989) has pointed out, many of the articles
that appeared in the *Zentralblatt für Psychotherapie* under Jung's

editorship go well beyond "ordinary," petit bourgeois anti-Semitism. There are repeated attacks on "Jewish" mental states and a
general lauding of "northern," Aryan psychology. There is a great
deal of praise for Hitler and the Nazi party and, in Masson's
opinion, even coded messages of support for measures such as the
extermination of mental patients. In any event, these articles
appeared long after the initial confusion over whether a statement
of support for the Nazis was to be printed in the *Zentralblatt*
proper or in the German national supplement, which, Jung said,
explained why his name appeared over such a statement. Masson's
point is that Jung must have known of the disgusting (and absurd)
nature of these further articles published in the years 1934–1939.
If he did nothing about it, it surely could not be because he was
completely divorced from the editorial policy of the *Zentralblatt*.
If he played no editorial role, surely he at least *read* it? If he didn't
read it, did nobody ever tell him what was in it?

There are several reasons why, knowing what was being published, Jung might have done nothing. First, he might have been in
full agreement with these views. But that would make him an overt
Nazi supporter and a rabid anti-Semite, and he denies both of
those charges. Second, he might have been playing a long-term
political game, continuing his strategy of helping Jewish psychotherapists to go on working. But there is no written or oral
evidence that he held back for this reason and, were it the case, I
think that there would be some evidence. Third, and I believe this
is the answer, Jung's position at the head of the German psychotherapy profession was too great an advantage to throw away. The
issue here is Jung's leadership. After all, Freud had once written to
Jung that psychoanalysis would never find its true status until it
had been accepted in Germany. The conquest of Germany was the
goal of the psychoanalytic conquistador.[3] History, and Hitler, put
that goal within Jung's grasp. (I shall look at Jung as a leader later
in the paper.)

JUNG AND NATIONAL PSYCHOLOGY

The main difficulty with Jung's work in the general area of
national psychology is an unwarranted expansion of his psychol-

ogy, and hence his authority as a leading psychologist, into complicated fields where psychology alone is an inadequate explanatory tool. This problem is exemplified in his treatment of the question of national psychology.

Jung's concept of the collective unconscious is open to abuse. There are connections between the collective unconscious and the notion of a "racial unconscious." For, in order for there to be racial psychologies of the sort Jung often seems to be describing, we have to advance a hypothesis of a racial unconscious. The reason for this is to be found in the nature of the collective unconscious itself. The truly collective aspect of the human psyche, which is what Jung refers to as "archetypal," is far deeper than any cultural manifestation, and far more difficult to put into words. For the level of archetype touches the psychosomatic basis of the human experience. But this makes a problem for Jung's theory because the universal and primary nature of the collective unconscious would imply a far greater degree of cultural homogeneity than we actually observe in the world.

Jung resolved this difficulty by claiming that there is a "collective psyche limited to race, tribe, and family over and above the 'universal' collective psyche."[4] This concept was depicted in Jolande Jacobi's book *The Psychology of C. G. Jung*, which was published in 1942 with Jung's express approval, by a "psychic genealogical tree" (see the figure on page 184) described as follows: "At the very bottom lies the unfathomable, the central force out of which at one time the individual psyche has been differentiated. This central force goes through all further differentiations and isolations, lives in them all, cuts through them to the individual psyche."[5] Above the "unfathomable ground," Jacobi arranges different strata, eight in all, like the layers of a cake: the central force, animal ancestors, primitive human ancestors, groups of people, nation, tribe, family, individual. Though she does not use the word *race*, it is clear from the text as well as from Jung's remarks quoted above that this is what is meant by "groups of people" (also referred to in the English translation as "human groups"—in the German original, *Volksgruppe*).

The hypothesis of a racial layer in Jung's model of the collective

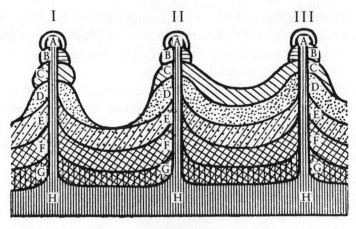

I. Single Nations
II and III. Groups of Nations (e.g., Europe)

A. Individual   E. Groups of People
B. Family   F. Primitive Human Ancestors
C. Tribe   G. Animal Ancestors
D. Nation   H. Central Force

Source: Diagram from Jolande Jacobi, *The Psychology of C. G. Jung*
(New Haven: Yale University Press, 1973), diagram XI, p. 34. Copyright
© 1973 by Yale University Press. Reprinted by permission of Yale
University Press.

psyche has caused as great a furor as his alleged anti-Semitism. As
a result, the serious charge of racism has been leveled against Jung
and his psychology. According to most modern definitions, racism
divides humankind into distinct and hierarchically gradable
groups on the basis of biological or quasi-biological characteristics.
A racist is therefore someone who believes that people of a
particular race, color, or origin are inherently inferior, so that their
identity, culture, self-esteem, views, and feelings are of less value
and may be treated as less important than those of the groups
believed to be superior.

The question is, does Jung's thought conform to this definition?

In a paper entitled "Jung: A Racist," Farhad Dalal thoroughly
surveyed Jung's writings, especially on Africa and Africans. He
concluded that Jung was indeed a racist in that he thought that
black people were inferior and not just different. Dalal understood

Jung to be saying that Africans lack a complete layer of consciousness altogether, that white people are inherently less "primitive"
and so individuation is reserved for them alone, and that modern
Africans can be used as evidence for his theories about the prehistoric human. All this, and more, is well documented by Dalal.

It has become clear to me that something goes very wrong with
Jung's thought when he goes beyond the boundaries of psychology
into what has been termed *racial typology*.[6] When Jung's African
stays an imaginal African, the African of dreams, or when Jung
studies African myth, he makes a richly creative contribution. But
when Jung generalizes about African *character,* and does so from
a solely psychological point of view, ignoring economic, social,
political and historical factors, then he spoils his own work,
inviting the severe criticism he has received.[7]

What was it that led Jung to spoil his own work, leaving him
open to the charge that his theories resemble Nazi ideology? When
Jung ceases to serve the psyche and finds a new master, he can
scarcely avoid being linked to the Nazis and castigated as an anti-
Semite. But I want to argue that it is *not* in the area of racial
psychology that we must search for an explanation of Jung's
behavior and attitudes in the 1930s. I think that it is far too general
and facile a conclusion to advance "race" as the linkage between
analytical psychology and Nazi ideology. There is more in Hitler's
theorizing than its undeniably racist element. There is also a
comprehensive political and historical theory, and it is hard to
disentangle the racial from the political ideas. The political dogma
certainly employs a racial viewpoint, but Hitler's racism also has a
political format, one that uses a *nationalistic* vocabulary and
focuses on the idea of the nation.[8]

The key questions that require answers are these: Why did Jung
get involved with German political affairs *in the way he did?* Why
did he feel *obliged* to publish his thoughts on "Jewish psychology"
at such a sensitive moment? Was there anything in the *structure* of
his work up until then that made his *active* involvement an inevitability? Simply to stigmatize (or possibly even to scapegoat) Jung
as a racist does not help us to address these issues. If we want to

know more about Jung, the Nazis, and anti-Semitism, then we have to explore the idea of nation, without in any way minimizing the question of Jung's racism.

Let us look again at the layers in Jacobi's diagram. Notice that at layer D, "nation," a quality change has come into the diagram. The introduction of the idea of the nation leads inevitably to the introduction of economic, social, political, and historical factors. For the national level of the psyche, unlike the deeper layers such as "animal ancestors," involves an economic, social, political, and historical construct of relatively modern origin: the nation. Now it should become clearer why I stress that "race" is too general a theme to serve as an overarching backdrop to our drama. When we look a little more closely at Jung's not-absolutely-collective layer of the collective unconscious, we find that it is not "race," not "tribe," and not "family" that engage Jung, but *nation*. Jung was intrigued by the idea of the "psychology of the nation" and by the influence of a person's national background, saying that the "soil of every country holds [a] mystery . . . there is a relationship of body to earth."[9]

When Jung wrote about America and the Americans in 1918, he introduced this idea that the land in or on which an individual lived influenced the psyche and the psychological development of that individual. "The mystery of the American earth" was so powerful that, according to him, it had even changed the physiognomy of the citizens. The skull and pelvis measurements of second-generation Americans were becoming "Indianized." It can be seen that Jung is not thinking solely along racial lines, for the immigrants from Europe and the indigenous Indians come from *different* races. No—living in America, living on American soil, being part of the American nation, all exert profound psychological and physiological effects. Though the effects may be described along roughly racial lines, they have not been caused by race; it is "the foreign land" that has "assimilated the conqueror."[10]

There is an important case that Jung wrote about in 1937 (a significant date considering the topic of this paper). A young woman from Europe had been born in Java. As an infant she had a local woman as an *ayah* (which Jung takes to mean a wet-nurse, though the term often describes a nanny). The patient returned to Europe to go to school and quite forgot her childhood, including her onetime fluency in Malay. During the analysis, the patient's dreams included imagery of a marked Indonesian kind. Jung claimed that "tantric philosophy" (about which he had recently been reading) was helpful in understanding the case. At one point in the case history, Jung comments that the patient had "sucked in the local demonology with the *ayah's* milk." Here the argument is based not on race but on the idea that "the earth and native culture constitute the matrix from which we evolve," to use Mary Loomis's words.[11] For Jung, earth plus culture equals nation.

In my view, Jung's account of the relations between a nation and the individuals who are part of it is inadequate. Jung frequently asserts that "nations are made up of individuals"[12] or, conversely, that "the psychology of the individual is reflected in the psychology of the nation."[13] Statements like these form the basis of Jung's argument that there is a "psychology of nations." But nationalism has as its social and political functions the overriding of individual distinctions (often *including* so-called racial differences within a single state). Far from being a phenomenon that is somehow secondary to the individual, the nation sets its stamp on her or him through its ideology and power structures—a closely textured web of assumptions about society and the individual's place in it, about morality, about the rules and concepts of behavior, about politics, about life itself. Although nationalism requires the equation of state and people, the one is not "made up" of the other. Of course, we should not forget that defining the differences between "nation," "state," and "people" is still a thorny problem. Germany's divided condition used to be referred to as "two states, one nation."

The modern idea of "nation" stems from the late eighteenth and early nineteenth centuries. The idea gradually arose that nationality was a natural possession of everyone and that a person could only participate in civic and political life as part of a nation. It has been argued that it was only when large-scale colonization produced encounters on a mass level with other cultures and colors that the idea of nation came into being;[14] the "other" defined the "self" as nation. Just as political allegiance had hitherto not been determined by nationality, so civilization had not been regarded as nationally defined. During the Middle Ages, civilization defined itself religiously and, in the Renaissance and the Enlightenment periods, the classical cultures of Greece and Rome became the yardsticks. When civilization started to be defined on the basis of nationality, it was felt for the first time that people should be educated in their own mother tongue, not in the language of other civilizations. Poets and scholars began to emphasize cultural nationalism. They reformed the national language, elevated it to literary status, and celebrated the traditional past of their native culture for nationalist ends.

The German nation, as such a cultural and political phenomenon, did not exist before the rise of Prussia at the end of the eighteenth century. German cultural nationalism has been portrayed as stressing instinct over reason; the power of historical tradition over modernization and democracy; the historical differences between nations over their common aspirations.[15] If we analyze typical nationalist ideology (Germany being only one example), we find that much more is involved than emphasis on the geographical unit. We also find an emphasis on some kind of an ethical principle, or at least ethical expression, and this is usually couched in comparative (and self-congratulatory) terms: our soldiers are the bravest, the quality of our family life is the finest, we have special rights, we have a special relationship to higher forces, our apple pie is the greatest, our upper lips are the stiffest. In other words, *nationalism always involves a form of psychological expression and self-characterization, and therefore nationalism requires the services of psychologists.*

It is my contention that, in C. G. Jung, nationalism found its psychologist and that, in spite of his concern with the racial unconscious, it is as a psychologist of nationhood that we should also understand Jung. He was a psychologist who lent his authority to nationalism, thereby legitimizing ideas of innate psychological differences between nations. Jung's "pan-psychism,"[16] his tendency, noted by many commentators, to see all outer events in terms of inner, usually archetypal dynamics, his neglect of economic, social, political, and historical factors, *finds its most extreme expression in the phrase "the psychology of the nation."* With this insight in mind, Jung's offensive generalizations about Jews can be seen in a new light. There are hardly any references to "Aryans" in Jung's *Collected Works.* But there are numerous references to Germany and, indeed, to most of the countries of the world. There are also frequent uses of the term "Germanic," and at first sight it seems that Jung has made the important distinction between Germany the nation-state and Germanic culture, an identifiable, communal, and ethnic tradition established over a very long time. If Jung had consistently made this distinction, we would be able to distinguish clearly the racial and nationalistic trends in his thought. For it is not my contention that Jung's racism is unimportant, rather that it is not the main thing to examine in connection with the Nazis and anti-Semitism.

Unhappily, the situation is extremely confused, and this cannot all be laid at the door of Jung's English translator. In the index to volume 10 of the German edition of the *Collected Works,* under *"Germanisch"* we find *s. auch Deutschland"* (*"see also* Germany"). In "Wotan," which is the piece of Jung's where the distinction is probably most needed, we find a sentence that has been correctly translated in the following manner: "Wotan is a *Germanic* datum of first importance, the truest expression and unsurpassed personification of a fundamental quality that is particularly characteristic of the *Germans.*"[17] Later we find a reference to "the Germans who were adults in 1914,"[18] so it does seem that Jung has a specific historical and geographical entity in mind when he writes of Germans and Germany. At one point, Jung even refers to himself as a "Germanic,"[19] if we attend to the German language original![20] But, after the war, Jung often recalled that he was Swiss, in contradistinction to being German. It follows that modern nations were very much in his mind, as well as large-scale supranational cultural groupings.

My further contention is that Jung exceeded his brief as the psychologist of nations. We have already seen how complex are the historical, economic, political, and cultural forces that go into nationalism. Jung's mistake was to expand his role as psychologist to the point at which the nation itself is regarded as a solely psychological entity and observed from a solely psychological point of view. This explains Jung's very positive and favorable interest in Count Hermann Keyserling's somewhat eccentric books, two of which he reviewed in the 1920s and '30s. In these popular works, Keyserling opined that each nation has a definite psychological character and that each contributes one feature to a sort of world personality. In one of these reviews Jung writes that "the 'nation' (like the 'state') is a personified concept that corresponds in reality only to a specific nuance of the individual psyche. . . . [The nation] is nothing but an inborn character. . . . Thus, in many ways it is an advantage to have been imprinted with the English national character in one's cradle. You can then travel in the most god-forsaken countries and when anybody asks, 'Are you a foreigner?' you can answer, 'No, I am English.' "[21]

Jung was also influenced by C. G. Carus, the early-nineteenth-century German philosopher, who thought that the relation of the passage of the sun to any given area influenced the character of those living there. What is more, according to Carus, new inhabitants of a geographical area acquire the characteristics of its previous, unrelated inhabitants. By this hypothesis, possession of land, a central feature of nationhood, is elevated to a mystical level. Here I would say that Jung followed Carus rather closely, as in his remarks about the "mystery" to be found in a country's soil. The Germans, according to Carus, acquire and recapitulate the development and achievements of the Caucasians, Persians, Armenians, Semites (sic), Pelasgians, Etruscans, Thracians, Illyrians, Iberians, Romans, and Celts. Carus is not advancing a racial theory, for biology plays little part in his formulations. For Carus, and for Jung, the concern is with psychology, not biology.

But Jung went too far, and as a result his ideas on national psychology degenerate into nothing more than typology. His method is to assemble lists of characteristics to serve as stepping stones toward a definition—of German or of Jew. It is exactly the same method that he used to define the psychological attributes of the two sexes.[22] He focuses upon what a Jew *is*, not upon what being a Jew is like. The emphasis is on classification by characteristics, emphasizing differences, not on the living experience of difference. Just as with the sexes, we find Jung promoting an ethos of complementarity, so that any two opposite lists combined produce an absolutely wonderful-sounding "wholeness." Jew and German seem to constitute two halves of a whole: rational, sophisticated, erudite city-dweller complementing irrational, energetic, earthy peasant-warrior. This is presented as something factual, revealed by an empirical, psychological method. At no point does Jung admit to being part of a myth-making process, nor does he claim a metaphorical intent.

Is this really psychology, or is it the use of psychological terminology and Jung's authority as a leading psychologist to convert anecdote, prejudice, and desire into definitory, typological statements? I shall return to that question at the end of the paper. For now I'd like to ask my readers to hold the idea of Jung as a psychologist of nations in their minds for a while so that I can turn my attention to certain relevant aspects of the theories of Adolf Hitler. Remember, we have been discussing the hypertrophy of psychology, *its* expansionism, its search for *Lebensraum*, "living space."

JUNG, HITLER,
AND THE PSYCHOLOGY
OF THE NATION

It is interesting to note that Hitler did not regard Germany as being composed purely of "Aryans." Rather, he hoped to increase the Aryan proportion of the population through genetic selection, deportation, and extermination. But, as I mentioned earlier, throughout Hitler's writings, it is clear that there is a pronounced nationalistic as well as a racial component in his thinking.[23] Hitler regarded all history as consisting of struggles between competing nations for living space and, ultimately, for world domination. The Jews, according to Hitler (who got it from Karl Lueger), are a nation and participate in these struggles, with the principal goal of world domination. He felt that because the Jews did not possess an identifiable geographical locality, it is the world or nothing for them. In fact, for Hitler, the nationalism of the Jews is "denationalism, the bastardization of other nations."[24] The Jewish nation achieves its goal of world domination by denationalizing existing states from within and imposing a homogeneous "Jewish" character on them—for instance, by its international capitalism and by its equally international communism. So, in Hitler's thinking, there is a tussle between wholesome nationhood and its corrupting enemy, the Jews.[25]

To summarize: First, a crucial aspect of *Hitler's* thinking is that the Jews represent a threat to the inevitable and healthy struggle of different nations for world domination. Second, *Jung's* view is that each nation has a different and identifiable national psychology that is, in some mysterious manner, an innate factor.

At first sight, juxtaposing these two points of view might seem innocuous or pointless or even distasteful in itself. It is certainly not my intention to make a straightforward comparison of Hitler and Jung. But if we go on to explore *the place of the Jews in Jung's mental ecology*, to find out where they are situated in his perspective on the world, then the juxtaposition of the two points of view takes on a far more profound significance. For my intention has been to see whether there is anything in the essence of Jung's thinking about the Jews, anything in its underlying structure and assumptions, that must lead him to anti-Semitism, perhaps forcing honest men and women to give up their interest in analytical psychology.

My perception is that the ideas of nation and of national difference form an interface between the Hitlerian phenomenon and Jung's analytical psychology. For, as the psychologist of nations, Jung's theorizing was threatened by the existence of the Jews, this strange nation without a land and, hence, in Jung's words of 1918, lacking a chthonic quality, a good relation to the earth.[26] Jung's whole approach to "the psychology of the nation" was threatened by this strange nation without cultural forms—that is, without *national* cultural forms—of its own and hence, in Jung's words of 1933, requiring a "host nation."[27] (A more detailed discussion of the difference between "culture" and "cultural forms" takes place below.)

What threatens Jung, in particular, can be discovered by inquiring closely into what he means when he describes "Jewish psychology." His use of the term is dramatically inconsistent.

First, there is Jewish psychology defined as the psychological characteristics to be found in a typical Jewish person, and not found in a typical member of another ethnic or racial group. Jung argues that everyone is affected by his or her background, and this leads to all kinds of prejudices and assumptions: "every child knows that differences exist."[28] One may disagree or agree with Jung's views on what Jews are like; I have already said that I do not consider such views to be psychological at all. The observation that there are differences in cultural tradition is not the same as the assertion that there are differences in the actual process of psychological functioning, and I do not think Jung manages to validate that assertion.

Jung's second use of this term "Jewish psychology" has a quite different and more provocative implication. Here he is referring to systems of psychology developed by Jews like Freud and Adler, systems that claim universal applicability and truth. Such a psychology is a "leveling psychology" in that it undermines the idea of national differences.[29] Such a psychology has erred in applying "Jewish categories . . . indiscriminately to German and Slavic Christendom."[30] We are tempted to make the "unpardonable mistake [of] accepting the conclusions of a Jewish psychology as generally valid."[31] It is not psychoanalysis that is the problem but *Jewish* psychoanalysis—rather a different thing.

Is Jung saying that the theories of psychoanalysis reflect Jewish psychology, meaning typical Jewish character traits, as exemplified in Freud himself? If so, he surely goes far beyond his habitual position that all psychological theorizing is a "subjective confession." Even the prejudice-ridden personal friction between Jung and Freud, which undeniably existed, would not explain why for Jung this became his reading of the whole of psychoanalysis.

It seems that, for Jung, there is an extra ingredient: the Jews as a group, typified by Freudian psychoanalysis, represent a strain of *psychological denationalization*, leveling out all national psychological differences. Psychoanalysis therefore occupies a place in Jung's mind *analogous* to the place occupied in Hitler's mind by capitalism and communism. The great fears are, respectively, of "leveling" and of "denationalizing." Jung and Hitler react to the Jews in differing ways, of course, but the leveling aim of Jewish psychology and the denationalizing aim of Jewish political and economic activity represent a similar threat to each of them. So each develops a similar obsession.

For Hitler it takes the form of an obsession with a Jewish "spirit," functioning as a pestilential bacillus, undermining the very idea of nation. For Jung it takes the form of an obsession with a Jewish psychology, capable of being imposed on all other ethnic groups and, above all, on all other national psychologies.

It might also be possible to juxtapose Hitler's geographical expansionism with Jung's psychological expansionism. The former would result from Hitler's feeling threatened by the Jews and the latter from Jung's feeling threatened by "Jewish psychology." However, this juxtaposition is more of an intuition than something that can be justified by an examination of the writings of the two men.

I mentioned that Jung's use of the phrase "cultural forms" rather than "culture" is significant. It can be seen that, for Jung, the missing elements in Jewish history and experience that would have made the emergence of Jewish cultural forms possible are those of nation and land. In a letter to C. E. Benda in 1934 he writes:

> Between culture and cultural form there is, as we know, an essential difference. The Swiss, for instance, as you rightly remark, are a people with a culture but no cultural form of their own. For this, as you rightly remark, certain conditions are needed, such as the size of a people and its ties to the soil, etc. . . . A people with no ties to the soil, having neither land nor homeland, is commonly called nomadic.[32]

Writing to James Kirsch in the same year, Jung once again emphasizes the importance of land and nationhood to the creation of cultural forms by pointing out that Jewish cultural forms might come into being in Palestine. Jung makes the interesting point in this letter that the Jews often become the carriers or even protectors of the culture in which they live, something that was certainly true of prewar Germany. However, I think many would agree that Jung did not know enough about Jewish culture to make some of these assertions. Be that as it may, the issue here has been to clarify the nature of the threat that the Jews present to Jung's conception of national psychological differences.

JUNG AND THE *FÜHRERPRINZIP*

I have criticized Jung for using his leadership and authority as a psychologist for nonpsychological purposes. I used the words "Jung's leadership" deliberately to raise the question of where Jung stood both as a leader and in relation to the theory and practice of leadership.

That Jung had a desire for leadership and behaved like the leader of a movement is still a contentious claim to make within analytical psychology. The part played by Jung's own desire for power in bringing about the break with Freud is often underestimated. Jung himself was emphatic that, unlike Freud, he had no ambition to be a leader and was not interested in forming a school of psychology, in actively spreading his ideas, or in training analysts. In my book *Jung and the Post-Jungians*, I sought to show that Jung displayed many of the features of a typical leader: sometimes maintaining his rule by dividing his followers, selecting individuals for particular support (often by writing forewords to their books), and eventually laying down rather tough academic criteria for the professional training of analysts. In 1935 Jung explicitly claimed Drs. W. M. Kranefeldt, Gustav Heyer, and Gerhard Adler as "members of my school."[33] How can we reconcile this with Jung's exclamation "Thank God I am Jung and not a Jungian"? Jung's denial of the existence of Jungians is often repeated by those most closely associated with him. I think that Jung's technique was to flatter his followers and hence bind them more closely to him, by maintaining that he did not want or have disciples; therefore, those involved with Jung could not possibly be mere disciples.

It can be argued that Jung relegated his leadership ambitions to his shadow. If so, then we may find something psychological and personal in Jung's keen interest in the *Führer*. But there is much more to it than that, and I want to contribute something more profound than the "wild" assertion that Hitler was Jung's shadow. After all, we are talking of the "decade of the dictators," so it is certainly not simply a personal issue for Jung.

In the late 1930s Jung was a prime mover in the drawing up of a list of propositions concerning the theory and practice of psychotherapy. The "Fourteen Points," also known as "Views Held in Common,"[34] were an attempt to bring unity to depth psychology. We can see now that the seemingly inherent tendency of depth psychology to fragment made this a forlorn hope, practically speaking. But we may well wonder at the use of a political catch phrase dating from the time of the formation of the League of Nations to characterize this effort. Jung wanted to be the dominant psychological theorist of the day. He regarded his approach to analysis as subsuming Adler's and Freud's.[35] Thus, any Jungian analysis would include the relevant features of an analysis of each of the other schools, although the vital last stage of analysis known as "transformation" was said to be possible only under the aegis of Jung's approach.

Bearing these reflections in mind, we can turn our attention to Jung's comments about *political* leadership, for example in the famous interview by Dr. Weizsäcker on Radio Berlin in 1933. Jung told his listeners, using the key word *Führer*, that "every great movement culminates in a leader."[36] Even more interesting is Jung's opinion that the prerequisite for successful leadership is self-knowledge: "If [the leader] doesn't know himself, how is he to lead others? That is why the true leader is always one who has the courage to be himself."[37]

Matthias von der Tann has made a careful linguistic analysis of Jung's remarks in this interview.[38] It was only in 1987 that the full German text of the interview once again became available in the public domain, and an important result of von der Tann's research is to highlight how the English translation consistently mutes Jung's imagery, making his remarks altogether more statesmanlike and less inflammatory.[39] Von der Tann demonstrates that on many occasions Jung used words and phrases that would have had a particular association for German listeners. These words and phrases echo Nazi ideology and propaganda and can be said to constitute a message: Jung supports the Nazi cause.[40]

Jung was the first to insist, in 1913, that a prospective analyst be analyzed (in what is nowadays called the training analysis).[41] Among the many reasons for this requirement is the observation that the patient can go only so far as the analyst has gone, psychologically speaking. So the analyst's neurosis is the brake on the patient's growth—or, as Jung said of the leader, "if he doesn't know himself, how is he to lead others?" As far as Jung's version of the *Führerprinzip* (the principle of unquestioned leadership) is concerned, I cannot think of a better short definition of individuation than "having the courage to be oneself."[42]

With the politics of intellectual endeavor in mind, I want to ask if there is really anything wrong with a great thinker trying to influence other people, promote his work, and be a leader. Why do Jungians continue to deny that Jung was actively involved in the ideological marketplace—for instance, in 1930s Germany, where the banning of Freud left a vacuum in depth psychology? There is obviously some strange investment in sticking to Jung's public version of himself: an unworldly, even other-worldly poetic genius, naively indifferent to professional and other kinds of politics, who had almost to be forced to become president of the International General Medical Society for Psychotherapy. One has only to read the Freud-Jung letters, in which Jung reveals himself as an enthusiastic "politician," to understand where the naiveté really lies. After all, Jung did not display much hesitation when asked by Freud to become president of the International Psycho-Analytic Association.

Jung was certainly not completely dominated by his desire for leadership. He really did seem able to value other people's points of view and, above all, he had a great capacity to tolerate uncertainty and not knowing. He is believable when he says that "agreement would only spell one-sidedness and desiccation" and that we need many theories before we get "even a rough picture of the psyche's complexity."[43] But Jung's elitism is always just below the surface, for nature is, after all, "aristocratic."[44] The idea of leadership, like that of nation, forms a psychological backdrop to the interplay of Nazis, Jews, Jungians, and Freudians that we have been examining. Nazi claims to leadership are self-evident; Jewish claims to primacy in the field of moral development are well known; the activities of the Freudian "committee," set up by Ernest Jones to ensure that defectors were not taken seriously, illustrate the Freudian desire for hegemony. The Jungian portion of this epidemic should be denied no longer.

ANALYTICAL PSYCHOLOGY AND RENEWAL

What about the future of analytical psychology? Reviewing the troubled and tragic history of psychoanalysis in Germany, Robert Wallerstein, then president of the International Psycho-Analytic Association, used these words: "we need to underline the implicit invitation (nay, demand) that all of us in psychoanalysis reflect together on what this means for our common humanity and where our psychoanalytic identities can fit meaningfully into it."[45] Similarly, can analytical psychologists employ psychological and critical reflections on Jung, anti-Semitism, and the Nazis so that some kind of personal and professional renewal results? Could this lead to a more productive engagement of analytical psychology, and also of depth psychology in general, with the public sphere and with culture?

Since Jung's death in 1961, analytical psychology *has* sought to renew itself, through contact with psychoanalysis, religion, classical mythology, even theoretical physics. But what about renewal from within, through the new discoveries that come from a self-directed psychological and critical attitude, an analytical working over and working through of the events of the past? Can analytical psychology learn from its founder's experiences? I suggest that renewal will not occur until Jungians resolve their work of mourning for Jung. Once again, I would add that Jungians are not alone in having problems disidentifying from the great man who still dominates their discipline. As Wallerstein said in a presidential address to the Freudian group: "For so many of us, Sigmund Freud remains our lost object, our unreachable genius, whose passing we have perhaps never properly mourned, at least not in emotional fullness."[46]

Only when Jung has been mourned can anything be learned from Jung the social and cultural phenomenon rather than from Jung the man, the flawed (and hence overanalyzed) leader. If this could be done and if we were then to attempt to sketch out a program of renewal for analytical psychology, what would that program look like?

DEPTH PSYCHOLOGY, DIFFERENCE, AND NATIONALISM

To begin with, I think it would help if depth psychologists of all persuasions were to cease expanding the national boundaries of the psychological kingdom and try to work cooperatively with their colleagues in the social sciences. This would mean stopping an abuse of our authority when we define the typical psychology of this or that group—Jews, Germans, African Americans, homosexuals, women, men. Whether we like it or not, depth psychology and politics are connected. As a recognition of that, we should consider expressly allying ourselves with marginal and so-called minority groups, for that is the category where we ourselves belong. We could contribute our limited but profound expertise to the achievement of their goals. Jung aligned himself with and sought power; we should align ourselves with the powerless. We would do this by using our analytical capacity to work on a clarification of the psychological experience of being Jew, German, African American, homosexual, woman, man. We would assist such groups in getting behind the defensive stereotypes imposed by a threatened dominant culture as we explore the nature of difference itself. It is subversive work, breaking the contemporary taboo on the discussion of certain differences (racial, national, ethnic). But it has to be done. After all, many of the most convincing objections to *Freudian* theory rest on a rejection of its supposedly universal generalizations, which are in fact suffused by the specific ambience of fin-de-siècle Vienna.

For I have not been arguing that there are *no* differences between nations (or between races, or between sexes, or between classes). But it is crucial that these differences not be defined or predefined. It is impossible to classify such differences; they are terra incognita. The analyst is not an authority or teacher who has a priori knowledge of the psychological implications of the patient's ethnic and cultural background. Rather he or she is a mediator who enables the patient to experience and express his or her *own* difference.[47] The one thing analysts are good at is getting people to talk about what they implicitly know but have not yet consciously expressed.

I think that Jung himself was trying, with an inadequate methodology and hence with mixed results, to make just this kind of analysis of difference. In 1934 he wrote to A. Pupato:

> The question that I broached regarding the peculiarities of Jewish psychology does not presuppose any intention on my part to depreciate Jews, but is merely an attempt to single out and formulate the mental idiosyncrasies that distinguish Jews from other people. No sensible person will deny that such differences exist, any more than he will deny that there are essential differences in the mental attitude of Germans and Frenchman. . . . Again, nobody with any experience of the world would deny that the psychology of an American differs in a characteristic and unmistakable way from that of an Englishman.[48]

Jung's view of the origins of the idiosyncrasies that constitute difference is that they come from (1) the individual, (2) the family, (3) the nation, race, climate, locality, and history.[49] *The seeds of a multidisciplinary approach are here.*

Moving out of the consulting room, depth psychologists could initiate a psychological exploration of a world in which racial strife is as destructive as national strife. Such a world urgently needs a pluralistic psychological model (or vision) in which difference is truly valued, in which diversity need not become the reason for schism, and in which competition and bargaining—between race, class, sex, nation—are given a new valency: as normative and mutually enriching. Moreover, there may even be a distinctly political value in trying to understand difference more profoundly. In the same letter of 1934, Jung wrote to Pupato:

> I would consider it most fortunate if, for example, Germany and France took the trouble to understand each other better and could appreciate and acknowledge each other's characteristic values. But the way things are, each explains the other in terms of the assumptions of its own psychology, as you can convince yourself daily by reading the French and German newspapers. That people are also all alike is by this time a familiar fact, but it leads to no misunderstandings. These come from the differences, which should therefore be a worthy subject of investigation.[50]

Here we can make *creative* use of the rejection by Jung of the imposition of psychology derived from the cultural experience of one group upon another.[51]

Alongside the many problems with Jung's ideas about nation and race that we have been tracking, there are also the seeds of a productive and useful approach to difference. Even if Jung's list-making method and his ideology of complementarity are suspect, his intuitions of the importance of exploring differences, preserving them, even celebrating them, remain intact. When I write of the renewal of analytical psychology, I mean *reconnecting to Jung's intuition about the importance of difference while discarding excessive dependence on "the opposites," on oppositional thinking, and, above all, on essentialism—the dogma that says that things are as they are because it's only natural for them to be that way.*

Concerning differences in national psychology, if we resist the temptation to indulge in typology and offer to a multidisciplinary endeavor *only* what we have learned as depth psychologists, then another kind of picture emerges. Generalizations about national character and psychology can be understood as a form of myth-making crucial to a sense of *Gemeinschaft* (community). National characteristics, or rather what are claimed as national characteristics, are revealed as metaphors and as part of the contemporary quest for *Gemeinschaft*. There is, these days, a yearning for a preindustrial time when societal relations seemed to have been governed by tradition and agriculture rather than by politics and commerce. The question of the psychological influence of the earth can be tackled psychologically and understood as a group's attempt to express its uniqueness, its own national difference. The stress on "earth" rather than race contains an exceedingly powerful antiracist potential, making a pluralistic vision of society psychologically viable. The differences that we inherit, culturally and biologically, are of value; modern desires for national identity reflect just that.

It is a matter of the very shape and texture of the countryside: "the old track fading on the hillside, the tumbled stone of a Saxon steading, winter sunlight on new ploughland, the strip of dark beneath the trees, the names repeating in a country churchyard."[52] That's England. Or, from a letter written by a Japanese scholar to his prime minister: "the Japanese spirit is to be found in sacred old rocks and pine trees . . . only the Japanese know instinctively how to live in harmony with nature."[53] The Romantic nature of such nationalistic expressions should not obscure their potentially revolutionary nature or their feelings for history. Though clearly in reaction to the evolution of modern societies, there is an aura of renewal and group rebirth that has a political significance; it need not lead inevitably toward fascism.

We should recall, however, that there is no such thing as a single, immutable "pure" national character; a belief in national "purity" can have only one disastrous outcome. The problem is exemplified in the word "blood." For example, when Jung writes that there is a Jewish psychology based on "blood and history,"[54] we need to see through "blood" to understand it as referring also to the shared history of a connected group of people. But sometimes "blood" is taken literally, and then the image of purity is bound to arise.

When the idea of national purity is abroad, we tend to forget the mutability of nationhood, the ways in which, over time, nations define and redefine themselves. If humanity did begin in one part of Africa, as many now think, then it is clear that the world as we find it is one station on an unknowably long journey. In Europe, the rise and decline of empires, city-states, and supranational federations is well documented but, as this mutability is anxiety-provoking, easily set aside. In India and in Africa, modern patterns of tribal organization and separation often turn out to be of surprisingly recent origin. For nations are ideas; Charles de Gaulle spoke of *une certaine idée de la France*. The mutability of nation-hood is another reason why the presence of depth psychologists is required: nation is a coruscating fantasy. But Jung's conception of the role of the psychologist was not sufficiently questioning of the apparent fixity of contemporary national arrangements.

I wrote the bulk of this paper in 1988, before the massive political changes in Eastern Europe had taken place and before the Baltic and Russian moves to secede from the Soviet Union had got under way. I could not have known then the extent to which discussion of nationalism and issues of national psychology would move into the foreground. For example, the question of German reunification positively reeked of an immense anxiety about the true nature of German national psychology (something that is more or less assumed to exist). Though unease about German national psychology is usually admitted to be subjective, difficult to catch in the nets of rationality, it is obviously an exceedingly potent factor in the debate.

Close on the heels of the upsurge of nationalism in Europe comes that classic, perennial parasite on nationalism—anti-Semitism. Whether in the rise of Pamyat in the Soviet Union, or the character defamation of the Hungarian Free Democrats (heavily defeated in the first free elections), or the demonstrations in Poland in 1990 for a Europe free of Jews, or the postrevolutionary murmurings in Rumania about getting rid of the Magyars and Jews, or the desecration in 1990 of Bertolt Brecht's tombstone in East Berlin (it was daubed with the words "Jewish pig," though he was not Jewish)—and not forgetting the wave of anti-Semitism in France at the same time or the scarcely disguised blaming of Jews in the United States for the materialistic excesses of the Reagan era—it is clear that whatever threatens and upsets people about the Jews has upped its work rate once again. I feel that the content of my paper on Jung and anti-Semitism takes on a new and depressing significance here. Could it be the Jewish images in Jung's mind in the 1930s that are also the problem today: the nomads with no cultural forms of their own; the Wandering Jews; world citizens; international communists (now, incredibly, reviled for their Marxism in the Eastern European countries and the Soviet Union); wily international capitalists; scholars with a poor relation to the earth but nevertheless protected by *internationally* recognized Ph.D's? Could it be these Jews, the ones who threatened both Jung and Hitler, these Jewish enemies of national difference, that are the problem?

Whatever the problem really is, there is no use in merely speaking out against nationalism, because that would be a simplistic and unrealistic response to such a complicated matter. Rather, we need to make a psychological distinction between different aspects of nationalism, or, putting it another way, between different nationalisms. On the one hand, we have nationalism serving a positive collective psychological function, socially progressive, historically liberalizing and democratizing, reconnecting people to their roots and traditions, celebrating differences in a cornucopia of languages. Nationalism is preferable to world empire or the played-out game of geopolitics dominated by the superpowers. But, on the other hand, we have what could be called "spiritualized nationalism," the creed of the *Kulturnation*, with the emphasis on kinship, blood, people (*Volk*), earth—the whole mysterious, mystifying Romantic lexicon. Spiritualized nationalism obliterates the social contract, constitutional rights, the political dimensions of life itself. What is collective and held in common is decreed by birth and not by consent. As Saint-Just said before his execution during the French Revolution, "There is something terrible about the holy love of one's nation, for it is so excessive that it sacrifices everything to the public interest, without mercy, without fear, without humanity."

As far as Germany in the 1930s was concerned, we can see that, without enemies, the *Volk* could not exist. Perhaps this dependence on the Other for national definition was more marked in German nationalism dating from the end of the eighteenth century, due to specific features of German political evolution. From a psychological perspective, the creation of an entity other to the nation facilitates the expression of national aggression because then the nation's Other serves as the object of aggression. The role of projection is also important; the *Volk*-identified nation evacuates what, unconsciously, it experiences as its undesirable features into the designated enemies (without and, as in the case of Germany and the German Jews, within). Complementarity plays its usual suspect role, so that German virtues are complemented by Russian (or Jewish) vices. In addition, though the *Volk* may sometimes seem all-powerful, it can be and often is manipulated by a leader or leadership class.

The Germany of the 1930s performed a collective psychological function for the rest of the world at that time, which, in some respects, the Holocaust continues to perform in our time. The great economic depressions of the 1920s and '30s brought suffering throughout the industrial world to ruling class and proletariat alike. The kind of national organization Hitler was evolving salved desires for retaliation and rage against the invisible Fates of economic forces on the part of both rulers and ruled in countries outside Germany. Those classes with aspirations for economic and political leadership saw these brought into concrete form by the alliance of the *Führerprinzip* with German industrial power, while those with little or no economic power could identify with the world historical role assigned by Hitler to members of his *Volk*. The final solution, even in its initial stages, met these needs. This might go some way to explaining the ambivalence of the world community at that time toward Hitler's expansionism—an ambivalence that continues to provoke guilt—a guilt that contributes to a preoccupation with the Holocaust. For the Holocaust was not only the supreme crisis of nationalism, anti-Semitism, and racism; it was also a crisis for industrialism and modernity itself.

I can see no alternative to saying that, at the present time, we do not have a satisfyingly full answer to questions of the influence of national (or ethnic, or racial) background upon individual psychology, or the part played by what we call "psychology" in the formation of what we call "nation." Psychologists can join with scientists, social scientists, and environmentalists in a study of these matters. If they do join up in this way, then I think Jung's contribution will prove seminal and valuable. As he wrote to James Kirsch in 1934, "Nationalism—disagreeable as it is—is a *sine qua non*, but the individual must not remain stuck in it. On the other hand, in so far as he is a particle in the mass he must not raise himself above it either."[55]

We have to use our judgment and make a distinction: nationalism can lead to paranoia and chauvinism, but it also leads to the undoubtedly healthy and positive desire not to be dominated by something or someone felt as foreign: a foreign suffocating mother, a foreign castrating father, a foreign, disciplinarian superego. We cannot eliminate competition and division between nations. But why should we? Pluralistic psychology shows us that competition and division, mediated by bargaining, are productive paths to follow.

CONCLUDING REFLECTIONS

My hope is that playing Jung through Hitler, Hitler through Jung, emotionally wearing though it undoubtedly is, will lead to our making a contribution to the contemporary celebration of difference.

Then analytical psychology can joyfully renounce the top table, the level of nation-states—for we have seen what a terrible mess we make when we try to sit there. But there is no need to retreat behind the barricade of the "clinical." We need, I think, to sit down with the materially disadvantaged and the socially frightened, as well as with educated analysands. We should be engaged when a Law of Return is passed and small ethnic groups gain or regain their lands; hence we should be engaged when an *intifada* erupts. We *should* be concerned with promised lands as well as with sovereign nation-states; with the people as well as with their leaders.

We may have to question the very way we work, for private practice with a privileged clientele is not politically neutral. Our way of working has affected our way of thinking. We may have to question our automatic preference for the inner world and our tendency to make "inner" and "outer" or "private" and "public" into polar opposites, rejecting multidisciplinary work as "unpsychological."

Before the war, Hitler proclaimed all German modern art to be "decadent." Officially approved realistic art was sponsored. Two exhibitions were organized—one of the degenerate and one of the official art. The degenerate exhibition was viewed by two million people, still the world record for any single art exhibition, whereas less than four hundred thousand attended the official exhibition.[56]

I have exhibited the decadent and degenerate side of analytical psychology. We have had reparation to make, and we have much to offer a depth psychology engaged with processes of political and cultural transformation.

Notes

I am grateful for the many helpful comments on earlier drafts of this paper from Matthias von der Tann and Fred Plaut in Berlin, Gustav Dreifuss in Haifa, Michael Vannoy Adams in New York, Bradley Te Paske in Santa Fe, Kendra Crossen in Boston, and Rosie Parker, Coline Covington, Rabbi David Freeman, and Rosemary Gordon in London. Responsibility for the views expressed is, of course, mine.

1. R. Bulka, Editorial, *Journal of Psychology and Judaism* 6, no. 2 (Spring/ Summer 1982), p. 79.

2. Donald Winnicott, *The Spontaneous Gesture: Selected Letters*, edited by F. Rodman (Cambridge & London: Harvard University Press, 1987), p. 4.

3. See C. G. Jung, *Letters*, vol. 1, p. 156; W. McGuire, ed., *The Freud/Jung Letters*, pp. 13, 38, 126, 166.

4. *CW* 7, para. 235.

5. Jolande Jacobi, *The Psychology of C. G. Jung* (London: Kegan Paul, Trench, Trubner, 1942), pp. 31–32.

6. M. Banton, *The Idea of Race* (London: Tavistock, 1977), p. 2.

7. See Andrew Samuels, "Comment on 'Jung: A Racist' by Dalal," *British Journal of Psychotherapy* 4, no. 3 (1988).

8. See S. Graham, *Hitler, Germans, and the "Jewish Question"* (Princeton: Princeton University Press, 1984), pp. 91–118; S. Haffner, *The Meaning of*

Hitler: Hitler's Uses of Power: His Successes and Failures (New York: Macmillan, 1979).

9. CW 10, para. 19.

10. CW 10, para. 103; written in 1927.

11. M. Loomis, "Balancing the Shields: Native American Teachings and the Individuation Process," *Quadrant* 21, no. 2 (1988): 37.

12. E.g., CW 10, para. 45.

13. CW 7, p. 4.

14. Banton, *The Idea of Race*, p. 13.

15. See H. Kohn, *The Idea of Nationalism* (Oxford: Oxford University Press, 1967).

16. CW 8, para. 29.

17. CW 10, para. 389; emphases added.

18. CW 10, para. 391.

19. CW 10, para. 19.

20. M. von der Tann, personal communication, 1989.

21. CW 10, para. 921.

22. See Andrew Samuels, *The Plural Psyche: Personality, Morality and the Father* (London & New York: Routledge, 1989), pp. 107–122.

23. This is also true of nineteenth- and twentieth-century anti-Semitism in general. See M. Marrus, "Popular Anti-Semitism," *Catalogue of the Dreyfus Affair: Art, Truth and Justice* (New York: Jewish Museum, 1987).

24. Quoted in Graham, *Hitler, Germans, and the "Jewish Question,"* p. 94.

25. This question of the nationhood of the Jews is still a pressing problem, especially in the context of Middle Eastern politics, as Gustav Dreifuss (personal communication, 1989) has reminded me.

26. CW 10, para. 18.

27. CW 10, para. 353.

28. CW 10, para. 1029.

29. Ibid.

30. CW 10, para. 354.

31. CW 7, para. 240n.

32. Jung, *Letters*, vol. 1, p. 201.

33. CW 10, para. 1060.

34. CW 10, para. 1072.

35. E.g., in the paper "Problems of Modern Psychotherapy," CW 16.

36. C. G. Jung, *C. G. Jung Speaking*, p. 79.

37. Ibid., p. 77.

38. M. von der Tann, "A Jungian Perspective on the Berlin Institute for Psychotherapy: A Basis for Mourning," *San Francisco Jung Institute Library Journal* 8, no. 4 (1989).

39. C. G. *Jung Speaking*, pp. 73–79.

40. Incidentally, the official English translation of the *Collected Works of C. G. Jung* contains many similar examples of sanitization.

41. CW 4, paras. 586–587.

42. See also Andrew Samuels, Foreword to *Essays on Contemporary Events*.

43. CW 16, para. 198.

44. CW 7, paras. 198, 235; CW 17, paras. 343, 345.

45. R. Wallerstein, "Psychoanalysis in Nazi Germany: Historical and Psychoanalytical Lessons," *Psychoanalysis and Contemporary Thought* 11, no. 2 (1987): 360–361.

46. R. Wallerstein, "One Psychoanalysis or Many?," *International Journal of Psycho-Analysis* 69, no. 1 (1988): 9.

47. Stanley Perelman, personal communication, 1989.

48. Jung, *Letters*, vol. 1, pp. 147–149.

49. CW 10, para. 1025.

50. Jung, *Letters*, vol. 1, pp. 147–149.

51. CW 7, para. 240n.

52. Lovibond quoted in I. Buruma, "England, Whose England?," *The Spectator*, September 9, 1989.

53. Ibid.

54. CW 10, para. 10.

55. In Jung, *Letters*, vol. 1, p. 162.

56. From the catalogue of the exhibition *Stationen der Moderne*, Berlin, 1988.

Jung
and Anti-Semitism

Paul Roazen

Paul Roazen is Professor of Social and Political Science at York University in Toronto. He is the author of six books on the history of psychoanalysis, including *Freud: Political and Social Thought* (1986), *Freud and His Followers* (1986), and *Encountering Freud: The Politics and Histories of Psychoanalysis* (1990), as well as the editor of several volumes, such as *Sigmund Freud* (1987).

Roazen observes in this paper that Jung has not received the recognition he deserves for his contributions to twentieth-century thought. As a historian, a non-Jungian, and a Jew, he concludes that Jung's political views have been responsible for a general resistance to his ideas, and insists that Jung must be held accountable for his statements.

The subject of Jung and anti-Semitism is not one that I approach with any eagerness. Since I am myself a Jew, although an inadequately practicing one, I am bound to have a special concern with the fate of the Jewish people in this most terrible of centuries.

On the other hand, I am also a student of the history of psychoanalysis, and I am convinced that Jung's stature in the story of the development of depth psychology has been badly misunderstood. Perhaps one anecdote can serve to illustrate the historiographical problem I believe we face. Once, during the course of a few luncheon discussions I had a few years ago with Paul Ricoeur in Toronto, we got onto the subject of his book *Freud and*

Philosophy. Since Ricoeur was both modest and self-critical about how he thought he had failed to achieve his objective in this book, I raised the subject of Jung. It seemed to me, and I told Ricoeur, that if he wanted to accomplish the philosophic purposes he had in mind, he would have been better advised to pick Jung as a central thinker instead of Freud. For Jung's view of the unconscious, rather than Freud's, seemed to me much closer to Ricoeur's thinking. The mention of Jung's name, however, posed a special perplexity to Ricoeur. For one could not in Paris, according to Ricoeur, read Jung; he was "on the Index" of forbidden books among French intellectuals.

Ricoeur is himself a Protestant, and one of his sons is a practicing psychoanalyst in France. I found Ricoeur sophisticated about the struggles within psychoanalysis in Paris, where so much is being published these days in connection with Freud, and yet Ricoeur seemed wholly unfamiliar with Jung's writings. And there was I, who had written on Freud, suggesting to Ricoeur the overlooked significance of Jung.

And yet as an intellectual historian I think it is impossible to divorce Jung's psychology from his politics. When I teach at my university the writings of Dostoevsky and Nietzsche, a standard question I ask is whether, and to what degree, their psychologies must need lead to their politics. Just as Freud himself admired Dostoevsky, without at all going along with his particular set of political beliefs, so it is possible, I think, to say of Jung that he made a great and lasting contribution to psychology, without ignoring the nature of his collaboration with the Nazis.

I should spell out more concretely why I consider Jung to be so important in the history of ideas. First of all, I do not think that Freud ever had a better critic than Jung. It is often said that Freud himself saw some of his own worst failings, and there is a good deal of truth in that proposition; yet Freud usually managed to handle all the possible objections to his own system of thought so masterfully that readers have been inclined to go along with his dismissal of the possible flaws in his psychology.

Jung, however, was to my knowledge the first to insist that authoritarianism was implicit in Freud's therapeutic technique.

Jung was also, doubtless in part because of his personal contact with Freud, the earliest to suggest that all analysts in the future be obliged to undergo training analyses. I should say that I am not by any means sure that this was such a good idea; the concept of a training analysis has had some unfortunate side consequences, in infantilizing candidates, for example, and ensuring their indoctrination into a particular teacher's way of doing things. It is of course for others than myself, since I have never been a clinician, to weigh the pros and cons of the institution of a training analysis.

I do believe, however, based on my own historical research, that not enough attention has been given to the whole vexed question of psychoanalytic education. Supervised psychoanalyses were invented precisely as a device to check the power that a senior training analyst is bound to have. But one finds so much sectarianism in psychoanalysis, right up until today, that it does not seem to me that previous devices have succeeded in being as effective as they should be. The literature keeps reinventing the wheel; one finds people from different schools of thought unaware of what others have been up to.

Two vignettes can illustrate what I have in mind. Once, during an interview with Jolande Jacobi in Switzerland in 1966, I raised the concept, then fashionable in orthodox psychoanalysis, of "regression in the service of the ego." Although Dr. Jacobi had known Ernst Kris personally in Vienna, and immediately understood the purport of what I described as his notion, she had not been familiar with it; she agreed with me that it bore striking similarities to Jung's own approach. To give another example, I recall Anthony Storr telling me after he had stayed in Chicago once that the Freudian analysts there seemed to have picked up some of Jung's ideas about how to proceed with short-term psychotherapy. The Chicago Psychoanalytic Institute was founded by Franz Alexander, and although I am confident that Dr. Alexander was not directly influenced by Jung, he had worked out ideas on his own in the 1940s that bore many analogies to those Jung had had a generation earlier. Ideological enemies of Franz Alexander, like the orthodox Kurt Eissler, would no doubt be delighted to hear of Jungian parallels in Alexander's work, but I am raising the analogy in connection with intellectual history rather than as an aspect of the partisan politics of sectarian squabbling.

Different schools of psychoanalysis are like ships passing in the night. Although it might seem that the two examples I have just given are instances of people who have grown up within Jung's framework not being aware enough of Freudian contributions, I am certain that the general neglect is much more the other way around. In my experience those who have been trained as Freudians are far less likely ever to have read Jung than Jungians are apt to be familiar with Freud.

Perhaps the most striking instance of this in my own research came in the course of an interview I once conducted with René Spitz in Switzerland. "You won't believe," he told me, what Jung once "claimed": Jung had told Dr. Spitz that he had invented the idea of a training analysis. Spitz considered this preposterous, and as far as I know Freudians today still agree with him. Yet some years ago I came across a passage in Freud's writings where he specifically credits "the Zurich school," meaning Jung, with that suggestion.

Since I have indicated some of my reservations about the drawbacks that I think have been associated with training analyses, I should immediately list some of the more unquestionably positive contributions that I think Jung was able to make. He understood, fifty years before it occurred to orthodox analysts, that clinically infantile material could be used as a defense. The idea that a preoccupation with the childhood past could become an evasion was only later dubbed by Max Schur as "resistance from below." Jung also knew that dreams were not just expressions of wishes and that they had to do with the dreamer's own self, not only past loved ones. Jung looked on the unconscious more constructively, and with less suspicion, than Freud did, and therefore Jung was likely, at least according to his theory, to take a more positive attitude toward the presence of symptoms.

In reality, of course, despite the difference in age between the two men, Jung and Freud shared much in common. If one reads some of Jung's social philosophy, it sounds strikingly like that of Freud himself, even though both men wrote their own works long after their association was over. And in Freud's *Moses and Monotheism*, for example, he commits himself to many views on the nature of symbols that sound to me very like Jung's. Although I do not have the space to document this point here, I am pretty sure that in their concrete clinical practices both Jung and Freud, despite their falling out, continued to share more things in common than one might expect.

But I am afraid that in the course of indicating mỳ respect for Jung's stature within intellectual history, I have drifted too far from the subject at hand: anti-Semitism. It is obviously a very good sign that Jungians are able publicly to face up to this problem. Yet I myself am put in a great deal of inner conflict in addressing this topic.

Anti-Semitism is a vast subject, extending throughout Western thought, and the variety of prejudices about Jews constitutes a matter on which I cannot hope to be expert. With Jung, however, we are dealing with a specific problem that arises uniquely in connection with mid-twentieth-century intellectuals. Henry Adams, for example, died too early for anyone to get terribly exercised about the specifics of what he thought about Jews. It would be ahistorical to consider his views in the light of later events. Anti-Semitism is a deeply rooted part of Western culture and has touched many otherwise admirable thinkers. Hannah Arendt once wrote that the rise of the Nazis had finally put an end to comments about Jews that once were considered culturally allowable; for as soon as it became possible to see that anti-Semitism could lead to gas chambers, then no respectable person could permit cracks about Jews that once might have been thought acceptably run-of-the-mill.

Other eminent figures in the middle of our century, besides Jung, have been caught in the same bind of having expressed morally compromising points about Jews that have a special status because of their timing. I take it mainly as a matter of authority that Martin Heidegger was a great philosopher; he is perhaps the most extreme example of the betrayal of an intellectual's ethics that comes to mind, since he actually joined the Nazi party; although he did not generalize about Jews, he allowed himself at least one negative reference to an individual academic as a Jew that struck other Nazis as so poisonous that it backfired. Ezra Pound's poetry is, I am told, a great work of world literature; yet Pound gave hundreds of perfectly dreadful broadcasts in behalf of Mussolini's regime, programs that sometimes were rebroadcast from Berlin. And then again, it has recently been discovered how Paul de Man, the eminent literary critic, wrote anti-Semitic newspaper articles in his youth during the German occupation of Belgium in World War II.

Of all these men, Jung is the only one I feel expert enough about to defend, in terms of the great contribution he made to psychology. If, however, I were French, and my family had endured World War II, I might well be in Ricoeur's position of not ever having read Jung. The closer one is to the Holocaust, the harder it becomes to take some distance toward the political views that Jung was associated with. I am, however, among the lucky ones, born on this continent; but the accident of geography and history does not spare me the obligation of thinking about the ethical implications that Jung's political commitments entail.

I should be more explicit. It is not correct to compartmentalize psychology and politics. At the same time we should not go to the other extreme and weigh everything on the scale of political judgment; it is the totalitarian regimes that have made all of reality subservient to politics. And yet, without overdoing the implications of what Jung wrote and did in the 1930s, it is indeed relevant to an overall appreciation of his standing.

The details of the controversy about Jung and anti-Semitism are already well known. Nevertheless, though I admire Robertson Davies's novels very much, I once read a book review of his in the New York Times in which he blankly repudiated the idea that Jung was an anti-Semite. Curiously enough, to me at least, it was Freud himself who first leveled this charge against Jung, in the course of Freud's polemic On the History of the Psychoanalytic Movement. As I recall from having studied the Freud-Jung correspondence, I detected no signs of such prejudice on Jung's part coming up in their exchanges. But I have no doubt that on Freud's side his enthusiasm about Jung as a disciple stemmed in part from Freud's own special kind of anti-Semitism, his concern that psychoanalysis not become exclusively a Jewish affair and that the movement be led by a Gentile. The bitterness of Freud's disappointment in Jung, and Freud's disillusionment with himself as a leader, can be found in the themes that were preoccupying Freud in *Moses and Monotheism.*

It is not easy for me to cite chapter and verse of what Jung wrote about Jews. In 1934 he argued:

> The Jew, who is something of a nomad, has never yet created a cultural form of his own and as far as we can see never will, since all his instincts and talents require a more or less civilized nation to act as host for their development. . . . The "Aryan" unconscious has a higher potential than the Jewish; that is both the advantage and the disadvantage of a youthfulness not yet fully weaned from barbarism. In my opinion it has been a grave error in medical psychology up to now to apply Jewish categories—which are not even binding on all Jews—indiscriminately to German and Slavic Christendom. Because of this the most precious secret of the Germanic peoples—their creative and intuitive depth of soul—has been explained as a mass of banal infantilism, while my own warning voice has for decades been suspected of anti-Semitism. This suspicion emanated from Freud. He did not understand the Germanic psyche any more than did his Germanic followers. Has the formidable phenomenon of National Socialism, on which the whole world gazes with astonished eyes, taught them better? . . . That is why I say that the Germanic unconscious contains tensions and potentialities which medical psychology must consider in its evaluation of the unconscious.[1]

I have no doubt that much of what Jung had to say has some validity to it; I think that the truth of the matter is that Freud's psychology is characteristically a Jewish one, and that this accounts for some of its strengths as well as for the defects in it that are in need of correction.[2] But the point is, and here I am speaking as a political scientist, the worst of what Jung wrote came in the early days of the rise to power of the Nazis in Germany. Worse still, Jung traveled there to deliver his message; he undertook to make political choices, for which he must historically be held responsible. It was a time when, it will be recalled, Jewish psychotherapists were being forced to flee abroad or were suffering in Germany.

Jung seems to have been politically naive, even stupid; but I must say that what often looks like stupidity can mask prejudice and conviction. In Jung's case it is not as if others in the field did not try to point out to him at the time where he was going wrong. Wilhelm Reich was among those who denounced Jung, as did Gustav Bally of Zurich, eliciting Jung's 1934 "Rejoinder to Dr. Bally." It was Erich Fromm, a man of the left, who advised me to consult with Dr. Bally in Zurich about Jung's politics. (Unfortunately Bally died too soon for me to have been able to see him.)

Jung always claimed that he had undertaken to accept the leadership of the German Medical Society for Psychotherapy in June 1933 in order to protect the profession, and the Jews who practiced it, from needlessly suffering during the ravages of the Nazi regime. I have no doubt that Jung helped many Jewish refugees from Germany to reestablish themselves abroad. But when, in 1935, the Dutch members of Jung's reconstituted international society refused on political grounds to act as hosts for a congress, Jung wrote to them that they were compromising the neutrality of science.

It is simply not the case, however, that when one is talking about the Nazis it is possible to sustain such an appeal to neutral science. The Dutch were, I think, morally right in refusing to collaborate with Jung's call. Those of us intellectuals who during the Vietnam war felt passionately that the war was immoral found ourselves experiencing utter frustration for years; it is not easy to point to more than a few mild acts of protest on our part. I do not claim to be myself some kind of political hero. But I do not think it is necessary to gloss over what Jung did. I cannot avoid calling a spade a spade.

After World War II it might have been possible for Jung to have better made amends for what had happened. According to the Index of the papers of the British Foreign Office, in 1946 a "booklet" existed that bore the title "The Case of Dr. Carl G. Jung—Pseudo-Scientist Nazi Auxiliary" by Maurice Leon, which outlined "Dr. Jung's connection with Nazis and Nazi Plans."

Evidently there were Foreign Office minutes on a "proposed trial as war criminal." I have not succeeded in obtaining this documentation, which as I recall was still covered by a rule restricting access to state papers. Even if this particular file turns out to be wholly innocuous, still it is striking to me that as far as I know Jung never adequately acknowledged the immorality of any of his conduct. It might have been logically possible for him to have owned up to having made an error in judgment; but he stuck to his guns and made a consistent argument in his own defense.

Politically we are not talking about small potatoes. It is not as if we were evaluating why a particular political leader failed to resign, for example, from a government doing business with Hitler; appeasement does differ from being a fellow traveler. We are not even discussing the question of going along with a government that pursues a course that we disapprove of, or even would prefer to dissociate ourselves from.

In my opinion the rise of the Nazis is the most significant political event of the twentieth century. It is appalling to find Jung in June 1933 remarking approvingly: "as Hitler said recently. . . ." In the same interview on Radio Berlin he referred to "the aimless conversation of parliamentary deliberations" that "drone on. . . ."[3] And, as Edward Glover long ago pointed out, in 1936 Jung said: "The SS men are being transformed into a caste of knights ruling sixty million natives."[4] I have not attempted, nor could I bear to do so, a comprehensive review of all of Jung's political commentary.

Hitler did not seize power by force, but was duly elected to office; and the regime he displaced was a democratic one. So that for me one of the most distressing aspects of the whole matter is that a people willingly chose Hitler, knowing his program beforehand. Those of us who like to believe in democratic processes, and the enlightenment we associate with higher education, have to face up to the fact that Nazism came in such a highly cultured community. Freud himself, when warned of the danger of Hitlerism in Germany, was in some sense sound to have dismissed the dread prospect on the grounds that "the nation of Goethe could never go to the bad."

No one could have appreciated the full horrors of the Nazis. But intellectual historians do rightly wonder about what elements in Western culture may have fed the long-term sources of Hitlerism. Can it be that an emphasis on the legitimacy of the irrational in psychology does also, when introduced to the world of politics, encourage Nazi-like movements? It would not be too speculative, I think, to suppose that some of Jung's ideas had enough echo in what he heard from Germany from 1933 on for him to think that his work might successfully fit in there. But to the extent that his actions were opportunistically motivated, he is not going to come off well on this particular score.

Many of you already know about the story of the children at an international school in Paris who were once asked to write essays on the elephant. The English boy wrote about hunting elephants in Africa. The German boy wrote "The Sorrows of a Young Elephant." The French child wrote "On the Love Habits of the Elephant." And the Jewish boy called his contribution: "The Elephant and the Jewish Question."

The issue of anti-Semitism, however, does seem to me especially pertinent to Jung's thought as a whole. I know I could have chosen to address myself more evasively to the subject of the "Lingering Shadows" conference. But I originally accepted the invitation to speak on the issue of Jung and anti-Semitism. It took me ages before I could sit down and write what little I had to say; I pondered the matter for months, each time putting the matter to the back of my mind, and more than once I cried out in anguish to myself: "What am I going to say!" I do not believe in pussyfooting, and yet I hope it is clear that I have not approached the topic in an embattled mood. I trust that what I have said will not, under the circumstances, seem offensive. But I have tried my best to address myself to the problem.

Each of us makes choices, and these decisions become deeds. We in North America know little of the tormenting moral problems that have wracked less fortunate societies. Hitlerism is the worst form of evil I can think of; and therefore, because of Jung's politics and their links to the Nazis, his genuinely great contributions to psychology can only be fully appreciated and evaluated once they are understood in terms of their association with his social views, and yet somehow ultimately detached from the politics of Hitler's regime. Just as it is possible, I think, to divorce Dostoevsky's psychology from his politics, so I hope Jung's psychology will endure in spite of his brand of anti-Semitism.

Notes

1. Quoted in Paul Roazen, *Freud and His Followers,* pp. 291–92.
2. See ibid., especially pp. 22ff.
3. *C. G. Jung Speaking,* pp. 77–78.
4. Ibid., p. 103.

Scapegoating:
The Double Cross

Ann Belford Ulanov

Ann Belford Ulanov is a Jungian analyst, faculty member and supervisor at the C. G. Jung Institute of New York, and Christiane Brooks Johnson Professor of Psychiatry and Religion at Union Theological Seminary in New York. She is the author of nine books, including *The Wisdom of the Psyche* and, with her husband, Barry Ulanov, *Cinderella and Her Sisters: The Envied and the Envying*.

Somehow, in the Judeo-Christian tradition, scapegoating and redemption have become inseparable. This is what Ann Ulanov means by "The Double Cross," and she demonstrates the presence of this dynamic in Old Testament sacrifice and dietary proscriptions, the crucifixion of Jesus, anti-Semitism, and attitudes toward Jung, concluding that "we only scapegoat those who redeem us." She examines the scapegoating phenomenon in attitudes toward the Jews and in shadow projection in general, and questions how Jung, who professed a passionate attention to the existence of real evil, could have at first been blind to the evils of Nazi Germany.

I

Scapegoating and anti-Semitism are not subjects we can speak about objectively. We can only speak of them out of suffering—unconsciousness, abysmal pain and terror, rage and guilt, and a persistent longing to glimpse a way through their thickets of fear, sadism, violence, and despair.

Two crosses are always involved in scapegoating. The first cross represents suffering: we are nailed to cross-purposes, assaulted, brought to helplessness before the brute fact of evil. The opposites we would embrace pull us apart. The consciousness we strive for is opposed by unconsciousness. The help we offer turns out to hurt. The opposites do not just coincide: they clash; they collide. We are caught in a complex of opposites.

The second cross is the double-cross, the trick by one we trusted, the betrayal by someone or something that we counted on. In scapegoating we say to the other: You carry the suffering and I will punish you for carrying it. Those we expect to help betray instead. Boatloads of Jews seeking refuge from the Holocaust were turned back from the shores of this country. Jung, the friend of many Jews, finally said to Rabbi Leo Baeck, "I slipped up."[1] Christians, who follow One who came to fulfill the law in love, often generate prejudice and persecution instead. The Jews, chosen by God, elected to be God's bride, seem left behind by God in the camps of Auschwitz and Dachau. The Jews, abandoned by neighbors and nations to abysmal suffering, appear to refuse to identify their suffering with the suffering of others—the miseries of blacks victimized by whites, of Ukrainians systematically starved by their government, of Cambodians massacred by the Khmer Rouge, of the millions buried alive in Soviet gulags.[2]

We must go further and ask whether we who are concerned to discuss anti-Semitism are prepared now to scapegoat Jung and Freud and other depth psychologists as a double cross, to evade our own scapegoating. It relieves us to point to the prejudice of others, and especially such esteemed others as Jung and Freud, on whose work many of us have built our own work. Ultimately we double-cross ourselves by betraying our friends and befriending what betrays us.

Finally, the two crosses are one. The redemptive cross and the scapegoat cross are the same—someone or something to draw off the misery. We only scapegoat those who redeem us: Jesus, the Jew on the cross, double-crossed; the Jews, chosen by God, crucified as a people.

In Judaism (Lev. 16:1–28) two offerings must always be brought to the Lord—two doves, two turtles, two pigeons, two bulls, two rams, and finally two goats. The first goat is a sin offering. Its blood is sprinkled within the veil of the Holy of Holies before the Mercy Seat upon the Ark, where Yahweh will appear in a cloud. This goat's blood atones at the holy place for the uncleanness and transgressions of the children of Israel. Then the goat's blood is sprinkled outside the Holy of Holies on the altar, and the goat is taken outside the camp and burned—its own holocaust.

The second goat stays alive and is driven into the wilderness after the priest confesses in words delivered over it the iniquities of the children of Israel. This goat, loaded down with these sins, is sent away into a land which is not inhabited, into the desert outside the boundaries of community. These are the precincts of Azazel, the goat deity dwelling in the desert, to whom the sin offering is dispatched. Later, Azazel is called the leader of the fallen angels, the author of all sin (Enoch 6, 8, 10). Like Prometheus, he also instructs humans in essential human crafts. In later Jewish, Gnostic, and Muhammadan traditions, Azazel is called the leader of all demons. He is associated with the chthonic, demonic forces, both generative and destructive, sexual and combative, that prevail outside the boundaries of Israel.[3]

One set of sins is burnt up outside the camp of Israel and the second set of sins driven away to the place beyond the bounds. We can see how the Jewish people have been identified with both goats, suffering holocaust and being driven outside the human community to the ends of the earth. More than any other people, they have been the archetypal scapegoat, carrying both kinds of crosses.

II

What then is scapegoating psychologically? This mechanism is well known to us. It forms a distinct chain of reactions that leads from personal repression to social oppression. Its defined sequence begins when we repress contents we dislike and dread. We disown them. We keep consciousness from such contents and we eject such contents from consciousness. Our ego recoils from connection to contents we feel are destructive to our ego position and from the disordered chaos from which such contents spring. We refuse consciousness to the annihilating forces we call evil. We either throw such contents out of consciousness into unconsciousness or we leave them blocked in unconsciousness, refusing them admittance to our awareness. Such refusal brings relief to our egos; we get rid, we think, of disturbing contents.

But such contents do not go away. They go unconscious. They remain in us as live bits of being, as volatile forces now out of reach of our ego and its restraining, civilizing effects. These contents regress and achieve still more powerful form, as a hungry dog we locked in a closet becomes a savage beast bent on killing to satisfy its hunger. A repressed content is like a tiny alligator we bring back from a Florida vacation that becomes increasingly inconvenient as it keeps on growing. We flush it down the toilet into our sewers. There it not only continues to grow but now, out of sight and out of reach, it joins all the other alligators flushed away by our neighbors. What we repress accumulates more life to itself, growing stronger, bigger, contaminating whatever else is in the unconscious. Pressure builds up that demands release into conscious life. Such contents burst out finally in projections onto others—usually those different from us, alien, because of physical appearance or sex or background, or distant from us because we deem them inferior or superior to us. All that our egos judge unacceptable hurls itself in projection onto our alien or distant neighbor. We identify our neighbors with that bit of ourselves we put onto and into them. Thus we inaugurate a relationship of projective identification with our neighbors. We feel we must control them because they carry a feared bit of ourselves and fear them because we cannot control them. They carry the package of unconscious contents we dread in ourselves. Rather, we want to see ourselves as identified with the values and ideals we hold most precious. We contrast our good to our alien neighbors' bad. We draw a boundary around the good with which our egos identify, outlawing the bad with which we identify our neighbors.

We can understand that the initial function of such repression and projection is to differentiate good from bad, to become conscious of what we hold as good and to bind our group into a community, distinguished from other groups. Such initial differ-

entiation and group consciousness might be all right, even further-
ing consciousness, if it did not go further, but it always does. For
the repressed material, the howling dogs and snapping alligators,
press to get out, press for contact. What begins as differentiation
only too soon leads to a wide gap between our conscious ego
identification with the good and our projective identification of
our alien neighbor with the bad.

The line is drawn, from repression to regression and contamination of unconscious contents, to projection and projective identification onto our alien neighbor, to attitudes of prejudice from
which grow acts of oppression, persecution, and finally, scapegoating. Like one or the other of the original scapegoats, the alien
neighbor is seen as the carrier of our sins we must get rid of in
order to keep intact our commitment to the good. In the ironies of
opposing consciousness and unconsciousness, we can indulge,
even act out in frenzy, all the badness we disown in the name of
defending the good. The disease attacks those who attack the
disease. In the name of our ideal we attack, violate, persecute, and
kill those on whom we have projected our badness. We are infiltrated by the very qualities we tried to control, depositing them in
our neighbor. What begins as initial differentiation of opposites
ends by making a wide split between us and them, a split which
soon becomes a yawning chasm filled with violence, misery, and
suffering. That happens because we are unable to hold in consciousness the opposing values of good and bad. If we identify
ourselves with the victims of such actions, we become the first
goat, we become the victims who are burnt up. In psychological
terms, we fall into masochism. If we identify with the ones who
accuse their neighbors, we see them as the second kind of scapegoat
and ourselves fall into sadism, attempting to purge the community
of their presence.

The temptations in scapegoating are double, and each brings its
own cross. To get out of the coincidence of opposites—of the good
and bad in each of us—we split them. To elude the cross of
accepting and suffering the bad and good mixed in us, we double-
cross our neighbor. Either way we avoid the real issue—what to do
in the face of evil, where to put the alligators, how to hold the

opposites within ourselves and our own community. In Jung's vocabulary, scapegoating introduces us to the shadow in ourselves, to the collective shadow in our society, and to the archetypal core that underlies the shadow.[4]

III

This connection between repression and scapegoating is true of all prejudices which are acted out in social oppression. What is specific to anti-Semitism? What do we repress and project and then identify with Jews? What is the specific archetypal core which informs and inflames the mechanism of scapegoating in anti-Semitism? The answer, in a word, is religion.

Although not at the center of the debate about anti-Semitism, often obscured by economic, political, and historical circumstances, and often put aside or denied by Jews in their self-appraisals, the religious issue rests in the background of anti-Semitism. It forms the distinct core of the package repressed by and projected onto the Jews.

Even to those who associate Judaism with ethnicity rather than faith, who see it as a culture rather than a religion, religion remains the inescapable fact, for this is a culture shaped by religion, whether it declares for or against the faith. The notorious resentment against Jews for their reputed intellectual superiority, for example, can be traced back to a religious origin. Judaism is the first of the three great monotheisms in human history, and the other two were clearly shaped by it. Islam itself traces its origins to Abraham. Jesus was a Jew.

Anti-Semitism is a religious scapegoating, not one of color, class, or sex. And religious scapegoating is the most violent of all because religion arranges the order of being. On the surface, anti-Semitism seems to follow the mechanisms of all prejudice—repression, regression, contamination, projection, projective-identification, prejudice, oppression, persecution, scapegoating.

At the core of anti-Semitism lies the specific archetype that ignites people against Jews. It is unmistakably religious. For the

Jews are a people chosen by God, a people who have said yes to God's choosing, who have engaged in life-long dramas in yea-saying and nay-saying, turning to God, turning away. They complain that it is God who turns away and abandons them. And yet they know at the same time God is steadfast in demands upon them and in love of them.

It is almost a commonplace to say that what has happened to Jews is what happens to God on earth. They have been hunted, hounded, excluded, trivialized, caricatured, mocked, betrayed, double-crossed. We persecute Jews because we persecute the addressing Ultimate, the calling to us to be Abraham or to be the bride, to be the feminine receiver and container who will make the transcendent manifest in this life.

Jung knew this addressing, this receiving womanliness. He described Yahweh as one whom we punch and kick back at for dislocating our hip, as with Jacob, or who plagues us as He did Job. Jung knew what a fearful thing it was to fall into the hands of the living God, to encounter the archetype of God in our own psyche. Such an experience is steel on stone, a defeat for the ego, and yet of such indescribable bliss, says Jung, that he will not, cannot breathe a word of it.[5]

The Jews symbolically represent those who want to say yes to God, a yes that will include questions, resistance, a simultaneous fighting and running away. In such speech with the divine, our bowels loosen, our stomachs heave, our voices fill up, our flesh trembles. We, like the Jews, dare now to be occupied with the Holy One who hovers over the Mercy Seat in the Holy of Holies, and we are frightened—and fascinated.

It is a miracle the Jews still survive, for they carry the projection of the primordial, not only our nay-saying to the center, which is our sin, which we put on the scapegoat we drive into the desert, but also our yea-saying, that part of us that aches for the center, that wants to look, to see who will come through to us.

Jung crafted his whole psychology around this center. He discovered that we carry within our own psyches such a center, a self that is not God but that within us which knows about God. It is a large knowing, a taste of that which transcends, not just the ego, but the whole psyche, the whole personal psyche, the whole group psyche.[6]

The deepest place of our dread of being is where the Jewish people stand, and they are persecuted for it. In them we persecute our own desire and fear of the center of being. In them we persecute our attraction to the center and our fear of it. What then happens when we scapegoat the Jews? We avoid compulsively, not only the mystery of our own shadows, both individual and collective, but the mystery of evil that we seek to eject from consciousness and project out of our communities.[7] That is the scapegoat we send into the desert. We also avoid the mystery of living in relation to the center and the burnt offering it seems to demand. That is the goat whose blood is offered at the altar.

We must look at one further thing that comes with all scapegoating, and particularly with anti-Semitism. Jews carry the necessity of drawing a boundary line when the finite comes in contact with the infinite. In repressing and projecting what we find bad, and thus insupportable, we are setting it off from the good. We are making boundary lines that help us to see evil and help protect us from its infectious nature. Such boundaries enhance consciousness and our sense of community.[8] To send the goat into the desert is to send it beyond the boundaries; To take the goat outside the camp to be burned is to define the boundaries of inside and out.

The anthropologist Mary Douglas tells us that this making of boundaries, which happens for example in the dietary law of Judaism, is an attempt to impose order on untidy experience.[9] It demarcates inside from outside, order from chaos, community from nameless wandering. Drawing boundaries marks off our belonging, living in relation to the center, from homelessness. God's blessing creates a space where being is always being-in-relation to the center, and distinguished from nonbeing, which is to say from not-being-defined-in-relation-to, but choosing self-definition instead. We will make the boundaries. We will determine good and evil. We will know it all. We become know-it-alls. Pulling loose from such boundaries means taking to ourselves, our little selves, the big power to say what is good and what is evil—

what was seen so unmistakably clearly in the death camps—the power to save or to kill.

Dietary laws in Judaism are like signs designed to inspire meditation upon what God has set apart as holy. Holiness is unity, integrity, completeness. Marion Milner, writing about painting, says the frame marks off a different kind of reality that is within the picture from what is outside. Our own psychoanalytical sessions do the same, marking off in time and space a special kind of reality that makes possible "that creative illusion that analysts call the transference."[10]

Drawing these boundaries, saying in effect that this is good and this is bad, this sacred, this profane, is possible only if connection to the transcendent is maintained. The goat's blood must be offered back to the Holy, whether at the altar or in the desert. When the scapegoating ritual pulls loose from the transcendent center, it falls into idolatry. Symbolic form becomes literal action, whether through inflation we identify with the chosen ones or through deflation become the literal victims of the double cross. When a ritual is literalized, it falls on real living people. Instead of asking what our relation is to the infinite, we take offense at those who claim a covenant: If we can destroy them, we can evade the whole question.

IV

Jung mixed up the boundary lines, became caught up in them, and paid for it in his own experience of the double cross of scapegoating, both as accuser—drawing whole peoples into types, which inflamed persecution against them—and as accused—where he suffered, and his name goes on suffering, the label of anti-Semitism. Jung, so sensitive to the complexity of opposites, who never wanted to leave one of them out, was enmeshed in a complex of opposites. His strengths and gifts double-crossed him, in his weaknesses, in his blind spots. Jung shows us through his experience what it means to say scapegoating delivers us into fully acknowledging our shadow in ourselves and in the collective of which we are a part. We do not acknowledge our shadow from a safe perch in an observer's chair. It means to be pitched into the muck, coming up covered with it, stinking of it, smeared in our eyes so we cannot see clearly. That is the shadow. We slip onto it and into it, as Jung said. And we hurt others because of it. Jung also shows us, in his experience of the self and of the God-image in him, that a cross awaits any of us who struggle to relate to the Ultimate. Jung tried to keep the opposites together, and fell into them and into their splitting apart.

For example, Jung tells us that individuation can only occur in relation to tradition, to the collective, to the prevailing *Zeitgeist* from which we must differentiate ourselves and then relate to again, more consciously. We must become aware of the subjective premise from which we see objective truth, and know that our premise is subjective, so that finally, he wrote, we know that our vision of truth is only a "subjective confession."[11] But Jung himself was caught in the texture of his times with its bedeviling anti-Semitism. He was strongly influenced by his personal collectivity— generations of Christian pastors with all the ambiguity and devi-ousness of Christianity seeing Judaism as both its foundation and its rival. Christ the Jew, killed by Jews. From another perspective, Jung remained embedded in centuries of Swiss traditions of neu-trality, product of a country that observed the clashing opposite views of other peoples and chose to stand apart, to preserve neutrality for itself. Thus under his editorship of the journal of the International General Medical Society for Psychotherapy, Jung published both Nazi and Jewish doctors, expecting that scientific insight would be generated out of their opposing views.[12] Jung did not see in any of these collective and ostensibly objective worlds his own subjectivity, which colored not only his view of the Jews but also his hope of gathering insight from a sharp opposition neutrally observed.

Another example of where Jung was both crossed and double-crossed between opposites is in the realm of symbol. His great insight is into the openness of the symbol. It points to and evokes the living experience of the unknown, but never defines it exactly.[13] Yet Jung himself falls victim to attempts to define whole peoples in restrictive ways, which fed not differentiation, reconciliation, or insight, but separation and persecution. Jung reminds us again and again to open ourselves to the person before us, not to try to know what a dream means ahead of time, like a recipe, not to apply reasoning to spiritual paradoxes. He even declares his own typology is suggestive, never prescriptive. Yet here is Jung applying restrictive categories to whole races.[14] Jung's great open consciousness, determined always to see the other, can also contribute to obliterating others by applying mass generalizations to them. Jung tells us repeatedly that the archetype is not a formula clapped onto persons, yet he himself falls victim to a fascination with the Wotan archetype and forgets the persons involved with the new invocation of it.[15]

Jung advocates the recovery to consciousness of the feminine mode of being, with his seminal insight into the contrasexual nature of the human, yet he himself suffered a benighted relation to his own anima during the Nazi years, as the "sick cow" dream and his illnesses of the heart show. Yet growth continued in him, and true openness, as his near-death vision makes clear. He saw himself being fed kosher food by a maternal anima figure, whom he joined in a "mystical marriage," seeing himself cast as "Rabbi ben Jochai, whose wedding in the afterlife was being celebrated."[16] Jay Sherry suggests that the sick-cow side of Jung's anima—the nurturing feminine with "life-promoting milk"—fell ill from Jung's fascination with the Wotan archetype, suddenly alive again in Nazi Germany, and from Jung's bitterness about Freud after the breakup of their relationship.[17]

Jung, noted for bringing insight into the feeling and sensate levels of the unconscious, was tripped up by the limitations of his own feeling and sensate functions.[18] He expressed his dubious views about archetypal factors in Jewish psychology at a time of racial fanaticism in Germany, where even to be a Jew was enough to put one's life in danger. To put forward for scientific discussion the topic of racial differences in such a climate, even to think in such terms, was a grave error. Jung missed on the feeling and sensate levels—in terms of his typology his own inferior functions—the reality of the evil being visited upon the Jews. He wrote and spoke about racial characteristics, both during and after the war, in a way that was bound to further inflame the persecution of a whole people. Caught in his own emotions about the Wotan archetype, and his own resentments against Freudian analysis, he did not see the harm he himself was causing.

Jung is singular among depth psychologists in his intense interest in evil, in taking up good and evil as moral categories, in probing the mystery of conscience.[19] Yet Jung did not at first recognize one of the greatest examples of evil in history when it confronted him in its immeasurable brutality. Jung's incessant protests and objections against the Christian understanding of the force of evil, as described in the doctrine of *privatio boni*, can be understood as that excessive protestation we all fall into when we are fascinated by something and cannot really see what it is that so absorbs us.[20] Jung insists that the doctrine misses the fact that evil really exists, that it is really there savaging our lives. To anyone who grasps the doctrine, Jung's reading grossly misses the point. But the point here is that Jung missed the brute facts of Nazi evil.

Perhaps the two missings—of evil in itself and of the Nazi evil—are linked. In the *privatio boni*, evil is indeed understood to exist, but in a very different way from good. Good is simply being in relation to God, related being, created being, being within the circle of dependent connections to the Creator. Evil denies that connection, seeks to destroy it, to defect from it. Evil exists as denial, betrayal, deficiency, a ruthless attempt to put "nothing" in the place of something.[21] Evil exists outside relation to a transcendent center, usurping the center for its own version and vision of reality. Isn't this exactly what the Nazis attempted?

Aniela Jaffé understands Jung's error about the Jews and about Nazism as the product of a one-sided consciousness. She says his "romantic consciousness" got caught in fascination with the objective psyche displayed in National Socialism, particularly through the Wotan archetype. The "classic" type of consciousness which, Jaffé says, Jung acquired toward National Socialism was not fooled for a moment.[22]

At first Jung missed the evil so clear to so many others in the rise of the Nazis because of his faith in his own theory of consciousness. He missed it because of his conviction that healing power is released when consciousness can expand to include all the opposites, when a small ego can behold the *complexio oppositorum* of the self. Jung described the self as the God-image within us manifest in the psyche. He described the self—his image of God—as the *coincidentia oppositorum* and as the *complexio oppositorum*. Jung faced cross and double cross when he equated his image of God with God. What he relied upon betrayed him, and he betrayed what he relied upon. Like any person who really risks encounter with the living God, Jung was stripped of his God-image. When we identify our God-image with what it points to, as in some ways some of the time we must, because our image acts as a bridge between us and that unknown center to which it leads, it will break beneath our feet, for what it leads to is radically different from our pictures of it.[23] Jung's faith in consciousness was betrayed. It did not work. It double-crossed him. Consciousness of the opposites and writing about them in categories of Aryan and Jew, of the Germanic and the Jewish, harmed instead of helping, brought attack instead of a healing clarity.

V

What is to be done? Jung slipped up because of areas in his large personality of incomplete individuation. They resulted, these areas of absence and deprivation, from the collective *Zeitgeist*, from his own tendencies to type instead of to see symbolically, from his own underdeveloped feeling and sensate functions, from his own anima problems, from the resulting blindness to the stark reality of Nazi evil, from his overdetermined reliance on consciousness of opposites. Do we, then, dismiss everything Jung has to say? Hardly. That would be for us to fall into the double cross—either accusing or defending Jung or thinking we can stay out of the whole mess with a neutrality only too much like his at its worst. Seeing Jung caught, we should turn to our own enmeshment in scapegoating, for anti-Semitism is still here, still active among us. What is so powerful about this particular brand of scapegoating that it persists still, after all the horrors of the Holocaust?

The specific scapegoating of anti-Semitism introduces us not only to our own evil in collective and individual form in the myth of expelling evil, but also to our own God-image, our own relation or lack of relation to the transcendent. Whether we are Jewish or not, whether we practice or repudiate religion, the spiritual question is constellated: What is our relation to the center?

One of the reasons anti-Semitism endures is that we all need to take up two issues: how to deal with the shadow and how to relate to the self. Jung's insights and Jung's cross and double cross will help us enormously here.

The shadow issue poses itself in a series of additional questions. How do we mark off boundaries to consolidate ego-consciousness without discriminating against those who have different boundaries? How do we differentiate without repudiating?[24] Or, to put the same issue in social terms, how do we each set off order from disorder without disowning our neighbors? How do we think in terms of a whole society while at the same time risking commitment to our particular part of society? How do we get rooted firmly in our soil and remain hospitable to those who root differently or in different earth?

Jung's failures and insights point the way. Our consciousness must develop differently. A double intercession matches the double cross. We intercede for shadow and for ego both. Consciousness intercedes for the left-out bits of shadow in our personality and in our society, while at the same time respecting our need for boundaries. Consciousness also intercedes on behalf of our ego-point-of-view in relation to the opposite points of view that live inside us and around us. The *complexio oppositorum* which Jung sees as essential comes home to us. It becomes our everyday reality. This is living toward the self. We try to intercede on behalf of what we believe in and on behalf of what others believe in too. For this we urgently need the help of the Hebrew Bible and the feminine mode of being.

To do this work with the shadow means neither expelling evil nor burning it up. It means not identifying with either scapegoat, for both are offerings to the transcendent—the altar deity or the desert deity. It means moving on to the Prophets and the Psalms in the Hebrew Bible, where God says, I do not want burnt offerings,

I want a broken and contrite heart; I do not want burnt offerings, I want a faithful and loving spirit. But to make this shift means changing the way we become conscious. The old way was to differentiate opposites—good from bad, us from them, inside boundaries from outside boundaries—by splitting them apart. But in that way the split widens to a point where we cannot bring the opposites together again, and millions of people perish in the gap left between them. Differentiation then turns into discrimination. Consciousness means repression. The opposites do not belong together as parts of a complex whole, coinciding all at once, but instead proceed serially, sequentially, to a killing exclusivity.

What the texts of the Hebrew Bible are after in the shift from burnt offering to heart offering is inclusion of a feeling, sensate, bodily kind of awareness, where, although different each from the other, we are still all members of the one body. This perception is fostered by the feminine mode of being that goes into the midst of living experience and differentiates aspects of it by a both-and instead of an either-or method of apprehension.[25] The split does not widen to expel opposites nor move to exclude any one of them. The opposites are held in tension to discern and integrate all of them.

The feminine mode of consciousness allows a holding in being of what one is separating in thought. It is a holding in feeling of what we discern differences in, a holding of boundaries to make space for the commitments of the particular persons and groups that together compose the whole. The feminine mode recognizes evil both without sentimentality and without enthusiasm for grand ways of fixing it. Evil is a fact to be reckoned with and, if necessary, to be fought or suffered. The feminine approach helps the ego in its space-making function, enlarging awareness so the coinciding opposites can be experienced as complexly related to each other and to the whole of which they are parts.[26] Those coinciding opposites make up different parts of our society, different groups rooted in different commitments, just as much as they make up different segments of each person's personality.

In gaining consciousness of our own scapegoating tendencies, and interceding for another way, we are pushed to become conscious of how we experience the center of existence, of how we experience what it is all for and thus what really matters.

This consciousness of our own images of the center, of what Jung calls our God-images, makes us struggle with mystery as it touches us. If we are in any way to lift from the Jews what history has scapegoated them for—self-conscious relation to the center— then we must take up that task, their task, ourselves, in our own groups, in our own lives.

This is not to say everyone must become a defined Jew—any more than Muslim or Christian or Buddhist or atheist. It is to say that we must direct our consciousness to the center and decide to struggle with it and about it, to know its great positive qualities, its abiding difficulties, ourselves. That will keep our neighbors safe from the unconscious spiritual burden that we only too easily project onto them.

If we take up this task we will know the cross and double cross, but differently now, as a necessary ritual in relation to the transcendent. We will enter that radical experience that Jung exemplifies, of disidentifying our God-images from God, for relating to the infinite means being stripped of our finite images of it. That which we rely upon will pin us to the cross and will double-cross us. We will be forced to identify what our images of God are, forced to disidentify them from the transcendent itself. This means simultaneously committing ourselves in time and space to belief in whatever our version of the center is and opening to whatever our symbols evoke and point to but never capture or define, let alone prescribe for others. It means drawing boundaries that are both binding and open-ended. In religious terms, it means witnessing rather than proselytizing. In psychological terms, we are brought to true consciousness of opposites, rather than coercion. This is a paradoxical knowing and unknowing simultaneously. It is a seeing into the dark ground of the God who presides over both goats, both crosses, within boundary and beyond, the world of deity and of desert.

Notes

1. Aniela Jaffé, "C. G. Jung and National Socialism" in *From the Life and Work of Jung*, pp. 97–98.

2. See Richard L. Rubenstein, *After Auschwitz: Radical Theology and Contemporary Judaism* (Indianapolis: Bobbs-Merrill, 1966); see also Richard L. Rubenstein and John K. Roth, *Approaches to Auschwitz: The Holocaust and Its Legacy* (Atlanta: John Knox, 1987); John G. Gager, *The Origins of Anti-Semitism* (New York: Oxford University Press, 1983); Rosemary Ruether, *Faith and Fratricide: The Theological Roots of Anti-Semitism* (New York: Seabury, 1974); R. M. Lowenstein, *Christians and Jews: A Psychoanalytic Study* (New York: International Universities Press, 1952).

3. *The Oxford Dictionary of the Christian Church* (London: Oxford University Press, 1974); see also Sylvia Brinton Perera, *The Scapegoat Complex: Toward a Mythology of Shadow and Guilt* (Toronto: Inner City Books, 1986), pp. 18–19, 89.

4. See Erich Neuman, *Depth Psychology and a New Ethic*, trans. Eugene Rolfe (New York: Putnam's, 1969; Boston: Shambhala Publications, 1990), *passim* for discussion of the many facets of repression and their effects on society. See also C. G. Jung, "Shadow," in *Aion*, CW 9, II, paras. 13–19.

5. See C. G. Jung, *Letters*, vol. 2, p. 156. See also C. G. Jung, *Mysterium Coniunctionis* 14, para. 778.

6. See C. G. Jung, *Psychological Types*, CW 6, paras. 789–790. See also C. G. Jung, *The Archetypes and the Collective Unconscious*, CW 9, I, paras. 5, 442, 572, 626.

7. See C. G. Jung, *Two Essays in Analytical Psychology*, CW 7, paras. 27, 35, 41–42, 70–78, 152–154, 185. See also C. G. Jung, *Psychology and Religion: West and East*, CW 11, para. 140; see also paras. 509–513, 738–789.

8. See Neumann, *Depth Psychology and a New Ethic*, pp. 64–66.

9. Mary Douglas, *Purity and Danger* (New York: Frederick A. Praeger, 1966), pp. 1, 4–5, 29, 50, 53–54, 57, 63–64.

10. Marion Milner, "The Role of Illusion in Symbol Formation," *New Directions in Psychoanalysis*, eds. M. Klein, P. Hermann, R. E. Money-Kyrle (New York: Basic Books, 1957), p. 86; also cited in Douglas, op. cit., p. 63.

11. See C. G. Jung, *Civilization in Transition*, CW 10, paras. 1025, 1034. See also C. G. Jung, *Modern Man in Search of a Soul*, trans. W. S. Dell and C. F. Baynes (New York: Harcourt, Brace & Co., 1933), p. 220.

12. See Jung, *Civilization in Transition*, paras. 1026–1032.

13. See Jung, *Letters*, vol. 1, pp. 32, 59; See also Jung, *Psychological Types*, paras. 814–829; see also Ann Belford Ulanov, *The Feminine in Jungian Psychology and Christian Theology* (Evanston: Northwestern University Press, 1971), chap. 5.

14. See Jung, *Civilization in Transition*, paras. 400–487.

15. See ibid., paras. 371–399 and especially 385, 391.

16. C. G. Jung, *Memories, Dreams, Reflections*, p. 294.

17. See Jay Sherry, "Jung, the Jews, and Hitler," *Spring*, 1986, pp. 170–174, for full presentation of this idea.

18. Jung, *Psychological Types*, paras. 595–609.

19. See Jung, *Civilization in Transition*, paras. 825–886.

20. See Jung, *Letters*, vol. 2, pp 52–54, 58–61, 71–73, 268, 281, 484, 519. See Jung, *Psychology and Religion: West and East*, paras. 274f, 451f, 470, 685.

21. For further discussion of this denying role of evil, see Ann Belford Ulanov, "The Devil's Trick," in *The Wisdom of the Psyche* (Cambridge: Cowley, 1988).

22. Jaffé, "C. G. Jung and National Socialism," p. 96. Jung describes the two kinds of consciousness, linking them with extraversion and introversion, in his *Psychological Types*, paras. 543, 544, 548, 549, 550.

    The romantic type tends to be extraverted, swift in his reactions, expressing himself and needing to make his presence felt, "because his whole nature goes outwards to the object. He gives himself easily to the world in a form that is pleasing and acceptable. . . ." Enthusiasm "flows out of his mouth." He appears interesting, empathetic. He publishes early and wants to make a name for himself.

    "The classic type is slow to produce, usually bringing forth the ripest fruit of his mind relatively late in life." He needs "to stand unblemished in the public eye" and does not set other minds on fire. He always keeps his personality in the background and tends to be introverted, hiding "his personal reactions and suppressing his immediate reactions." He lets "his work speak for him and does not take up the cudgels on its behalf." He seals his lips over enthusiasm and appears commonplace.

    As usual with any typology, neither of these descriptions fits Jung precisely. But Jaffé's referral to them as helping to explain Jung's trials with the Nazis is most interesting.

23. See Ann Belford Ulanov, *Picturing God* (Cambridge: Cowley, 1986), pp. 164–171, 179–184.

24. See Ann Belford Ulanov, "When Is Repudiation Differentiation?," unpublished paper, 1987.

25. See Ann Belford Ulanov, *The Feminine in Jungian Psychology and in Christian Theology*, Part III; see also "Between Anxiety and Faith: The Role of the Feminine in Paul Tillich's Theological Thought," in *Tillich on Creativity*, ed. G. Kegley (Lanham: University Press of America, 1989).

26. See Ann Belford Ulanov, "The Ego as Spacemaker," unpublished paper, 1981.

My Siegfried Problem— and Ours: Jungians, Freudians, Anti-Semitism, and the Psychology of Knowledge

Michael Vannoy Adams

Michael Vannoy Adams is Associate Provost and Lecturer in Humanities in the University at the New School for Social Research, where he teaches in the Graduate Faculty of Political and Social Science, Eugene Lang College, and Parsons School of Design.

In this revised version of the paper he delivered at the "Lingering Shadows" conference, Adams addresses the antagonism between Jungians and Freudians as derivative of two personality cults and holds up as an example the efforts of Sabina Spielrein to go beyond the personal differences of these two thinkers and to recognize the combined contributions they have made to depth psychology. Adams asks, in regard to Jung's theory of the collective unconscious, whether collective psychological differences do exist between groups and, if so, whether we can discuss them without value judgment or "imputation of superiority and inferiority." He concludes that, while cultural differences no doubt exist, natural (or innate) differences are too uninformative to be significant, and any theory of collective psychology based on these differences can too easily be pressed into the service of discrimination and prejudicial projections.

It is especially appropriate that the "Lingering Shadows" conference on Jungians, Freudians, and anti-Semitism took place at the New School for Social Research in New York City. This site was the location of the "University in Exile," which was established by the New School in 1933. The New School for Social Research was the first American university to organize a systematic effort to rescue European scholars and intellectuals from fascism. Much of the persecution and oppression was, of course, anti-Semitic. In 1934, the University in Exile was formally constituted as the Graduate Faculty of Political and Social Science.[1] Today, the New School for Social Research remains committed to upholding the democratic values and the principles of free inquiry and expression that inspired it to found the University in Exile. Academically, the Graduate Faculty continues to emphasize a distinctive style of interdisciplinary social science that combines theoretical and historical reflection in the European tradition with American methods of empirical research.

In 1954, there was another relevant event at the New School. Jolande Jacobi, a Jewish Jungian analyst from Zurich and a colleague of Jung's for many years, was giving a series of lectures. At one of the lectures there was a disruption—a scene with boos, hisses, shouting, and heckling—when a member of the audience stood up and repeated the charges that Jung was anti-Semitic. Jacobi replied, "I am a Jewess and my husband is a Jew. Does anyone here believe that I would defend Dr. Jung if he were anti-Semitic? We thrashed out charges against Dr. Jung at my first lecture."[2] So there are historical vibrations at the New School— and thirty-seven years later we are still thrashing out the same charges.

My own interest is certainly in anti-Semitism but equally in Jungians and Freudians. If I may quote from a letter that I wrote to the *New York Times*, I can state my position succinctly:

> There were theoretical differences between Freud and Jung, but it is deplorable when these continue to be racialized, personalized, and politicized. Freudians and Jungians should engage in amicable and beneficial conversation about these differences. Rather than simply awake from the nightmare of history in the

twentieth century, they should reinterpret the original dream of psychoanalysis as an impartial science of the unconscious.[3]

I should emphasize that when I use the word *psychoanalysis*, I use it generically, as a synonym for *depth psychology*—all the varieties of it, including both the Freudian and Jungian schools of psychoanalytic thought.

The split between Freud and Jung persists as a split between Freudians and Jungians. A personality conflict, a theoretical difference, has resulted in a personality cult—or, more precisely, two personality cults, where charisma plays a certain part and where there's identification, idealization, even idolization. I confess to having been, in the past, a member of the Melville Society. *Moby-Dick* is one of my interests, and Melville is, too.[4] Henry A. Murray, one of those rarities who was both a Jungian and a Freudian—and also a Melvillian—was a member of the Melville Society.[5] I used to go to the meetings, at which men would wear necklaces of shark's teeth or ties with little white whales on them. I used to joke that one day one of them would walk in with a peg leg. They really identified with Melville.

I read recently that there is one remaining giant picture of Chairman Mao in Beijing and that there's now discussion about removing it. I'm not an iconoclast. I like icons. I think that one of Chairman Mao there is perfectly all right. I went to the Andy Warhol retrospective exhibition at the Museum of Modern Art recently, and there were lots of Chairman Maos there. We have room for one image of the Chairman. But Freud has been dead fifty-two years now, Jung has been dead thirty years, and it is time to put an end to the personality cults in psychoanalysis.

I used to believe that the split between Freud and Jung, between Freudians and Jungians, was a tragedy. I no longer think so. I simply feel that it's a shame and a pity. I have even realized that there may be one advantage to the split. Different schools of psychoanalytic thought can perform an important function by bringing into clear, sharp focus different theoretical positions that might otherwise be blurred. I am not urging the reunification of psychoanalysis as a whole. I am merely advocating a friendly dialogue, in a free and open spirit, between different schools of psychoanalytic thought.

My position is very like Sabina Spielrein's.[6] Spielrein has been mentioned as one of Jung's lovers. To what extent she may have been, I am unsure. Even if there was no affair as such, there was, at the very least, a certain intimacy. Spielrein is an extremely interesting person in relation to the issue of Jungians, Freudians, and anti-Semitism. She herself was Jewish, and her great-grand-father and grandfather were rabbis in Russia. She started out in analysis with Jung and ended up as an analyst with Freud and the Freudians. In priority of discovery, she was a precursor of Freud in the theory of the death instinct. After the split between Freud and Jung, she continued to correspond with both analysts. In the belief that Freud and Jung shared more in common than they either acknowledged or imagined, she urged—to no avail—a reconciliation.

What impresses me most about Spielrein is not this attempt at mediation between Freud and Jung but the intellectual quality of the questions that she poses about the precise relationship between *theoretical differences and interpretative preferences*, for this is the epistemological issue that remains fundamental to the current divisions among the various schools of psychoanalytic thought. In a wonderfully persistent way, Spielrein presses Jung to specify practical criteria for using one theory rather than another, for choosing one interpretation rather than another. On what basis, in a particular case, should one value this alternative over that? For instance, when—and why—should one prefer an Adlerian inter-pretation (will to power) or a Freudian interpretation (wish for sex) or a Jungian interpretation (task in life)? What evidence, Spielrein asks Jung, would verify or refute these alternatives?

I know of no other analyst who, in the years immediately after the split between Freud and Jung, maintains quite such an equita-ble attitude. In the effort to exclude prejudice and to exercise properly independent discrimination, Spielrein is not only tolerant but also seriously inquisitive in the pursuit of knowledge, espe-cially as it pertains to the practicalities of interpretative prefer-ences. She never commits the fallacy of confusing Freud and Jung with psychoanalysis. Among analysts at the time, Spielrein is a model of nonpartisan rectitude.

For Spielrein, the Jungian-Freudian controversy is one aspect of an "Aryan-Semitic" problem for which she seeks a psychoanalytic solution in the interpretation of several "Siegfried" dreams. From as early as 1909 until at least 1918, the attempt to secure a definitive interpretation of these dreams assumes singular impor-tance for Spielrein. In the dreams, the "Aryan" Jung and the "Semitic" Spielrein together produce a child, Siegfried. This Sieg-fried child is an Aryan-Semitic hero. Spielrein and Jung discuss what the dreams might mean. The question becomes: Is this to be a real child or a symbolic child, a physical child or a psychical child, a literal child or a figurative child? In Jungian terms, should the dreams be interpreted on the objective level or on the subjec-tive level? Is the "procreative" in this case a metaphor for the "creative"?

In 1912 Spielrein interprets the child metaphorically when she sends Jung the manuscript that she has written on the death instinct, a study that she explicitly identifies as "the product of our love, the project which is your little son Siegfried."[7] By this time in the relationship, Spielrein obviously accepts the impossibility of having a real child by Jung. She interprets Siegfried as a symbolic child, a sublimation of the sexual into the intellectual, of body into mind. Freud suggestively reinforces this interpretation when he remarks to Spielrein, "You could have the child, you know, if you wanted it, but what a waste of your talents, etc."[8] (According to the hierarchical logic of sublimation, of course, intellect is "higher" and sex "lower.")

Spielrein—who expresses the conviction that giving birth to Siegfried as either a real or a symbolic child is an act of equal value, the one neither higher nor lower than the other—asks Jung a very serious question about the relative cogency of alternative interpretations: Does the unconscious ever provide any indications as to which interpretation, the real or the symbolic, is accurate?[9] Does the unconscious offer any clues as to the correct choice, or does it simply present a dream for consideration and leave it to the conscious to reflect on it—and perhaps act on it in a decisive way?

In a dream, does having a child mean what it says, or does it mean, say, having a career—as a psychoanalyst? For example, might having a child mean writing a manuscript on the death instinct or perhaps even integrating the Jungian and Freudian theories of the unconscious? Thus Spielrein writes to Jung: "My Siegfried problem, for instance, might just as well yield a real child as a symbolic Aryan-Semitic child—for instance, a child that resulted from the union of your and Freud's theories."[10] In the Siegfried dreams, Spielrein and Jung together—perhaps physically, perhaps only psychically—are to produce a heroic Aryan-Semitic child—and perhaps also, at the same time, a purely theoretical Jungian-Freudian child.

One may, of course, dismiss these dreams as merely the product of a romantic infatuation. I prefer to regard them as an instance of the unconscious spontaneously striving to address, through Spielrein and Jung, the collective ethnic issue. In this sense, Spielrein and Jung are the epitome of both a difficulty and an opportunity on a scale much vaster than the individual. They represent the hope, before Hitler and the Holocaust, that a humane relationship between "Aryans" and "Semites" would produce heroic results—one of the practical consequences being, on the theoretical level, psychoanalysis.

In 1918, four years after the split between Freud and Jung, Spielrein writes to Jung about Freud:

> Now, then, you are so extraordinarily valuable in my eyes that I
> should not like to see you become narrowly partisan. It is very
> possible that Freud will never understand you when you propose
> innovative theories. In his lifetime Freud has accomplished such
> extraordinary things, and he has enough to keep him occupied
> for the rest of his days, simply working out the details of his vast
> edifice. You, on the other hand, are still capable of growth. You
> can understand Freud perfectly well if you wish to, i.e., if your
> personal affect does not get in the way. The Freudian theories
> were, are, and will remain extraordinarily fruitful. . . . You
> should have the courage to recognize Freud in all his grandeur,
> even if you do not agree with him on every point, even if in the
> process you might have to credit Freud with many of your own

accomplishments. Only then will you be completely free, and only then will you be the greater one. You will be amazed to see how markedly your entire personality and your new theory will gain in objectivity through this process.[11]

In 1914, at the time of the split, Spielrein writes to Freud about Jung: "You, Professor Freud, and he have not the faintest idea that you belong together far more than anyone might suspect."[12] The same could be said today of Freudians and Jungians. Something is wrong when members of one school of psychoanalytic thought neither read nor cite the works of members of another school and when so few members of one school are friends with members of another school—as, for example, Joseph Wheelwright and Erik Erikson have been for so many years.

After the split with Freud, on December 18, 1913, Jung had his own Siegfried dream:

> I was with an unknown, brown-skinned man, a savage, in a lonely, rocky mountain landscape. It was before dawn; the eastern sky was already bright, and the stars fading. Then I heard Siegfried's horn sounding over the mountains and I knew that we had to kill him. We were armed with rifles and lay in wait for him on a narrow path over the rocks.
>
> Then Siegfried appeared high up on the crest of the mountain, in the first ray of the rising sun. On a chariot made of the bones of the dead he drove at furious speed down the precipitous slope. When he turned a corner, we shot at him, and he plunged down, struck dead.
>
> Filled with disgust and remorse for having destroyed something so great and beautiful, I turned to flee, impelled by the fear that the murder might be discovered. But a tremendous downfall of rain began, and I knew that it would wipe out all traces of the dead. I had escaped the danger of discovery; life could go on, but an unbearable feeling of guilt remained.
>
> When I awoke from the dream, I turned it over in my mind, but was unable to understand it. I tried therefore to fall asleep again, but a voice within me said, "You *must* understand the dream, and must do so at once!" The inner urgency mounted until the terrible moment came when the voice said, "If you do

not understand the dream, you must shoot yourself!" In the drawer of my night table lay a loaded revolver, and I became frightened. Then I began pondering once again, and suddenly the meaning of the dream dawned on me. "Why, that is the problem that is being played out in the world." Siegfried, I thought, represents what the Germans want to achieve, heroically to impose their will, have their own way. "Where there is a will there is a way!" I had wanted to do the same. But now that was no longer possible. The dream showed that the attitude embodied by Siegfried, the hero, no longer suited me. Therefore it had to be killed.

After the deed I felt an overpowering compassion, as though I myself had been shot: a sign of my secret identity with Siegfried, as well as of the grief a man feels when he is forced to sacrifice his ideal and his conscious attitudes. This identity and my heroic idealism had to be abandoned, for there are higher things than the ego's will, and to these one must bow.

These thoughts sufficed for the present, and I fell asleep again.[13]

Through a process of unconscious identification, the personal epitomizes the collective. In this case, Jung states a definite interpretative preference for the "symbolic" over the "real." In Jung's dream, "Siegfried" has no external, objective referent. "Siegfried" does, however, have an internal, subjective significance. (This is an exemplary instance of the basic distinction that Jung articulates between interpretation on the objective level and interpretation on the subjective level.) As a hero, Siegfried is a concrete image of an abstract type (be it archetype or stereotype). Rhetorically, Siegfried is a personification of an attitude that Jung contends is typically Germanic. The unconscious compensates the ego, persuades Jung to commit a homicide that is a suicide, convinces him to shoot the hero and kill the will, which is Siegfried, which is—as it were— Jung (not the physical but the psychical Jung). Or, as I prefer to say: In *imaginal psychoanalysis*, if one understands the dream, one shoots the self figuratively; if one does *not* understand the dream, one takes the revolver from the drawer of the table and shoots the self literally.[14]

On November 29, 1982, a few months after the publication of

A Secret Symmetry: Sabina Spielrein between Jung and Freud, I had my own Siegfried dream:

> I have received a letter from Sigmund Freud. The letter has to do with whether analysis is scientific or not. There is a joke to the first two sentences of the letter. The second sentence says: "If that's not a contradiction in terms . . ." [as if it were a contradiction in terms to imagine that analysis is scientific]. I am surprised that Freud has the sort of sense of humor that can joke about the scientific status of analysis. Either the letter also has something to do with Freud agreeing to see me, or else I have found out from him in some other way when he will have some time to see me. I wait with a woman (perhaps my mother, although this part of the dream is vague, and I may only be guessing) for Freud to arrive. When the hour comes, and when some minutes have passed, it occurs to me that Freud is not supposed to come to me—I am supposed to go to him. After all, he is an old, decrepit man who should not be expected to make the difficult effort to come to me. Furthermore, he has a reputation, and who, after all, am I?
>
> The scene shifts, and I am on a subway, elevated above ground, with a woman—my wife, I believe. We see city buildings below. I realize that the letter was not from Sigmund Freud but from Sieg Friedmann, another analyst, whose office is below, in one of the buildings.

I do not propose to interpret my Siegfried dream—other than to note that there is a pun "Sig[mund] Freud/Sieg Fried[mann]" that probably comprises a number of homonymic permutations. Is Sieg Friedmann (the man who is—and is not—simultaneously "Sig Freud/Sieg Fried") perhaps the man who aspires to combine, as an analyst, both "Sig Freud" (Freudian) and "Sieg Fried" (Jungian) theories, methods, concepts, sensibilities? I cite my Siegfried dream only to emphasize that Spielrein's Siegfried problem is *my* Siegfried problem—and, if I may say so, *ours*: both Jungians' and Freudians'. Ours is the problem of *Sieg* ("Victory") and *Fried[e]* ("Peace"). Surely, the solution is neither in "war" between Jungians and Freudians nor in the "defeat" of one or the other school of psychoanalytic thought.

In discussing certain issues—and I would count anti-Semitism as one of them—I believe that we have a responsibility to apply words to things with particular precision, if for no other reason in this case than as a demonstration of respect for those who have suffered so much from anti-Semitism, especially in this century. The narrowness or the broadness of the application of words to things has been a controversial topic in psychoanalysis from the very beginning. The prime example, of course, is the dispute over the proper extension of the word *sexual*—or *psychosexual*. Similarly, as a graduate student in England in the early 1970s, I got very tired of hearing certain individuals casually and indiscriminately call virtually everybody with a different opinion "fascist." When we use serious words, words with extreme value, we depreciate that value by applying them too expansively to things. In this sense, *anti-Semitic* is one of the serious words that we should reserve exclusively for serious applications. I believe that it is simply too valuable a word for us to do otherwise.

Psychoanalysis in both the Freudian and Jungian versions is an interpretative method that inevitably delves into motives. The real motives are not manifest—they're latent; the real motives are ulterior, or unconscious. The real significance is hidden (according to Freud); or it's unknown (according to Jung). Implicit in the concepts of "overdetermination" and "overinterpretation" is an assumption that the unconscious is multivalent in terms of motivation. In order to understand Jung's or anyone else's motives, one must question them. As Paul Ricoeur says, psychoanalysis (by which he means Freudian analysis) is an interpretative method that belongs to "the school of suspicion."[15]

All the schools of psychoanalytic thought, including Jungian analysis, are intrinsically reductive in this sense, insofar as they tend not to accept what anyone says at face value. Face value is only a facade; behind that facade is the real significance. Psychoanalysis is not a surface psychology; it is a depth psychology, and underneath the surface is the real significance.[16] Nothing is ever only what it seems, and nobody ever means only what he says. So, in this case, how should one interpret Jung's disclaimer "I am no anti-Semite"? Psychoanalysis cannot accept it at face value; it has to be suspicious. At the very least, it has to add the qualifier, "*Consciously*, I am no anti-Semite." But unconsciously?

The concept of resistance further complicates matters. In psychoanalysis, one invariably means something different from, something more than, even something opposite to what one says. "The lady doth protest too much, methinks" becomes "The patient doth resist too much, methinks." The more one protests the accusation, the more one proves it. The more one resists the interpretation, the more one confirms it. In defending oneself, one is simply being "defensive."

However, in what only appears to be a contradiction in terms, psychoanalysis also acknowledges that the unconscious itself is the quintessential defense. In this regard, the unconscious constitutes a general theory of defense in the context of which the insanity plea is simply a special case. If one is not conscious of one's anti-Semitic motives, for example, then one is not morally responsible for one's words or deeds. In short, according to psychoanalysis, one is culpable only to the extent that one is conscious.

Now, consider these cases, which involve intent, motive, and effect and which constitute an attempt to differentiate the issue of anti-Semitism semantically:

1. Someone who is *with conscious intent* anti-Semitic and *says* that he is. Hitler and the Nazis never say, "I am no anti-Semite." They proudly and publicly declare that they are anti-Semites—and, in advocating the "final solution," they are genocidally so.

2. Someone who is *with conscious intent* anti-Semitic but says that he is *not*. When this individual says, "I am no anti-Semite," he is either a liar or a hypocrite.

3. Someone who is *by unconscious motive* (not with conscious intent) anti-Semitic and says that he is *not*. This individual is only involuntarily an anti-Semite. The unconscious motive is either hidden from him or unknown to him.

4. Someone who is *in equivalent effect* (neither with conscious intent nor by unconscious motive) "anti-Semitic"

and says that he is *not*. This individual is only consequen-
tially an "anti-Semite"—an anti-Semite so to speak. In
this instance, conscious intent and unconscious motive are
irrelevant insofar as the observable effect is, for all practical purposes, identically pernicious.

5. Someone who is *not* by any definition anti-Semitic and
says that he is *not*.

In evaluating the charges that recur and persist in spite of vehement
denials by Jung and various Jungians, including a considerable
number of Jewish Jungians who knew Jung personally, we have a
responsibility to recognize both the extreme value and the semantic
complexity of the word *anti-Semitism*. A person may be incorrect
without being immoral; an individual may be foolish without
being evil.

Freud emphasizes the distinction between psychical reality and
external reality—which includes factual, historical reality. In psychoanalysis, external reality by no means provides the necessary
and sufficient evidence to verify or falsify an interpretative proposition. The correspondence theory of truth is simply not applicable
in a conclusive way in psychoanalysis. When Freud discusses
psychical reality, he posits the existence of "phylogenetically inherited schemata, which, like the categories of philosophy, are concerned with the business of 'placing' the impressions derived from
actual experience." These schemata are similar if not identical to
what Jung calls archetypes. Freud continues by describing the
circumstances under which such a schema may exert a dominant
influence over external reality:

> Wherever experiences fail to fit in with the hereditary schema,
> they become remodelled in the imagination—a process which
> might very profitably be followed out in detail. It is precisely such
> cases that are calculated to convince us of the independent
> existence of the schema. We are often able to see the schema
> triumphing over the experience of the individual.[17]

As Freud characterizes the schemata that alter experience and that
force external reality to conform to psychical reality, they are

natural rather than cultural categories: archetypes rather than stereotypes.

I prefer to say that the individual vision of external reality is mediated—that is, *psychically constructed*—by schemata, categories, or "types" (be they archetypes or stereotypes), which, if not naturally inherited, are so culturally ingrained in the unconscious that they might as well be. Thus I speak of *the psychical construction of reality*. It is the psychical construction of reality that explains why we have such difficulty with the issue of Jungians, Freudians, and anti-Semitism and why no amount of facts from the history of the twentieth century seems likely to resolve the controversy once and for all. Ultimately, this is not a factual, historical question; it is an interpretative, psychological question. Perfectly sincere individuals will have different interpretations of the psychology of Jung, of Freud, of Jungians, of Freudians, and of anti-Semitism.

My interest in the construction of reality happens to coincide, perhaps synchronistically, with my first knowledge of the very existence of the New School for Social Research, where I now work, twenty-one years later. I became interested in how reality is constructed (rather than given) in 1970, when I read a book by two New School professors. The title was *The Social Construction of Reality*. The authors, Peter L. Berger and Thomas Luckmann, acknowledged that they were writing about reality in the tradition of another New School professor, Alfred Schutz.[18] They approached the problem of reality from the perspective of the sociology of knowledge. In this regard, what I advocate for psychoanalysis (that is, for both Jungian and Freudian analysis) is a *psychology of knowledge* that would adequately address the issue of how reality is psychically constructed.

I prefer to emphasize cultural rather than natural categories (for example, ethnic rather than "racial" categories). Addressing the issue in this manner is similar to what Wilhelm Dilthey was attempting when, instead of writing a critique of pure reason as Immanuel Kant had done, he proposed writing a critique of historical reason—by which he meant a critique of historical categories, or a critique of cultural categories.[19] In my opinion, Jung's most important contribution as an analyst is his insistence that the psyche has a collective as well as an individual dimension. It may be, however, that Jung's conception of collective psychology is one that we now need to reconsider—and perhaps reformulate.

The issue is: Do collective psychological differences exist? If so, can we discuss these differences with an attitude of mutual respect? Can we emphasize cultural differences rather than any putative natural differences? Can we affirm what Tzvetan Todorov calls "difference in equality" and repudiate imputations of superiority and inferiority?[20] The question of cultural differences is difficult enough to discuss sensibly without complicating matters with dubious propositions about natural differences—including "racial" differences. (As Todorov notes, although racism exists, "races" do not.)[21]

In this regard, allow me to relate an anecdote. A few years ago, several Jungians formed a study group in Zurich to investigate the question of whether one could discern in dreams indications of collective psychological differences. In the group were a number of Jewish Jungians with an interest in discovering in the unconscious any evidence of a distinctively "Jewish" psychology. One day a member of the group—an American Jewish woman from New York—suddenly announced, "At last I've had a Jewish dream. Last night," she proudly declared, "I dreamed of lox and bagels." Although Woody Allen would surely have appreciated the dream, the members of the study group immediately disqualified it. It was not, in the opinion of the group, typically Jewish. It was American, New York—Yiddish perhaps—but not intrinsically "Jewish," whatever that might ultimately mean.

I am not denying that natural categories exist. I am merely asserting that they exist at a level of generality so abstract that they convey hardly any concrete information. It is this paucity of information that tends to render these categories ineffectual and irrelevant. Natural categories such as "racial" ones (in contrast to cultural categories such as ethnic ones) are so vague and elusive that virtually the only purpose they serve is an utterly trivial and inconsequential one—or a vicious one, as an excuse for invidious distinctions and an opportunity for prejudicial projections.

Cultural categories are much more readily accessible as sources of pertinent information. Because it is difficult if not impossible to discuss natural categories to any satisfactory effect, it is especially significant that cultural categories afford such an impressively ample explanation of the diversity of the psyche. There is simply no need to resort immediately to natural categories to account for the existence of these differences. Cultural categories more than suffice in this respect—and quite properly emphasize *the conventionality of collective differences.*

I believe that in applications of the comparative method (for example, the Jungian method of amplification), differences are almost always of more intrinsic interest than similarities or identities. In recent years, Gregory Bateson and Jacques Derrida have emphasized the decisive importance of "difference."[22] Differences have more intrinsic interest than similarities or identities precisely because differences have more information to convey. Because the comparative method tends to reduce differences to similarities or identities, psychoanalysis (and perhaps especially Jungian psychoanalysis) needs to develop a deliberately *contrastive method* and apply it to contemporary issues of collective psychology—for example, to the topics of diversity, pluralism, and multiculturalism.

I want to leave you with one final image. Leo Baeck's name is often mentioned in connection with the subject at issue. Baeck was the rabbi of Berlin and a person who, after having entered the Theresienstadt concentration camp at the age of sixty-nine, finally emerged a survivor. He was also the individual who, after a two-hour confrontation with Jung in Zurich after the war, accepted Jung's acknowledgment that he had "slipped up" (apparently a reference to Jung's misjudgment in the early 1930s that, following a period of political excess, Germany might, after all, be capable of something positive)—and who, on that basis, renewed his friendship with Jung. While reflecting on the issue of Jungians, Freudians, and anti-Semitism, I looked again at the beautiful book

C. G. *Jung: Word and Image,* which includes a photograph of Jung and Baeck sitting and talking together at the 1947 Eranos Conference. I leave it to you to decide how many words that one picture is worth.

Notes

1. See Peter M. Rutkoff and William B. Scott, *New School: A History of the New School for Social Research* (New York: Free Press, 1986), pp. 84–106, and Alvin Johnson, *Pioneer's Progress* (Lincoln: University of Nebraska Press, 1960), pp. 332–348.

2. Vincent Brome, *Freud and His Early Circle* (New York: William Morrow, 1968), pp. 150–151.

3. *New York Times,* June 11, 1988.

4. See, for example: Michael Vannoy Adams, "Ahab's Jonah-and-the-Whale Complex: The Fish Archetype in *Moby-Dick,*" *ESQ* 28, no. 3 (3rd Quarter 1982): 167–182; "Madness and Right Reason, Extremes of One: The Shadow Archetype in *Moby-Dick,*" *Bucknell Review* 31, no. 2 (1988): 97–109; "Getting a Kick Out of Captain Ahab: The Merman Dream in *Moby-Dick,*" *Dreamworks* 4, no. 4 (1984/85), 279–287; "Whaling and Difference: *Moby-Dick* Deconstructed," *New Orleans Review* 10, no. 4 (Winter 1983): 59–64.

5. Murray is perhaps best known for having invented the Thematic Apperception Test (TAT). As I understand it, what originally inspired Murray to develop the TAT was the chapter in *Moby-Dick* entitled "The Doubloon," in which several sailors project various subjective significances onto the gold coin that Captain Ahab has nailed to the mast as a reward for the first member of the crew to sight the White Whale. For more of Murray on Jung, Freud, and Melville, see *Endeavors in Psychology: Selections from the Personology of Henry A. Murray,* ed. Edwin S. Shneidman (New York: Harper and Row, 1981). See in particular "Jung: Beyond the Hour's Most Exacting Expectation" (pp 79–81) and "What Should Psychologists Do About Psychoanalysis?" (pp. 291–311)—in which Murray says that the conflict between different schools of psychoanalytic thought, including the Freudian and Jungian schools, has been so severe that "now it is quite impossible for the protagonists of one dogma to appreciate the values and validities of others" (300).

6. See Aldo Carotenuto, *A Secret Symmetry.*

7. Ibid., p. 48.

8. Ibid., p. 71.

9. In *The Visions Seminars* (Zurich: Spring Publications, 1976), II:317, Jung

interprets a woman's vision that is curiously parallel to Spielrein's dreams. Both the vision and the dreams involve a child. As if in answer to the question that Spielrein poses about interpretative preference, Jung says that this particular vision does provide—imagistically—a quite specific indication as to which interpretation is accurate: "Should it be a real child or an imaginary child? . . . She is inclined to think it should be real, but this vision says its conception starts from a seed in her eye, and from that she will never have a real child. It will be visionary or spiritual."

10. Carotenuto, *A Secret Symmetry*, p. 86.

11. Ibid., p. 85.

12. Ibid., p. 112.

13. C. G. Jung, *Memories, Dreams, Reflections*, pp. 180–181. Another version of his Siegfried dream appears in C. G. Jung, *Analytical Psychology: Notes of the Seminar Given in 1925*, ed. William McGuire (Princeton: Princeton University Press, 1989), pp. 56–57:

> At the last lecture I told you of my descent into the cavern. After that came a dream in which I had to kill Siegfried. Siegfried was not an especially sympathetic figure to me, and I don't know why my unconscious got engrossed in him. Wagner's Siegfried, especially, is exaggeratedly extraverted and at times actually ridiculous. I never liked him. Nevertheless my dream showed him to be my hero. I could not understand the strong emotion I had with the dream. . . .
>
> This was the dream: I was in the Alps, not alone, but with another man, a curious shortish man with brown skin. Both of us carried rifles. It was just before dawn, when the stars were disappearing from the sky, and we were climbing up the mountain together. Suddenly I heard Siegfried's horn sound out from above, and I knew that it was he we were to shoot. The next minute he appeared high above us, lit up by a shaft of sunlight from the rising sun. He came plunging down the mountainside in a chariot made of bones. I thought to myself, "Only Siegfried could do that." Presently, around a bend in the trail, he came upon us, and we fired full into his breast. Then I was filled with horror and disgust at myself for the cowardice of what we had done. The little man with me went forward, and I knew he was going to drive the knife into Siegfried's heart, but that was just a little too much for me, and I turned and fled. I had the idea of getting away as fast as I could to a place where "they" could not find me. I had the choice of going down into the valley or further up the mountains by a faint trail. I chose the latter, and as I ran there broke upon me a perfect deluge of rain. Then I awoke with a sense of great relief.
>
> The hero, as I told you, is the symbol of the greatest value recognized by us. Christ has been our hero when we accept the principles of his life as our own principles. Or Herakles or Mithras becomes my hero when I am determined to be as disciplined as they were. So it appeared as if Siegfried were my hero. I felt an enormous pity for him, as though I myself had been shot. I must then have had a hero I did not appreciate, and it was my ideal of force and efficiency I had killed. I had killed my intellect, helped on to the deed by a personification of the collective unconscious, the little brown man with me. In other words, I deposed my superior function.

14. For an alternative, Freudian interpretation that combines a father/son conflict and patricidal death wish, see Nandor Fodor, *Freud, Jung, and Occultism* (New Hyde Park: University Books, 1971). The point of departure for Fodor is the proposition that Siegfried in the dream represents Jung: "So Siegfried was himself. The father of Siegfried was Sigmund. He was then Sigmund's son. Freud had treated him like a son, and Siegfried was a play on Sig Freud. It was Freud whom he killed in the dream, a dramatization of his death wish and remorse at carrying out the unconscious aggression against the father of psychoanalysis who wanted to make him his Crownprinz and heir. In his megalomania he wanted to step into Freud's place without delay and owe him nothing" (p. 23). In the opinion of Fodor, the Siegfried dream is an example of the profundity of repression. By means of a pun ("Siegfried/Sig Freud"), the dream represents a desire on the part of Jung to kill Freud. It is unconscious "hostility to Freud" that motivates not only the dream but also the misinterpretation of the dream by Jung: "When it appeared in really unmistakable terms in the Siegfried dream, his mind went blank to the real interpretation, even though the understanding of the dream was said to be, by a voice sounding in his mind, a matter of life and death to him" (p. 108).

15. Paul Ricoeur, *Freud and Philosophy: An Essay on Interpretation*, trans. Denis Savage (New Haven and London: Yale University Press, 1970), pp. 32-35.

16. It is true that Jung explicitly repudiates the distinction between manifest and latent content as well as the idea of the facade: "What Freud calls the 'dream-facade' is the dream's obscurity, and this is really only a projection of our own lack of understanding. We say that the dream has a false front only because we fail to see into it. We would do better to say that we are dealing with something like a text that is unintelligible not because it has a facade—a text has no facade—but simply because we cannot read it. We do not have to get behind such a text, but must first learn to read it" (*CW* 16, p. 149). Nevertheless, it seems to me that the distinction between surface and depth psychology—not to mention the very idea of the unconscious—necessarily implies that we are ignorant of, perhaps innocent of, what really motivates us. Psychoanalysis has compelled us to acknowledge that we do not always immediately know all the real motives.

17. *Standard Edition* 17, p. 119.

18. See Peter L. Berger and Thomas Luckmann, *The Social Construction of Reality: A Treatise in the Sociology of Knowledge* (Garden City, N.Y.: Doubleday, 1966), and Alfred Schutz, *Collected Papers*, Volume 1: *The Problem of Social Reality*, ed. Maurice Natanson (The Hague: Martinus Nijhoff, 1962), and Volume 2: *Studies in Social Theory*, ed. Arvid Brodersen (The Hague: Martinus Nijhoff, 1964).

19. See H. A. Hodges, *Wilhelm Dilthey: An Introduction* (London: Routledge and Kegan Paul, 1949) and *The Philosophy of Wilhelm Dilthey* (London:

Routledge and Kegan Paul, 1952). See also H. P. Rickman (ed.), *Wilhelm Dilthey: Selected Writings* (Cambridge: Cambridge University Press, 1976).

20. Tzvetan Todorov, *The Conquest of America: The Question of the Other*, trans. Richard Howard (New York: Harper and Row, 1984), p. 249.

21. Tzvetan Todorov, " 'Race,' Writing, and Culture," in *"Race," Writing, and Difference*, ed. Henry Louis Gates, Jr. (Chicago and London: University of Chicago Press, 1986), pp. 370–371.

22. Gregory Bateson, "Form, Substance, and Difference," *Steps to an Ecology of Mind: Collected Essays in Anthropology, Psychiatry, Evolution, and Epistemology* (Northvale, N.J., and London: Jason Aronson, 1987), pp. 454–471, and Jacques Derrida, "Difference," *Speech and Phenomena*, trans. David B. Allison (Evanston, Ill.: Northwestern University, 1973), pp. 129–160. See also Michael Vannoy Adams, "Deconstructive Philosophy and Imaginal Psychology: Comparative Perspectives on Jacques Derrida and James Hillman," in Rajnath (ed.), *Deconstruction: A Critique* (London: Macmillan, 1989), pp. 138–157, and *Journal of Literary Criticism* 2, no. 1 (June 1985), pp. 23–39.

Thoughts and Memories
of C. G. Jung

Werner H. Engel

Werner H. Engel, M.D., a psychiatrist and Jungian analyst, is a Life Fellow of the American Psychiatric Association. He was born in Berlin in 1901, worked as a farmer, and came to the United States as a refugee from the Nazis in 1940. During the war, he volunteered for the U.S. Army Rehabilitation Service; from 1957 to 1977 he served as a psychiatric examiner to the German General Consulate for restitutions for victims of the Nazis. He was president of the New York Association for Analytical Psychology (1965–1972) and was founder and medical director of the C. G. Jung Training Center Clinic (1975–1983).

As a participant in the "Lingering Shadows" conference, Dr. Engel was invited to submit his paper to this book, although he did not present it at the conference. He presents here his perspective on Jung and the Nazi era through personal reminiscences of Jung and memories of conversations with several of his Jewish followers. This is the story of a Jew, a survivor of Nazi Germany, a psychiatrically trained physician, and a Jungian analyst who has found in Jungian psychology a meaningful context in which to place the events of his personal life. Not disregarding the shadow element in Jung, Dr. Engel faces it in full recognition of the special category of Jung's personality.

The 1989 conference "Lingering Shadows: Jungians, Freudians, and Anti-Semitism" brought memories to my mind that I regard as milestones in my relationship to Jung's person and Jung's work.

I am aware that such memories are necessarily incomplete and subjective.

In Berlin, in 1929, when I was twenty-eight years old, a meaningful coincidence had brought me to my first analyst, James Kirsch, M.D. In 1933, before leaving for Palestine to flee the Nazis, Kirsch called my attention to the presence of C. G. Jung in Berlin, where I saw Jung for the first time.

I remember Jung's next time in Berlin in 1934. He was giving a seminar in the Architects' Building which was located on a very wide street, I believe, Hardenbergstrasse. Through that street a military parade was scheduled for the reception of Mussolini by Hitler.

Jung had started speaking when the parade came nearer and nearer, brass, drums, and all else increasing. He was standing on the stage, with the usual big Nazi flag on his left side and, on a chair to his right, a uniformed Nazi officer who had been assigned to monitor the lecture according to the ruling for assemblies. Soon, with the noise growing louder and louder, Jung had to stop. Only we who were seated in the front could hear what he said in his normal, well-grounded voice: *"Lassen wir die Weltgeschichte ruhig an uns vorbeimarschieren!"* (Let world history quietly pass us by). His stress was on the *vorbei* ("by").

Now, the word *vorbei* in German has both a literal and a connotative meaning. Literally, as I translated above, Jung merely stated that world history was passing by. But *vorbei* can also connote the hope that something will be over. This is precisely the meaning we heard Jung express, in a rather tongue-in-cheek manner: his hope that this Nazi period of world history would soon be over.[1] Those of us sitting in the front, in fact, were so sure that Jung had implied this second meaning that we were staring in fearful tension at the SS-officer. He was as close to Jung as we were. Had he noticed what Jung had so forcefully expressed with his *"vorbei"*? We had expected some consternation or even some action, as he was there to guard against exactly what had just happened. Yet there was not a move—so he was apparently under the fascination of what happened outside those windows.

I was most powerfully impressed by Jung's sentence. Something in me knew that I had heard the real Jung, and that knowing has crystallized more and more over time.

Jung strongly believed in that *vorbei*. At the time, he shared that belief with an unknown number of others: that Germany would wake up to see what was going on. A strong idea of transition, a strong belief in transformation toward what he wished Germany to be, must have been on his mind in those dark and beclouded days. That man whom I just had seen and heard was certainly not a Nazi.

Marie-Louise von Franz, known as a sharp-thinking critic, has stated that in all the years that she knew Jung personally, from 1933 to his death, she "never perceived the slightest conscious or unconscious trace of any such attitude . . . referring to the oft-repeated slander that Jung was a National Socialist and/or anti-Semitic."[2] She speaks of a "therapeutic optimism" that must be considered before Jung's mistakes are to be discussed. Jung had "admitted his illusions about people when it came to Nazism and he could never have imagined that such abysmal evil could come to the surface and break out."[3]

In the same year, 1934, Jung acted directly against the most basic Nazi rulings and principles, the destruction of anything Jewish, when he officially reinvited Jewish psychotherapists, whom the Germans had *gleichgeschaltet* (i.e., deprived of their professional standing and more), back into his international organization by using his position as president to make a basic change of the constitution of this organization. He announced this change at the time of the Congress in Bad Nauheim, in the midst of Nazi ruling. The publication of this pro-Jewish constitutional change could not be released in Nazi Germany and was therefore added as a special unbound page of the *Zentralblatt für Psychotherapie* for subscribers outside Germany. This page was used by Ernest Harms for his paper "Carl Gustav Jung—Defender of Freud and the Jews," in which he revised widespread misconceptions about Jung.

Harms, the chief editor of the scientific journal *The Nervous Child*, had been my coordinator when I was in charge of a psychiatric child guidance clinic in New York City. I remember that he reported difficulties in finding the special page containing

Jung's reinvitation to the Jewish therapists in New York City libraries, but had found it in an out-of-town library. He left the question open whether anyone in New York City might have been interested in preventing Jung's pro-Jewish activities from being known in wider circles.

That article by Harms is a well-researched history of Jung's activities around the year 1934 and could well be a compensation for the various misinterpretations of that period. Jung has frequently described the difficulties he had taken on himself in this chaotic period. They do not need repetition. I was in Berlin, my birthplace, during the Hitler years from 1933 to 1940, because various emigration attempts had failed for political reasons. Only later, in New York, in Zurich, and other places, did I hear or read about Jung's activities for the support and assistance given to Jews and his organized efforts to help assure the victory of the Western Powers. I am not sure whether Jung has received proper credit for these various activities.

I have rather experienced the opposite. What I mean is what I prefer to call the "formula" with the wording: "How can you . . ." Innumerable times and at a great variety of places where I met with Jews, I met with the "How can you . . ." formula. That means: How can you who are a good Jew associate with that Nazi or anti-Semite Jung!

The basis for this formula is the archetypal concept: treason, with in-built duplicity: treason against my collective, my tribe on the one hand; treason against my inner knowing, my conviction, on the other. This was where the silent memory from the noisy moment of the "*vorbei*" found its proper place, and its answer: Who of the questioners really wants to know who that man Jung really is, or was? Very few; the rest just simply knew better, they had read it all.

I remember when Dr. M. Esther Harding, an outstanding representative of Jung in New York, once arrived with pounds of anti-Jungian letters and articles, her years-long collection. Today such a collection would be much heavier. There is a great amount of energy invested there, even—or especially—when it appears repetitive. It is certainly worth examining. To be satisfied with describing a person from his dark side only, his or her shadow, does not show the total person. But the method is of great interest and frequently applied. It does not leave room for the light—for values. It is the method of anti-Semitism: you isolate and enlarge the shadow qualities, even invent or project them, and you diminish, neglect, or deny what is valuable and acceptable. That is the nature of the prejudicial element in anti-Semitism. It expressed itself clearly in that special formula "How can you . . . !"

The difference was that this time it was not pointing at a Jew, but at the non-Jewish Jung.

In a more organized form, the principle of concentrating on the shadow without leaving much space for the positive values of a person and his work can even appear under the title "Lingering Shadows" here relating to "Jungians, Freudians, and Anti-Semitism." Unless a listener is well aware of what Freud as well as Jung actually means for our time, facing the volume of those lingering shadows could lead to a distortion of the image of these personalities.

On the other hand, there is no doubt about the necessity of clarifying and truthfully researching those elements that could have an influence on freeing the emotions that may have blocked the acceptance of the total personalities of either of these two highly creative men.

The emotional element of acceptability is also the basis for loyalty toward a person, which may contain the acceptance of unified opposites of dark shadow and bright light. This factor— acceptance—may well be preceded by a painfully felt dilemma which faces the individual with a special task of healing, starting with the internal one.

In my early analytical years 1929 to 1933 and later I had established my collection of Jungian books and related literature that were ready to be packed when the American consulate proceeded with the acceptance of affidavits for visa to the United States, where my wife's family had resettled. The time was 1938 when I found out that whatever I wanted to take out of Germany would undergo inspection in my district of Berlin. I also heard that the inspectors were not all alike in letting the restricted Jungian books pass, but mine was especially strict and to try to bribe him could be deadly.

A friend, Heinz Westmann, who had fled to England before his goods could be packed, had asked me to be present at the packing of his lift-van. That inspector, I found out, was open to financially supported persuasion, and so my bookcase with Jungian books went first to England. One thing was clear: the Nazis had learned between 1933 and 1938 that Jung was not one of them, but the opposite, a declared anti-Nazi. The inspectors knew that Jung's books were blacklisted. The Nazis knew in 1938 what some people do not seem to know fifty years later.

Besides the paper by Harms, many efforts have been made to study the life of Jung around 1934. There are individual statements like "Jung, the Jews, and Hitler" by Jay Sherry in *Spring* 1986 and repeated chapters on Jung and National Socialism in the books of Aniela Jaffé and many others.

I was highly impressed by James Kirsch's paper "Reconsidering Jung's So-Called Anti-Semitism."[4] Kirsch, an outstanding Jewish Jungian analyst from Berlin, deeply rooted in his Judaism, had known Jung since 1928 and, with some interruptions, had worked with Jung in Zurich about once a year for decades, until Jung's death. His paper brings, with great openness and clarity, the facts that have contributed to Jung's reputation as an anti-Semite, including the "quite devastating" fragment of a letter to W. M. Kranenfeldt.

Kirsch concludes that Jung's unacceptable and insufficiently informed statements derived from residues of his tragic and painful relationship to Freud, and that facing the immensely powerful god-image of Yahweh in his later book *Answer to Job* had resulted in conquering in depth any residues of potential anti-Semitic traces. "Through this brutal act of fate he finally overcame the anti-Semitic feelings which originally had been activated in him through his experience of Freud."[5] In his way Kirsch has worked out that the Jewish question was for Jung not a matter of politics, but essentially a deeply intrapsychic experience with its consequences.

In this connection it could be said that the attempts of Emma Jung and Sabina Spielrein to accomplish a reconciliation of these two men, Jung and Freud, in an early period would have been most senseless if they, two women who knew Jung intimately had noticed anti-Semitism in Jung's motivations.

In my conversations with Siegmund Hurwitz, a Jewish Jungian in Zurich deeply involved in Kabbalah studies, he told me what happened in 1939 when Hitler was preparing to march into Austria. Freud was in Vienna. Jung and the Riklin family, of whom the son was a friend of Hurwitz, prepared a basis for an escape for Freud to Switzerland or any safe place, and the son of Riklin traveled to Vienna to Freud's house to deliver the monetary support in person. At the door he received the answer that Freud would not accept help from his enemies.[6]

It would certainly be a daring speculation to imagine what could have resulted from that invitation if Freud had not reacted with that basically not surprising rejection. Jung may have had an extraordinary potentiality of a totally new contact in mind, maybe even a reversal of the father-son transference on a higher spiritual level.

But all that stayed was prolonged pain.

Hurwitz also confirmed to me that Jung, occasionally with Hurwitz's assistance, had undergone intensive studies to deepen his knowledge of Judaism, including Isaac Luria's kabbalistic writings.

In this connection it is of interest that on November 16, 1937, Jung wrote to Professor M. H. Goering, editor of the *Zentralblatt für Psychotherapie* in Berlin. Jung had heard that Goering planned a book review of the author Rosenberg, who had made the statement that the Jews have contempt for mysticism. Jung responded that this was an extremely regrettable error for anyone who knew Jewish history, especially Chasidism. He said that no mention should be made of such writing: "I cannot cover such derailments (*Entgleisungen*) with my name."[7]

When the time for him had come, Jung must have felt a powerful urge to rebuild or restore the personal side of his relationship with a most highly qualified and most deeply rooted representative of Judaism. That opportunity arose when Rabbi Leo Baeck came to Zurich. Rabbi Baeck had stayed, caring for his congregation in

Berlin, until the Nazis deported him and them to the concentration camp Theresienstadt, where he stayed until the last ones were freed.

Great credit is due to Aniela Jaffé for having given, in her well-known essay "Jung and National Socialism," a most impressive description of the highly important meeting of Jung and Rabbi Baeck. She let Gershom Scholem from Jerusalem tell the story.

Aniela Jaffé writes:

> Those who had an opportunity to converse with Jung personally were in a better position than an outsider to see the shadow side of this great researcher and to accept it. As evidence of this, I will quote from a letter which Gershom Scholem wrote to me in 1963 and has kindly permitted me to publish. It reports a conversation he had about Jung with Leo Baeck. With this report of a subjective experience I will end my attempt to give an account and interpretation of the facts.

Jerusalem
7 May 1963

Dear Mrs. Jaffé:

As you are so interested in the story of Baeck and Jung, I will write it down for your benefit and have no objection to being cited by you in this matter.

In the summer of 1947 Leo Baeck was in Jerusalem. I had then just received for the first time an invitation to the Eranos meeting in Ascona, evidently at Jung's suggestion, and I asked Baeck whether I should accept it, as I had heard and read many protests about Jung's behavior in the Nazi period. Baeck said: "You must go, absolutely!" and in the course of our conversation told me the following story. He too had been put off by Jung's reputation resulting from those well-known articles in the years 1933–34, precisely because he knew Jung very well from the Darmstadt meetings of the School of Wisdom and would never have credited him with any Nazi and anti-Semitic sentiments. When, after his release from Theresienstadt, he returned to Switzerland for the first time (I think it was 1946), he therefore did not call on Jung in Zurich. But it came to Jung's ears that he was in the city and Jung sent a message begging him to visit him, which he, Baeck, declined because of those happenings. Whereupon Jung came to his hotel and they had an extremely lively talk lasting two hours, during which Baeck reproached him with all the things he had heard. Jung defended himself by an appeal to the special conditions in Germany but at the same time confessed to him: "Well, I slipped up"—probably referring to the Nazis and his expectation that something great might after all emerge. This remark, "I slipped up," which Baeck repeated to me several times, remains vividly in my memory. Baeck said that in this talk they cleared up everything that had come between them and that they parted from one another reconciled again. Because of this explanation of Baeck's I accepted the invitation to Eranos when it came a second time.

Yours sincerely,

G. Scholem[8]

Siegmund Hurwitz had later told me that not only Scholem but also Rabbi Baeck had joined Jung at an Eranos meeting at Ascona. In addition, James Kirsch reported that Baeck stayed in Jung's home for two weeks in 1947.[9]

When leaders so deeply rooted in Judaism as Rabbi Leo Baeck and Gershom Scholem were able to accomplish the final healing of their relationship with Carl Jung, those who cannot might consider going more deeply and seriously into themselves, assisted by the inner opening for meeting the total personality of this man Jung.

The powerful energy that had driven Jung not to let Leo Baeck go without the opportunity to meet him face to face must have been harbored in Jung since those years around 1934. "*Ausgerutscht*," which appears translated as "slipped up," means much more than the simple "slipped up" to a Swiss mountain climber, as Jung was. It means to lose one's footing, and in the quest to conquer those great Swiss mountains, to lose one's footing is an occurrence of truly serious and potentially deadly nature. It was of a matter on such a level that Jung referred to when he said, "*Ich bin ausgerutscht.*" For him, the "slippings" of 1933–34 were now seen as the tragic and deadly serious missteps that they had been. And it was to this context and to this meaning that Leo Baeck must have resonated in their important meeting of reconciliation.

Jung did not believe in whitewashing. Aniela Jaffé has, in a different connection, preserved Jung's opinion by the following: *"Keiner darf sich vom andern 'die Würde seiner Schuld' nehmen lassen."* (No one shall allow another to deprive him of the dignity of his guilt.)[9]

The question of loyalty to Jung played a significant role in my relationship to Jewish Jungian analysts in my early years. It was clear that each one had found his or her own loyalty to Jung in an individual way.

Specifically I remember such loyalty discussions with James Kirsch in New York and Los Angeles, Max Zeller in Berlin, Gerhard Adler in London, Ernst Bernhard in Rome, and with Erich Neumann on his balcony looking out to the Mediterranean in Tel Aviv. The meeting with Erich Neumann at which we discussed loyalty to Jung stands sharply in my memory because of the wide and beautiful expanse of the Mediterranean visible from that balcony. In more recent years Julia Neumann remarked to me how sad she was that that very view was obscured by new buildings that had gone up.

The memory of that wide view corresponds symbolically to my memory of the inner attitude that leads to the acceptance of Jung as a total personality. These five Jewish analysts whom I have mentioned had all originally come from Berlin.

Some extended analytical work with Rivkah Schaerf (later to become Rivkah Kluger) in Zurich had led, on the basis of a dream, to the first of my many trips to Israel.

I have mentioned six Jewish names of analysts, early followers of Jung. If I wanted to extend that list beyond those six I would have to mention a very long list of analysts, all devoted Jewish followers of Jung. The length of that list could well remind one of the fact that for a while the group of Freud was described by others and himself as representative of a "Jewish science." Considering the length of that list, one can well say that here Jung is not too far behind Freud, as far as Jewish followers are concerned.

The meeting between Jung and Baeck was personal, eye-to-eye between these two great men.

I want to conclude with an account of my last meeting

with Jung in 1954, an encounter that struck me then and has remained with me ever since as being representative of that outstanding man.

I had had many sessions with Emma Jung at that time. A frequent topic had been the many forms of pain. She even wanted to be informed about the various patents of American reclining chairs, apparently stimulated by her desire to sit and rest more comfortably, maybe related to an early discomfort that may have foreshadowed her tragic end only one year later.

I remember that my topic on this particular occasion was my seven Hitler years in Berlin and, later, my mother's suicide in Berlin. My mother took her life after receiving the order to report to Alexanderplatz, which meant concentration camp, unaware that my visa and ticket for her to the United States were in the mail, to arrive the next day.

Then Emma Jung stood up, walked around her long table, and stretched out her hand. I, standing, took her guiding hand, and she led me all the way to Jung's room. She opened the door, said my name, and when Dr. Jung, from his seat, gestured to me to be seated, she had left.

Jung's strong voice was nearly inaudible. I heard, in the beginning, a few words relating to his German origin. The rest was silence, with powerful waves of silent communication between us. No way to say whose pain, whose darkness, was around—and no need. Three and a half decades later there is no loss of intensity.

I had felt at the start surrounded by a sea of pain and very slowly entered the inconceivable deepening of the numinosum in that nonexisting time.

The comradeship in silence with this radiant man whose universal creativity had given my life guidance and meaning was on a level far out of the reach of the categories of those "lingering shadows."

For me, what was felt as grace was the recognition that a time shared in human comradeship, in deepest silence, was more convincing of the true category of that extraordinary man than any reading or even speaking could be or have been.

This communion of silence was a powerful bridge from the

totality of one man's life to that of another and even, potentially, into life beyond. That silence, that uniting communication took its own time, and when I had the feeling that it was time to go, I arose in silence, no words, no formalities. I just got up and left, filled with the numinosity of that utterly powerful togetherness.

A last look at the well-known inscription over the front door— "*Vocatus atque non vocatus, Deus aderit*" (Called or not called, the God will be present)—and I was out in great silence on the walkway to the street, into the little world of Seestrasse.

Notes

1. From Hella Adler in London I learned how Gerhard Adler, who had been present, had described Jung saying those same words: "with a twinkle in his eyes."

2. Marie-Louise von Franz, C. G. *Jung: His Myth in Our Time* (New York: G. P. Putnam & Sons, 1975), pp. 63–64.

3. Ibid.

4. In *The Arms of the Windmill: Essays in Analytical Psychology* (1981).

5. Ibid., p. 25.

6. For details, see Robert S. McCully, Letters, *Quadrant* 20, no. 2 (1987): 73–74. Conversation with Riklin Jr.

7. C. G. Jung, *Briefe*, vol. 1, 1906–1945 (Freiburg: Walter Verlag, 1972), p. 302.

8. Aniela Jaffé, "Jung and National Socialism," in *Jung's Last Years and Other Essays*, pp. 96–99.

9. James Kirsch, Interview with David Serbin, *Psychological Perspectives*, Fall 1985, p. 172.

10. Aniela Jaffé, *Aus Leben und Werkstatt von C. G. Jung* (Zurich: Rascher Verlag, 1968), p. 120.

On the Relationship between Erich Neumann and C. G. Jung and the Question of Anti-Semitism

Micha Neumann

Micha Neumann, M.D., is a psychiatrist, Professor of Psychiatry at the Sackler School of Medicine of Tel Aviv University, and medical director of Shalvata Mental Health Center in Israel. His parents, Julie and Erich Neumann, were both enthusiastic followers of Jung. The fact of Jung's close relationship to Erich Neumann, who was both a Jew and a Zionist, stands in sharp contrast to the allegations of anti-Semitism and pro-Nazi sympathies that have been leveled against Jung.

In this paper, Dr. Neumann portrays the relationship between his father and Jung through reference to their extensive correspondence. He emphasizes that Erich Neumann exhorted Jung to become more aware of Jewish religion and culture, and regrets the fact that Jung never did this. It is clear, however, that Jung very much valued his relationship to Neumann and encouraged him in his work.

Dr. Neumann compares his father's relationship to Jung with that of Freud to Jung, and finds Jung to be the more compassionate and less ethnocentric mentor. While Jung's relationship to Neumann seems free of anti-Semitic prejudice, his writings and actions around the year 1934 definitely were not. Dr. Neumann suggests that Jung never came to terms with this aspect of his shadow.

Since the time of my childhood Jung was a central and positive figure in our family. His photographs decorated my father's desk. His name, whenever mentioned by my parents, reflected respect, love, and friendship. I perceived his presence as that of a friend and teacher.

As I was growing up, the rumors that Jung was pro-Nazi and an anti-Semite disturbed me a great deal. When I finally asked my parents about these accusations, they became embarrassed and defensive. They said the accusations were unjust but admitted that Jung made mistakes and that he had been misunderstood.

I learned that my father had worked with Jung during the years 1933–1934 in Zurich. My parents left Germany for Palestine a short while after the Nazi takeover in Germany. Before their departure they witnessed brutal anti-Jewish demonstrations, propaganda, and persecution. My father told me that he tried to convince Jung of the terrible danger of the Nazi movement, of the brutality and inhumanity of the Nazis. He asked Jung to express himself openly and clearly against their ideologies and especially their anti-Semitic ideas and policies. He admitted that he failed to change Jung's attitude. My father warned him that if he kept quiet at such a bad time for the Jews, then it would always be remembered and he would never be forgiven. Jung, believing in the qualities of the German collective unconscious, insisted that something positive might still emerge from the situation.

My father pleaded with Jung to learn more about Judaism so that he could have a deeper understanding of Jewish roots, culture, and psychology. Jung was a far more willing student of Far Eastern culture than of Jewish culture, which was much nearer to his own. My father expected Jung to apply his great wisdom, creativity, and knowledge in order to be more closely involved with the present Jewish problem.

Even though Jung promised my father that he would study Judaism, he never really kept his promise. My parents, although understandably disappointed, regarded Jung's "oversight" as only an error, an aberration, a blind spot. This did not change a bit their very positive attitude toward Jung. "Even great men make mistakes," they said, and their love and admiration for Jung was not diminished. When I talked about these matters in my own analysis (a Freudian psychoanalysis), my analyst said, "Every anti-Semite has his own good Jews." He had no doubts about Jung's anti-Semitism.

The relationship between Freud and Jung and their painful breakup captured my interest, and in 1986 I published an article about this fascinating subject in the *Hebrew Journal of Psychotherapy*. I found myself intensely involved in the father-son relationship between Freud and Jung. I regarded the relationship between Jung and Erich Neumann also as a father-son relationship. I could not resist delving deeper into this matter and exploring it. For me, as a psychoanalyst and a Jew, Freud is the great-grandfather who was in a bitter conflict with Jung, my father's spiritual father. I decided to study these problems and reach my own conclusions.

After my mother's death in 1985, I found the correspondence between Erich Neumann and Jung. This same correspondence was the basis for an article I wrote about the Jung-Neumann relationship. And, coincidentally, it was just when I finished this paper that I received the invitation to speak on the delicate problem of Jung and anti-Semitism at the "Lingering Shadows" conference. You can imagine my excitement about this synchronicity.

When I read Jung's article "Zur gegenwärtigen Lage der Psychotherapie," published in the *Zentralblatt für Psychotherapie* at the beginning of 1934, I was quite shocked at his aggressive anti-Semitic expressions and pro-Germanic, pro-Aryan, pro–National Socialistic opinions and beliefs. To think that all this was written and published in German at the time when the Nazis were carrying out their evil anti-Semitic and anti-democratic plans in Germany made it even worse. This article aroused much criticism in the Jewish world and especially among Jung's Jewish disciples and colleagues. I studied Jung's correspondence from the year 1934 with these Jewish friends and found additional expressions that I could not avoid regarding as anti-Semitic. And finally there was a letter from Jung to his former assistant in Berlin, Dr. Kranefeldt, a Nazi, dated February 9, 1934. This letter was full of contemptuous and sarcastic anti-Semitic remarks and expressions.

For me to realize that all these anti-Semitic ideas and terminologies were expressed at the same time that my father lived in Zurich and worked with Jung was shocking. Equally disturbing was the fact that, during that same period, while Jung held the Nazis in high regard and expressed such negative feelings against "the Jews," he also felt affection, respect, and even friendship toward my father.

Could my analyst have been right when he said, "Every anti-Semite has his good Jews whom he regards as exceptions, as different from the rest of the Jews"? How can it be explained that at the individual level Jung helped Jews and supported them, while at the collective level he was so completely indifferent and insensitive to their tragedy?

There must have been a scotoma, a blind spot, in Jung's psyche that was responsible for these outstanding discrepancies in his attitude and his behavior. The roots of this problem can be traced back to Jung's complicated, conflict-laden, and unanalyzed relationship with Freud. There were not only father projections on Freud but also strong elements of unconscious religious contents. He identified himself unconsciously with Nazi symbols, ideology, and anti-Semitism. He believed in the positive collective "Germanic soul," to which he felt he belonged. Is it not true that Jung's shadow remained repressed and cut off from his own consciousness?

In that same year, 1934, Jung declared his willingness to relate to the Jewish problem and to concentrate on the very special conditions in Palestine through his correspondence with my father, who had immigrated to Palestine. He even mentioned these promises and intentions in his letter to James Kirsch dated May 26, 1934. Through reading the correspondence between Jung and my father I uncovered a different aspect of his attitude to his Jewish pupil Erich Neumann. Could this be the same anti-Semite who collaborated with the Nazis and believed in their future?

My father's first letter to Jung was written in the summer of 1934. It is a long and very interesting letter in which he tells Jung all about his first impressions and strong feelings as a new immigrant in Palestine and about his first encounter with the Jews there.

The letter is very open, warm, and friendly. Neumann ends it by writing: "Dear Dr. Jung, as always it seems to me to be too cheap to thank you for all that I received from you. My ambition encourages me to give you as a gift of gratitude a creation of my own. I do not think it is difficult for me to say thank you, but it seems too little."

On August 12, 1934, Jung replied in a letter that has not been published:

> I do not think that the Jews suffered from a collective neurosis until the emancipation. The question is whether or not the emancipation influenced them in the direction of neurotization. The group, social, and national perception of the Jews until their emancipation was to some extent parallel to the spiritual and political situation of the Christians during the Middle Ages. With the liberation of the Christians from the authority of the church, archetypes awakened to life, and the Christian world is still busy assimilating them. In Germany this awakening brought manifestations of a new kind of paganism, which hearkens back to the distant past of the Germans and is a concession to the might of the ancient archaic pagan archetypes. Therefore, I believe that the Jews, who were emancipated from the authority of their religion, are threatened in a similar way from the awakening to life of their collective unconscious. One awakening archetype is no doubt connected to the land, hence the spiritual need of Zionism. To the extent that these awakening archetypes do not undergo digestion, assimilation, and integration, a neurotic situation can easily ensue. In the Western Christian world, neurotic restlessness is clear and apparent. . . .
>
> . . . I know that the Jewish problem is a serious subject that concerns you, while for me the psychic life of the individual and his mental situation are the most important issues. You can be assured that I will devote myself to your problem with all the means at my disposal. I feel it is especially important to discuss the complexity of modern culture and the spiritual situation in Europe with a Jew just like yourself. You know the situation in Europe well and yet think from a point of view that is different than mine, and you stand on your own archetypal ground. By the

way, I was very intrigued by your dreams as a result of your encounter with Palestine. This is a real psychic blood transfusion.

Now comes an amazing passage:

Jacob, in contrast to Esau, constitutes a symbolic attempt at collective individuation or, better, a stage in a collective development, as, for instance, historically Hitler is an attempt at collective individuation for the German, or mythologically, Jesus, Mithras, Attis, Osiris, etc. You are therefore quite right to look at the problem as a whole from the side of the collective unconscious and grasp Jacob as a symbolic exponent of the *Volkspsychologie*.

Further passages of this unpublished letter say:

The non-Jews as "citizens of the world" cannot fall into an "outside" *(Aussen)* because they are already in the outside. Their number and the fact that they own the land are a counterbalance against the danger of the within. . . . Through his mere existence the Jew draws attention to these unpleasantnesses. Thus he falls into the shadow zone of the non-Jewish masses. They do not need self-defense (except in emergency situations) and only a small amount of intuition and therefore have a stronger perception for sensation and aesthetic perception (in order to enjoy their safe life).

. . . In this way the Christians fall into the shadow of the Jews and are assured of their secret contempt, because they live in an immoral peace with all that the Jews may desire but is forbidden to them. . . . Only with the liberalization—i.e., the disintegration of Christianity with the enlightenment—did the Jew receive the counter-gift of the Danaer (the Greeks), emancipation, and with it, the tradition, contradictory and God-alien joy of the world, which is always the fruit of living in physical safety.

The letter ends with the sentence: "What is the meaning of *Galuth* [exile]? A riddle."

In this letter, Jung impressed me as completely different from the Jung who expressed pro-Nazi and anti-Jewish prejudices. His observations about the influence of emancipation on the Jewish

awakening archtypes is anything but anti-Semitic. His willingness
to discuss Jewish problems and issues with Neumann is clear and
friendly. No ambivalence or animosity against the Jews can be
found.

The only striking passage in this letter is Jung's fantastic comparison between Jacob as a symbolic "stage in a collective [Jewish]
development, and "Hitler as an attempt at collective individuation
for the Germans." I believe that this most unfortunate passage
from Jung's letter to Neumann is the reason for its exclusion from
the published Jung letters. Yet it is interesting and astonishing to
note that in August 1934 Jung still attributed to Hitler such
significance as a collective individuation for the Germans.

The following passages are from a letter from Neumann to Jung
dated May 19, 1935:

> . . . I have stubbornly decided not to let you loose, and I want to
> warn you once again. I have a solid intention not to let you rest
> with the Jewish problem and, if necessary, I will regain the racial
> qualities of stubbornness and flexibility that I have lost. All this
> in order that you will lead me into the depth of these questions in
> such a manner that I will not be forced to see you in too narrow
> a light and too removed from Judaism. It seems that I have a
> confession to make, even though it is unpleasant for me to do so.
> Before I came to you in Zurich, I was a bit sad because I could
> not find a Jewish spiritual authority that I could accept as a
> teacher. Unfortunately I regarded it as typical of the present
> spiritual bankruptcy of Judaism and its inability to present me
> with a spiritual Jewish figure whom I could regard as a teacher.
>
> Only when at your side was that something which is prototypical
> of my situation revealed to me. It is written that the Jews have to
> go to "one of the righteous of the nations." Perhaps this is the
> reason they have none of their own. This Jewish situation and the
> beginning of mutual relationships and exchange of ideas between
> us are what make our correspondence so vital to me.

Neumann is still hoping that Jung, the teacher, will come closer
to Judaism and lead him to the depth of the Jewish problem. He
goes so far as to regard him as "one of the righteous of the

nations," and this at the same time that Jung was under heavy attack for being pro-Nazi and anti-Semitic. This title, *michasidei umot ha-olam* (one of the righteous of the nations of the world), was given by the State of Israel after the Holocaust to those non-Jews who risked their lives and their families during the Second World War in order to save Jewish lives from a certain death.

In another letter to Jung, dated October 19, 1935, Neumann writes:

> . . . The work on Jewish contents is slow and difficult. Only slowly do I grasp in which points analytical psychology cannot be the sole ground on which I stand. This does not mean that I am not standing on this ground and that I cannot grasp its main meaning. What I comprehend today, more than before, is the fact that Jungian analytical psychology itself stands on its own ground, which is something so obvious that it is not conscious of it. Switzerland, Germany, the West, Christianity; this is no discovery, and yet it is for me. I have to learn to differentiate myself, and that is very difficult for me, especially when so much weight is just on the other side (the Western Christian). It certainly is easier to assimilate as "your Jews" are doing, but thus the assimilant Jews keep distant from their individuation, which must, in spite of everything, be based on our own archetypal collective foundations, which are different because we are Jews.
>
> I see a danger for me in analytical psychology. This is the danger of betrayal to my own Jewish foundations, for something that is more beautiful, wider, and more modern. Only a final realization of analytical psychology can prevent me from this danger. The temptation is regression instead of individuation (the golden calf instead of a "bad" Jehovah). Not in vain did you work so seriously on Christianity, but you lack knowledge and understanding of Judaism.
>
> . . . The obviousness of the fact that you are Swiss, a Christian, and a man of the West prevents you, and not only you, in a vital sense from understanding that we Jews are Jews. Do you not underestimate the significance of this difference in the analyses of your Jewish patients? It is true that you once expressed your

disgust at the phenomenon of self-betrayal, but you never wrote about it and focused on the problem of Jewish identity. Do not regard this as insolence, but rather as a question. This matter is of extreme importance to me.

. . . If you want to use the Jews as the yeast of European culture, they are really quite useful in this function, but in this way they remain *"Kultur Juden,"* psychologically without their own foundations, that is, without a potential for individuation. There must be a return to the land, as political Zionism demands, as well as a psychological return. In Europe the individuation of the Jews is impossible.

Here again Neumann deplores Jung's lack of knowledge and understanding of Jews, Judaism, and the problem of Jewish identity. He implores Jung to delve more deeply into these issues. He wants Jung to understand Zionism and its necessity and the fact that in Europe, true individuation of the Jews in the Jungian sense is really impossible. It is interesting to see how Neumann insists on the differences between Jews and non-Jews, a difference that, when pointed out by Jung, was regarded as anti-Semitic.

Jung soon replied to Neumann's letter on December 22, 1935.

. . . What the European Jews do, I know already, but what the Jews do on archetypal soil, that interests me extraordinarily. . . . The *"Kultur Juden"* are always on the road to being "not Jews." You are quite right, the way does not go from good to better but first downward, to the historical roots. I demand that most of my Jewish patients pay attention to the fact that they are obviously Jews. I would not do it if I did not see so often Jews who imagine themselves to be something else. For those to be Jewish is some kind of personal insult. . . .

. . . Your very positive conviction that the Palestinian soil is vital for a Jewish individuation is dear to me. How does the fact that the Jew lived generally much longer in other countries, rather than just in Palestine, relate to your conviction? Even Moses Maimonides preferred Cairo, though he could live in Jerusalem. Can it be that the Jew is so very used to being not a Jew, that he needs the Palestinian soil *in concreto* in order to be reminded of his being Jewish? I can, however, only enter with difficulty in my mind into a soul that did not grow on any soil.

Here we can see that Jung was indeed interested in Zionism and that he dearly regards the notion of Jewish individuation through a return to the land. Even his critical question regarding the Jewish preference for living in the Diaspora cannot be regarded as hostile. Jung's remark about his inability to identify with "a soul that did not grow on any soil" again demonstrates his personal difficulty in, perhaps even his resistance to, empathizing or identifying himself with the Jews and their history and culture, but that too cannot be regarded as anti-Semitism.

After *Kristallnacht* Neumann wrote a painful letter to Jung dated December 15, 1938.

> I do not know if you can imagine how difficult it is to maintain an inner relationship with a man who naturally feels, at most, a superficial connection to the events that injure all of us Jews. . . . It is understandable and natural for me to know that you live on quite a different level than ours. . . . On the other hand, it makes the approach difficult, though I am deeply convinced that I do not have to reproach you too much for being a distanced observer. I am sure you are involved in the events (as I experience daily) through your practice with your patients. Still I feel the need to write to you once again in order to sustain within me the feeling that even for a Jew like myself there still exists some piece of Europe.

I was considerably impressed by Neumann's almost desperate efforts to keep up his positive relationship with Jung. His hope to involve Jung seriously and deeply in Jewish issues failed, as did his expectation that Jung, following the aftermath of the terrible *Kristallnacht*, would speak out clearly against the Nazi persecution of the Jews. Even after *Kristallnacht*, which was a cruel physical assault on the Jews and their existence in Germany, Neumann continues to defend Jung. He is deeply convinced that he does not have to "reproach Jung too much for being a mere observer from afar." He makes a tremendous effort to hold on to Jung and sustain the feeling that even for a Jew like Neumann himself, "there still exists some piece of Europe." Jung represents this good piece of Europe that Neumann is so dependent on.

Jung's speedy response came on December 19, 1938:

> You must not imagine that I retired to the snow-covered heights, above world events. I am even deeply involved and follow daily the newspapers on the Palestinian question and think often about my acquaintances there, who have to live in this chaos. . . . I have also predicted awful things for Germany, but when they really happen, it still will seem to me to be unbelievable. It can be said that here everyone is deeply shocked by what is going on in Germany. I have a lot to do with Jewish refugees and am permanently occupied with finding a place for all my Jewish acquaintances in England and in America. In this way I am in continuous connection with the events of our time. . . . I think you must be very careful concerning your opinion about your specific Jewish experiences. Truly there do exist specific Jewish traits in this development, but the specific Christian or Jewish traits have only a secondary significance. . . . Especially small is the difference between a typical Protestant and a Jewish psychology as far as the historical problem of time is concerned. Individual and race-related differences play only an insignificant role. . . . It seems to me that the specific Jewish trait as well as the specific Christian trait could best be discovered in the way and manner in which materials from the unconscious are accepted by the subject. According to my experience it seems that the resistance of the Jew against them is more rigid, and therefore the attempt to resist much more vehement. I do not mean by this more than a mere subjective impression.

I was struck by Jung's insensitivity to Neumann's plea. In his opening words he does not refer to *Kristallnacht* but rather speaks of the restlessness in Palestine. Later Jung writes that like everyone else in Switzerland he too is shocked by what is going on in Germany, but he offers no word of sympathy for the cruel fate of the German Jews, though he is very busy helping them. He goes on to say that the specific Christian or Jewish traits have only secondary significance. He writes that "race-related differences play only an insignificant part." Yet Jung insists on his subjective impression that the Jews are more resistant to materials from the unconscious than the Christians. Still, these views, which he reserves as subjective, could by no means be regarded as anti-Semitic.

On December 16, 1939, several months after the outbreak of the Second World War, Jung wrote to Neumann: "We here are naturally very much impressed by the direct danger of war in our own country, but in the meantime everything is still suspended. . . . In my lectures I deal with the Oriental position regarding the Yoga philosophy and the Western position regarding the Ignatian *Exercitia spiritualia*."

As can be seen, it's business as usual for the Swiss, neutral Jung. Only after the beginning of the Second World War did Jung finally give up his position as the president of the International Psychotherapeutic Society, which practically ceased to exist at that time.

On January 13, 1949, Jung wrote to Jorg Firtz, an editor of *Die Weltwoche,* about Neumann and his book *Depth Psychology and a New Ethic:* "When I recommend his book, I do so mainly because he [Neumann] demonstrates what consequences can be reached when the ethical problem is exposed and explored without consideration and to the end. It should be taken into account that Neumann is a Jew and hence knows Christianity only from the outside, and in addition, we should know that it was demonstrated to the Jews in the most drastic manner 'that evil is always projected on the outside' as Neumann claims." Jung continues:

> But I am not the same Neumann, who was driven and pushed by a cruel destiny into a belligerent counterposition. If by doing so he brings difficulty to the world, causing some people to suffer, I am not astonished and I will not consider it disgraceful. . . . I also cannot be sorry should the so-called Christians suffer a little. They certainly deserve it. One always speaks about Christian morality, and I would once like to see the person who really performs it. Even toward Neumann they do not show the most quiet understanding, let alone "love for thy neighbor."

In this letter Jung is really supportive and empathic with Neumann the Jew. He claims that the Christians should suffer and that

they deserve it. He attacks the Christians for lacking some understanding of Neumann and his ideas. Could it be that Jung also
referred to himself, as a Christian who should suffer for his
support of the Nazis and for his lack of empathy and understanding for the Jews, who themselves suffered so much from Christian
compassionate love?

In a letter to Neumann dated August 28, 1949, Jung writes:
"However, you have the tendency to judge the unconscious too
pessimistically. It would be advisable to add to each negative
comment a positive one; otherwise one may be impressed by a
catastrophic tragedy without mercy from above. This would not
be in keeping with the experience: 'God helps the courageous.' "

These remarks demonstrate the difference in mentality and
approach between Jung and Neumann, the Jew who is still under
the catastrophic impact of the Holocaust. Neumann, like the Jew
Freud (who was also accused of being too pessimistic in his views
of human nature and unconscious drives), sees the terrible dangers
of an unrestrained, unbalanced, and erupting unconscious. In
contrast, the naive and optimistic Swiss Jung really believes that
"God helps the courageous."

On July 1950 Neumann wrote to Jung on his seventy-fifth
birthday:

> In this little country [Israel], which is remote in many aspects
> and in many others productive and with good prospects for the
> future, I internally stand in solitude with a disintegrated Europe
> at my back and an Asia, dangerous in its awakening, in front of
> me. Just in such a situation, the connection with you meant to
> me vital support of decisive importance. . . . You were for me an
> internal guide, and this comforted me, especially because I, as a
> human being and a Jew, live, as you know, and experience things
> in many senses in a different and even opposite manner than you.
> Beyond the "incidents" and unpleasantnesses, I was always left
> with a feeling of inner connection to you which is stronger than
> you imagine.

This letter demonstrates again why Jung's support meant so much
to Neumann. The feeling of inner connection to Jung was more

important than their different human experiences as Jew and Christian, and the incidents and unpleasantnesses that occurred between them.

On December 5, 1951, Neumann wrote to Jung about his not yet published book *Answer to Job:* "This is a book that conquered me to my depth. I think it is the most beautiful and deepest of all your writings. It can be said that it is not really a book. It is a dialogue and dispute with God, similar to that of Abraham, when he argued with God about the fate of Sodom. For me personally it is like an accusation sheet against God, who allowed six million of his people to be killed." Neumann is so enthusiastic about Jung's *Answer to Job* that he goes so far as to compare Jung to Abraham, the Jewish patriarch. Neumann identifies completely here with Jung in his charge against the Old Testament Jewish God Jehovah.

Jung's reply to Neumann's letter came soon, on January 5, 1952: "I thank you very much for your friendly letter and for the way that you understand me. This compensates for a thousand misunderstandings."

On February 28, 1952, Jung wrote to Neumann about his book *Amor and Psyche:* "I must humbly tell you how much your *Amor and Psyche* made me happy. It is excellent and written with a most powerful involvement." Here we can see that Jung, the generous, benevolent teacher and friend, supports Neumann and rewards him by admiring his strong involvement and his excellent work. How much Jung must have yearned for a similar attitude from Freud toward his work some forty years earlier. How different the father-son relationship of Freud and Jung from that of Jung and Neumann.

On October 11, 1958, Neumann wrote to Jung: "My relationship to you, as you know, does not depend on writing letters or conversations—better to say, is not dependent on them anymore—but each encounter with you always gives me a feeling of profound confirmation that cannot be found anywhere else." In another passage he says: "For me there exists a deep central attachment only with you yourself, and concerning all that is related to the mission of my work." Neumann feels no ambivalence toward Jung. He is now fifty-three years old, a writer and researcher who is much respected on his own merits. Yet he is very grateful for the "feeling of profound confirmation" he receives from Jung, which he cannot find anywhere else.

Neumann wrote his last letter to Jung on February 19, 1959, after reading Jung's manuscript for *Memories, Dreams, Reflections.* "For me it is the most beautiful of all your works, though I must admit that this has personal reasons. Of all that I have ever read, I cannot think of anything that is closer to my life perception and experience. . . . I have a life feeling that is very similar to that which speaks from your book."

In this letter we see not only that Neumann is grateful and admiring, but that he also feels deeply, beyond all the differences of religion, nationality, mentality, and age, that they share a very similar life experience. This letter, which was written two years before his death, best describes the depth and closeness that Neumann felt in his relationship with Jung.

Jung's last letter to Neumann is dated March 10, 1959: "Dear friend, For your deep and detailed letter from February 18, 1959, many thanks. . . . Without the reflecting consciousness of man, the world is of a gigantic meaninglessness. Man, according to our experience, is the only creature that can at all understand *meaning.*" This was the last letter ever exchanged between them and the only one in which Jung addressed Neumann as *Lieber Freund* (dear friend).

Erich Neumann died on November 5, 1960, after a short illness, in Tel Aviv. He was fifty-six years old.

Jung died on June 6, 1961, after a short illness, in his house in Küsnacht. He was eighty-six years old.

The relationship between Jung and Neumann was much closer and simpler than the very complicated, ambivalent relationship between Freud and Jung. Jung respected Neumann and supported him. He regarded him as a colleague, an equally creative personality, one who would continue and expand his work, and not as a dangerous adversary. He even defended Neumann to a certain extent against envious and competative disciples in Switzerland.

The fact that Neumann was a Jew did not diminish in any way

Jung's friendship toward him. Neumann's being Jewish did not increase his value in Jung's eyes, as was the case with Freud, who saw in Jung, the Christian, a real asset for the young science of psychoanalysis.

On the other hand, I cannot say that the fact that Neumann was a Jew and Jung a Christian did not play an important role in their relationship. It certainly had great meaning and significance, but anti-Semitism or philo-Semitism had nothing to do with it. Jung respected and appreciated the fact that Neumann was a proud Jew, a Jew who stood on his archetypal and collective roots. Jung believed in Neumann's Zionism as part of his true individuation and was enthusiastic about the return of the Jews to their native soil and roots.

Neumann guarded the positive relationship with Jung as something very delicate and precious. Jung symbolized for him the last and only positive spiritual bond between himself, the Jew, and treacherous Europe. He ignored, or perhaps even denied, the accusations that Jung was anti-Semitic.

Reading their correspondence carefully, I can detect no trace of anti-Semitism. Jung was objective toward the Jews and the Jewish problem. He disappointed Neumann because he did not get deeply involved in the Jewish question, as Neumann had expected, but almost all his expressions in the correspondence were free of anti-Jewish resentment or prejudice.

On the other hand, when reading about Jung's actions in 1934, and what he wrote, and knowing what was going on at that time in Germany and with the Jews, I am convinced that Jung was anti-Semitic in the full sense of the word. He was so at least until after the Second World War. His anti-Semitism was deeply rooted in his unconscious and erupted vehemently in the thirties, just when anti-Semitism took its most brutal form in Germany. In Jungian terms, I would say that anti-Semitism was a component of Jung's shadow. It seems that he never came to grips with this aspect of his shadow. He never realized and confronted himself with his anti-Semitism and thus never suffered from the integration of this part of his shadow into his whole personality. Jung himself did not realize the full individuation and integration that he taught and sought all his life. Jung's anti-Semitism is an example of how even in a great mind, when it has not been fully analyzed by an "other," there still lurk strong, unconscious, dark forces struggling without resolution.

Lingering Shadows:
A Personal Perspective

Aryeh Maidenbaum

Aryeh Maidenbaum, Ph.D., a Jungian analyst, received his doctorate in history from the Hebrew University in Jerusalem and a Diploma in Analytical Psychology from the C. G. Jung Institute in Zurich. He is Executive Director of the C. G. Jung Foundation for Analytical Psychology in New York as well as an analyst in private practice. He also teaches courses on dreams and Jungian psychology and is on the faculty of New York University and Herbert H. Lehman College of the City University of New York.

After discussing his personal difficulties in approaching this topic, and the path he took to Jung from his Orthodox Jewish background, Dr. Maidenbaum outlines his conclusions based on an examination of the record and interviews with people who had firsthand experience of the issues. He points to several areas that leave an inconclusive or conflicted impression, including the existence of a secret quota system for Jewish members of the Analytical Psychology Club of Zurich, which existed from the 1930s perhaps until as late as 1950. He concludes that, although Jung did not make policy for the club, he certainly must have known about the existence of the quota policy and clearly made no attempt to eliminate it. Thus, although Jung's own personal relationships with his Jewish students was unquestionably free of personal prejudice (indeed, at one point he went so far as to intervene on their behalf for admission to the club), on a public, collective level his refusal to address the topic is far from admirable.

This is a paper I did not want to write, on a topic I did not want to deal with, about a man whose psychology and ideas have played a most important part in my life. I come from a strong Orthodox

Jewish background, and to this day Jewish history, culture, and tradition are a paramount aspect of the world I live in. Jung's psychology, in fact, helped me reconnect to my own Jewish roots and become a better Jew in the process. To have to deal with confronting this volatile and emotional issue of Jung's alleged anti-Semitism is not an easy task for me.

I discovered Jung through Rivkah Kluger, who was my first Jungian analyst, in Haifa, Israel. Dr. Kluger, whose own analysts included both Jung and Toni Wolff, was a very special woman, close to Jung and Jung's colleagues and friends in Zurich. In addition to being a Jungian analyst, Dr. Kluger was a scholar and student of Jewish and Near Eastern religion. In fact two of her books, *Psyche and Bible* and *Satan in the Old Testament,* deal with building bridges to the world of the Bible through the application of Jung's ideas. Through Rivkah, a woman I loved dearly, I learned much about not only Jung's psychology but Jung the man. Certainly, to her, as someone who knew him well, there was no possible way he could be viewed as anti-Semitic.

My first indication that Jung's attitude toward Jews was in question came when, after completing my Ph.D. at the Hebrew University in Jerusalem, I applied for a postdoctoral grant. My request was initially approved, but afterward, when I indicated that I intended to use it for the purposes of study at the C. G. Jung Institute in Zurich, I was put on notice that this was not acceptable. Apparently, one of the committee members insisted that Jung had been not only anti-Semitic but a Nazi as well. I soon learned that this was a widely held view.

Through Rivkah's help, I was able to address the issue and refute some of the more blatantly false and ugly smears. It helped that Gershom Scholem had documented his own connection to Jung and had attended the Eranos Conferences, which Jung had been so much a part of. The committee ultimately approved my request, and I spent the next three years in Zurich, eventually completing my training as a Jungian analyst.

In Switzerland during these years, I was fortunate enough to meet, work, and study with a number of analysts who had been close to Jung, some of whom had even been in analysis with him.

It was to these people, among others, that I turned, when the conceptualization of the "Lingering Shadows" conference became a reality, and the research I was engaged in took various turns and unexpected twists. It was for this reason as well that I enlisted the aid of a friend and colleague, Stephen Martin, to help plan the conference and conduct the research interviews in Zurich. We tried to keep an open mind in relation to the material at hand and approach this subjective problem on an objective level. We tried to be conscious of that aspect of the "transference" which might have inclined those who were in analysis with Jung to personalize their experiences and neglect to put the larger picture in perspective. In many ways, I have had to be careful and treat my own transferences (both positive and negative) in a similar manner, for I too feel personally connected to several of the people we interviewed, some of whom were quite involved with Jung during the turbulent earlier years and whose own actions are now coming into question. Dr. Martin helped me greatly in this process.

During the course of our research, interviews, and discussions, several conclusions have emerged for us:

1. Jung was neither a Nazi sympathizer nor a rabid, overt anti-Semite. Accusations along these lines are false and either unknowingly ignorant or maliciously slanderous.

2. Jung, as a consequence of accepting the presidency of the General Medical Society for Psychotherapy, was in fact able to reorganize that predominantly German group and, in theory, enable German Jewish psychotherapists to join a newly formed international organization, with Jung as president. How many Jewish psychotherapists actually joined the newly formed international organization is not known.

3. Jung did, in fact, help many Jewish people, both personally and professionally, throughout his life, including the period in question.

4. Jung however, was genuinely taken for a time with what he psychologically took to be a potentially positive resurgence in German nationalism during the early 1930s.

5. As part and parcel of this political activity, Jung had his own

(perhaps opportunistic) agenda—to promote his ideas and himself. As many participants in the conference have agreed, the time has come to acknowledge this. From international activity to forming Jung institutes, Jung was understandably interested in seeing the work he was so involved in brought to a greater audience and attain widespread recognition.

6. Notwithstanding the shadow aspect of Jung's own personal positions, there appear to be "lingering shadows" among Freudians in their accusations against Jung. He is often portrayed as being guilty of much more heinous crimes than was the case. More often than not, even rudimentary knowledge of Jung's life and activities is lacking, leading us to understand that resistance to Jung's psychology and ideas plays more than a token role in this. In short, it is easier to discredit the man than deal with his psychology.

7. Finally, Jung himself said: "The greater the light, the greater the shadow." Jung, being indeed a "great light," had quite a large shadow, some of it revolving around his own attitude toward Jews, more on a larger, cultural, perhaps even *unconscious* level than personal, but there nevertheless. As a result of this, he got himself into trouble by picking an inappropriate moment in history to discuss the Jewish psyche—a time, moreover, in which he still knew very little about Jewish history, tradition, mysticism, or even as he put it, "cultural form." Undoubtedly, his complex and ambivalent attitude toward Jews was connected to his personal experience with Freud and his followers. Nevertheless, there appears to be no doubt that Jung did have his personal prejudices in this regard quite apart from Freud and the psychoanalytic movement.

There is nothing startling in reaching such conclusions. Even the most faithful and loyal of Jungians would accept this if they took the time to sift through the myriad primary and secondary sources available. There are, however, several areas that were particularly troubling, and we were hard pressed to explain them away.

First, what has troubled many Jungians all along has been the lack of a clear, distinct public statement by Jung dealing with his actions and more questionable pronouncements during the 1930s. And while he did disassociate himself from National Socialism and the politics of Germany, even in later years he did not unequivocally express regrets or show any understanding toward the sensitivities of Jews regarding his own, at best naive, earlier attitudes. In all likelihood, his personal admission to Rabbi Leo Baeck that he had "slipped up" must have been accompanied by a great deal of mutual soul searching for Baeck to have accepted Jung's apology.[1] But publicly, neither Jung, nor Baeck for that matter, ever said anything that would lead us to believe that Jung had come to terms with his own "Jewish shadow" issue of earlier years. In fact, even in his essay "After the Catastrophe," Jung discusses the Nazi distortions of "pseudo-scientific" race theories but neither mentions his own prewar writings, which lent themselves to similar misuse, nor directly refers to either the Holocaust or the catastrophe that had befallen the Jews of Europe.

Nevertheless, a most enlightening comment for one such article came from Siegmund Hurwitz. Dr. Hurwitz, eighty-six, is a deeply committed Jew who has written extensively on analytical psychology and Jewish topics. He told us that during the course of his own analysis with Jung (which took place over a period of ten years) he told Jung how troubled he was by some of Jung's earlier writings on the Jewish psyche, including the timing of his 1934 article entitled "The State of Psychotherapy Today," in which he discusses the differences between "Jewish" and "German" psychology. Jung's reply to Dr. Hurwitz was: "Today I would not write this article in this way. I have written in my long life many books, and I have also written nonsense. Unfortunately, that was nonsense."

This was as close as we could get to an acknowledgment by Jung that there was anything wrong with what he had written and published in that period.

A second area that merited further investigation was the infamous manifesto written by Matthias Goering and inserted without Jung's knowledge and permission in the December 1933 edition of the *Zentralblatt*. It contained, in the words of Aniela Jaffé, "a declaration . . . by which the German branch of the society committed itself to Hitler's political and ideological principles."[2] Jung, as president of the international society, was the nominal editor of the journal. However, the journal itself was published in Leipzig, so that neither Jung nor C. A. Meier, his assistant at the time, could prevent what happened.

Unquestionably, this was done without Jung's knowledge. What troubled us was why Jung did not either write an editorial himself in a subsequent issue renouncing it and disassociating the international society from such a declaration, or even resign. We put the question to Dr. Meier, who made several points. First, Jung did no work at all on the journal. His understanding was that Meier would bear total responsibility, so that if anyone should have done something, it was Meier. And second, both Meier and Jung felt it was better to simply ignore the incident to avoid risking the breakup of the international society, which was able to protect Jewish psychotherapists.

In truth, acceptable answers for Jung's failure to make a public statement during or after the war do not exist. In general, the question—which we put not only to Meier but to a number of Jung's colleagues—as to why Jung did not apologize, renounce the 1933 *Zentralblatt* editorial, and/or resign the presidency elicited much defense but shed little new light. One possibility put forward was that Jung's anger at being attacked for an anti-Semitic bias he did not have pushed him in the direction of silence. Surely, if this was a factor, it served him poorly in the long run.

Notwithstanding Jung's private silence, an additional discovery during the course of our research proved even more difficult to come to terms with. Indeed, it was harder to ignore, owing to its overt content, rather than any omission. I am referring to the secret agreement limiting the number of Jews who could be accepted as members of the Analytical Psychology Club of Zurich. The club, with a membership of some fifty analysands of Jung and those active in Jung's circle, was a group that met regularly to hear lectures, discuss topics of Jungian interest, and socialize. Jung himself had no official capacity in the club but did attend meetings, and it is safe to assume that any policy decisions had to have his acceptance, if not blessings.

The document in question, dated December 1944, stated that, when possible, members of the Jewish faith should not exceed 10 percent and that "guests" (a separate category of membership that bestowed attendence but not voting privileges) should limit Jewish participation to 25 percent. It is important to note that this was an appendix to the by-laws, signed by members of the executive committee and apparently *not* circulated publicly to the club members. The president of the club at this time (and in fact for many years) was Toni Wolff, who, along with Linda Fierz David, is acknowledged to have been the prime mover behind this restriction. Naturally, the question that has to be answered is whether or not Jung knew about this restriction. There is no question but that he did.

After many hours of interviews and additional informal investigation, we realized there were no consistent or acceptable answers as to why this restriction was adopted. The date in question (December 7, 1944) was disturbing, but better understood in light of an acknowledgment that this policy had been unofficially in effect since the 1930s and only formalized in 1944. However, the reasons and justifications are far more difficult to pin down. Several of the responses of club members and even signatories were as follows.

There was a widespread fear of the club's becoming dominated by foreigners—a euphemism for German Jewish refugees who had made their way to Switzerland. Another rationale put forward was that Toni Wolff and Linda Fierz David (whose grandfather, incidentally, was rumored to have been Jewish) feared for Jung's life in the event that the Nazis invaded Switzerland. If Jungian institutions were kept free from a significant Jewish membership, they felt, both Jung and club members would be done a service.

Another reason put forward was that this had been an irrational time, in which a feeling of genuine hysteria prevailed. Most of those interviewed, including Jewish analysts, emphasized that unless one had lived in Switzerland during this period, one could not understand it. Several individuals remarked that there had been a feeling that an invasion by Germany was imminent. In short, Toni Wolff and Linda Fierz David, nicknamed "The Goddesses" in the club, were afraid Jung would be sent to a concentration camp if the Germans invaded and found too many Jewish Jungians in the club.

Finally, it has been suggested that this restriction was a form of "differentiation" and not "discrimination," an attitude that Jung himself held. Too many Jews would have changed the nature of the organization, and there was an obligation on the part of its officers to protect the Swiss character of the club.

To us, admittedly from the perspective and safety of over forty years' distance, none of these reasons is acceptable, although they all provide some psychological insight into the thought processes of the signatories. In this regard it is important to put some perspective on our findings—specifically, the additional research we feel is still needed before drawing definitive conclusions.

First and foremost is the question, not of whether Jung knew, but to what extent he was culpable. The fact that he knew is indisputable. Almost every person interviewed acknowledged that Jung was aware of the quota system then in effect. However, Jung's relationship to both the club and his individual Jewish analysands was a complex one. For example, Aniela Jaffé related the story that when her membership came into question, Jung made it clear that if she were not accepted as a member of the club, he would resign and have nothing to do with it. She was, naturally, accepted. Siegmund Hurwitz tells of the incident in 1950 when his membership came into question—a membership, ironically, that was sponsored and encouraged by Toni Wolff. When it was brought to Dr. Hurwitz's attention that he was being accepted despite the fact that Jewish membership was restricted, he informed Jung (who at first tried to defend the statute) that he was withdrawing his application, as he did not want to be a part of a club with such a policy. Jung called Hurwitz several weeks later and told him that the rule had been eliminated and he could now apply.

Amazingly, the elimination of the Jewish quota took place in 1950, five years after the end of the war. Thus, the nuances, as is always the case with Jung, are not so simple. Furthermore, the idea of a quota system was neither new nor limited to Switzerland, though given Jung's own history with the "Jewish issue," and coming *after* his meeting with Baeck, one would have expected him to be more conscious by this time (i.e., 1945–50).

When individuals active in the club were asked why this restriction had not been eliminated sooner, the response was that it had been forgotten about and not paid attention to—again, another area that clearly needs further research. For example, how many Jewish versus non-Jewish members were admitted during those years? Was there indeed a restrictive pattern in place as late as 1950? Unfortunately, when Stephen Martin and I tried to pursue this ourselves by examining the records of the club, we were told that the records were in shambles, making it impossible to piece anything together.

In concluding, none of the people we interviewed was particularly proud of this piece of the club's history, and several were shocked, as they themselves had never seen this in writing before. Both Siegmund Hurwitz and Aniela Jaffé, for example, informed us that while they knew of the restrictions, this was the first time they had seen the document itself. And C. A. Meier, one of the signatories, acknowledged that such restrictions were in place since the 1930s but had no recollection of formally signing a document. His comment was that this should be taken in the context of its time, though when pressed he openly admitted that in retrospect it was an "ugly" thing.

Finally, however, what was heartening to us both was the honesty and trust shown by those we interviewed—individuals who are truly important figures in Jungian history. Their willingness to meet with us, openly discuss the topic, share their recollections, and confront this unpleasant shadow dimension of Jung was very touching. At times it was a painful experience, and we regretted having to witness their inner suffering. An excerpt from a letter sent to me by one of the individuals interviewed illustrates this point: "I myself felt tormented during the interview since I was in a difficult conflict between my loyalty to Jung and the necessity to tell the truth."

I know that many Jungians who are concerned with these issues

300 LINGERING SHADOWS

carry similar feelings. Nevertheless, I feel confident that this is what Jung himself would have approved of—the search for truth, for conscious and unconscious realities.

Notes

1. Aniela Jaffé, "C. G. Jung and National Socialism," in *From the Life and Work of C. G. Jung,* p. 100.
2. Ibid., p. 81.

Shadows and Light:
Closing Reflections on Jung
and Jungian Psychology

Philip T. Zabriskie

In this revised version of his remarks offered at the end of the "Lingering Shadows" conference, Philip Zabriskie, a Jungian analyst and former president of the C. G. Jung Foundation and the C. G. Jung Institute of New York, speaks of his feelings in dealing with these issues about Jung, and he reflects upon several different aspects of racism and its widespread manifestation in our century. The principal question he then sets out to answer is whether Jung's approach to the psyche leads, as some charge, to discriminatory or racist thinking. He examines three basic Jungian principles that are sometimes held to lead to such attitudes. He concludes that, far from leading to racism (unless greatly misused), they in fact are essential to understanding the psyche, its strengths, and its dangers.

My task is to respond to the material brought forth at the "Lingering Shadows" conference.

Though this is a formal paper, the initial responses are inescapably from the heart. I am a Jungian analyst. This is a professional designation, but it means more; it means that I acknowledge great personal as well as professional debt to Jung. My own life has been affected, changed, deepened by experience opened by Jungian psychology. My work is grounded fundamentally on Jung's understanding of the psyche. While one may learn much from other theoreticians, none is more practical or as profound. And there is always an awesome amount yet to learn from Jung—one can reread his works and continue to be surprised, to be informed, to be enlightened.

It is, however, a fact of life for a Jungian to be presented from time to time with questions about Jung's alleged anti-Semitism. Sometimes the questions come with serious concern, sometimes with curiosity, sometimes with malice. In any case, they persist. The "Lingering Shadows" conference was organized and held in order to examine the record as fully as possible. Allegations have been exaggerated and misused over the years. It is, nevertheless, necessary, and it has been difficult and painful, to deal directly with these issues in Jung's life and work.

Part of our pain is no doubt confusion, for we Jungians, individually and collectively, are still working through our transferences to Jung. And there is much to work with and work through. He was not only our analyst (directly for some, for many only once or twice removed); he was also a public figure, a teacher and theoretician, and a particular individual with his own predilections and characteristics. Inescapably we know far more about him than one ordinarily would know about one's analyst, and some of it is disturbing. Many have worked through these issues before now, and some have shared a portion of that experience— James Kirsch, for example, and Gerhard Adler, and Werner Engel, who at the conference uttered the poignant and powerful question, when speaking of Jews who were with Jung in the thirties: "Why did we stay? For all we knew and debated, why did we stay?" It is hard to imagine at what depth that question must have been asked and met. Now it is the turn of the next generations to deal for ourselves with whatever matters we need to examine, such as that which has been the subject matter of the conference and of this volume. And whatever else may be true about the times and about Jung's own attitudes, decisions, and values, we are dealing here with what, in the light of history, appears to have been a serious failure of, in Jungian terms, the feeling function.

Confronting these questions about Jung has produced sadness and anger, and occasionally defensiveness. We want to defend

Jung in order to defend his theories, his rightness about so much, his great gifts to us, indeed to defend ourselves. But defensiveness does not seem necessary now (except in response, on occasion, to grossly exaggerated attacks based themselves on distortions of feeling or fact). We are now past the fundamentalist stage of Jungian thought, which he surely would welcome.

Beyond facing Jung, what of us Jungians? We are his heirs, affected, in the unconscious as well as consciously, by the problematic aspects of his psyche as well as by his gifts. Whether from that influence or from ourselves, are our shortcomings or failures also likely to be in the realm of feeling? In our day, do we underestimate our power drives, our projections of inferiority, our unconscious sadism? Do we tend to call ambition courage? Do we look past what is actually happening (in analysis, in relationships, in history) because our eye is set too fast on what it all means, whether in terms of mythic structure or clinical theory? What *is* our ongoing Jungian shadow? It is, I think, likely to be a feeling problem or a mix of feeling problems.

Aside from the particular issue on which the conference focused, the material has made it abundantly clear that Jung's feet were flat on the ground of the history of his time, his part of the world, his land and class. In many ways, far more than most mortals, he rose to a height where he could see over much of that; but no man or woman can entirely transcend his or her history, neither its strengths nor its evils.

The whole relation of history to psychology is a vastly interesting and important area of reflection and study. There are examples of such reflection in this volume (Roazen, Cocks, Williamson, Dieckmann, Ulanov, Samuels, Neumann). Sometimes the focus of study is on the effect of an individual's psychology on his or her behavior and on the larger environment or history around them. Sometimes the focus is on the effect of the archetype constellated in the collective psyche on the visible history of a given time or area. It becomes ever more clear that we cannot understand a person or a group without understanding the historical context. It also becomes clear that we cannot understand a period of history or a development in history (e.g., anti-Semitism) without some theory of archetypes, some willingness to search for underlying psychic forces that work under and through—and significantly shape—the empirical factors of economics, politics, conscious ideas, individual personalities, and all their interminglings.

Returning to the central issue under consideration in this book, it is important to set forth several complicated dimensions of the dreadful phenomenon of anti-Semitism or racism generally. While I know that anti-Semitism is not entirely understood as a subcategory of racism, here I shall be speaking of attitudes and complications that are in fact characteristic of racism in whatever form.

First, racist attitudes may be conscious or unconscious, and the unconscious attitudes may differ markedly from those held consciously. Many commentators at the conference, for example, said that if Jung had anti-Semitic feelings or attitudes, they were very largely unconscious—which is not to say insignificant. Indeed this raises the question of one's responsibility for one's *un*conscious attitudes. Plainly it is not possible to take responsibility for attitudes that remain unconscious. But once life or fate or analysis make one conscious, Jung's consistent position is that we *must* then take responsibility for attitudes which have previously been unconscious, and for actions or damage done as a result of them. It is not so much a question of blame or blameworthiness—that has more to do with one's ego or conscious malice or ill intent. This is a difficult distinction to make quickly, but it is important in a climate which is eager to assign blame or innocence. It is often an important issue clinically, when we are learning about unconscious shadow projections or unconscious plots or actions which we have perpetrated in our past. It is then a matter of moral and psychological growth not endlessly to blame oneself (i.e., to dwell on guilt and how much one deserves punishment), but to accept responsibility for what took place (i.e., to acknowledge and to suffer in due measure for participation and consequences, and to make amends if possible). Prior unconsciousness is not an excuse: Part of our anguish or plight about Jung is that we do not know how much in later days he took responsibility for what seem to have been earlier unconscious attitudes about Jews and Jewish culture. On that subject he kept silence. His silence is hard on us, yet we cannot assume we know what was inside of it. He generally accepted the weight of his shadow once alerted to it; but we cannot know about this. He did call the Holocaust "the most monstrous crime of all ages,"[1] but this says little about his own earlier expressions. In any case I think it may be said that he gave more *outward* sign of being aware of the horrors of the Germanic shadow than of the sufferings of the Jewish people.

Second, racism involves issues of both individual and collective attitudes, and what one thinks individually may not be consistent with how one acts as part of a group.

For example, a man, when interacting personally with an individual of another race, may not be racist at all, but when thinking or talking about that person's whole group or race, he may be plainly biased (again, consciously or unconsciously). I expect this was true of Jung in relation to Jewish culture, at least until he was profoundly educated by James Kirsch, Erich Neumann, and others. It is clear, I believe, that he was quite free of anti-Semitic prejudice when it came to individual Jews or indeed when he was laboring on behalf of Jewish therapists in Germany. I find no evidence that this was a disguise for power ambitions in the arena of German psychotherapy. Such a charge rings of projection onto him, rather than an accurate reading of his psychology. I think the same about the vicious and quite ungrounded accusations that he was pro-Nazi. But he did in the middle thirties write in indisputably patronizing and prejudicial ways about Jewish culture.

Jung himself often spoke about this contrast between individual and collective attitudes, describing how group or mass complexes and emotions could reduce or overwhelm an individual's capacity to make thoughtful and conscious decisions. In the heat of the outrage or passion of a multitude, people not uncommonly do or say things they would never do or contemplate individually. Jung was so aware of this as a contemporary problem that he stressed again and again that the only protection against mass infection was deep consciousness of one's own shadow and a growing individual grounding in the Self.

It can further be said about individual and collective attitudes that an individual may be nonracist but be part of a group, institution, or class that is decidedly racist. This was true of a number of patrician slaveholders in the antebellum South. It is true of virtually all of us in the white middle class who consider ourselves personally nonracist but who live and live well in our racist society. It was the point at the heart of Reinhold Niebuhr's great book, *Moral Man and Immoral Society*. A major question immediately confronts us: What is one's responsibility for the attitudes of one's group, especially if they differ from one's private views? Without trying to answer that fully, we can say at least that it is crucial to be conscious of the projections inherent in the group attitude and to face those first in one's own self; one cannot simply assume one's own innocence. Having confronted the inner issue, one then goes to the familiar but usually difficult and ambiguous problem of deciding whether to stay within the group and attempt to change its attitudes, simply to survive if it appears truly too dangerous to protest and there is no escape, or to disaffiliate, with all the risks of self-righteousness and impotence, then to join or create an opposition.

Third, the twentieth century may well warrant the epithet "The Century of Racism," and this for two reasons:

One is because we have seen so much of it. Widespread racism, both conscious and unconscious, has been acted out by individuals, mobs, parties, societies, and governments, by people of many races and ethnic groups against many other peoples in a great many parts of the globe.

The other reason for the epithet is that we have become so much more aware of racism—as a stance and as an evil. In this century many groups and individuals have come to realize and struggle with what racism is, and of how racist we have been, often without knowing it. I am thinking of people who by and large have not considered themselves racist and may have learned it with shock. We have been told in no uncertain terms, we have been exposed; to some degree we have awakened. For instance, can we who are white read what was written in the 1950s by "good" white people about black-white relations without cringing at the paternalism, condescension, and smug superiority beneath the words about tolerance and community? In fact, as this century approaches its end, we learn that we—practically all of us—white, black, Jew, Gentile—are or have been racist in some measure. But in the Western world most of the weight of responsibility for this evil falls on the dominant white citizenry of Christian and European identity or background. Is this white liberal guilt? Yes. And it is well warranted; but it had best not be paralyzing.

Now I want to proceed to a different matter, to an issue first raised at the conference by Professor Paul Roazen, namely: did (or do) Jung's theories lead necessarily to anti-Semitism, conscious or otherwise, and to an underestimation of evil such as that of the Nazis?

Naturally, we say no; if it were so, we could not be Jungians. But we must pursue the matter further, for the question is seriously posed about Jungian psychology and warrants serious consideration.

I find three themes in Jung's work that provoke such a question. The first has to do with his great interest in what we might call the psychology of peoples, that is, the way in which the collective psyche manifests itself not so much in humanity as a whole but in a particular people, an ethnic community, a "race." The second theme is the value Jung placed on the irrational or nonrational aspects of psychic life, not merely the strength or influence of such aspects but their *value*. The third theme has to do with Jung's thoughts about, or the way he talked about, good and evil.

1. Jung in the late twenties and thirties often pressed the matter of the psychology of peoples. For example, in 1927 he described how he experienced the psychology of Americans (white Americans) as different from that of Europeans, and he asserted that the difference derived from the psychological impact of contact with blacks and American Indians. That contact, he maintained, even if strongly registered only in the unconscious, changed the archetypal energies alive in the psyche of American whites.[2]

More urgently he endeavored to comprehend Germanic psychology. This was, and for some time had been, a heavy matter for him, for he was of course Germanic, and yet he dreaded some of the most prominent elements in that psychic formation, especially the tensions in it, its propensity to unbridled violence. "Germany," he said in 1946, "has been a problem to me ever since the first World War."[3] Already in 1918 he had written, "As the Christian view of the world loses its authority, the more menacingly will the 'blond beast' be heard prowling about in his underground prison, ready at any moment to burst out with devastating consequences."[4]

At the same time we know that Jung, like Nietszche, believed that this same restless, youthful, violence-prone energy carried what could be most constructive, most creative in the Germanic psyche. Characteristically he feared that if one were to dissolve or repress these volatile aspects, one would also neutralize the creative. He knew this combination was exceedingly dangerous, especially when the people who possessed it had been beaten in war, humiliated, and subject to great misery. He knew in his bones that Germany was "a land of spiritual catastrophes."[5] He knew all this was uneasily present in his own psyche; he was involved in the problem; it was part of him. Put another way, he knew (I believe) that violent Wotan was a genuine aspect of his own shadow, his own individually and his own as one grounded in the Germanic collective psyche. He was conscious of it; he was conscious of its violence if not of its anti-Semitic ingredient, and he knew it was terrible.

He also spoke from time to time of Jewish psychology, usually as a contrast to Germanic psychology, and sometimes as a way of characterizing differences of attitude between himself and Freud. These passages, which have been examined elsewhere in this volume, typically conveyed a sense of definite difference between Jewish and Germanic psychology. Often the difference was described with deep respect for what he experienced as a certain maturity in the Jewish psyche born of many centuries of struggle and consciousness. Yet without doubt some of his statements (until the middle thirties) also suggested unconscious prejudice, ignorance, condescension, and a sense of superiority, especially in relation to creativity or originality. Furthermore, his timing was catastrophic. It looks as if his poor extraverted feeling never grasped the terrible inappropriateness and danger of pressing such discussions at that time and place.

But what about now?

Today many intelligent, enlightened people say: Do not talk about differences. Ethnic stereotypes are still the source of terrible harm. In a recent issue of the *New York Review of Books,* Conor Cruse O'Brien wrote of the continuing danger of a sense of "folk," especially when linked to nationalism or racism. Does the very idea that the unconscious crystallizes in different ways among different peoples in itself lead to racist or nationalistic attitudes?

I think not. Rather I believe that generations of psychic experience give rise to shapes and patterns of psyche that are not everywhere the same. To be French is to be generally human *and also* something specific. Likewise, to be Irish or Chinese or Italian or, within America, to be of and from the Deep South. The psychologies are not altogether the same. And the historical, psychological characteristics or differences, the uniquenesses, are important ingredients in one's identity. It is therefore valuable to try to understand in some measure the nature of those differences. Erich Neumann, for one, according to the material presented at the "Lingering Shadows" conference by Micha Neumann, spoke of the seriousness and the importance of such an effort. However, the notion of ethnic differences continues to be a charged matter, because it has been used so terribly to mask, assert, and exercise claims of superiority. Nevertheless, if we maintain an attitude of care and thoughtfulness that avoids universals and facile stereotypes, and that does not use any such analyses for power purposes, I believe we can indeed make rich use of the idea of the collective psyche manifesting in particular ways among particular peoples. Clinically, for example, it can be crucial to understand ancestral influences in an individual's psychology that do not derive specifically (or not only) from his or her parents, but from generations of psychic experience in that person's "tribe."

2. Regarding the question of the weight and value Jung placed on nonrational dimensions of human experience, Roazen's question is, "Can it be that an emphasis on the legitimacy of the irrational in psychology does also, when introduced to the world of politics, encourage Nazi-like movements?" (page 220). He was careful to say, "when introduced to the world of politics," but he

had rightly earlier insisted that one cannot compartmentalize one's ideas. To prevent a fundamental theory about the nature of human psychology from being applied in the political realm, one would have to modify it drastically or eliminate it. Would Jung do that? And did his emphasis on "the legitimacy of the irrational" lead to anti-Semitic writings or actions?

On the central theoretical point Jung was convinced and passionate. It was (and is) fundamental to his theory of the psyche that

- there is an unconscious;
- it contains elements that are personal (i.e., deriving from that individual's particular experience, e.g., with mother and father) and non-personal (i.e., drawn from wider or older strata of collective human experience, constellated in the psyche of this specific individual but not deriving from his or her particular history);
- within the unconscious there are complexes and archetypes from which arise on the one hand neuroses and destructive energies, and on the other hand imaginative capacities, healing symbols, and wondrous creativity.

In his student days Jung had parted company with modern rationalism on this score. He also consistently criticized contemporary protagonists of religion, who, in an effort to come to terms with science and modern thought, abandoned the ancient religious sense of the reality of the nonrational or transpersonal depths.

As time went on, this became a major point of conflict with Freud. In *Memories, Dreams, Reflections* he recalled Freud saying of his sexual theory, "We must make a dogma of it, an unshakeable bulwark . . . against the black tide of mud of occultism."[6] Jung believed what Paul Roazen suggested in his comments, that Freud was laying down a fundamental challenge to Western civilization, with the goal of overthrowing Christianity and Christian ethics. In truth Freud was convinced that psychoanalysis, with its scientific basis, would overthrow, or render obsolete, all Western religion,

Christian and Jewish, for it was the best and last bastion against all forms of nonrational superstition, which he called occultism, and which (he was persuaded) only deluded, providing neither illumination nor strength to deal with the inevitable hardships and tragedies of life. Jung opposed this position with great determination, not as a fundamentalist Christian but as one persuaded that there are levels and forces of reality deeper, more ancient, more powerful than any amount of rational sophistication or courage can control or comprehend. These forces, he believed, profoundly affect our lives, for good or ill, for good *and* ill. And these forces have been represented from time immemorial in religious symbolism. Jung placed great value on the task of developing some measure of conscious relation to these transpersonal realities both as the route toward individuation and as the only reliable safeguard against their capacity for destructiveness and delusion.

Freud, it seems, came to represent to Jung not only the lost and abandoning father but the dangerous brother who must be opposed, the one who knew *so much* that was true and then denied what appeared to Jung to be most true. Freud's rationalism, his irreligion, was what Jung so disliked.

This is important in relation to the question of anti-Semitism because Jung came to think of Freud not only as a nineteenth-century rationalist but as a latter-day secularized Jewish rationalist, which Freud indeed was and professed to be. Jung believed that most contemporary rationalism had no sense of the unconscious at all, whereas psychoanalysis, which had rediscovered a portion of the unconscious, might, with its ancient Jewish history and background, have understood not only the personal but also the transpersonal depths of the psyche. However, Jung concluded, Freud's antireligious secularism deprived psychoanalysis of that insight. Jung's attack was really on Freud's secularism, but his irrational inference was to equate such secularized depth psychology with "Jewish psychology" and to devalue it. "Irrational" here suggests a shadow projection, and I think Freud may have been the embodiment of a passionate, antireligious shadow in Jung's own psyche. This shadow would become visible not in secular attacks against religion but in his wrath against God, especially God as Jung saw Him in the Old Testament, the God of Abraham, Isaac, and Jacob (see *Answer to Job*).

Jung's intensity about the issue of a religious versus a secular attitude was immediately linked to his central convictions about psychology. Further, he believed that the debate went to the very heart of the dangerous crisis faced by culture and civilization in the twentieth century. He believed that crisis was especially acute in the Germanic world. He was persuaded that he must take part in the debate, and he attempted to address it often. In a letter in March 1934 Jung wrote to Max Guggenheim that "Freud once told me, very rightly: The fate of psychotherapy will be decided in Germany."[7] One notable effort to engage in the debate about that fate was the 1934 essay "The State of Psychotherapy Today," the very essay that contains some of the most disturbing statements about Jewish psychology.[8] Most of this paper is a treatise on the nature of neurosis. In it Jung asserts that psychotherapy, in order to have a valuable future, must not see neurosis as viewed by Freudian psychoanalysis, namely as a problem to be resolved, to be rid of. Rather, psychotherapists must see that the psyche contains its creativity *within* the very areas of illness. Thus, one must work not to dissolve neuroses but to understand their meaning, to understand what the psyche is endeavoring to express in a fragmented or distorted way. In that sense, a "neurosis [is] our truest and most precious possession."[9] Within the complex at the heart of a neurosis is a conflict that contains some of the energies that have most to do with one's inner truth and individuality. Solve or get around the neurosis, reduce it rationalistically, and psychotherapy will accomplish not healing but a different version of just what the neurosis was doing, namely masking one's deepest truth. In this sense, Freudian psychology, said Jung, "continues the baleful work that is going on in every neurotic: destruction of the bond between men and the gods,"[10] without which we lose all chance to heal or transform an individual or the collective psyche.

It seems to me that we who are involved in analytical psychology must value the objective psyche as Jung did, or go against our deepest experience. While we prize the hard-won gifts of consciousness and rationality, we also look for and depend upon the movements and manifestations of the nonrational, the unconscious. We wrestle with what is destructive there and also draw from its life-giving waters. We hold to a religious attitude about life and the psyche; we know there is another order of reality in or behind or under the explicate one. Ancient images of the pleroma or of alchemical operations proceeding in the dark symbolize profound realities. This may engage us in debate with Freudian theories (and with a good many other theories and philosophies as well). But that debate does not exclude great appreciation for those theories nor readiness to learn from them, despite deep disagreement on the major point. And this debate has nothing to do specifically with Judaism—secularized or religious.

For Jungians, the answer to warnings about the dangers of the greed, cruelty, and destructiveness in what is nonrational in the psyche is not repression or liberal rationalism (overwhelmingly the majority responses in our culture) but rather consciousness. The gods—the invisible, transpersonal forces in the psyche, known more by the symbols they produce than by logic—torment and inspire us. Growth, the way forward, is not to deny them, but to be aware of them, so that we are not blindly driven by their furies but rather open to their constructive powers.

There is risk and danger in this line of thought. It may take one away from the guidance or constraints of laws and conventions. There are no guarantees of safety or nonhurtfulness. Following this line has led Jung and Jungians into areas of work, art, and relationship that have been rich and rewarding, but also undoubtedly—for our complexes do not cease on occasion to possess us—into illusions or actions that have been very harmful. So we are continually drawn back to affirmations of the importance of ego development and ego responsibility. But this affirmed, I believe that Jungians will always be characterized by a certain individualistic or unpredictable or exploratory streak, which we can own if, and only if, our dedication to consciousness is profound and consistent.

3. Finally (and briefly, for much has been written about this element of Jung's thought), many have felt that Jung's convictions

about good and evil contributed to his seeming inability accurately to see and to fight against palpable evil, notably the evil of Nazism.

Jung wrestled with the problem of evil all his life, and with increasing urgency and depth through the thirties and forties, and later as in the short, passionate *Answer to Job* (1952), the long, alchemically based *Mysterium Coniunctionis* (1955), and his re-action to the East-West split and the nuclear danger, *The Undis-covered Self* (1957). Responding to his work, many critics have feared or insisted that reflection upon evil that leads to a sense of darkness and evil in the very Godhead inevitably reduces the sharpness and courage necessary to enlist in the ancient and perpetual war of good against evil.

It may be that Jung's convictions about the need to contain the opposites played some part in his apparent failure for a time to recognize the extent and the unmitigated nature of Nazi evil. But if true, it must be added that the problem was not that he underestimated evil, but rather he overestimated the capacity of the psyche (individual and collective) to contain and control it. In fact, from the middle 1930s through the rest of his life he protested about the tendency in most religious, philosophical, and political communities to underestimate the reality and the dimensions of evil, in individuals and especially in collective entities or move-ments. The two targets that he continually attacked were, on the one hand, the attitude that the evil is in the other person or group and the good in me or us (projection of the shadow) and, on the other hand, the medieval doctrine of *privatio boni* (evil as the absence of good), which he believed conditions one to believe that evil does not actually have substance. At the same time, while indeed confronting the ubiquitous and horrifying reality of evil, he insisted that it is no answer to drop what we have learned about the importance of containing the opposites, and instead to split them or go back to a simplistic view of good against evil. That is the borderline defense; good and evil cannot be so disentangled. Rather, Jung held, we are required to ponder, to suffer the problem in ourselves and in life, in order that we can indeed endeavor to hold the opposites within and without when that is the task, and/ or resist what appears to be *most* destructive when that is necessary. This is easy enough to say; it is a life undertaking to honor. And I think Jung was right in believing that we cannot do so fully unless we appreciate that these opposites go to the depths of reality, that there is no place beyond which we can say, Now we are free of evil and conflict. We know there is no guarantee against the evil that must be faced or the evil that is also in us and the harm that we do. Work on consciousness of the shadow is truly an endless task, the beginning, middle, and end of the great opus of connection with the Self.

So my answer to the large question posed by Paul Roazen is complicated. I think Jung's theories and values were surely related to his entering into German and Jewish issues as and when he did; but he went into those actions and debates not only with clear convictions, but also (a) with old and inadequate ideas of Jewish culture and perhaps (it cannot be excluded) with some unconscious ingredient of anti-Semitism, and (b) with a shadow that was antireligion or, deep in his psyche, anti-God, and that he projected onto Freud or what he thought of as secularized Jewish psychology. His theories about the unconscious and the nonrational do not require, do not themselves contain, either an anti-Semitic attitude or the shadow projection. It is therefore possible, indeed it is necessary, both truly to value his fundamental insights and not to fall into unconscious prejudice or projection. I profoundly believe Jung's basic point of view to be fundamentally valid and crucially important both clinically and in one's understanding of history and society. About racism, conscious and unconscious: we all carry our shame; we carry the continuing task of becoming and remaining conscious of the psyche's dark and projective tendencies. For we can be certain that there remain many forms of darkness that we shall surely encounter in the world and in ourselves in our day and generation.

Notes

1. C. G. Jung, "After the Catastrophe" (1945), CW 10, para. 406.
2. C. G. Jung, "Mind and Earth" (1927), CW 10, esp. paras. 94ff.

3. C. G. Jung, "Preface to 'Essays on Contemporary Events' " (1946), CW 10, p. 178.

4. C. G. Jung, "The Role of the Unconscious" (1918), CW 10, para. 17; also quoted by Jung in his "Epilogue to 'Essays on Contemporary Events' " (1946), CW 10, para. 458.

5. C. G. Jung, "Wotan" (1936), CW 10, para. 391.

6. C. G. Jung, Memories, Dreams, Reflections, p. 150.

7. C. G. Jung, Letters, vol. 1, p. 156.

8. CW 10, paras. 333–370.

9. Ibid., para. 359.

10. Ibid., para. 367.

Part Three

WORKSHOP ON JUNG AND ANTI-SEMITISM

Eleventh International
Congress of the IAAP
Paris, 1989

Remarks for the
Workshop on Jung
and Anti-Semitism

Jerome S. Bernstein

Jerome S. Bernstein is a Jungian analyst and clinical psychologist with a private practice in Washington, D.C. He has been vice-chairman of the C. G. Jung Institute of New York and is founding president of the C. G. Jung Analysts Association of Greater Washington, D.C. He is the author of *Power and Politics: The Psychology of Soviet-American Partnership.*

As Chairman of the two-day workshop on Jung and anti-Semitism, held at the eleventh congress of the International Association for Analytical Psychology in Paris on August 31 and September 1, 1989, Jerome Bernstein speaks of the issue of Jung's alleged anti-Semitism as a wound that has not yet healed—a fact that all of Jung's followers, but particularly the Jews among them—must contend with. In his remarks opening and closing the workshop, he presents his own experiences, emotions, reflections, and ongoing struggle with this troublesome legacy.

OPENING REMARKS FOR THE WORKSHOP

Day One

I would like to share a recent personal experience with you. In June 1989, my first book was published—certainly an important event in my life. It received its first newspaper review in the *Los*

Angeles Times. In the opening lines, the reviewer, Russell Jacoby, wrote: ". . . Jung was—to put the best face on it—confused by the politics of his day. In Nazism he glimpsed an ecstatic Wotan; he babbled about the creative Aryan unconscious and the inferior Jewish psyche." Jacoby went on to ridicule and dismiss as inane various aspects of my book. In short, his antipathy for Jung—I should say, Jung's shadow—and also the brilliance of Jung's thought, which the reviewer could not grasp, caused him to use my book for Jung-bashing. I felt smeared with Jung's shadow. And the value of my book as a new model for looking at superpower conflict and the collective unconscious as it manifests at the macro level of international relations was denigrated as well. So much for those who say that the issue of Jung's anti-Semitism is history and has no relevancy in the context of the contemporary *Zeitgeist.*

I will not present here my own views about Jung and his alleged anti-Semitism. Rather, I would like to talk about how it is that this workshop came to be—what I have come to realize as a spiritual and intellectual awakening, which has germinated and is unfolding within our own community.

For me this story goes back to my personal analysis in the early 1970s. When I first heard the assertion that Jung was anti-Semitic, I was dismayed. I took the issue to my analyst and asked him about it. With great authority and reassurance, he said that there was no truth to the charge, that it was slanderous, and that at most, Jung in the genesis of his own theories of archetypes and the collective unconscious had become momentarily psychically in-fected—fascinated with an archetype. Since my analyst was Jewish, and had had dealings with Jung himself, I thought the issue was put to rest.

The next chapter for me was at the International Congress for Analytical Psychology in Jerusalem in 1983. A spontaneous meet-ing took place one evening about the topic of the emotional impact of a meeting in the city of Jerusalem. As it turned out, about a third of the meeting consisted of Jews, about a third Germans, and about a third others. The meeting soon turned into an extremely emotional connection between Germans and Jews, and there was lots of talk about fear, about guilt, about victims, about grief and loss. Also, there were lots of tears. I remember my shock at hearing one analyst two or three times matter-of-factly refer to Jung as anti-Semitic. The most disturbing thing of all, for me, was that no one challenged his assertions. One analyst even made mention of Jung's pro-Nazi leanings, and again no one challenged such a shocking statement. Those words lingered with me a long while. Though it may seem naive, I did not know what to think about these allegations. My projections onto Jung were assaulted, if not cracked.

One outcome of that encounter was that the group wanted the rest of the Congress to know that an important event had occurred that evening. I was designated along with a German woman to report to the group at the next morning's plenary session. To my dismay the request to make such a report was met with profound and angry opposition by a segment of the Israeli delegation. I was personally subjected to outrageous and insulting shadow projections and assault on my character as a Jew. I had become a traitor to my own people, it was said. I could hardly believe—although I did understand—the controversy in which I found myself. I experienced that assault on my character and my integrity as personally very hurtful. As a child I had the experience of being stoned because of my Jewishness. With the assault on my character at the Congress, I found myself confronted with a Jewish shadow problem that took on some of the ugliness of anti-Semitism. In the end, a five-minute report was given at the next day's plenary session, but not without vociferous objections by some, and not without a confrontational vote on the floor to bring the matter before the Congress.

I was shaken by that experience. It was only in the last year and a half that I realized that part of what I had encountered there in Jerusalem was Jung's—and our, yours and mine—undealt-with shadow problem. Although I was not able to attend the Berlin Congress, I noted with some dismay from the Congress proceedings that there was little if any focus on the specific issue of Jung's alleged anti-Semitism and pro-Nazi leanings, and not a single paper dealt with it at a Congress whose theme was the shadow. (I later learned that there was a workshop held on the subject.)

Thus, after the initial request for papers went out for the 1989 Paris Congress, I wrote Rosemary Gordon and suggested that a workshop on Jung and anti-Semitism be held. (Independently of my letter to Rosemary Gordon and unaware of the proposal for this workshop, Stephen A. Martin and Aryeh Maidenbaum of the Jung Foundation of New York put together the three-evening "Lingering Shadows" program in March of 1989.)

It is my hope that this two-day workshop will address not only the important—and, I think, easier-to-deal-with—historical question of Jung's behavior between 1933 and his death. To limit our focus to historical events would be to do little more than to enjoin the argument at the level of Jung's non-Jungian attackers, one of whom—a respected psychiatrist—went so far as to compare Jung to Joseph Mengele.

We are all here in this room because we have been wounded, individually and/or collectively, by this shadow problem and by the man—a man we all respect at one level or another. Some of us displace our hurt through anger onto Jung; some of us blindly defend Jung, to avoid our hurt and anger; some of us would rather discuss Jung's alleged anti-Semitism without taking a deeper look at our own prejudices; and some of us would just as soon not deal with it at all. I wish to remind all of us that this is a *workshop*. The intent is for all of us, collectively, to process our own thoughts, feelings, emotions, and blindnesses with each other. We have been and remain wounded by this issue, and the only way to heal is for us to look into the darkness that hurts, and to explore together what light we can find and extricate from that darkness.

I would leave you with this question: It is one thing to address Jung's shadow in the 1930s in the context of a world radically different and much more unaware than our own. But what can we, as analytical psychologists, say of ourselves, with our claim to greater consciousness and sensitivity to shadow issues, when we realize that it has taken until 1989 to begin to take our own dirty laundry out of the hamper and to examine it in depth?

Day Two

The theme of today's workshop, broadly, is how do we deal with our wound and where do we go from here.

Aryeh Maidenbaum and Marga Speicher in their presentations in different ways described the wound we have experienced as a result of Jung's anti-Semitism. They both posed the rhetorical question, "Where do we go from here?"

Andrew Samuels pointed to a direction—beyond Jung the man—to a greater commitment among Jungians to working with so-called minority groups.

Here I would like to add some personal comments. I believe that we cannot move beyond Jung the man, although we can make some of the other commitments Andrew Samuels would like us to make, before we fully process our wound—which includes, ultimately, conscious mourning and forgiveness, or conscious refusal to forgive what we cannot forgive. For Jung was a father figure to us all. How would we react if any of us were to discover, after his death, that our personal father was anti-Semitic or had made statements that indicated even a brief enchantment with Nazism. What would we say to a patient in our consulting room who had the same problem?

However, it takes considerable time to absorb the shock of profound betrayal. Marga Speicher has witnessed that it took her at least forty years to come to terms with anti-Semitism in her own country, Germany. I think it is clear that it has taken Jungians collectively over fifty years to begin that process in earnest.

There is some danger in moving too quickly from this process. The next generation of Jungians will be sufficiently removed from the history, from the emotion, and from Jung the man. It will be easier to leave this issue and the work that it calls on us to do on ourselves—individually and collectively—for dry chapters in biographies of Jung.

Most of us call ourselves Jungian analysts—we carry the name of our intellectual and, yes, our spiritual father in our very identities as professionals. When people allude to Jung's anti-Semitism and to his alleged Nazism, it goes into me personally, similarly to the way that it might if they were talking about my personal father.

And what do we do when an outsider charges that Jung was anti-Semitic and pro-Nazi and as a result discredits the entire body of analytical psychology? Up until now, I have never known how to deal with that problem in a way that feels fully satisfactory to me. What I have seen others do is rush to Jung's defense, or argue the details of how anti-Semitic he was or he wasn't; how he could have sounded pro-Nazi but really wasn't, and so forth. Or perhaps we should ignore the question altogether and just press forward with the development of our craft and let the issue recede into the background.

For myself, I don't think that is either possible or desirable. Non-Jungians will not let the issue recede and will continue to cast out the body of analytical psychology as they continue to appropriate as their own its most fundamental and penetrating concepts and ideas.

But there is a bigger question here. We are all, in one sense or another, healers. And there is something to be healed here. Adolf Guggenbühl-Craig, in his important book *Power in the Helping Professions,* cautioned us Jungians about becoming inflated with the symbol of the wounded healer. And he was right. That symbol in its positive manifestation suggests a healing empathy that derives from personal woundedness. This paradoxical image also suggests a psyche and a soul that in spite of itself wounds out of its own limitations, deprivation, and woundedness. Jung was a wounded healer who sometimes wounded those he healed and taught. In this instance, the issue is anti-Semitism. In other contexts it has been his relationships with patients and colleagues, such as Toni Wolff and Sabina Spielrein. (And haven't some of us done the very same thing from time to time—wounded someone we were trying to heal?) I believe that until we have adequately addressed this aspect of Jung's shadow—his alleged anti-Semitism—we will carry a collective depression and guilt about it. Certainly the overwhelming attendance at the two days of the workshop is one indication of the personal and professional importance of this issue to all of us.

At the same time, we are all at this workshop because we feel more healed by Jung than wounded by him. If today I were confronted by one of Jung's detractors, I would say, "Yes, it does appear that Jung engaged in anti-Semitic behavior. That was wrong. It wounded him and it has wounded me. I have come to be able to forgive him for that as I have some others and I continue to mourn its truth. But I have to tell you, too, that he has given to me—and I think to the world—much more than he has wounded us. Ironically, for me personally it was through my own Jungian analysis that the Jewish aspects of my own spiritual self were redeemed. On balance, Jung's redemption of the spiritual dimension as an integral part of human self-definition far outweighs his anti-Semitic behavior.

There is, I think, another observation that is worth mentioning. Within a family, a wound to the family by one of the parents often has the effect of drawing the rest of the family together into a closer union. I felt such a bond emerging from the first day of our workshop.

EPILOGUE

As might be expected, responses of participants in the two-day workshop varied widely. Although there was some discussion about whether Jung was in fact anti-Semitic, there was general acceptance (with the notable exception of Thomas Kirsch's presentation) that his behavior was at some level anti-Semitic. Importantly, notwithstanding Jung's acknowledged assistance to specific individual Jewish friends and colleagues, it was established and accepted as fact that Jung knew about and condoned a quota on the number of Jewish members who would be admitted to the Psychology Club of Zurich. (See the Ribi correspondence referred to below.)

It is significant, I feel, that the running current before, during, and after the workshop centered on the tension—still within our community—over whether or not Jung's position on anti-Semitism is significant on grounds other than historical interest. Responses on this score ranged widely—both on the part of presenters and within the larger group of participants in the two days of the workshop.

Andrew Samuels, in his presentation, took the position that notwithstanding Jung's anti-Semitism, as a community we must move beyond Jung the man and that we must focus on what we as analytical psychologists can do to prevent such bigotry from occurring. He raised the important question of whether there is something inherent in the nature of analytical psychology itself that lends itself to bigotry and, without directly answering that question, suggested some ways to ensure that our craft does not inadvertently so lend itself.

The second day of the workshop was particularly noteworthy in that it seemed to highlight the tensions around this issue within the Jungian community. Adolf Guggenbühl-Craig's presentation, enthusiastically received by workshop participants, did much to move the issue beyond Jung the man, by grounding Jung in his "petit bourgeois humanity" and in his human shadow. At the same time, while acknowledging that Jung was anti-Semitic, and condemning him for being so, he asserted:

> The dark sides of Jung should not affect us at all. We should not care about them. We should not worry about them. For us, the second generation, the dark sides of Jung are a pseudo-issue, a non-event. If it affects us all the same, then there is something wrong with us. We have to search them in ourselves. If we get worked up by the contradictions in Jung's character, we are bad Jungian psychologists. We miss some essential points of Jungian psychology. . . .
>
> The disappointment [in Jung] is in us a kind of a lack of psychological consciousness. . . . Is there something inherent in the psychology of Jung that could lead to anti-Semitism or Nazism? That's the only issue we have to worry about. . . .
> (Quoted from official tape of workshop proceedings)

This position was troubling for a number of participants. It poses the question as to whether or not the integrity of a great man is of consequence to his followers and to the community of humankind as a whole. Is it irrelevant that when an individual looks a great man—a great healer—in the eye and says, "Your actions hurt me," as Erich Neumann did repeatedly in his correspondence with Jung, the silence on the part of the great man is of no import? Is it inconsequential how people view the body of Jung's work because they cannot get beyond Jung's shadow to the importance of his body of thought? More broadly stated, is moral consciousness an essential ingredient in healing a wounded psyche and in the development of human thought, particularly as regards Jungian thought and approaches to healing?

It takes courage on the part of Jungian analysts to pursue the unpopular and painful work of exploring the shadow of a great man and a hero/father figure. Carl Jung was a great man, one of the great thinkers of this century. But he was a man, not a god, and as he pointed out, great men have great shadows. It seems to me that it honors Jung the great man that we, his followers, honor his teachings—to integrate the shadow, lest it thrash us from behind—more than his failings as a human being. It also honors Jung's work to separate it out from the shadow of the man, so that it becomes less easy for his detractors and those who fear the implications of his theories to throw out the body of his work along with their rejection of his shadow.

While virtually all of the workshops and papers at the IAAP Congress in Paris dealt with clinical and related issues, the Workshop on Jung and Anti-Semitism was the only one that reached beyond this narrower focus to a topic of general interest. The topic is of such import to the Jungian community that the Paris workshop drew nearly four hundred attendees over two days.

As a Jew, and as an analytical psychologist, I have come to believe that anti-Semitism (like any other prejudice) is an attitude more than just a behavior. As a Jew I often know an anti-Semite when he enters the room, even before he utters a word. The attitude broadcasts itself. At a feeling level, Jung does not feel like the stereotypical anti-Semite to me. However, there is no question in my mind, as a result of the Paris workshop and the "Lingering Shadows" conference in New York, that he engaged in some anti-Semitic behavior.

My personal conclusion is that Jung suffered from a profoundly deficient—perhaps a pathologically deficient—feeling function. I draw this observation from the body of literature written about Jung, his own writings, the information presented at the "Lingering Shadows" conference, and my own discussions (not about his alleged anti-Semitism) with some of Jung's family. A deficient feeling function best explains Jung's paradoxical behavior with

James Kirsch and Erich Neumann—concerned and helpful on the one hand and callously silent on the other. His defective feeling function left him particularly vulnerable to the anti-Semitism endemic in German Swiss culture and to the anti-Semitic *Zeitgeist* prevalent in most of Western culture at the time, as well as to those anti-Semitic elements in his personal shadow.

My most critical judgments of Jung on this score have to do less with what he did and said than with what he did not do and did not say. Even after World War II, his oft-quoted statement "I slipped up" seems insultingly inadequate as an explanation for his behavior. It belies a woeful insensitivity to the events and reflects his failure to take a stance on the moral issues of the times. It seems to me that personal vanity—what Guggenbühl-Craig refers to as his "petit bourgeois humanity"—and a defective feeling function more fully explain Jung's behavior toward Jews than just dismissing him as a stereotypical anti-Semite.

It is significant that the Paris workshop concluded with a theme of opposites. The very last response made in the workshop proceedings was by John Beebe of San Francisco, who stated his conviction that seeking some act of atonement from the Psychology Club of Zurich regarding the quota put on Jewish membership in the club during the period from the 1930s to 1950 is essential for moving forward and for healing. Dr. Beebe's position clearly implies that not only the integrity of the man but our own integrity as a community of Jungian analysts makes a difference. His suggestion was met with approbation by those in attendance.

After the workshop on Jung and anti-Semitism at the Congress, the following letter was sent to Alfred Ribi, President of the Psychology Club of Zurich. Dr. Ribi's reply and my response are presented below.

November 6, 1989

Dear Dr. Ribi:

As you may be aware, the XIth International Congress of the IAAP was held between August 28 and September 2, 1989, in Paris, France. On August 31st and September 1st, a Workshop entitled

"Jung and Anti-Semitism" was held as part of the Congress program. I was Chairman of that workshop.

Although there were three workshops which ran concurrently, the workshop on Jung and Anti-semitism was far and away the most heavily attended, each of the two workshops having to be moved to larger rooms to accommodate a standing room attendance. There were over 150 attendees at the first day of the workshop and nearly 250 at the second. I mention the heavy attendance to give you some notion of the importance attached to this topic by the international analytic community.

I have enclosed my introductory notes for the opening of the workshop. These remarks will give you some idea of the history and genesis of the workshop that was recently held in Paris and another meeting, entitled "Lingering Shadows," which was held at the C. G. Jung Foundation in New York in March of this year.

One of the facts that was reported at the Paris workshop was that the Analytical Psychology Club of Zurich imposed a secret quota (10%) on the maximum number of Jews who may hold membership in the Club at any one time. This quota was enforced unofficially since the thirties, was formalized in 1944, and remained on the record until 1950 when, finally, it was rescinded. I have enclosed a copy of a paper by Dr. Aryeh Maidenbaum, Executive Director of the C. G. Jung Foundation of New York, who did the research on this question (along with another analyst, Dr. Steve Martin, of Philadelphia, Pennsylvania), which documents this history.

There was considerable discussion of this issue during both days of the Paris workshop. (Indeed, one attending analyst was so disturbed by this revelation that she declared that she would have to consider resigning from the IAAP because of Jung's complicity in such an onerous policy on the part of the Club.)

It is noteworthy that the final comment made at the close of the second day of the workshop was one by John Beebe, M.D., a San Francisco analyst. He observed that, from the Jewish perspective, atonement for a sin is essential, both for the healing of the one injured by the act and for the perpetrator of the act itself. He noted that, as far as anyone knew, the Analytical Psychology Club of Zurich has never offered any statement of regret or any other act of atonement for such an injurious policy. He suggested that the present Club make some such expression. After consultation with various people who were present, it was decided that as Chairman

of the workshop, I would convey the sentiments of those in attendance and would forward a formal request for some expression of
atonement by the Club. (I wish to be clear that this request is from
the attendees of the two-day workshop and is not the result of
formal action by the IAAP.)

As I have written this, I have been reminded of Joseph Campbell's
observation that the word "atonement" structurally is composed of
the words "at-one-ment." Symbolically, I think that Dr. Beebe's
suggestion provides an opportunity to begin a process of healing
which has been long overdue.

Should you wish additional information concerning the Paris
workshop or the Lingering Shadows program held in New York
earlier this year, I will be glad to forward papers, backup research
material, etc., for your edification.

The proceedings of the Paris Congress will be published next year
in a book. I am in the process of preparing material on the workshop
for forwarding to the editor of that volume. It would be both
appropriate and timely to have some response to this formal request
to the Analytical Psychology Club of Zurich which emanated from
the workshop to include in that package of material which I will
forward to the editor.

If I can be of assistance, please don't hesitate to contact me.

Sincerely yours,

Jerome S. Bernstein, M.A.P.C., NCPsyA.
Chairman, Workshop on Jung and Anti-Semitism
XIth Congress of the IAAP

Dr. Ribi did respond to my letter, and we have had two additional subsequent exchanges of letters as of April 1991. In our last
exchange, Dr. Ribi declined to have our postworkshop correspondence published because it was an "afterthought" and not part of
the formal IAAP conference.

In his response to my letter of November 6, 1989, Dr. Ribi
pointed out that the general membership of the Club was not
informed of the secret actions of its executive committee regarding
a Jewish quota during the period in question, 1944–50. Furthermore, it was his belief that the present Club membership could not
be held responsible for the secret actions of the Club's executive

committee in the 1940s. At the same time he informed me that the Club was appointing a historian to research the history of the Club, including the period in question, and that he would keep me posted on their findings.

In our further correspondence I emphasized that more than a technical assessment of blame for those actions of the Club during such a difficult period in history was called for. The IAAP workshop attendees conveyed that what is called for is a feeling gesture of "atonement"—at the least a public disavowal by the Club of the actions of the Executive committee of that period to heal the moral and psychological wound to the Jungian community as a whole. Only by dissociating itself from this past discriminatory act in its history can the Club finally close the door on this subject. Although it is true that no discriminatory policy has been part of the Club's history since 1950, it is also true that its history during the period 1944–50 has remained a festering shadow issue for the Club and the Jungian community as a whole. This conclusion is attested to by the reaction of attendees at the Paris workshop. The concern here is not just the moral stance of the Club, but rather the moral stance of the Jungian community at large, both in its own eyes and in the eyes of the world. As analyst-healers, our job is not to blame, but to attempt to heal those wounds that hurt. This is no less true of our own community than it is of the patients whom we see in our consulting rooms.

I have written Dr. Ribi to urge that the work of the Club's historian be completed in time for a joint report to the XIIth IAAP Congress, to be held in Chicago, Illinois, in the fall of 1992.

Jung, Anti-Semitism, and the Nazi Regime

Marga Speicher

Marga Speicher, Ph.D., a Jungian analyst in private practice in New York City and Englewood, New Jersey, is on the faculty of the C. G. Jung Institute and of the C. G. Jung Foundation in New York. She is Chairperson of the Institute's Board of Trustees. In this paper Dr. Speicher describes her personal connection to the subject of anti-Semitism and the Nazi regime. She details her own personal path to consciousness on this issue and urges the Jungian community to deal straightforwardly with this component of Jung's shadow.

Why did I agree to serve as a panelist in the workshop that seeks to explore Jung's relation to Germany in the early 1930s and his stance toward Nazism and anti-Semitism? A personal matter led me to agree readily: one of the major struggles in my life has centered on facing the issue of Germany in World War II, of Nazism, and of the anti-Semitism that exploded so virulently and that led to holocaust and genocide. Fate stuck me right in the middle of this thorny issue; and I came to the workshop to bring the personal dimension to bear on our topic. I will speak about what coming to terms with Nazism and anti-Semitism, with the collective shadow, has involved for me as a person and what it involves for me as a Jungian analyst.

I was born in Germany in 1934 and grew up in a Catholic family in a small industrial town. In my family I was told of the

Nazis as a godless regime opposed to religious practice. My father was censured for being a practicing Catholic. I directly experienced the existence of the police state. As a Catholic, I prayed during the Good Friday liturgy "for the conversion of the unbelieving Jews," as all Catholics did until the reforms of Vatican II. I knew of Jews only in an abstract sense; the term was not connected to any individual person.

Immediately after the war in 1945, we were confronted with the horrible occurrences of the Holocaust. The textbooks issued by the Occupation forces contained stories of concentration camps and death camps that profoundly marked my eleven-year-old psyche. However, while the horrors of the Holocaust were thrust into the eleven-year-old's being, the subsequent years of schooling were notable for the lack of study of Nazism, anti-Semitism, and the Holocaust. From what I understand now, this silence on recent history was typical of German education in the late 1940s and early 1950s. There was focus on current events—the establishment and workings of the postwar democracy and the movement toward European unity.

I came to the United States in 1956 and spent the next fifteen years in South Texas acquiring a professional education and working as a psychotherapist. I moved to New York City in 1972. It was then and there that life forced me to confront squarely my German background, anti-Semitism, the Holocaust: collective shadow and collective guilt. These were issues that I had managed to avoid, contents that I had split off and had let sink into the unconscious, where they were wreaking havoc with my life.

A concern for dealing at a deeper level with blockages in my life led me at that point into another analytic exploration. New York City, with its large Jewish population, where the annual Holocaust Remembrance Week not only is observed in synagogues but enters public consciousness, provided the outer stimulus for the confrontation that I had avoided for so long.

Jung's essay "After the Catastrophe" (1945) was profoundly meaningful to me. Jung speaks at length about collective guilt: of German collective guilt and of European collective guilt. And he calls for an acknowledgment of psychic participation in the fall into shadow, lest a person "compound his [*sic*] collective guilt by the sin of unconsciousness." He speaks of the need for "a proper *rite de sortie,* a solemn admission of guilt" so that we can "escape the contaminating touch of evil."[1]

In my inner confrontation, it became essential for me (1) on a personal level, to recall as much as I could of the years I spent in Germany during and after the war; (2) on a wider level, to know as much as I could of Nazism, anti-Semitism, Holocaust, and genocide; (3) most importantly, to come to a personal stance in relation to collective issues.

My personal confrontation with Nazism, anti-Semitism, Holocaust, and genocide occurred about thirty years after the war's end, when I was around forty years old. It was a late confrontation and I have asked myself, "Where was I, psychically, in the interim?" The details of that answer are not relevant to this discussion, but the fact of the delay needs to be noted. A few years after this confrontation, I met and married a Jewish man. With and within that important relationship, life did thrust me closer to the experience of the Jewish minority in Western civilization.

When I look at our topic, the relation of the Jungian community to Jung's position toward Nazism and anti-Semitism, I see an odd similarity between the course that awareness of collective shadow issues took in my life and the course that our communal awareness of Jung's shadow issues has taken so far and where it is today. Both share a long period of silence; an awakening to the issue at the IAAP Congresses in Jerusalem and Berlin, where outer environment contributed to the raising of the questions; the conference in New York, aptly called "Lingering Shadows"; and the present workshop on Jung and anti-Semitism at the Paris IAAP Congress.

What was Jung's position in regard to anti-Semitism and the Nazi regime? I have reviewed much of the available material and listened carefully to the material presented at the New York conference. It is my belief at present that Jung shared in the anti-Semitism that was rampant throughout Europe and that his position toward Nazism in its early years, on one hand, was naively apolitical and, on the other hand, was fed by overly optimistic views of the archetypal energies that he saw activated.[2]

We can look at Jung's anti-Semitism in terms of his family history, of the culture of his time, and especially of the intellectual environment at the turn of the century. We can also see how the conflicts with Freud and the remnants of disappointment, hurt, and anger after their parting contributed to his ethnocentric emphasis on the differentiation between Jewish and Germanic psychology, which pervades his statements of the 1920s and early 1930s. We can, furthermore, see how Jung, in the 1930s, seized the opportunity to focus on his contributions to psychotherapy that were acceptable in the Germany of the 1930s when Freudian views had fallen into political disfavor irrespective of their merit. I do not believe that Jung was anti-Semitic on a person-to-person basis nor that he held conscious anti-Semitic views. Jung's orientation was firmly German-Swiss and Protestant-Christian. In the underground waters of that orientation there flowed ethnocentrism and anti-Semitism that remained unconscious, in shadow, but that influenced his views and actions. The ethnocentrism and anti-Semitism in Jung formed a background attitude similar to the racism and ethnocentrism of many today who are consciously neither racist nor ethnocentric.

When we look at Jung's relation to Germany in the early 1930s, we see that Jung was taken by the archetypal dynamic of Wotan, which he saw as underlying the nationalistic stirrings in Germany. He valued its awakening and held hopes that it would yield long-term positive contributions.[3] It is easy for any of us at any time not to see clearly the earthly reality whenever we focus on archetypal energies.

In the 1930s, Jung fell into shadow, into the anti-Semitism lurking in the psychic underground waters, and into the fascination with the potential of an archetypal awakening in Germany. He also fell into the shadow of being apolitical. He said repeatedly that he was a physician and not a political man.[4] He overlooked or ignored the fact that he lived in a body politic, like it or not, and that every action or nonaction makes a political statement, overtly or covertly. This is especially evident in the life of a prominent person; and Jung was a prominent person.

I wish Jung had spoken out strongly against anti-Semitism. I know that there was censorship and fear in Switzerland, especially in the 1940s, as the Swiss tried to stay uninvolved in the European conflicts. Nonetheless, I wish Jung had spoken out against anti-Semitism. I wish Pius XII had spoken out. I wish leaders in the United States had spoken out and had acted firmly and directly to aid persecuted groups in Germany and under German occupation. I am grateful for each person, prominent or unknown, who did speak out as well as for each person in the underground and Resistance who was able to stand against the tide.

Jung did not speak out clearly and publicly against anti-Semitism because he fell into shadow. That is the human condition.

Jung defended himself vigorously against charges of anti-Semitism and acquiescence. In 1946, he published a long list of excerpts[5] out of his earlier writing to show how he had foreseen and warned against the eruptions in Europe. He had seen and named the archetypal dynamics in their positive and in their negative aspects, but he had not attended actively and publicly to the horrible human manifestations. It has been said: "Too much psychology, not enough political action." Jung's reply to that point would be, again, that he is a physician, not a political man. But that is an easy reply: we are all involved in the political world, be it by action or omission. Omission is also a political act.

Jung wrestled with the events of Nazism and of the Holocaust. In "After the Catastrophe" in 1945, he wrote: "While I was working on this article I noticed how churned up one still is in one's own psyche. . . . I must confess that no article has ever given me so much trouble, from a moral as well as a human point of view. I had not realized how much I myself was affected. . . . This inner identity or *participation mystique* with events in Germany has caused me to experience afresh how painfully wide is the scope of the psychological concept of *collective guilt.*"[6] He speaks of participation in collective shadow that is to be faced by the German and by the European, and he calls for recognition, consciousness, a *rite de sortie.*[7] One can read the essay as his way of acknowledging collective shadow and collective guilt that touched him also.

I do not know whether Jung ever wrestled with the anti-Semitism in his shadow. I have not seen an indication of such a struggle in anything I have read or heard. I have seen denial in his writings.

What I miss in Jung is a clear acknowledgment that he had fallen into the shadow of anti-Semitism, of fascination with archetypal energies, of the apolitical stance. I wish he could have come to a clear, open acknowledgment of the fall into shadow. (We do not know what his private acknowledgment might have been.)

What is my relation as a Jungian analyst to Jung's shadow issues? The very same as for all shadow issues: to see them, know them, and name them; to acknowledge them as human and let them be what they are: shadow—without condoning or whitewashing or denying. That is the stance we take toward shadow: know it, name it, be with it, and then ask: how do I live with it? what does it require?

Jung died in 1961, twenty-eight years ago. World War II ended in 1945, forty-four years ago. The most questionable period in Jung's life falls into the early and mid-1930s, about fifty-five years ago. The time is here in which we as a Jungian community[8] can see and name Jung's shadow issues of anti-Semitism, fascination with archetypal energies, the apolitical stance; the time also in which we can seek to understand the dynamics as far as we can; and the time in which we can grow through this process. Why have we as a community stayed away from this process for so long? Where have we been, psychically, in the interim? Shadow issues claim to be recognized. When we block them out, a price has to be paid.

I want to urge us as a Jungian community to give the necessary recognition and acknowledgment to Jung's shadow, his anti-Semitism, his fascination with archetypal energies, and his apolitical stance as well as to the shadow of the Jungian community in those very same matters. We have to ask ourselves continually: (1) Where do the underground waters of ethnocentrism, anti-Semitism, racism flow at the present time? (2) When and where does our recognition of archetypal energies turn into fascination and cause us to lose sight of earthly reality? (3) Where do we claim an apolitical stance in a rather routine manner without due consideration of the political impact of such a position?[9]

Such an exploration of Jung's fall into shadow can lead us, on the one hand, to a better understanding of shadow, personal and archetypal, individual and collective, and, on the other hand, to a better understanding of the ever-present pitfalls inherent in personal and communal life as well as to the pitfalls inherent in the theoretical and philosophical positions we hold.

I will close with Jung's words from "After the Catastrophe": "We must all open our eyes to the shadow who looms behind contemporary man [*sic*]. . . . It is indeed no small matter to know of one's own guilt and one's own evil, and there is certainly nothing to be gained by losing sight of one's own shadow. . . . Anything that remains in the unconscious is incorrigible; psychological corrections can be made only in consciousness."[10]

Notes

1. C. G. Jung, "After the Catastrophe," *CW* 10, paras. 400–443. The quotations are from paras. 404 and 410.

2. It is beyond the scope of this brief paper to present the basic data on which my conclusions are based. The data are contained in Jung's writings as published in the *Collected Works* and in his letters. A critical review and evaluation of Jung's views, words, and actions can be found elsewhere in this book. See especially Appendix A, "Significant Words and Events."

3. C. G. Jung, "Wotan," *CW* 10, paras. 371–399.

4. In responding to criticism over his involvement with the General Medical Society for Psychotherapy in Germany and with the International General Medical Society for Psychotherapy in the 1930s, Jung refers to himself as uninterested in politics but only interested in assisting the German psychotherapists. For instance, he wrote to Abraham Aaron Roback on 29 September 1936: "As a matter of fact, I am quite unpolitical."

5. C. G. Jung, "Epilogue to 'Essays on Contemporary Events," *CW* 10, paras. 458–487.

6. Jung, "After the Catastrophe," *CW* 10, para. 402.

7. Ibid., paras. 404, 411.

8. While individuals in our midst have struggled with these issues, as a com-

munity we have been silent about them. It is important that we see Jung the man separate from Jung the original creative thinker and psychologist; that we see and name the flaws of the man while we reap the benefits of his psychological creativity, which are the basis of our professional orientation.

9. I am speaking of the position that each of us as an individual holds in relation to these issues. As a community, we have not called much attention to the manifestations of these issues in our individual lives. That is a lacuna. In regard to political matters, I consider it important that each person's consciousness and conscience direct her or his political stance. I am not thinking of these issues in terms of taking action or expressing views as a group nor as so-called psychological experts.

10. Jung, "After the Catastrophe," CW 10, para. 440.

Reflections on Jung and Anti-Semitism

Adolf Guggenbühl-Craig

Adolf Guggenbühl-Craig is a psychiatrist and Jungian analyst in Zurich, Switzerland, and the author of several books, including *Power in the Helping Professions* and *Eros on Crutches: Reflections on Psychology and Amorality*. In his contribution to the workshop, he suggests that we should not be alarmed by Jung's anti-Semitism, as it was a byproduct of his bourgeois Protestant background and in no way detracted from his psychological genius. He urges us to confront our need for an idealized, shadowless father figure in Jung, and to accept that he was, ultimately, simply an ordinary person of his time.

Guggenbühl-Craig makes the uniquely Jungian argument that generalizations about nations and races are valid in that they are ultimately mythological in nature, and therefore true expressions of collective fantasy.

The center of our discussion seems to be the impact of Jung's anti-Semitism on the credibility of his ideas, and the injuries that we have suffered as a result of Jung's darker side. I may be the wrong person to talk about this topic, as I feel neither injured nor disappointed by Jung.

In 1943, when I was twenty years old, I started to read Jung. My father warned me, "Why are you interested in that man? Don't you know that he is a anti-Semite, he flirts with Nazism, he flatters rich ladies, and who knows what else?" At that time I had the same political ideas as my father. For both of us anti-Semitism was *the* crime. We knew that the Germans had begun to exterminate the Jews. I was at that time so shocked by this fact that I started to learn Yiddish, a feeble attempt to honor the threatened Jewish people. And I continued, in spite of my father, to read Jung.

My father's opinions of Jung were not particularly original. He had never read Jung himself. His psychological hero was Freud. The ideas he had about Jung were collective, shared by a large number of Swiss, who saw in Hitler's Germany a deadly danger for Switzerland and the whole liberal democratic world. When later, as a psychiatrist, I joined the Jungians, my father was very disappointed. He could never fully understand how I could betray my family and myself by joining what to him was a half-fascistic crowd. That's why, to use James Hillman's images, I was never a white, innocent Jungian; I was "yellow" from the beginning. But all the same, the topic interests me: How do the dark sides of Jung affect us, as Christians and as Jews, or whatever our identity may be? I will try to give a precise answer to this question now and go into details later.

The dark sides of Jung should not affect us at all. We should ignore them; they should not worry us at all. For us, the second-generation Jungians, the dark sides of Jung are a pseudo-issue, a non-event. If it affects us all the same, then there is something wrong with us. We have to examine ourselves to find out what is wrong.

But first of all, let us turn to Jung. As far as I can see, Jung was certainly anti-Semitic, but in a less ideological, conscious, yet deeper way than Andrew Samuels believes. Everyone in Europe, with perhaps the exception of the Italians, was anti-Semitic in the last century, and in the centuries before that, as well as in this century. Anti-Semitism was and is part of the collective mythology, originating from the Christian religion. The Jews were considered to be the killers of Jesus Christ. James Kirsch has written very convincingly about the religious roots of Jung's anti-Semitism. (See the article by James Kirsch in this volume.)

Jung was on the one hand a psychological genius and on the other hand a very average middle-class man, a bourgeois, with all the mythological beliefs, images, and ideas that this class possessed. Anti-Semitism was, and partially still is, the darker side of this belief system. There are many bright sides too: ideas of freedom, justice, decency, honesty, social justice, democracy, and so on. The anti-Semitism of Jung was a sheer banality, part and parcel of the collective he belonged to.

As an ordinary man, Jung displayed positive and negative sides. He was, for instance, an appeaser: don't make the beast angry, don't anger Hitler, and so forth. Again, this was a typical collective attitude. Europe was, until 1939, largely dominated by appeasers. Remember Chamberlain's "Peace for our time" after Munich? "Be nice to the beast, save your skin," amounted to an argument in favor of survival at all costs.

Appeasement is not always a mistake; it is one way to deal with the dark forces around and within us. Heroes have done as much damage, and as much good, as appeasers—and in the collective psyche, sometimes the appeaser is stronger, while at other times the hero is.

Jung was intellectual, again in a very collective way. Intellectuals are much inclined to admire power. The French speak of a *"trahison des clercs,"* a phrase that translates literally as "treason of the clergy" or "of the intellectuals." We should not forget that hundreds of European intellectuals, writers, and sophisticated professors paid homage to Stalin while he was walking knee-deep in the blood of Russian peasants. They admired even his macabre purges. While Mao was killing millions of Chinese farmers, many intellectuals went on praising him as the creator of a new and better world. This admiration of power among intellectuals is probably a compensation for their fascination with the spirit. Obviously, not all intellectuals are blinded by power; there are always a few original individuals who can resist it. But the bulk of them, insofar as they are part of the intellectual collective, tend to be attracted by power.

And so Jung, as a collective intellectual, was fascinated by Hitler and Mussolini. This is not very original. But even the greatest genius can only be original in a small part of his psyche; the bigger part belongs to the collective psyche. And Jung, at least after the Second World War, did not follow the collective crazes for the mass murderers Stalin and Mao.

I repeat: Jung had many sides. On one side he was a unique psychological genius, on the other side he was an average member of the upper middle class, an anti-Semite, an appeaser, and sometimes an intellectual who admired power.

However, if we are chagrined by the contradictions in Jung, we are not true Jungian psychologists; we are then missing some points of Jungian psychology, because Jung taught us the following: human beings are many-sided, composed of many archetypes, psychoids, complexes, all of them having their own consciousness. The different sides might have little to do with each other, not only in schizophrenics, but in all of us.

In dealing with my wife, my children, and my friends, I have to take all sides into account. With Jung this is not the case. Jung was not my friend. His contradictory sides might have been a problem for his analysands, but his aura was so overpowering that often the critical faculties of his analysands melted away and they slipped into an eternal happy glorification of the master. We Jungians today have to listen to his genius; the rest should be of no interest to us.

There was a movement in American literary criticism that coined a phrase, "The author is 'out,' " meaning that personal information about a writer is of no interest, and only his or her work counts. This certainly applies to Jung.

But we still have to ask: why this disappointment in Jung? Why is this disappointment so widespread among Jungians? I believe that this disappointment stems from a deep need for a perfect leader, a perfect saint, someone who guides us, who becomes a guru. And so, if a genius appears, we make him into a saint, a prophet, and a leader. But even though we are psychologists and know about archetypes, we are still not conscious of this longing for the messiah or for the second coming of Christ. We are then, of course, disappointed when our hero, apart from being a genius, turns out to be a very average human being.

Nevertheless, I must confess that I was very disturbed a few years ago when the changes in the statutes of the Jungian club in Zurich during the war, limiting the number of Jewish numbers, were revealed. What the club did—whoever the club was at that time—is very difficult to understand. It was similar to kicking a dying man in the face. But then again, who wants to throw the first stone?

Granting Jung his shadow of collective beliefs frees us from our messianic projection onto him. Yet there is another important issue, which has been raised by Andrew Samuels: is there something inherent in the ideas of Jung that could lead to anti-Semitism or to Nazism? That is, in my opinion, the only issue that we have to worry about, and this only within limits. By way of comparison, Christianity contains inherent ideas that, when misunderstood and abused, led to the burning of thousands of men and women as witches and to pogroms, and yet some of us are still Christians.

Andrew Samuels has mentioned Jung's fascination with nations. He thinks that this fascination should be suspect. Here I have to defend Jung. In this instance I see evidence of his psychological genius.

Nations are a very impressive psychological phenomenon. It makes no difference if Germany only existed officially since 1871, or if already in olden times one spoke of the *"römischen Reich deutscher Nation"* (the Roman empire of the German nation), or if the Italians became a nation only in the nineteenth century, or if the British nation is really four nations. The fact is that in the past centuries, millions of people died in Europe and elsewhere for their nation, often voluntarily. Today in the U.S.S.R. the last cohesive colonial empire is being threatened by nationalism. Nations are an extremely powerful phenomenon and, like all important psychological phenomena, they cannot be explained; they can only be approached by mythological images.

We all talk about the characteristics of different nations. For instance, we say that the Italians have lots of feelings, the French are rational, the Swiss are sober, the English are gentlemen and ladies; but it is pure mythology. I hope that Jung realized this when he talked about Germans and Jews in this way. This talk about the characters of nations and peoples is all fantasy—extremely powerful fantasy. Maybe Jung was at times inclined to take these fantasies too literally; from the point of view of Jungian psychology, these fantasies can be treated as pure mythological images.

The problem of the different characteristics of groups and nations, of women and men, is not whether they are inborn or acquired, but that they are a powerful collective phenomenon of mysterious origin, only able to be described by mythology. Jung tried to do just that, to understand this powerful phenomenon by the collective fantasies and the mythologies lying behind them.

The collective fantasies, or at least the fantasies of some nations, became ill during this century, as we saw in Nazi Germany. Our job as psychotherapists, analysts, and psychiatrists is to treat psychotics and neurotics, with the help of the insight analytical psychology gives us. Our job is not only to talk to ladies and gentlemen about their fancy dreams—or only to train trainees to become, in turn, training analysts for trainees. When we have patients with delusions, hallucinations, horrible perversions, it's no use pointing to reality. First we have to join with the psychopathology of the patient and accept it. We even have to do this half unconsciously, and only when we make this connection and become fascinated can we go further with the patient and eventually help him or her.

Jung, the genius, did exactly that. He let himself be drawn into the collective madness of Nazism, of which anti-Semitism was only a part. He was fascinated, by the phenomenon, and out of this fascination he was able to formulate and describe precisely what this phenomenon was and is. His little book *Wotan* is still, even today, the best, most frightening mythological description of Nazism. All other explanations, based on economy, inflation, sociology, and the like, look poor compared with the tremendous mythological images by which Jung tried to approach National Socialism. Jung was in many ways a very average man, but once he was caught be a psychological phenomenon, his genius always got the better of him.

But now you may ask: What can we do when we are attacked because of the dark sides of Jung? To that question I can only answer: If you are afraid of being attacked, you should not become analysts or psychotherapists, but honest accountants at Lafayette or Marks and Spencer.

We can forget about the little average collective man Jung, the appeaser, anti-Semite, and admirer of power. We have mainly to be inspired by Jung's passion for psychology. I say passion, not detached observation, but burning, even self-damaging passion for the human psyche in all its appearances.

Jung and the Jews
Personal Reflections

Thomas B. Kirsch

Thomas B. Kirsch, M.D., is a Jungian analyst in private practice in Palo Alto, California. He is President of the International Association for Analytical Psychology and Clinical Associate Professor of Psychiatry at Stanford University Medical School.

Dr. Kirsch argues that, while Jung's attitudes toward Jews were neither uncomplicated nor above reproach, his contributions to the field of psychology were not based on racist preconceptions, and any evaluation of his legacy should not be influenced by judgments of his personality or prejudices.

Anti-Semitism is a subject that has been associated with Jung since the rise of Nazism in the 1930s. It is used by his detractors to discount his theories of the psyche, while on the other hand his followers have defended him, saying that there is nothing to these rumors. Every time one thinks the subject has died, it is resurrected by a new generation with the idea of getting to the truth of the matter. This is the first time that the subject has been discussed at the international level, and it is really a good thing that we are doing it. However, I would caution us not to become obsessed with the topic. There is that tendency.

I am often asked to speak on this topic as I am Jewish and both my parents, James and Hilde Kirsch, were in analysis with Jung during the time that he was allegedly anti-Semitic. My parents left

Germany in 1933, going to Palestine and England and finally settling in Los Angeles. They had contact with Jung from 1929 until his death in 1961. I must say that my parents never felt a trace of anti-Semitism in their own personal dealings with him. They always felt that because of their experience of the unconscious and Jung they were able to understand what was going on in Nazi Germany and to leave. They had many Jewish colleagues during that period who had similar experiences, and I do not believe friends and colleagues like Erich Neumann, Aniela Jaffé, Gerhard Adler, and many others would have stayed with Jung had they experienced him as being anti-Jewish.

I do not think that Jung's attitude toward Jews was simple. On one hand, he held the typical collective European prejudice of the time toward Jews. This was endemic. On the other hand, he had been an early champion of Freud and psychoanalysis at a time when it was quite unpopular. He also had a strong erotic countertransference to Sabrina Spielrein, a Russian Jew, and this preceded his relationship with Toni Wolff. Also, I have the definite impression that Jung was never able to satisfactorily work out his relationship with Freud. In a recent interview with John Freeman, the man who interviewed Jung in *Face to Face,* Freeman states that, in subsequent visits with Jung, he would always come back to his relationship with Freud.[1] It remained unresolved for Jung all his life.

Let us move away from the past and ask how the issue of Jung's alleged anti-Semitism affects us today. How is it when I am with a patient? Does it make me feel that I might be less a Jungian because Jung had some complex, perhaps terribly negative feeling toward Jews? No. It makes absolutely no difference, and the thought never crosses my mind. On the other hand, I am often reminded in a session that I am Jewish, and there is a debt of gratitude that through Jung and my analysis, by which I mean the understanding of complexes in a transpersonal archetypal sense, I have come to a deeper understanding of my Jewish roots and their relationship to other cultures and religions.

Let me offer two examples. The first was from early in my practice. The patient came to me as a general psychiatrist but not as a Jungian. At the end of the first hour he asked me if I was Christian. I thought for a moment and then answered that, no, I was not a Christian, but I did have a respectful attitude toward religion and religious phenomena. Analysis had prepared me to be able to manage this conflict, and although I was uncomfortable saying it at the time, it also felt all right. He seemed satisfied with my response. The second example was more difficult. The patient was a long-term analytic case. He was non-Jewish and his parents had been anti-Semitic during his youth. As part of his rage in the transference, he expressed how he hated to pay me because he hated to have his money supporting Zionist causes. He knew that I was Jewish, and he imagined me being a big supporter of Israel. He identified unconsciously with his own father and saw me as the stereotyped Zionist Jew. I did not want to answer him directly because it seemed important to hear out his fantasy about me. At the time I felt deeply wounded by his remarks, but they also helped me to see the level of the wound in his relationship to his father, who had similarly attacked him in his childhood. We were able to work analytically on this issue, and I am grateful that we both could stand the tension. Again, my own Jungian analysis and Jung's attitude toward the psyche, as I had learned it, helped me remain analytic under this kind of pressure.

I would now like to move on to another area. I think it may be the case that the Jew has a different expression of the transference than many others, and this has to do with a difference in the relationship to land and earth. The Jews have a long history of being uprooted from their own land, and as a consequence they have developed a tendency to focus on personal relations in the family. This, of course, intensifies the personal nature of the transference. (This type of marginality was completely alien to Jung, the Swiss, who was thoroughly rooted in the land of his ancestors. The transference-countertransference relationship tends to be more long-lasting, intense, and personal for Jews, because it repeats their family pattern and also serves as a compensation for the lack of attachment to the land. Obviously, there are other aspects to this complex, multilevel issue, but with respect to the differences between Freud and Jung, this observation can contribute some understanding. Although both men realized the critical nature of transference in analysis, the relative amount of time spent on it during analysis was quite different. For Freud it was the fulcrum of analysis, whereas Jung wanted to discuss and interpret it as little as necessary.

Where Jung's alleged anti-Semitism does become an issue for me is in teaching settings or public situations. The question often arises, what about Jung and his anti-Semitism? We cannot change a long history of bitterness between psychoanalysts and analytical psychologists. What to do with this question? (1) One can offer the personal fact that there were many Jewish people working with Jung during those difficult times of the 1930s and 1940s. (2) Jung's concepts of the archetypes and collective unconscious are not racially or nationalistically bound, and Jung is talking about universals in mankind. (3) The attacks on Jung and allegations of anti-Semitism are a way to discount Jung's theories, and therefore one does not have to read him: "Oh, Jung, he was a Nazi, so you don't need to know him." This was one of the major findings of the "Lingering Shadows" conference. Jung is dismissed because one doesn't need to know him, and one does not need to feel guilt about that. (4) Analytical psychology is no longer only the work of one person, so that one should study the field and not the person.

There are cycles about this issue, and every generation needs to work it through anew. There is no one piece of incontrovertible evidence that is going to settle it once and for all. It is almost all hearsay evidence. The Analytical Psychology Club in Zurich had a quota in 1944, but so did lots of other institutions at that time. The quota limited Jews, but it did not exclude them. Also, we do not know exactly what Jung's own role in this provision was. So we are left with hints that Jung did not exhibit exemplary behavior toward Jews. I do not think he liked the law-giving aspect of Judaism, and he only became aware of the mystical traditions of Judaism late in his life. In any case, we are left with this shadowy aspect of Jung's life to deal with, and as time goes on it becomes harder to ascertain what is fact and what is fiction.

We should only worry if there were some reason to believe that

Jung's theories and practice had some racist leanings, but that is not the case. In the meantime we are left with the legacy of Jung the man.

Note

1. John Boe, "Pleasing and Agreeable: An Interview with John Freeman," *San Francisco Jung Institute Library Journal* 8, no. 4 (1989): 75–84.

APPENDIXES

APPENDIXES

Significant Words and Events

Compiled by
Michael Vannoy Adams
& Jay Sherry

1856

Freud is born on May 6, 1856.

1866–1868

In *The Interpretation of Dreams,* Freud relates an anecdote:
"I may have been ten or twelve years old, when my father began to take me with him on his walks and reveal to me in his talk his views upon things in the world we live in. Thus it was, on one such occasion, that he told me a story to show me how much better things were now than they had been in his days. 'When I was a young man,' he said, 'I went for a walk one Saturday in the streets of your birthplace; I was well dressed, and had a new fur cap on my head. A Christian came up to me and with a single blow knocked off my cap into the mud and shouted: "Jew! get off the pavement." ' 'And what did you do?' I asked. 'I went into the roadway and picked up my cap,' was his quiet reply. This struck me as unheroic conduct on the part of the big, strong man who was holding the little boy by the hand" (*Standard Edition,* 4: 197).

1875

Jung is born on July 26, 1875.

1901

In *Glory Reflected: Sigmund Freud—Man and Father,* Martin Freud relates another anecdote:

"Unhappily, towards the end of our holiday there was an ugly and depressing incident which remains strongly marked in my memory. My brother Oliver and I were fishing one morning on the opposite side of the lake a few yards from the high-road which ran somewhat above the lake's level. A number of men had been watching us from the road, something which meant little to us: because fishermen are often watched by passers-by. We were shocked and considerably surprised when the men began abusing us, shouting that we were Israelites—which was true—that we were stealing fish—which was untrue—and being very offensive indeed.

"We ignored them, refusing to reply; and we went on with our fishing. After a time, the men were met by other people with whom they marched off. Nevertheless, the joy in our fishing had gone and we returned home earlier than usual with less fish caught. We told father about it all, and he became very serious for a few moments, remarking that kind of thing could happen to us again, and that we should be prepared for it.

"That same afternoon father had to go to Reichenhall and, as usual, Oliver and I rowed him across the lake to the highway to save him part of the walk. The men who had abused Oliver and me that morning were now reinforced by a number of other people, including women, and stood on the road near the primitive landing-place, apparently prepared to block the way to Reichenhall. As we moored the boat, they began shouting anti-Semitic abuse.

"Father, without the slightest hesitation, jumped out of the boat and, keeping to the middle of the road, marched towards the hostile crowd. When he saw me following him, he commanded me in so angry a voice to stay where I was that I dared not disobey. My mild-mannered father had never spoken to me in anything but kindly tones. This display of anger, as I thought it, upset me more than all the abuse of the strangers. Nevertheless, I took an oar from the boat, swung it over my shoulder and stood by, ready to join any battle that might develop. It is unlikely that this armed reserve of one boy with an oar impressed the enemy very much. They numbered about ten men, and all were armed with sticks and umbrellas. The women remained in the background, but cheered on their men-folk with shouts and gestures.

"In the meantime, father, swinging his stick, charged the hostile crowd, which gave way before him and promptly dispersed, allowing him a free passage. This was the last we saw of these unpleasant strangers. We never found out from where they came nor what their object had been in waylaying father.

"This unpleasant incident made a deep impression on me; the impression was so deep that after more than fifty-five years I can still recall the faces of these crusaders in racial hatred. Time has, undoubtedly, distorted their outline but without blurring them; they remain fiendishly ugly. But there is no evidence that father was affected in the least. He never recalled the incident at home, and I am not aware that he ever mentioned it in any of his letters to our family or friends" (pp. 70–71).

1906

Jung initiates a correspondence with Freud by sending him a copy of *Diagnostic Association Studies*.

1907

Freud and Jung meet for the first time when Jung visits Vienna.

1908

Freud to Abraham, May 3, 1908:

"Please be tolerant and do not forget that it is really easier for you than it is for Jung to follow my ideas, for in the first place you are completely independent, and then you are closer to my intellectual constitution because of racial kinship, while he as a Christian and a pastor's son finds his way to me only against great inner resistances. His association with us is the more valuable for that. I nearly said that it was only by his appearance on the scene that psychoanalysis escaped the danger of becoming a Jewish national affair."

Abraham to Freud, May 11, 1908:

"I freely admit that I find it easier to go along with you rather than with Jung. I, too, have always felt this intellectual kinship. After all, our Talmudic way of thinking cannot disappear just like that." (Gerhard Adler quotes Jung as saying: "The Talmudists go to Freud, the Cabbalists come to me." "Analytical Psychology and the Principle of Complementarity," in Joseph B. Wheelwright, ed., *The Analytic Process*, p. 114.)

Freud to Abraham, July 20, 1908:
"On the whole it is easier for us Jews, as we lack the mystical element."
(See also David Bakan, *Sigmund Freud and the Jewish Mystical Tradition.*)

Freud to Abraham, July 23, 1908:
"May I say that it is consanguineous Jewish traits that attract me to you? We understand each other. . . .
". . . I nurse a suspicion that the suppressed anti-Semitism of the Swiss that spares me is deflected in reinforced form upon you. But I think that we, as Jews, if we wish to join in, must develop a bit of masochism, be ready to suffer some wrong. Otherwise there is no hitting it off. Rest assured that, if my name were Oberhuber, in spite of everything my innovations would have met with far less resistance."

Freud to Abraham, December 26, 1908:
"Our Aryan comrades are really completely indispensable to us, otherwise psychoanalysis would succumb to anti-Semitism."

1909

Freud and Jung travel to the United States to deliver lectures at Clark University and to receive honorary doctorates.

1910

The Second International Psychoanalytic Congress is held in Nuremberg on March 30–31. Freud proposes Jung as president of the International Psychoanalytic Association. Viennese analysts hold a protest meeting, and Freud addresses the group. In *Sigmund Freud: His Personality, His Teaching, and His School* (New York: Dodd, Mead, 1924), Fritz Wittels quotes Freud as follows: " 'Most of you are Jews, and therefore you are incompetent to win friends for the new teaching. Jews must be content with the modest role of preparing the ground. It is absolutely essential that I should form ties in the world of general science. I am getting on in years, and am weary of being perpetually attacked. We are all in danger.' Seizing his coat by the lapels, he said, 'They won't even leave me a coat to my back. The Swiss will save us—will save me, and all of you as well' " (p. 140). Jung is elected president.

Freud to Ferenczi, April 24, 1910:
Commenting on an assertion that the emphasis on sexuality in psycho-analytic theory merely reflects the sensuality of Vienna, Freud says: "There one hears just the argument I tried to avoid by making Zurich the center. Viennese sensuality is not to be found anywhere else! Between the lines you can read further that we Viennese are not only swine but also Jews. But that does not appear in print."

1912

Jung delivers lectures at Fordham University and publishes *Symbols of Transformation*. These mark his intellectual divergence from Freud.

Freud forms the Committee, with Ferenczi, Abraham, Jones, Sachs, and Rank as members. In *The Life and Work of Sigmund Freud*, Jones says: "I became, of course, aware, somewhat to my astonishment, of how extraordinarily suspicious Jews could be of the faintest sign of anti-Semitism and of how many remarks or actions could be interpreted in that sense. The members most sensitive were Ferenczi and Sachs; Abraham and Rank were less so. Freud himself was pretty sensitive in this respect" (2: 163). Jones also says: "A Gentile would have said that Freud had few overt Jewish characteristics, a fondness for relating Jewish jokes and anecdotes being perhaps the most prominent one. But he felt himself to be Jewish to the core, and it evidently meant a great deal to him. He had the common Jewish sensitiveness to the slightest hint of anti-Semitism and he made very few friends who were not Jews. He objected strongly to the idea of their being unpopular or in any way inferior, and had evidently suffered much from school days onward, and especially at the University, from the anti-Semitism that pervaded Vienna. It put an end forever to the phase of German nationalistic enthusiasm through which he passed in early years" (1: 22). (See also Jones, "The Psychology of the Jewish Question," *Miscellaneous Essays* 1: 284–300).

Freud to Ferenczi, July 28, 1912:
Freud acknowledges that he has failed to unite "Jews and goyim in the service of psychoanalysis." He says: "They separate themselves like oil and water."

Freud to Rank, August 18, 1912:
Freud says that he had wanted to accomplish the "integration of Jews and anti-Semites on the soil of psychoanalysis."

1913

Freud proposes to Jung that they end personal relations, and Jung agrees. They maintain professional relations until 1914.

Freud to Abraham, May 13, 1913:
Freud says that the publication of *Totem and Taboo* "will serve to cut us off cleanly from all Aryan religiousness."

In *The Life and Work of Sigmund Freud,* Jones says: "Maeder wrote to Ferenczi that the scientific differences between the Viennese and the Swiss resulted from the former being Jews and the latter 'Aryans.' Freud advised Ferenczi to answer on the following lines [Freud to Ferenczi, June 8, 1913]. 'Certainly there are great differences between the Jewish and the Aryan spirit [*Geist*]. We can observe that every day. Hence there would assuredly be here and there differences in outlook on life and art. But there should not be such a thing as Aryan or Jewish science. Results in science must be identical, though the presentation of them may vary. If these differences mirror themselves in the apprehension of objective relationships in science there must be something wrong' " (2: 149).

1914

Jung resigns as president of the International Psychoanalytic Association. He and Freud end professional relations.

Freud publishes *On the History of the Psychoanalytic Movement* and says of Jung that "he seemed ready to enter into a friendly relationship with me and for my sake to give up certain racial prejudices which he had previously permitted himself" (*Standard Edition* 14: 43).

Jung publishes "The Role of the Unconscious," in which he distinguishes between Jewish and Germanic (or "Aryan") psychology (CW 10: 3–28):
"Christianity split the Germanic barbarian into an upper and a lower half, and enabled him, by repressing the dark side, to domesticate the brighter half and fit it for civilization. But the lower, darker half still awaits redemption and a second spell of domestication. Until then, it will remain associated with the vestiges of the prehistoric age, with the collective unconscious, which is subject to a peculiar and ever-increasing activation. As the Christian view of the world loses its authority, the more menacingly will the 'blond beast' be heard prowling about in its under-

ground prison, ready at any moment to burst out with devastating consequences. When this happens in the individual it brings about a psychological revolution, but it can also take a social form.

"In my opinion this problem does not exist for the Jews. The Jew already had the culture of the ancient world and on top of that has taken over the culture of the nations amongst whom he dwells. He has two cultures, paradoxical as that may sound. He is domesticated to a higher degree than we are, but he is badly at a loss for that quality in man which roots him to the earth and draws new strength from below. This chthonic quality is found in dangerous concentration in the Germanic peoples. Naturally the Aryan European has not noticed any signs of this for a very long time, but perhaps he is beginning to notice it in the present war; and again, perhaps not. The Jew has too little of this quality—where has he his own earth underfoot? The mystery of earth is no joke and no paradox. . . .

"The soil of every country holds some such mystery. We have an unconscious reflection of this in the psyche: just as there is a relationship of mind to body, so there is a relationship of body to earth. I hope the reader will pardon my figurative way of speaking, and will try to grasp what I mean. It is not easy to describe, definite though it is. There are people—quite a number of them—who live outside and above their bodies, who float like bodiless shadows above their earth, their earthy component, which is their body. Others live wholly in their bodies. As a rule, the Jew lives in amicable relationship with the earth, but without feeling the power of the chthonic. His receptivity to this seems to have weakened with time. This may explain the specific need of the Jew to reduce everything to its material beginnings; he needs these beginnings in order to counterbalance the dangerous ascendency of his two cultures. A little bit of primitivity does not hurt him; on the contrary, I can understand very well that Freud's and Adler's reduction of everything psychic to primitive sexual wishes and power-drives has something about it that is beneficial and satisfying to the Jew, because it is a form of simplification. For this reason, Freud is perhaps right to close his eyes to my objections. But these specifically Jewish doctrines are thoroughly unsatisfying to the Germanic mentality; we still have a genuine barbarian in us who is not to be trifled with, and whose manifestation is no comfort for us and not a pleasant way of passing the time. Would that people could learn the lesson of this war! The fact is, our unconscious is not to be got at with over-ingenious and grotesque interpretations. The psychotherapist with a Jewish background awakens in the Germanic psyche not those wistful and whimsical residues from the time of David, but the barbarian of yesterday, a being for whom matters suddenly become *serious* in the most unpleasant way. This annoying peculiarity of the barbarian was also apparent to Nietzsche—no doubt from personal experience—which is why he thought highly of the Jewish mentality and preached about dancing and flying and not taking things seriously. But he overlooked the fact that it is not the barbarian in us who takes things seriously—they become serious for him. He is gripped by the daemon. And who took things more seriously than Nietzsche himself?

"It seems to me that we should take the problem of the unconscious very seriously indeed. The tremendous compulsion towards goodness and the immense moral force of Christianity are not merely an argument in the latter's favor, they are also a proof of the strength of its suppressed and repressed counterpart—the antichristian, barbarian element. The existence within us of something that can turn against us, that can become a serious matter for us, I regard not merely as a dangerous peculiarity, but as a valuable and congenial asset as well. It is a still untouched fortune, an uncorrupted treasure, a sign of youthfulness, an earnest of rebirth. Nevertheless, to value the unconscious exclusively for the sake of its positive qualities and to regard it as a source of revelation would be fundamentally wrong" (pp. 12–14).

1926

Freud delivers an address to the B'nai B'rith:

"That you were Jews could only be agreeable to me; for I was myself a Jew, and it had always seemed to me not only unworthy but positively senseless to deny the fact. What bound me to Jewry was (I am ashamed to admit) neither faith nor national pride, for I have always been an unbeliever and was brought up without any religion though not without a respect for what are called the 'ethical' standards of human civilization. Whenever I felt an inclination to national enthusiasm I strove to suppress it as being harmful and wrong, alarmed by the warning examples of the peoples among whom we Jews live. But plenty of other things remained over to make the attraction of Jewry and Jews irresistible—many obscure emotional forces, which were the more powerful the less they could be expressed in words, as well as a clear consciousness of inner identity, the safe privacy of a common mental construction" (*Standard Edition* 20: 273–274).

1928

Jung publishes *The Relations between the Ego and the Unconscious* and discusses the collective psyche in terms of racial differences (CW 7: 121–241):

"Thus it is a quite unpardonable mistake to accept the conclusions of a Jewish psychology as generally valid. Nobody would dream of taking Chinese or Indian psychology as binding upon ourselves. The cheap accusation of anti-Semitism that has been levelled at me on the ground of this criticism is about as intelligent as accusing me of an anti-Chinese prejudice. No doubt, on an earlier and deeper level of psychic development, where it is still impossible to distinguish between an Aryan, Semitic, Hamitic, or Mongolian mentality, all human races have a common collective psyche. But with the beginning of racial differentiation essential differences are developed in the collective psyche as well. For this reason we cannot transplant the spirit of a foreign race *in globo* into our own mentality without sensible injury to the latter, a fact which does not, however, deter sundry natures of feeble instinct from affecting Indian philosophy and the like" (152 n.).

1930

Jung becomes honorary vice-president of the General Medical Society for Psychotherapy.

Freud writes a preface for the Hebrew translation of *Totem and Taboo:*
"No reader of [the Hebrew version of] this book will find it easy to put himself in the emotional position of an author who is ignorant of the language of holy writ, who is completely estranged from the religion of his fathers—as well as from every other religion—and who cannot take a share in nationalist ideals, but who has yet never repudiated his people, who feels that he is in his essential nature a Jew and who has no desire to alter that nature. If the question were put to him: 'Since you have abandoned all these common characteristics of your countrymen, what is there left to you that is Jewish?' he would reply: 'A very great deal, and probably its very essence.' He could not now express that essence clearly in words; but some day, no doubt, it will become accessible to the scientific mind" (*Standard Edition* 13: xv).

1932

Jung travels to Egypt and Palestine.

1933

Hitler is named Chancellor of Germany.

Ernst Kretschmer resigns as president of the General Medical Society for Psychotherapy. Jung agrees to serve as president on condition that the organization be renamed the International General Medical Society for Psychotherapy and that it be reconstituted to enable Jewish psychotherapists barred from the German national section to join the international society directly as individual members with equal rights. In an editorial in the society's journal, Jung writes: "The differences which actually do exist between Germanic and Jewish psychology and which have long been known to every intelligent person are no longer to be glossed over, and this can only be beneficial to science. . . . At the same time I should like to state expressly that this implies no depreciation of Semitic psychology, any more than it is a depreciation of the Chinese to speak of the peculiar psychology of the Oriental" (CW 10: 533–534).

Jung gives an interview on Radio Berlin and discusses the importance of consciously responsible individuals as leaders of collective movements (C. G. *Jung Speaking*, pp. 59–66):
"The self-development of the individual is especially necessary in our time. When the individual is unconscious of himself, the collective movement too lacks a clear sense of purpose. Only the self-development of the individual, which I consider to be the supreme goal of all psychological endeavor, can produce consciously responsible spokesmen and leaders of the collective movement. As Hitler said recently, the leader must be able to be alone and must have the courage to go his own way. But if he doesn't know himself, how is he to lead others? That is why the true leader is always one who has the courage to be himself, and can look not only others in the eye but above all himself" (p. 64).
"Times of mass movement are always times of leadership. Every movement culminates organically in a leader, who embodies in his whole being the meaning and purpose of the popular movement. He is an incarnation of the nation's psyche and its mouthpiece. He is the spearhead of the phalanx of the whole people in motion. The need of the whole always calls forth a leader, regardless of the form a state may take. . . . It is perfectly natural that a leader should stand at the head of an elite, which in earlier centuries was formed by the nobility. The nobility believe by the law of the nature in the blood and exclusiveness of the race" (p. 65).

In "Carl Gustav Jung and the Jews: The Real Story," *Journal of Psychology and Judaism* 6, no. 2 (Spring/Summer 1982): 113–43, James Kirsch relates the following anecdote:

"During his stay in Berlin in May, 1933, Jung was invited to see Dr. Goebbels, the infamous minister of propaganda. Jung went and the following conversation occurred:

> *Goebbels:* You wanted to see me, Dr. Jung.
> *Jung:* No. You wanted to see me.
> *Goebbels:* No. You wanted to see me.

"Jung turned around and left Goebbels' office—and vomited!!! From there he came to my house for lunch where my wife had prepared an ocean fish. He ate with excellent appetite!" (p. 135).

1934

Jung publishes "The State of Psychotherapy Today" and again distinguishes between Jewish and Germanic psychology (*CW* 10: 157–173):

"Freud and Adler have beheld very clearly the shadow that accompanies us all. The Jews have this peculiarity in common with women; being physically weaker, they have to aim at the chinks in the armour of their adversary, and thanks to this technique which has been forced on them through the centuries, the Jews themselves are best protected where others are most vulnerable. Because, again, of their civilization, more than twice as ancient as ours, they are vastly more conscious than we of human weaknesses, of the shadow-side of things, and hence in this respect much less vulnerable than we are. Thanks to their experience of an old culture, they are able, while fully conscious of their frailties, to live on friendly and even tolerant terms with them, whereas we are still too young not to have 'illusions' about ourselves. Moreover, we have been entrusted by fate with the task of creating a civilization—and indeed we have need of it— and for this 'illusions' in the form of one-sided ideals, convictions, plans, etc. are indispensable. As a member of a race with a three-thousand-year-old civilization, the Jew, like the cultured Chinese, has a wider area of psychological consciousness than we. Consequently it is *in general* less dangerous for the Jew to put a negative value on his unconscious. The 'Aryan' unconscious, on the other hand, contains explosive forces and seeds of a future yet to be born, and these may not be devalued as nursery romanticism without psychic danger. The still youthful Germanic peoples are fully capable of creating new cultural forms that still lie dormant in the darkness of the unconscious of every individual—seeds bursting with energy and capable of mighty expansion. The Jew, who is something of a nomad, has never yet created a cultural form of his own and as far as we can see never will, since all his instincts and talents require a more or less civilized nation to act as host for their development.

"The Jewish race as a whole—at least this is my experience—possesses an unconscious which can be compared with the 'Aryan' only with reserve. Creative individuals apart, the average Jew is far too conscious and differentiated to go about pregnant with the tensions of unborn futures. The 'Aryan' unconscious has a higher potential than the Jewish; that is both the advantage and the disadvantage of a youthfulness not yet fully weaned from barbarism. In my opinion it has been a grave error in medical psychology up till now to apply Jewish categories—which are not even binding on all Jews—indiscriminately to Germanic and Slavic Christendom. Because of this the most precious secret of the Germanic peoples—their creative and intuitive depth of soul—has been explained as a morass of banal infantilism, while my own warning voice has for decades been suspected of anti-Semitism. This suspicion emanated from Freud. He did not understand the Germanic psyche any more than did his Germanic followers. Has the formidable phenomenon of National Socialism, on which the whole world gazes with astonished eyes, taught them better? Where was that unparalleled tension and energy while as yet no National Socialism existed? Deep in the Germanic psyche, in a pit that is anything but a garbage-bin of unrealizable infantile wishes and unresolved family resentments. A movement that grips a whole nation must have matured in every individual as well. That is why I say that the Germanic unconscious contains tensions and potentialities which medical psychology must consider in its evaluation of the unconscious. Its business is not with neuroses but with human beings—that, in fact, is the grand privilege of medical psychology: to treat the whole man and not an artificially segregated function. And that is why its scope must be widened to reveal to the physician's gaze not just the pathological aberrations of a disturbed psychic development, but the creative powers of the psyche labouring at the future; not just a dreary fragment but the meaningful whole" (pp. 165–66).

Jung publishes "A Rejoinder to Dr. Bally" (CW 10: 535–544):
"About three years ago I was elected honorary [vice-] president of the General Medical Society for Psychotherapy. When, owing to the political

upheaval, Professor Kretschmer resigned from the presidency, and the Society like so many other scientific organizations in Germany received a profound shock, some leading members pressed me—I may say, fervently—to take the chair. This, I would expressly emphasize, was the presidency not of the *German* but of the *International* Society. . . . Thus a moral conflict arose for me as it would for any decent man in this situation. Should I, as a prudent neutral, withdraw into security this side of the frontier and wash my hands in innocence, or should I—as I was well aware—risk my skin and expose myself to the inevitable misunderstandings which no one escapes who, from higher necessity, has to make a pact with the existing political powers in Germany? Should I sacrifice the interests of science, loyalty to colleagues, the friendship which attaches me to some German physicians, and the living link with the humanities afforded by a common language—sacrifice all this to egotistic comfort and my different political sentiments?" (pp. 535–536).

"If the doctors of Petersburg [*sic*] or Moscow had sought my help I would have acceded without hesitation, because I am concerned with human beings and not with Bolsheviks—and if I was then inevitably branded a Bolshevik it would have bothered me just as little" (p. 539).

"Admittedly I was incautious, so incautious as to do the very thing most open to misunderstanding at the present moment: I have tabled the Jewish question. This I did deliberately. My esteemed critic appears to have forgotten that the first rule of psychotherapy is to talk in the greatest detail about all the things that are the most ticklish and dangerous, and the most misunderstood. The Jewish problem is a regular complex, a festering wound, and no responsible doctor could bring himself to apply methods of medical hush-hush in this matter.

"As to the difference between Jewish and 'Aryan-Germanic-Christian-European' psychology, it can of course hardly be seen in the individual products of science as a whole. But we are not so much concerned with these as with the fundamental fact that in psychology the object of knowledge is at the same time the organ of knowledge, which is true of no other science. It has therefore been doubted in all sincerity whether psychology is possible as a science at all. In keeping with this doubt I suggested years ago that every psychological theory should be criticized in the first instance as a subjective confession. For, if the organ of knowledge is its own object, we have every reason to examine the nature of that organ very closely indeed, since the subjective premise is at once the object of knowledge which is therefore limited from the start. This subjective premise is identical with our psychic idiosyncrasy. The idiosyncrasy is conditioned (1) by the individual, (2) by the family, (3) by the nation, race, climate, locality, and history.

"I have in my time been accused of 'Swiss wooden-headedness.' Not that I have anything against possessing the national vices of the Swiss; I am also quite ready to suppose that I am a bigoted Swiss in every respect. I am perfectly content to let my psychological confession, my so-called 'theories,' be criticized as a product of Swiss wooden-headedness or queer-headedness, as betraying the sinister influence of my theological and medical forbears, and, in general, of our Christian and German heritage, as exemplified for instance by Schiller and Meister Eckhart. I am not affronted when people call me 'Teutonically confused,' 'mystical,' 'moralistic,' etc. I am proud of my subjective premises, I love the Swiss earth in them, I am grateful to my theological forbears for having passed on to me the Christian premise, and I also admit my so-called 'father complex': I do not want to knuckle under to any 'fathers' and never shall (see 'queer-headedness').

"May it not therefore be said that there is a Jewish psychology too, which admits the prejudice of its blood and its history? And may it not be asked wherein lie the peculiar differences between an essentially Jewish and an essentially Christian outlook? Can it really be maintained that I alone among psychologists have a special organ of knowledge with a subjective bias, whereas the Jew is apparently insulted to the core if one assumes him to be a Jew? Presumably he would not have one assume that his insights are the products of a mere cipher, or that his brain emerged only today from the featureless ocean of non-history. I must confess my total inability to understand why it should be a crime to speak of 'Jewish' psychology.

". . . Are we really to believe that a tribe which has wandered through history for several thousand years as 'God's chosen people' was not put up to such an idea by some quite special psychological peculiarity? If no differences exist, how do we recognize Jews at all?

". . . All branches of mankind unite in one stem—yes, but what is a stem without separate branches? Why this ridiculous touchiness when anybody dares to say anything about the psychological difference between Jews and Christians? Every child knows that differences exist.

"It seems to be generally assumed that in tabling the discussion of ethnological differences my sole purpose was to blurt out my 'notorious' anti-Semitism. Apparently no one believes that I—and others—might also have something good and appreciative to say. . . .

"I express no value-judgments, nor do I intend any veiled ones. I have been engaged for many years on the problem of imponderable differences which everybody knows and nobody can really define. . . .

"Consequently I am amused to find myself cast in the role of the nitwit who is unable to spot a single difference between Jews and Christians. . . . I would like to bring the parties together round a conference-table, so that they could at last get to know and acknowledge their differences. Very often this sort of knowledge is the way to understanding" (pp. 539–542).

"But, my public will object, why raise the Jewish problem today of all days and in Germany of all places? Pardon me, I raised it long ago, as anybody knows who is acquainted with the literature. I did not speak about it only since the revolution; I have been officially campaigning for criticism of subjective psychological premises as a necessary reform in psychology ever since 1913. This has nothing to do with the form of the German state. If I am to be exploited for political ends, there's nothing I can do to stop it. Or can anyone stop anything he pleases in Germany? It is rather late in the day for my critical attitude to attract attention only now, and it is, alas, characteristic that it should be construed in such a way as to suggest that Nazism alone has lent wings to my criticism. It is, I frankly admit, a highly unfortunate and disconcerting coincidence that my scientific programme should, without any assistance of mine and against my express wish, have been lined up with a political manifesto. But an event of this kind, although regrettable in itself, often has the consequence of ventilating problems which would otherwise be sedulously avoided" (p. 543).

Jung to W. M. Kranefeldt, February 9, 1934:
". . . As is known, one cannot do anything against stupidity, but in this instance the Aryan people can point out that with Freud and Adler specifically Jewish points of view are publicly preached, and as can be proven likewise, points of view that have an essentially corrosive character. If the proclamation of this Jewish gospel is agreeable to the government, then so be it. Otherwise there is also the possibility that this would not be agreeable to the government. . . ." (the portion of a letter published by the auction house of I. A. Stargard, Marburg, Germany, Catalogue No. 608, and reprinted in the *International Review of Psycho-Analysis* 4 [1977]: 377).

Jung to A. Pupato, March 2, 1934:
"The question I broached regarding the peculiarities of Jewish psychology does not presuppose any intention on my part to depreciate Jews,

but is merely an attempt to single out and formulate the mental idiosyn-crasies that distinguish Jews from other people. No sensible person will deny that such differences exist, any more than he will deny that there are essential differences in the mental attitude of Germans and French-men. . . . Again, nobody with any experience of the world will deny that the psychology of an American differs in a characteristic and unmistaka-ble way from that of an Englishman. . . . To point out this difference cannot possibly, in my humble opinion, be in itself an insult to the Jews so long as one refrains from value judgments. If anyone seeking to pin down my peculiarities should remark that this or that is specifically Swiss, or peasant-like, or Christian, I just wouldn't know what I should get peeved about, and I would be able to admit such differences without turning a hair. I have never understood why, for instance, a Chinese should be insulted when a European asserts that the Chinese mentality differs from the European mentality. . . .

"It is my opinion that the peculiarity of the Jews might explain why they are an absolutely essential symbiotic element in our population. If there actually were no differences between them and other people, there would be nothing to distinguish them at all. . . . It must after all be supposed that a people which has kept itself more or less unadulterated for several thousand years and clung onto its belief in being 'chosen' is psychologically different in some way from the relatively young Germanic peoples whose culture is scarcely more than a thousand years old.

"It is true that I fight Freud's psychology because of its dogmatic claim to sole validity. The monotony of Freudian explanations obliterates the wealth of differences that do indeed exist. I am persuaded that I am not doing another person a favour by tarring him with the brush of my subjective assumptions. If I want a proper knowledge of his nature I must ascertain where and to what extent he is different from me. Then only is it possible for me to know him really objectively. I would consider it most fortunate if, for example, Germany and France took the trouble to understand each other better and could appreciate and acknowledge each other's characteristic values. But the way things are, each explains the other in terms of the assumptions of its own psychology, as you can convince yourself daily by reading the French and German newspapers.

"That people in some respects are also all alike is by this time a familiar fact, but it leads to no misunderstandings. These come from the differences, which should therefore be a worthy subject of investigation."

Jung to B. Cohen, March 26, 1934:
"Your criticism of my lack of knowledge in things Jewish is quite justified. I don't understand Hebrew. But you seem to impute a political

attitude to me which in reality I do not possess. I am absolutely not an opponent of the Jews even though I am an opponent of Freud's. I criticize him because of his materialistic and intellectualistic and—last but not least—irreligious attitude and not because he is a Jew. In so far as his theory is based in certain respects on Jewish premises, it is not valid for non-Jews. Nor do I deny my Protestant prejudice. Had Freud been more tolerant of the ideas of others I would still be standing at his side today. I consider his intolerance—and it is this that repels me—a personal idiosyncrasy."

Jung to Max Guggenheim, March 28, 1934:
"As a psychotherapist I cannot be indifferent to the future of psychotherapy. Its development in Germany will also be crucial for us. Freud once told me, very rightly: 'The fate of psychotherapy will be decided in Germany.' To begin with it was doomed to absolute perdition because it was considered wholly Jewish. I have broken this prejudice by my intervention and have made life possible not only for the so-called Aryan psychotherapists but for the Jewish ones as well. What with the hue and cry against me it has been completely forgotten that by far the greatest number of psychotherapists in Germany are Jews. People do not know, nor is it said in public, that I have intervened personally with the regime on behalf of certain Jewish psychotherapists. If the Jews start railing at me this is shortsighted in the extreme and I hope you will do what you can to combat this idiotic attitude. The existence of the Society for Psychotherapy, which has very many Jewish members, is now assured, also the membership of Jewish doctors. Actually the Jews should be thankful to me for that, but it seems that the—as you say—paranoid attitude prevents them from seeing clearly. . . . The understandable opposition of the Jews to the Hitler regime now makes it quits: everything German is outlawed, regardless of whether people are involved who are entirely innocent politically. I find that shortsighted too."

Jung to E. Beit von Speyer, April 13, 1934:
"I have fallen foul of contemporary history. From abroad one can hardly have anything to do with Germany without becoming politically suspect on one side or the other. People now think I am a blood-boltered anti-Semite because I have helped the German doctors to consolidate their Psychotherapeutic Society and because I have said there are certain differences between Jewish and so-called Aryan psychology which are mainly due to the fact that the Jews have a cultural history that is 2,000 years older than the so-called Aryan. There has been a terrific shindy over this."

Jung to James Kirsch, May 26, 1934:

"We can also record the satisfying fact that at my suggestion a special provision was adopted whereby German Jewish doctors can individually join the International Society. They have thus become members with equal rights.

"I need hardly go into the other rumours. It is a downright lie to quote me as saying that Jews are dishonest in analysis. Anyone who believes I could say anything so idiotic must think me extraordinarily stupid. Neither have I addressed Hitler over the radio or in any other manner, nor have I made any political statements.

"With regard to my opinion that the Jews so far as we can see do not create a cultural form of their own, this opinion is based on (1) historical data, (2) the fact that the specific cultural achievement of the Jew is most clearly developed within a host culture, where he very frequently becomes its actual carrier or its promoter. This task is so specific and demanding that it is hardly conceivable how any individual Jewish culture could arise alongside it. Since very specific conditions do in fact exist in Palestine, I have inserted a cautious 'so far as we can see' in my sentence. I would in no wise deny the possibility that something specific is being created there, but so far I do not know it. I simply cannot discover anything anti-Semitic in this opinion.

"Coming to your suggestion that I should write a special work on this question, this has already been anticipated, as I have proposed a correspondence with Dr. Neumann, who has worked with me and is now also in Palestine, that will deal with all controversial questions. So far I have heard nothing from him.

"The Jewish Christ-complex is a very remarkable affair. As you know, I completely agree with you in this matter. The existence of this complex makes for a somewhat hysterical attitude of mind which has become especially noticeable to me during the present anti-Christian attacks upon myself. The mere fact that I speak of a difference between Jewish and Christian psychology suffices to allow anyone to voice the prejudice that I am an anti-Semite. . . . This hypersensitivity is simply pathological and makes every discussion practically impossible. As you know, Freud previously accused me of anti-Semitism because I could not abide his soulless materialism. The Jew directly solicits anti-Semitism with his readiness to scent out anti-Semitism everywhere. I cannot see why the Jew, unlike any so-called Christian, is incapable of assuming that he is being criticized personally when one has an opinion about him. Why must it always be assumed that one wants to damn the Jewish people?

Surely the individual is not the people? I regard this as an inadmissible method of silencing one's adversary. In the great majority of cases I have got along very well with my Jewish patients and colleagues. It happens with other people, too, that I have had to criticize the individual, but they do not ascribe it to the fact that they are English, American or French. However, there is one exception worth mentioning, and that is the German. It has happened more than once that when I criticized a German he immediately concluded that I hate the Germans. . . .

". . . You ought to know me sufficiently well to realize that an unindividual stupidity like anti-Semitism cannot be laid at my door. You know well enough how very much I take the human being as a personality and how I continually endeavour to lift him out of his collective condition and make him an individual. This, as you know, is possible only if he acknowledges his peculiarity which has been forced on him by fate. No one who is a Jew can become a human being without *knowing* that he is a Jew, since this is the basis from which he can reach out towards a higher humanity. This holds good for all nations and races. Nationalism— disagreeable as it is—is therefore a *sine qua non,* but the individual must not remain stuck in it. On the other hand, in so far as he is a particle in the mass he must not raise himself above it either. As a human being I am a European, as an atom in the mass I am a Swiss bourgeois, domiciled at Seestrasse 228, Küsnacht near Zurich."

Jung to Gerhard Adler, June 9, 1934:
"Best thanks for your detailed letter, the tenor of which I find completely acceptable. I have pointed out in several places in my article that Freud does not appear to me as the typical exponent of the Jewish attitude to the unconscious. In fact I expressly state that his view of it is not binding for all Jews. Nevertheless there is something typically Jewish about his attitude, which I can document with your own words: 'When a Jew forgets his roots, he is doubly and triply in danger of mechanization and intellectualization.' With these words you have laid your finger on exactly what is typically Jewish. It is typically Jewish that Freud can forget his roots to such an extent. It is typically Jewish that the Jews can utterly forget that they are Jews despite the fact that they know they are Jews. That is what is suspicious about Freud's attitude and not his materialistic, rationalistic view of the world alone. Freud cannot be held responsible for the latter. In this respect he is simply a typical exponent of the expiring 19th century, just like Haeckel, Dubois-Reymond, or that *Kraft und Stoff* ass Büchner. These people, however, are not as completely

rootless as the Jewish rationalist, for which reason they are also much more naive and therefore less dangerous. So when I criticize Freud's Jewishness I am not criticizing the *Jews* but rather that damnable capacity of the Jew, as exemplified by Freud, to deny his own nature. Actually you should be glad that I think so rigorously, for then I speak in the interests of all Jews who want to find their way back to their own nature. I think the religious Jews of our time should summon up the courage to distinguish themselves clearly from Freud, because they need to prove that spirit is stronger than blood. But the prejudice that whoever criticizes Freud is criticizing the Jews always demonstrates to us that blood is thicker than spirit, and in this respect anti-Semitism has in all conscience learnt much from the Jewish prejudice.

"As to my assertion that the Jews have not created a 'cultural form' of their own, please note that I did not say 'culture.' I expressly stated that the Jews have a culture nearly 3,000 years old, but one can have a culture without possessing a cultural form of one's own. For instance, Switzerland has a culture but no cultural form. It has still to be proved conclusively that the Jews have ever created a cultural form of their own. At any rate they haven't in the last 2,000 years. It is also difficult to see how a relatively small folk ranging from India through Europe to America would be in a position to create such a form. I came across the same objection in a letter from a Jew a few days ago. Considering the proverbial intelligence of the Jews it has always seemed to me incomprehensible that they can no longer see the simplest truths because they are blinded by hypersensitivity. Blood is undoubtedly thicker than spirit, but, as you very rightly say, it is a tremendous danger for the Jew to get lost in the viscosity of sheer materialism."

Jung to C. E. Benda, June 19, 1934:

"I wonder what can have caused you to misconstrue my article to the point where you consider it necessary to defend Jewish culture against me. No one is more deeply convinced than I that the Jews are a people with a culture. Between culture and cultural form there is, as we know, an essential difference. The Swiss, for instance, are a people with a culture but no cultural form of their own. For this, as you rightly remark, certain conditions are needed, such as the size of a people, its ties to the soil, etc. In my opinion the Bible is not a cultural form but a document.

"A people with no ties to the soil, having neither land nor homeland, is commonly called nomadic. If you will submit these two points to which you took exception to unprejudiced scrutiny, you will probably come to the conclusion that there is no unjustified criticism in them. Had I said of the Jews what I said of the Germans in the same article, there might have been some cause for excitement, since 'barbarism' comes close to a value judgment.

"That psychoanalysis is, so to speak, a Jewish national affair is not my invention but Freud's. When I wrote my book *Wandlungen und Symbole der Libido* [*Symbols of Transformation*] and deviated at one point from orthodox theory, Freud suddenly accused me of anti-Semitism. From this I must conclude that I had somehow trespassed against the Jews. This prejudice has stuck to me ever since and has been repeated by all Freudians, thereby confirming every time that psychoanalysis is in fact a Jewish psychology which nobody else can criticize without making himself guilty of anti-Semitism."

1935

Jung delivers a series of lectures at the Tavistock Clinic in London (CW 18: 1–182):

"Who would have thought in 1900 that it would be possible thirty years later for such things to happen in Germany as are happening today? Would you have believed that a whole nation of highly intelligent and cultivated people could be seized by the fascinating power of an archetype? I saw it coming, and I can understand it because I know the power of the collective unconscious. But on the surface it looks simply incredible. Even my personal friends are under that fascination, and when I am in Germany, I believe it myself, I understand it all, I know it has to be as it is. One cannot resist it. It gets you below the belt and not in your mind, your brain just counts for nothing, your sympathetic system is gripped. It is a power that fascinates people from within, it is the collective unconscious which is activated, it is an archetype which is common to them all that has come to life. . . . We cannot be children about it, having intellectual and reasonable ideas and saying: this should not be. That is just childish. This is real history, this is what really happens to man and has always happened, and it is far more important than our personal little woes and our personal convictions. I know highly educated Germans who were just as reasonable as I think I am or as you think you are. But a wave went over them and just washed their reason away, and when you talk to them you have to admit that they could not do anything about it. An incomprehensible fate has seized them, and you cannot say it is right, or it is wrong. It has nothing to do with rational judgment, it is just history" (p. 164).

Jung to Erich Neumann, December 22, 1935:
"The 'cultivated Jew' is always on the way to becoming a 'non-Jew.' You are quite right: the way does not go from good to better, but dips down first to the historical data. I usually point out to most of my Jewish patients that it stands to reason they are Jews. I wouldn't do this had I not so often seen Jews who imagined they were something else. For them 'Jewishness' is a species of personal insult.

". . . I find your very positive conviction that the soil of Palestine is essential for Jewish individuation most valuable. How does this square with the fact that Jews in general have lived *much longer* in other countries than in Palestine? Even Moses Maimonides preferred Cairo Fostat although he had the opportunity of living in Jerusalem.

"Is it the case that the Jew is so accustomed to being a non-Jew that he needs the Palestinian soil *in concreto* to be reminded of his Jewishness? I can scarcely feel my way into a psyche that has not grown up on any soil."

1936

The Berlin Psychoanalytic Institute ceases to exist as an independent entity.

Jung prepares a press release for a trip to the United States (CW 18: 564–565):
"I make this statement in order to disillusion any attempt to claim me for any particular political party. I have some reason for it, since my name has been repeatedly drawn into the political discussion, which is, as you best know, in a feverish condition actually. It happened chiefly on account of the fact that I am interested in the undeniable differences in national and racial psychology, which chiefly account for a series of most fatal misunderstandings and practical mistakes in international dealings as well as in internal social frictions. In a politically poisoned and overheated atmosphere the sane and dispassionate scientific discussion of such delicate, yet most important problems has become well-nigh impossible. To discuss such matters in public would be about as successful as if the director of a lunatic asylum were to set out to discuss the particular delusions of his patients in the midst of them" (pp. 564–565).

Jung to Abraham Aaron Roback, September 29, 1936:

"Concerning my so-called 'Nazi affiliation' there has been quite an unnecessary noise about it. I am no Nazi, as a matter of fact I am quite unpolitical. German psychotherapists asked me to help them to maintain their professional organization, as there was an immediate danger that psychotherapy in Germany would be wiped out of existence. It was considered as 'Jewish science' and therefore highly suspect. Those German doctors were my friends and only a coward would leave his friends when they are in dire need of help. Not only did I set up their organization again but I made it clear that psychotherapy is an honest-to-God attempt and moreover I made it possible for Jewish German doctors, being excluded from professional organizations, to become immediate members of the International Society at least. But nobody mentions the fact that so many perfectly innocent existences could have been completely crushed if I had not stepped in.

"It is true that I have insisted upon the *difference* between Jewish and Christian psychology since 1917, but Jewish authors have done the same long ago as well as recently. I am no anti-Semite."

Jung to Roback, December 19, 1936:

"Unfortunately the political events in Germany have made it quite impossible to say anything reasonable about the most interesting difference between Jewish and non-Jewish psychology. The disinterested discussion of this most interesting difference is well-nigh impossible in our time of a new barbary. One risks being labelled as anti-Semite or pro-Semite without being heard at all."

Jung publishes "Wotan" and proposes an archetypal explanation for Nazism (*CW* 10: 179–193):

"We are always convinced that the modern world is a reasonable world, basing our opinion on economic, political, and psychological factors. But if we may forget for a moment that we are living in the year of Our Lord 1936, and, laying aside our well-meaning, all-too-human reasonableness, may burden God or the gods with the responsibility for contemporary events instead of man, we would find Wotan quite suitable as a causal hypothesis. In fact I venture the heretical suggestion that the unfathomable depths of Wotan's character explain more of National Socialism than all three reasonable factors put together" (p. 184).

"The impressive thing about the German phenomenon is that one man, who is obviously 'possessed,' has infected a whole nation to such an extent that everything is set in motion and has started rolling on its course towards perdition.

"It seems to me that Wotan hits the mark as an hypothesis. . . . He is a fundamental attribute of the German psyche, an irrational psychic factor. . . . Despite their crankiness, the Wotan-worshippers seem to have judged things more correctly than the worshippers of reason. Apparently everyone had forgotten that Wotan is a Germanic datum of first importance, the truest expression and unsurpassed personification of a fundamental quality that is particularly characteristic of the Germans. . . . The emphasis on the Germanic race (vulgarly called 'Aryan'), the Germanic heritage, blood and soil, the Wagalaweia songs, the ride of the Valkyries, Jesus as a blond and blue-eyed hero, the Greek mother of St. Paul, the devil as an international Alberich in Jewish or Masonic guise, the Nordic aurora borealis as the light of civilization, the inferior Mediterranean races—all this is the indispensable scenery for the drama that is taking place and at bottom they all mean the same thing: a god has taken possession of the Germans . . ." (pp. 185–186).

"It is above all the Germans who have an opportunity, perhaps unique in history, to look into their own hearts and to learn what those perils of the soul were from which Christianity tried to rescue mankind. Germany is a land of spiritual catastrophes, where nature never makes more than a pretence of peace with world-ruling reason. . . . Because the behaviour of a race takes on its specific character from its underlying images we can speak of an archetype 'Wotan.' As an autonomous psychic factor, Wotan produces effects in the collective life of a people. . . . It is only from time to time that individuals fall under the irresistible influence of this unconscious factor" (p. 187).

"All human control comes to an end when the individual is caught in a mass movement. Then the archetypes begin to function. . . . But what a so-called Führer does with a mass movement can plainly be seen if we turn our eyes to the north or south of our country" (pp. 189–190).

1937

Jung to J. Wilhelm Hauer, June 7, 1937:
"I myself have personally treated very many Jews and know their psychology in its deepest recesses, so I can recognize the relation of their racial psychology to their religion, but it would be quite beyond me to relate Islam or the ancient Egyptian religion to its devotees as I lack any intimate knowledge of Arab and Egyptian psychology."

1938

In *Jung, His Life and Work: A Biographical Memoir,* Barbara Hannah describes a cooperative effort by Swiss Jews and Jungians to convince Austrian Jews, including Freud, to leave after the Anschluss:

"Franz Riklin, Jr.—at that time nearing thirty and just starting his medical career—was chosen by some exceedingly rich Swiss Jews to go into Austria *at once,* with a very large sum of money, to do all that he could to persuade leading Jews to leave the country before the Nazis had time to start persecuting them. Franz said he was largely chosen for this work because of his exceedingly Teutonic appearance: no one would suspect him of any connection with the Jews. He also was a very resourceful young man who would obviously be adept at throwing dust in the eyes of the Nazis and at persuading the Jews to take advantage of the opportunity. In general he was *exceedingly* successful in carrying out this mission, but in one place, where he perhaps most wanted to succeed, he failed entirely.

"Before he left Zurich, his father, Franz Riklin, Sr., had pressed him to try above all to persuade Freud to leave Austria and to take advantage of the most unusual facilities which he could offer. His father had known Freud very well in the old days. Both he and Alfons Maeder had left the Freudian group at the same time as Jung, but none of that counted anymore in comparison with Dr. Riklin's very human wish to see his old friend in safety.

"Franz Jr. went to see Freud as soon as he got to Vienna and explained the situation to him. He was bitterly disappointed when Freud answered: 'I refuse to be beholden to my enemies.' Franz had been a very young child when Freud visited his parents, but he remembered him well. He did his best to persuade Freud that neither his father nor Jung felt any enmity toward him; on the contrary, he said, they really only wanted to know that he was safe. He also pointed out that there was no need for Freud to stay in Switzerland, for once there he could travel wherever he liked. It was all to no avail. Freud merely repeated that he would accept no favors from his enemies. The Freuds were very friendly to Franz himself; he was much too young to have been involved in the quarrel. They even asked him to dinner before he left Vienna, but nothing he could say was able to shake Freud's iron determination.

"This was a great disappointment to young Franz, for he knew how much it would disappoint his father, who was counting on him to bring Freud back with him. He knew that Jung, of whom he had always been particularly fond, would also be very sorry. The latter, however, had known Freud better than the Riklins. He was sad but not surprised. When reproached, as he sometimes was, for not doing more to help Freud leave Austria, Jung always replied: 'He would not take help from me under any circumstances' " (pp. 254–255).

In *Quadrant* 20, no. 2 (1987): 73–74, Robert S. McCully provides another version of the event:

"Sometime in the middle 1960s, Franz Riklin, Jr., came to the United States on an invited lecture tour, and when he came to New York, he spoke to the psychiatric faculty at Cornell University Medical College–The New York Hospital on the topic of depression. At the time I was an associate professor there, and was asked by the departmental chairman to act as host to Dr. Riklin, and to see to his entertainment following his presentation. We spent the afternoon together talking a good deal about Jung, the man, since I was also at the time a senior analytical trainee at the New York C. G. Jung Institute. Later we had dinner together, and the charge was an honor and a pleasure for me.

"Dr. Riklin described the details of his journey from Zurich to Vienna on Freud's behalf. Both his father and Jung combined five thousand dollars of their own funds, which they wished to give to Freud so that he, a sick man soon to die, could get out of Vienna and to England. Riklin told me that he was chosen because he was young and quite Nordic in appearance, and his mission into Nazi territory could be a dangerous one. He had the cash in a money belt. After arriving in Vienna he went to the Freud residence. While it may have been the case, he did not mention to me any other aim attached to his journey, other than to present the monies to Freud. Miss Hannah writes that wealthy Swiss Jews got together monies to take to Austria to help leading Jews get out of the country. It could have been so, but he did not include that in his report on his adventure to me. I got the distinct impression that his father and Jung provided the money from their own funds, and I am certain the amount was five thousand each. It would be a bit different for history if the monies were personally from Riklin, Sr., and Jung than from wealthy Jews in Switzerland as Miss Hannah presents it.

"Riklin, Jr., then said to me he knocked on the door, and it was answered, opened cautiously part way by Freud's daughter Anna. Riklin, Sr., had known Freud well in the old days. Dr. Riklin explained to Miss Freud that he had come from Zurich on behalf of his father and Jung in order to make a present of some monies to her father. She did not ask young Riklin into the house and simply said she would speak to her father. She returned to the door and said her father would not receive him. Young Riklin again pleaded his cause, hoping to provide the aid to her father that brought him there. The door was about half open as he spoke to Anna, when Freud himself stepped to the door saying, 'I refuse to be beholden to my enemies.' Riklin virtually begged him to take the gift, while Freud only repeated he would accept no favors from enemies. Riklin said he was met with such hostility that he departed, returning to Switzerland with the unaccepted monies."

The Vienna Psychoanalytic Institute is dissolved.

Freud leaves Austria for England.

Jung to Erich Neumann, December 19, 1938:
"I am right in the thick of it and every day I follow the Palestine question in the newspapers and often think of my friends there who have to live in this chaos. Unfortunately I foresaw all too clearly what was coming when I was in Palestine in 1932. I also foresaw bad things for Germany, actually very bad, but now that they have come to pass they seem unbelievable. Everyone here is profoundly shaken by what is happening in Germany. I have very much to do with Jewish refugees and am continually occupied in bringing all my Jewish acquaintances to safety in England and America. In this way I am in ceaseless touch with contemporary events.

"I am very interested in what you have told me about your plans for work. Your experiences exactly parallel those I have had in Europe for many years. But I think you should be very cautious in judging your specifically Jewish experiences. Though it is true that there are specifically Jewish traits about this development, it is at the same time a general one which is also to be found among Christians. It is a general and identical revolution of minds. The specifically Christian or Jewish traits are only of secondary importance. Thus the patient you want to know about is a pure Jew with a Catholic upbringing, but I could never with absolute certainty characterize his symbolism—insofar as I have presented it—as Jewish although certain nuances occasionally seem so. When I compare his material with mine or with that of other academically trained patients one is struck only by the astonishing similarities, while the differences are insignificant. The difference between a typically Protestant and a Jewish psychology is particularly small where the contemporary problem is concerned. The whole problem is of such overwhelming importance for humanity that individual and racial differences play a minor role. All the same, I can very well imagine that for Jews living in Palestine the direct influence of the surroundings brings out the chthonic and ancient Jewish element in a much more pregnant form. It seems to me that what is specifically Jewish or specifically Christian could be most easily discovered in the way the unconscious material is assimilated by the subject. In my experience the resistance of the Jew seems to be more obstinate and as a result the attempt at defence is much more vehement. This is no more than a subjective impression."

1939

Jung publishes an interview in which he diagnoses the dictators (C. G. Jung Speaking, pp. 115–135):

"Few foreigners respond at all, yet apparently every German in Germany does. It is because Hitler is the mirror of every German's unconscious, but of course he mirrors nothing from a non-German. He is the loudspeaker which magnifies the inaudible whispers of the German soul until they can be heard by the German's unconscious ear.

"He is the first man to tell every German what he has been thinking and feeling all along in his unconscious about German fate, especially since the defeat in the World War, and the one characteristic which colors every German soul is the typically German inferiority complex . . ." (p. 118).

"In a way, the position of the Germans is remarkably like that of the Jews of old. Since their defeat in the World War they have awaited a Messiah, a Savior. That is characteristic of people with an inferiority complex. The Jews got their inferiority complex from geographical and political factors. They lived in a part of the world which was a parade ground for conquerors from both sides, and after their return from their first exile to Babylon, when they were threatened with extinction by the Romans, they invented the solacing idea of a Messiah who was going to bring all the Jews together into a nation once more and save them.

"And the Germans got their inferiority complex from comparable causes. They came up out of the Danube valley too late, and founded the beginnings of their nation long after the French and the English were well on their way to nationhood. They got too late to the scramble for colonies, and for the foundation of empire. Then, when they did get together and make a united nation, they looked around them and saw the British, the French, and others with rich colonies. . . .

"This was the *original* source of the German inferiority complex which has determined so much of their political thought and action and which is certainly decisive of their whole policy today. It is impossible, you see, to talk about Hitler without talking about his people, because Hitler is only the German people" (p. 122).

"If he is not their true Messiah, he is like one of the Old Testament prophets: his mission is to unite his people and lead them to the Promised Land. This explains why the Nazis have to combat every form of religion besides their own idolatrous brand" (p. 123).

"As a physician, I have not only to analyze and diagnose, but to recommend treatment.

"We have been talking nearly all the while about Hitler and the Germans, because they are so incomparably the most important of the dictator phenomena at the moment. It is for this, then, that I must propose a therapy" (p. 131).

"So I say, in this situation, the only way to save Democracy in the West—and by the West I mean America too—is not to try to stop Hitler. . . . You can only hope to influence the direction of his expansion.

"I say let him go East. Turn his attention away from the West, or rather, encourage him to keep it turned away. Let him go to Russia. That is the logical *cure* for Hitler" (p. 132).

"Our interest in it is simply that it will save the West. Nobody has ever bitten into Russia without regretting it. It's not very palatable food. It might take the Germans a hundred years to finish that meal. Meanwhile we should be safe, and by we, I mean all of Western civilization" (p. 133).

Jung has a dream at the time of the Hitler-Stalin pact.

E. A. Bennet records this version of the dream on March 29, 1946, after visiting Jung:

"He was in a vast field with, in the distance, buildings like barracks. The place was filled with hordes of buffalos (i.e., Germans). He was on a mound, and Hitler was on another mound. He felt that as long as he fixed his gaze on Hitler all would be well. Then he saw a cloud of dust in the distance, and horsemen—Cossacks—rounding up the buffalos and driving them out of the field. Then he woke up and was glad, for he knew that Germany would be beaten by Russia. This, he said, was a collective dream, and very important" (*Meetings with Jung*, p. 14).

Esther Harding records another version of the dream on June 8, 1948, after visiting Jung:

"He found himself in a castle, all the walls and buildings of which were made of trinitrotoluene (dynamite). Hitler came in and was treated as divine. Hitler stood on a mound as for a review. C.G. was placed on a corresponding mound. Then the parade ground began to fill with buffalo or yak steers, which crowded into the enclosed space from one end. The herd was filled with nervous tension and moved about restlessly. Then he saw that one cow was alone, apparently sick. Hitler was concerned about this cow and asked C.G. what he thought of it. C.G. said, 'It is obviously very sick.' At this point, Cossacks rode in at the back and began to drive the herd off. He awoke and felt, 'It is all right' " (C. G. *Jung Speaking*, p. 181).

In the account that Harding provides, Jung interprets the dream as follows:

"He emphasized that Hitler was treated as *divine*. Consequently, he felt, we had to view him like that, that Hitler is not to be taken primarily as a human man, but as an instrument of 'divine' forces, as Judas, or, still better, as the Antichrist must be. That the castle was built of trinitrotoluene meant that it would blow up and be destroyed because of its own explosive quality. The herds of cattle are the instincts, the primitive, pre-human forces let loose in the German unconscious. They are not even domestic cattle, but buffalo or yaks, very primitive indeed. They are all male, as is the Nazi ideology: all the values of relationship, of the person or individual, are completely repressed; the feminine element is sick unto death, and so we get the sick cow. Hitler turns to C.G. for advice, but he limits his comment to the diagnosis, 'The cow is very sick.' At this, as though the recognition of the ailment released something, the Cossacks burst in. Even before that, the herd had been disturbed and nervous, as indeed the male animal is if separated too long or too completely from its complement, the female. The Cossacks are, of course, Russians. From that, C.G. said, he deduced that Russia—more barbaric than Germany, but also more directly primitive, and therefore of sounder instinct—would break in and cause the overthrow of Germany" (C. G. *Jung Speaking*, pp. 181–182). (See also Jay Sherry, "Jung, the Jews, and Hitler," *Spring 1986*, pp. 170–174).

In *Jung, His Life and Work*, Hannah comments on the dream as follows:

"We were all home again and Jung was at Bollingen when the news of the unholy alliance of Germany with Russia burst upon a horrified Europe. Jung was further disturbed by a most indigestible dream which he had immediately afterward. He dreamed that Hitler was 'the devil's

Christ,' the Anti-Christ, but that nevertheless, as such, he was the *instrument of God*. He told me it took him a long time and much effort before he was able to accept this idea. Although Jung had been occupied with the idea of the dark side of God since his childhood, it was still many years before he finally faced the problem in *Answer to Job,* and the idea that a dangerous madman like Hitler could be the instrument of God was still far from his consciousness when he had this dream" (pp. 264–265).

Freud publishes *Moses and Monotheism* and discusses differences between Jews and non-Jews (*Standard Edition* 23: 1–137):
"The poor Jewish people, who with their habitual stubbornness continued to disavow the father's murder, atoned heavily for it in the course of time. They were constantly met with the reproach 'You killed our God!' And this reproach is true, if it is correctly translated. If it is brought into relation with the history of religions, it runs: 'You will not *admit* that you murdered God (the primal picture of God, the primal father, and his later reincarnations).' There should be an addition declaring: 'We did the same thing, to be sure, but we have *admitted* it and since then we have been absolved.' Not all the reproaches with which anti-semitism persecutes the descendants of the Jewish people can appeal to a similar justification. A phenomenon of such intensity and permanence as the people's hatred of the Jews must of course have more than one ground. It is possible to find a whole number of grounds, some of them clearly derived from reality, which call for no interpretation, and others, lying deeper and derived from hidden sources, which might be regarded as the specific reasons. Of the former, the reproach of being aliens is perhaps the weakest, since in many places dominated by anti-semitism today the Jews were among the oldest portions of the population or had even been there before the present inhabitants. This applies, for instance, to the city of Cologne, to which the Jews came with the Romans, before it was occupied by the Germans. Other grounds for hating the Jews are stronger—thus, the circumstances that they live for the most part as minorities among other peoples, for the communal feeling of groups requires, in order to complete it, hostility towards some extraneous minority, and the numerical weakness of this excluded minority encourages its suppression. There are, however, two other characteristics of the Jews which are quite unforgivable. First is the fact that in some respects they are different from their 'host' nations. They are not fundamentally different, for they are not Asiatics of a foreign race, as their enemies maintain, but composed for the most part of remnants of the Mediterra-

nean peoples and heirs of the Mediterranean civilization. But they are none the less different, often in an indefinable way different, especially from the Nordic peoples, and the intolerance of groups is often, strangely enough, exhibited more strongly against small differences than against fundamental ones. The other point has a still greater effect: namely, that they defy all oppression, that the most cruel persecutions have not succeeded in exterminating them, and, indeed, that on the contrary they show a capacity for holding their own in commercial life and, where they are admitted, for making valuable contributions to every form of cultural activity.

"The deeper motives for hatred of the Jews are rooted in the remotest past ages; they operate from the unconscious of the peoples, and I am prepared to find that at first they will not seem credible. I venture to assert that jealousy of the people which declared itself the first-born, favourite child of God the Father, has not yet been surmounted among other peoples even today: it is as though they had thought there was truth in the claim. Further, among the customs by which the Jews made themselves separate, that of circumcision has made a disagreeable, un-canny impression, which is to be explained, no doubt, by its recalling the dreaded castration and along with it a portion of the primaeval past which is gladly forgotten. And finally, as the latest motive in this series, we must not forget that all those peoples who excel today in their hatred of Jews became Christians only in late historic times, often driven to it by bloody coercion. It might be said that they are all 'mis-baptized.' They have been left, under a thin veneer of Christianity, what their ancestors were, who worshipped a barbarous polytheism. They have not got over a grudge against the new religion which was imposed on them; but they have displaced the grudge on to the source from which Christianity reached them. The fact that the Gospels tell a story which is set among Jews, and in fact deals only with Jews, has made this displacement easy for them. Their hatred of Jews is at bottom a hatred of Christians, and we need not be surprised that in the German National-Socialist revolution this intimate relation between the two monotheist religions finds such a clear expression in the hostile treatment of both of them" (pp. 90–92).

"We may start from a character-trait of the Jews which dominates their relation to others. There is no doubt that they have a particularly high opinion of themselves, that they regard themselves as more distinguished, of higher standing, as superior to other peoples—from whom they are also distinguished by many of their customs. At the same time they are inspired by a peculiar confidence in life, such as is derived from the secret ownership of some precious possession, a kind of optimism: pious people would call it trust in God.

"We know the reason for this behaviour and what their secret treasure is. They really regard themselves as God's chosen people, they believe that they stand especially close to him; and this makes them proud and confident. Trustworthy reports tell us that they behaved in Hellenistic times just as they do to-day, so that the complete Jew was already there; and the Greeks, among whom and alongside of whom they lived, reacted to the Jewish characteristics in the same way as their 'hosts' do to-day" (pp. 105–106).

Freud dies on September 23, 1939.

1940

In *Jung, His Life and Work,* Hannah recounts the following incident:
"Here we learned what had caused the Jungs to take their grandchildren and daughter-in-law so suddenly to the mountains. He had been telephoned from a very high place in Bern, late the night before, and asked to leave Zurich immediately. The Swiss authorities had learned that Jung's name was on the Nazi blacklist and they did not want the Germans to have an opportunity to capture him. . . . That morning, moreover, he had been called by a friend in the High Command of the army who said that Switzerland was almost sure to be attacked that very day" (p. 269).

1944

Jung suffers a heart attack and while recuperating experiences a number of ecstatic visions (*Memories, Dreams, Reflections,* pp. 293–294):
"Toward evening I would fall asleep, and my sleep would last until about midnight. Then I would come to myself and lie awake for about an hour, but in an utterly transformed state. It was as if I were in an ecstasy. I felt as though I were floating in space, as though I were safe in the womb of the universe—in a tremendous void, but filled with the highest possible feeling of happiness. 'This is eternal bliss,' I thought. 'This cannot be described; it is far too wonderful!'

"Everything around me seemed enchanted. At this hour of the night the nurse brought me some food she had warmed—for only then was I able to take any, and I ate with appetite. For a time it seemed to me that she was an old Jewish woman, much older than she actually was, and that she was preparing ritual kosher dishes for me. When I looked at her, she seemed to have a blue halo around her head. I myself was, so it seemed, in the Pardes Rimmonim, the garden of pomegranates, and the wedding of Tifereth with Malchuth was taking place. Or else I was Rabbi Simon ben Jochai, whose wedding in the afterlife was being celebrated. It was the mystic marriage as it appears in the Cabbalistic tradition. I cannot tell you how wonderful it was. I could only think continually, 'Now this is the garden of pomegranates! Now this is the marriage of Malchuth with Tifereth!' I do not know exactly what part I played in it. At bottom it was I myself: I was the marriage. And my beatitude was that of a blissful wedding.

"Gradually the garden of pomegranates faded away and changed. There followed the Marriage of the Lamb, in a Jerusalem festively bedecked. I cannot describe what it was like in detail. These were ineffable states of joy. Angels were present, and light. I myself was the 'Marriage of the Lamb.'

"That, too, vanished, and there came a new image, the last vision. I walked up a wide valley to the end, where a gentle chain of hills began. The valley ended in a classical amphitheater. It was magnificently situated in the green landscape. And there, in this theater, the *hierosgamos* was being celebrated. Men and women dancers came onstage, and upon a flower-decked couch All-father Zeus and Hera consummated the mystic marriage, as it is described in the *Iliad*."

1945

Jung publishes "After the Catastrophe," in which he addresses the issues of collective guilt, inferiority, and hysteria in relation to the archetype of the shadow (*CW* 10: 194–217):

"While I was working on this article I noticed how churned up one still is in one's own psyche, and how difficult it is to reach anything approaching a moderate and relatively calm point of view in the midst of one's emotions. No doubt we should be cold-blooded and superior; but we are, on the whole, much more deeply involved in the recent events in Germany than we like to admit. . . . I must confess that no article has ever given me so much trouble, from a moral as well as a human point of view. I had not realized how much I myself was affected. There are others, I am sure, who will share this feeling with me. This inner identity or *participation mystique* with events in Germany has caused me to experience afresh how painfully wide is the scope of the psychological concept of *collective guilt*. So when I approach this problem it is certainly not with any feelings of cold-blooded superiority, but rather with an avowed sense of inferiority" (pp. 194–195).

"If only people could realize what an enrichment it is to find one's own guilt, what a sense of honour and spiritual dignity! But nowhere does there seem to be a glimmering of this insight. Instead, we hear only of attempts to shift the blame on to others—'no one will admit to having been a Nazi.' The Germans were never wholly indifferent to the impression they made on the outside world. They resented disapproval and hated even to be criticized. Inferiority feelings make people touchy and lead to compensatory efforts to impress. . . . Inferiority feelings are usually a sign of inferior feeling—which is not just a play on words. All the intellectual and technological achievements in the world cannot make up for inferiority in the matter of feeling. The pseudo-scientific race-theories with which it was dolled up did not make the extermination of the Jews any more acceptable . . ." (p. 202).

"A more accurate diagnosis of Hitler's condition would be *pseudologia phantastica*, that form of hysteria which is characterized by a peculiar talent for believing one's own lies. . . . Hitler's theatrical, obviously hysterical gestures struck all foreigners (with a few amazing exceptions) as purely ridiculous. When I saw him with my own eyes, he suggested a psychic scarecrow (with a broomstick for an outstretched arm) rather than a human being. . . . But the German people would never have been taken in and carried away so completely if this figure had not been a reflected image of the collective German hysteria. It is not without serious misgivings that one ventures to pin the label of 'psychopathic inferiority' on to a whole nation, and yet, heaven knows, it is the only explanation which could in any way account for the effect this scarecrow had on the masses" (pp. 203–204).

"But we must not forget that we are judging from today, from a knowledge of the events which led to the catastrophe. Our judgment would certainly be very different had our information stopped short at 1933 or 1934. At that time, in Germany as well as in Italy, there were not a few things that appeared plausible and seemed to speak in favour of the regime. An undeniable piece of evidence in this respect was the disappearance of the unemployed, who used to tramp the German highroads in their hundreds of thousands. After the stagnation and decay of the post-war years, the refreshing wind that blew through the two countries was a tempting sign of hope" (p. 205).

"We must all open our eyes to the shadow who looms behind contemporary man. . . . As to what should be done about this terrifying apparition, everyone must work this out for himself. It is indeed no small matter to know of one's own guilt and one's own evil, and there is certainly nothing to be gained by losing sight of one's shadow. When we are conscious of our guilt we are in a more favourable position—we can at least hope to change and improve ourselves. As we know, anything that remains in the unconscious is incorrigible; psychological corrections can be made only in consciousness. Consciousness of guilt can therefore act as a powerful moral stimulus. In every treatment of neurosis the discovery of the shadow is indispensable, otherwise nothing changes" (pp. 215–216).

"The question remains: How am I to live with this shadow? What attitude is required if I am to be able to live in spite of evil?" (p. 217).

1946

Jung gives a talk, "The Fight with the Shadow," on a British Broadcasting Corporation program (CW 10: 218–226):

"Hitler was the exponent of a 'new order,' and that is the real reason why practically every German fell for him. . . . Like the rest of the world, they did not understand wherein Hitler's significance lay, that he symbolized something in every individual. He was the most prodigious personification of all human inferiorities. He was an utterly incapable, unadapted, irresponsible, psychopathic personality, full of empty, infantile fantasies, but cursed with the keen intuition of a rat or a guttersnipe. He represented the shadow, the inferior part of everybody's personality, in an overwhelming degree, and this was another reason why they fell for him.

"But what could they have done? In Hitler, every German should have seen his own shadow, his own worst danger. It is everybody's allotted fate to become conscious of and learn to deal with this shadow. But how could the Germans be expected to understand this, when nobody in the world can understand such a simple truth?" (p. 223).

In the epilogue to *Essays on Contemporary Events*, Jung characterizes Nazism as a mass psychosis (CW 10: 227–243):

"When Hitler seized power it became quite evident to me that a mass psychosis was boiling up in Germany. But I could not help telling myself that this was after all Germany, a civilized European nation with a sense of morality and discipline. Hence the ultimate outcome of this unmistakable mass movement still seemed to me uncertain, just as the figure of the Führer at first struck me as being merely ambivalent. It is true that in July 1933, when I gave a series of lectures in Berlin, I received an extremely unfavourable impression both of the behaviour of the Party and of the person of Goebbels. But I did not wish to assume from the start that these symptoms were decisive, for I knew other people of unquestionable idealism who sought to prove to me that these things were unavoidable abuses such as are customary in any great revolution. It was indeed not at all easy for a foreigner to form a clear judgment at that time. Like many of my contemporaries, I had my doubts" (p. 236).

"National Socialism was one of those psychological mass phenomena, one of those outbreaks of the collective unconscious about which I had been speaking for nearly twenty years. The driving forces of a psychological mass movement are essentially archetypal. Every archetype contains the lowest and the highest, evil and good, and is therefore capable of producing diametrically opposite results. Hence it is impossible to make out at the start whether it will prove to be positive or negative. My medical attitude towards such things counselled me to wait, for it is an attitude that allows no hasty judgments, does not always know from the start what is better, and is willing to give things 'a fair trial.' Far from wishing to give the beleaguered consciousness its death-blow, it tries to strengthen its powers of resistance through insight, so that the evil that is hidden in every archetype shall not seize hold of the individual and drag him to destruction. The therapist's aim is to bring the positive, valuable, and living quality of the archetype—which will sooner or later be integrated into consciousness in any case—into reality, and at the same time to obstruct as far as possible its damaging and pernicious tendencies. It is part of the doctor's professional equipment to be able to summon up a certain amount of optimism even in the most unlikely circumstances, with a view to saving everything that it is still possible to save. He cannot afford to let himself be too much impressed by the real or apparent hopelessness of a situation, even if this means exposing himself to danger. Moreover, it should not be forgotten that Germany, up till the National Socialist era, was one of the most differentiated and highly civilized countries on earth, besides being, for us Swiss, a spiritual background to which we were bound by ties of blood, language, and friendship" (p. 237).

1948

The state of Israel is founded.

Jung writes a memorandum, "Techniques of Attitude Change Conducive to World Peace," in response to a request from UNESCO (CW 18: 606–613):
"Hitler's enormous psychological effect was based upon his highly ingenious method of playing on the well-known national inferiority complex of the Germans, of which he himself was the most outstanding example" (p. 607).

1949

Jung gives an interview in response to articles in the *Saturday Review of Literature* in which he is accused of being pro-Nazi and anti-Semitic (C. G. Jung Speaking, pp. 192–200):
"It must be clear to anyone who has read any of my books that I never have been a Nazi sympathizer and I never have been anti-Semitic, and no amount of misquotation, mistranslation, or rearrangement of what I have written can alter the record of my true point of view" (p. 193).
"During this fateful time the Nazis played double with my name. On the one hand, my name was placed on their blacklist on account of various things I had written which they could not swallow, as, for instance my lecture on the 'Theory of Complexes,' held in Bad Nauheim in May 1934, in which I paid tribute to Freud. Still later, my Swiss publisher received news that my books were banned and destroyed. On the other hand, the Nazis were only too pleased to publicize my name, as a Swiss feather in their caps, in an effort to prop their waning reputation in the eyes of the world. Many false and conflicting rumors were circulated about me: that I was anti-Semitic, that I was a Jew, that I was Hitler's doctor, etc., etc." (pp. 198–199).

1957

Jung to Edith Schroder, April [?] 1957:
". . . I must remark that many important things could be said about the theme you propose, 'The Significance of Freud's Jewish Descent for the Origin, Content, and Acceptance of Psychoanalysis,' if only the problem could be treated on a very high level. Racial theories and the like

would be a most unsatisfactory foundation, quite apart from the futility of such speculations. For a real understanding of the Jewish component in Freud's outlook a thorough knowledge would be needed of the specifically Jewish assumptions in regard to history, culture and religion. Since Freud calls for an extremely serious assessment on all these levels, one would have to take a deep plunge into the history of the Jewish mind. This would carry us beyond Jewish orthodoxy into the subterranean workings of Hasidism (e.g., the sects of Sabbatai Zwi), and then into the intricacies of the Kabbalah, which still remains unexplored psychologically. The Mediterranean man, to whom the Jews also belong, is not exclusively characterized and moulded by Christianity and the Kabbalah, but still carries within him a living heritage of paganism which could not be stamped out by the Christian Reformation.

"I had the privilege of knowing Freud personally and have realized that one must take all these facts into consideration in order to gain a real understanding of psychoanalysis in its Freudian form.

"I do not know how far you are acquainted with these various sources, but I can assure you that I myself could carry out such a task only in collaboration with a Jewish scholar since unfortunately I have no knowledge of Hebrew.

"In view of the blood-bespattered shadow that hangs over the so-called 'Aryan understanding of the Jew,' any assessment that fell below the level of these—as it may seem to you—high-falutin conditions would be nothing but a regrettable misunderstanding, especially on German soil.

"Despite the blatant misjudgment I have suffered at Freud's hands, I cannot fail to recognize, even in the teeth of my resentment, his significance as a cultural critic and psychological pioneer. A true assessment of Freud's achievement would take us far afield, into dark areas of the mind which concern not only the Jew but European man in general, and which I have sought to illuminate in my writings. Without Freud's 'psychoanalysis' I wouldn't have had a clue."

1961

Jung dies on June 5, 1961.

1963

Gershom Scholem to Aniela Jaffé, May 7, 1963:
"In the summer of 1947 Leo Baeck was in Jerusalem. I had then just

received for the first time an invitation to the Eranos meeting in Ascona, evidently at Jung's suggestion, and I asked Baeck whether I should accept it, as I had heard and read many protests about Jung's behavior in the Nazi period. Baeck said: 'You must go, absolutely!' and in the course of our conversation told me the following story. He too had been put off by Jung's reputation resulting from those well-known articles in the years 1933–34, precisely because he knew Jung very well from the Darmstadt meetings of the School of Wisdom and would never have credited him with any Nazi and anti-Semitic sentiments. When, after his release from Theresienstadt, he returned to Switzerland for the first time (I think it was 1946), he therefore did not call on Jung in Zurich. But it came to Jung's ears that he was in the city and Jung sent a message begging him to visit him, which he, Baeck, declined because of those happenings. Whereupon Jung came to his hotel and they had an extremely lively talk lasting two hours, during which Baeck reproached him with all the things he had heard. Jung defended himself by an appeal to the special conditions in Germany but at the same time confessed to him: 'Well, I slipped up'—probably referring to the Nazis and his expectation that something great might after all emerge. This remark, 'I slipped up,' which Baeck repeated to me several times, remains vividly in my memory. Baeck said that in this talk they cleared up everything that had come between them and that they parted from one another reconciled again. Because of this explanation of Baeck's I accepted the invitation to Eranos when it came a second time."

Appendix B

Bibliographic Survey

Jay Sherry

Freud's assertion in *On the History of the Psychoanalytic Movement* (Standard Edition, 14: 43) that Jung had given up "certain racial prejudices" when they undertook their collaboration is the starting point for the case of Jung's alleged anti-Semitism. The literature has taken many forms: letters to the editor, articles, comments made in passing, treatment in psychology books and biographies. The aim of this essay is to provide a chronological survey of the literature not discussed elsewhere in this book.

The first important period occurred in the 1930s after Jung had become president of the International General Medical Society for Psychotherapy. A Swiss psychiatrist, Dr. Gustav Bally, wrote an article for the *Neue Züricher Zeitung* on February 27, 1934, entitled "Deutschstämmige Psychotherapie?" in which he challenged Jung's participation in an organization with a large German membership that had embraced the Nazi ideology. Jung responded soon after in the same newspaper with a thorough defense of his actions. This response, "A Rejoiner to Dr. Bally" (CW 10, paras. 1016–34), is essential reading for anyone with an interest in this topic, as is Jung's "The State of Psychotherapy Today" (CW 10, paras. 333–370), the most widely quoted article regarding the controversy. The latter triggered a heavy correspondence and prompted responses from three of Jung's closest Jewish followers in *Judische Rundschau* (Berlin). In number 43 (May 29, 1934),

James Kirsch disagreed with Jung that Jews were nomads, suggesting rather that they were a restless people and that Jung had
mistaken a stereotypical image of the Jews for what is essential to
their identity. This view was countered by Erich Neumann in
number 48 (June 15, 1934), where he said that Jung's observations
about Jews would be as important as Zionism in their developing
a modern identity. In number 62 (August 15, 1934) Gerhard Adler
wrote that Jews "must find by way of the inner experience the
connection to the chain of ancestors. Jung has shown a way to do
that for all people, Jews and non-Jews; where he attacks the Jews
he does this insofar as they are negative and uprooted; is he anti-
Semitic for this reason?"

After the war the controversy broke out anew in the United
States, where there were intellectual scores to settle. The opening
shot was fired by Frederic Wertham in a book review in the *New
Republic* (December 4, 1944), where he wrote, "Jung has become
one of the most important influences on fascist philosophy in
Europe" (p. 774). The tempo picked up in the following year when
S. S. Feldman wrote a one-page critique of Jung in the *American
Journal of Psychiatry* (September 1945, p. 263) in which he
contrasted quotations from Jung's prewar and postwar writings to
convey a sense of Jung's opportunism.

In 1946 Jung's most vociferous critic appeared on the scene.
A. D. Parelhoff published a three-part article, "Dr. Carl G. Jung—
Nazi Collaborationist," in *The Protestant* (I: June-July, pp. 22–
28; II: August-September, pp. 26–31; III: February-March, 1947,
pp. 17–30). In what appears, even to critics of Jung, to be a
pathological diatribe with little or no factual support, Parelhoff
attributed to Jung every evil imaginable, including the accusation
that Jung had sought to establish Hitler as a seer and "had openly
allied himself with an already functioning organization of sadistic
degenerates and murderers" (I, p. 26). Parelhoff continued his
attacks into the 1950s. A letter to the *New Statesman* (London,
May 17, 1958) elicited a response from Gerhard Adler, who
questioned Parelhoff's sincerity and concluded, "There are many
Jews and refugees among us. . . . None of us has ever experienced
anything but friendship and active support—also against the Na-

zis—from Jung. To all of us the ill-founded presentation of Jung as anti-Semite and pro-Nazi is just utter ignorance or, worse, slander" (May 24, 1958, p. 667).

The charges against Jung were kept in the public eye for much of 1949 by two articles by Robert Hillyer in the *Saturday Review of Literature* (June 11 and 18). Their main focus was to condemn the awarding of the Bollingen Prize for Poetry to Ezra Pound, who had been arrested after the war for making profascist radio broadcasts and who was then being held at St. Elizabeth's Hospital, a federal institution for the insane). Jung's name was dragged in because the prize was named after his retreat home on Lake Zurich. Hillyer conjured up a grand conspiracy plot in which the committee represented a sinister clique bent on imposing a new cultural authoritarianism. Hillyer got most of his information from Parelhoff but recalled, "I had one personal contact with Dr. Jung's Nazism. At the luncheon during the Harvard Tercentary of 1936, Dr. Jung, who was seated beside me, deftly introduced the subject of Hitler, developed it with alert warmth, and concluded with the statement that from the high vantage point of Alpine Switzerland Hitler's new order in Germany seemed to offer the one hope of Europe" (June 11, p. 10). A solid discussion and critique of this affair can be found in William McGuire's *Bollingen* (Princeton University Press, 1982, pp. 208–216).

The July 30, 1949, issue of the *Saturday Review of Literature* contained a pair of articles about Jung, one supportive, by Philip Wylie, and the other critical, by Frederic Wertham. Ignoring Jung's positive accomplishments in helping Jewish analysts, Wertham wrote, "I am talking about the Fascism of Carl Gustav Jung. Nobody who knew the facts was surprised when, in 1933, after Hitler came to power, Jung took over the two important positions in psychotherapy. . . . But the Nazis had a difficult job of finding a psychotherapist or psychoanalyst with a big name. Everybody knew that only Jung would lend himself to such a step. For this act was a major political event in the cultural conquest of Central Europe by the Nazis. . . . [Jung] hoisted the swastika banner in a scientific field . . ." (p. 7).

Wertham continued his attack in the October 1949 issue of the

American Journal of Psychotherapy in an article entitled "The Road to Rapallo." Repeating many of his previous charges, he opined that "Bollingen has become the symbol of cultural fascism" (p. 587). This prompted a round of letters pro and con in the January and April 1950 issues. Jung himself responded to all this in an interview with Carol Baumann that first appeared in December 1949 and was later published in *C. G. Jung Speaking* (Princeton University Press, 1977, pp. 192–200).

By the 1960s the controversy was to be found less often in periodicals but was beginning to find itself in the secondary literature. Indicative of this shift was Edward Glover's *Freud or Jung?* (Cleveland: Meridian Books, 1963), much of which had appeared in *Horizon* (nos. 106, 107, and 111). His evaluation of Jung's views on politics (pp. 146–53) misinterprets Jung's analysis of Nazism as an endorsement of it. Alexander and Selesnick's *History of Psychiatry* (New York: Harper and Row) appeared in 1964 and unfortunately repeated the standard one-dimensional account of Jung's alleged anti-Semitism in its appendix B (pp. 407–409).

In conjunction with the centennial of Jung's birth in 1975, several biographies by close followers were released. Laurens van der Post's *Jung and the Story of Our Time* (New York: Pantheon Books) focused on the Wotanic forces in Germany that had attracted Jung's interest (pp. 22–25, 194–199): "Nonetheless, a vulgar mythological use of the personal story of Freud and Jung themselves continues and it is in the mythological abuse of the story of their relationship, I believe, that lies the real explanation of this continuation of the campaign against Jung for having been pro-Nazi and anti-Semitic" (p. 197). Van der Post recommended that people read Aniela Jaffé's article "C. G. Jung and National Socialism," which appears in her book *The Life and Work of C. G. Jung,* recently republished by Daimon Verlag; but this same article provoked a strong reaction from Marie-Louise von Franz in *C. G. Jung: His Myth in Our Time* (New York: Jung Foundation/ G. P. Putnam's Sons, 1975): "I knew Jung personally from 1933 until his death and I never perceived the slightest conscious or unconscious trace of any such [anti-Semitic] attitude. . . . Jung once confessed to Leo Baeck himself: 'I slipped up' (on the slippery ground of politics). Jaffé uses this occasion to speak of a 'shadow' of Jung's which, in her account, was mixed up in the matter. To me this seems to be an opinion taken from thin air" (p. 63).

The renaissance of occultism in the "new age" movements of the 1970s resulted in viewing this controversy from the point of view of Jung's affinity with romanticism and the occult. An article by S. Grossman in the *Journal of European Studies* 9 (1979, pp. 231–259) concludes by saying, "If Jung was interested in racial archetypes, he was even more interested in exploring the archetypes which were common to all of humanity . . . a broader view of Jung's relationship to National Socialism shows it to be the product of his racial supposition, of the romantic tendencies in his psychological theories, of his personal and professional conflict with Freud, and of his wariness of socialism" (pp. 255 and 256). In 1977 Dusty Sklar's *Gods and Beasts: The Nazis and the Occult* appeared (reissued as *The Nazis and the Occult* by the Dorset Press in 1989). She asserted that "the reigning attitudes in Germany expressed mystical affinities with which Jung was very much at home. . . . His high degree of tolerance for the 'shadow' side of human nature, a necessary complement to reason, may have caused him to cast the Nazis in a romantic light" (p. 139). Her one-sided account is marred with factual errors, including the misidentification of the General Medical Society for Psychotherapy as the "German Medical Society" (p. 135). A more focused investigation of the occult dimension based on solid historical research can be found in James Webb's *The Occult Establishment* (Richard Drew Publishing, Glasgow, 1981). He emphasized Jung's connection with Jacob Wilhelm Hauer, a German occultist who lectured at Eranos in the 1930s and who founded the German Faith Movement, about which Jung wrote in his Wotan article. Webb concluded by saying, "If his critics have falsely accused Jung of holding 'Nazi views,' this is at least partly because the Zurich psychologist talked in the language of contemporary illuminism, in whose alarming accents certain criminally eccentric politicians in Germany had also been thoroughly schooled" (p. 401).

In 1980, Walter Kaufmann's *Discovering the Mind*, volume 3:

Freud versus Adler and Jung (McGraw-Hill, New York), was posthumously published. It contains a trenchant critique of Jung as a person and as a theoretician and deserves careful reading. His analysis of Jung's statements about Jews and Nazi Germany is to be found in section 68 (pp. 387–394), where he asserts that "Jung's writings on [Jewish psychology] and, more generally, Jung's attacks on Freud are a wound that we cannot hush up if we want to understand Jung" (p. 393).

The publication of Aldo Carotenuto's *Secret Symmetry*, Morris West's *The World Is Made of Glass*, and D. M. Thomas's *The White Hotel* in the early 1980s led to a renewed public interest in the Freud-Jung relationship. Sabina Spielrein's emergence as a significant participant in the early psychoanalytic movement added a new dimension to this already complex relationship. In the *Voice Literary Supplement* of October 1982, Melvyn Hill used this triangle as the framework for another highly emotional attack on Jung. It is filled with unsubstantiated allegations, such as the claim that "Freud had told Jung that in order for them to work together, Jung would have to make enormous effort to overcome his racial prejudice" (p. 14). Hill reinforces the fantasy image of Jung created by his most extreme critics, who link him personally to Nazi death camps: "The Nazis, in other words, cured Jung of his paranoid transference onto Freud by giving him the chance to act it out. For Jung as for others, Nazism legitimated a relentless, unrelieved envy that led to a barbaric desire to destroy. In fact it was he and his Nazi friends who felt so weak and cowardly that they had to find defenseless victims on whom to prove their invincible strength" (p. 15).

A similarly off-the-mark attack is made in passing by Paul Johnson in *A History of the Jews* (Harper and Row, New York, 1987): "The 'scandal' of Freud and his teachings was an important collateral proof of the Nazi case, since (it was argued) they removed moral guilt from sexual promiscuity and so increased it. Thus Freud enabled Jews to gain greater access to Aryan women. Here, Jung was able to come to Hitler's assistance by drawing a distinction between Freudian-Jewish psychiatry and the rest" (pp. 473–474). Jeffrey Masson, who gained notoriety in Janet Malcolm's *In the Freud Archives,* published an extended critique of Jung in *Against Therapy* (Atheneum, New York, 1988, pp. 94–112). He concludes with this observation: "With its coercion and disdain for the real traumas that real people experience, there is a deep strain of fascism running through Jung's psychotherapy" (p. 111).

Just as controversy erupted when Jung's name was linked to Pound's in 1949, an article about Martin Heidegger's Nazi affiliation led to a renewed debate about Jung in 1988, in the *New York Times* letters to the editor (March 15, April 15, May 3, May 21, and June 11). What is so striking, and sad, is how little progress has been made over the past forty years in clarifying the facts and interpretations of this controversy. The heavy emotional investment over the years has made it resistant to any real resolution. The "Lingering Shadows" conference and this book have been an effort to change the tenor of this debate from accusation to investigation, and from denial to an acknowledgment of Jung's mistaken opinions. What emerges, in the end, is that Jung was all too human but far from the criminal that some have portrayed him as. His personal connection with numerous Jewish analysands and students leaves no doubt that many of the accusations leveled against him had no factual basis; yet even his most ardent admirers have come to understand that Jung, too, had a shadow side. What remains paramount is the need to separate Jung's personal shortcomings from his psychology and ideas. The time has come, even for his detractors, to separate the message from the messenger.

References

WORKS CITED

Alexander, Franz, and Sheldon Selesnick. *A History of Psychiatry*. New York: Harper and Row, 1964.

Bally, Gustav. "Deutschstämmige Psychotherapie?" *Neue Zürcher Zeitung*, 1934.

Bennet, E. A. *Meetings with Jung, 1946–61*. Zurich: Daimon Verlag, 1985.

Carotenuto, Aldo. *A Secret Symmetry: Sabina Spielrein between Jung and Freud*. Translated by Arno Pomerans, John Shepley, and Krishna Winston. New York: Pantheon Books, 1982.

Cocks, Geoffrey. *Psychotherapy in the Third Reich: The Göring Institute*. Oxford & New York: Oxford University Press, 1985.

Dalal, Farhad. "Jung: A Racist." *British Journal of Psychotherapy* 4, no. 3 (1988).

Feldman, S. S. "Dr. C. G. Jung and National Socialism." *American Journal of Psychiatry*, September 1945, p. 263.

Freud, Sigmund. *On the History of the Psychoanalytic Movement*. Standard Edition 14.

———. *The Standard Edition of the Complete Psychological Works of Sigmund Freud*. Edited and translated by James Strachey. 24 vols. London: Hogarth, 1957.

Freud, Sigmund, and Karl Abraham. *A Psycho-Analytic Dialogue: The Letters of Sigmund Freud and Karl Abraham, 1907–1926*. New York: Basic Books, 1965.

Freud, Sigmund, and C. G. Jung. *The Freud/Jung Letters*. Edited by W. McGuire. Princeton: Princeton University Press, 1974; London: Routledge and Kegan Paul, 1976.

Giegerich, Wolfgang. "Postscript to Cocks." *Spring*, 1979.

Glover, Edward. *Freud or Jung?* Cleveland: Meridian Books, 1963.

Groesbeck, J. "A Jungian Answer to: 'Yaweh as Freud.'" *American Imago.* Fall 1982.

Grossman, S. "C. G. Jung and National Socialism." *Journal of European Studies* 9 (1979): 231–259.

Hannah, Barbara. *Jung, His Life and Work: A Biographical Memoir.* New York: G. P. Putnam's Sons, 1976. Boston: Shambhala Publications, 1991.

Harms, Ernest. "Carl Gustav Jung—Defender of Freud and the Jews." *Psychiatric Quarterly,* April 1946, pp. 1–32.

Haymond, Robert. "On Carl Gustav Jung: Psycho-social Basis of Morality during the Nazi Era." *Journal of Psychology and Judaism* 6, no. 2 (Spring/Summer 1982).

Hill, Melvyn. "Women, Jews, and Madness." *Voice Literary Supplement,* October 11, 1982.

Jaffé, Aniela. "C. G. Jung and National Socialism." In *From the Life and Work of C. G. Jung.* Translated by R. F. C. Hull and Murray Stein. Einsiedeln, Switzerland: Daimon Verlag, 1989. Also in *Jung's Last Years and Other Essays.* Dallas: Spring Publications, 1984.

Jung, C. G. "After the Catastrophe." *CW* 10.

———. "Answer to Job." *CW* 11.

———. "The Archetypes and the Collective Unconscious." *CW* 9.

———. *C. G. Jung: Letters.* Edited by Gerhard Adler and Aniela Jaffé. 2 vols. Princeton: Princeton University Press, 1973.

———. *C. G. Jung Speaking.* Edited by W. McGuire & R. F. C. Hull. Princeton, N.J.: Princeton University Press, 1977; London: Picador, 1980.

———. *The Collected Works of C. G. Jung,* 20 vols. Bollingen Series No. 20. Princeton: Princeton University Press, 1953–1979.

———. "Epilogue to 'Essays on Contemporary Events.'" *CW* 10.

———. *Essays on Contemporary Events: Reflections on Nazi Germany.* Princeton: Princeton University Press, 1989; London: Routledge, 1989.

———. "Memorandum for UNESCO (1947/48)." *CW* 18.

———. *Memories, Dreams, Reflections.* Edited by Aniela Jaffé and translated by Richard and Clara Winston. New York: Vintage Books, 1965.

———. "Mysterium Coniunctionis" *CW* 14.

———. "Psychological Types." *CW* 6.

———. "Psychology and Religion: West and East" *CW* 11.

———. "A Rejoinder to Dr. Bally." *CW* 10.

———. "The Role of the Unconscious." *CW* 10.

———. "The State of Psychotherapy Today." *CW* 10.

———. "Two Essays in Analytical Psychology." *CW* 7.

———. "Wotan." *CW* 10.

Kirsch, James. "C. G. Jung and the Jews: The Real Story." *Journal of Psychology and Judaism* 6, no. 2 (Spring/Summer 1982).

———. "Jung's Transference on Freud: The Jewish Element." *American Imago* 41, no. 1 (Spring 1984).

———. "Reconsidering Jung's So-Called Anti-Semitism." In Estelle Weinreid et al., eds., *Arms of the Windmill: Essays in Analytical Psychology in Honor of Werner H. Engel.* Baltimore: Lucas, 1983.

Masson, Jeffrey Moussaieff. *Against Therapy.* New York: Atheneum, 1988; London: Collins, 1989.

Parelhoff, A. D. "Dr. C. G. Jung—Nazi Collaborationist." *The Protestant* I (June/July 1946); II (August/September 1946); III (February/March 1947).

Roazen, Paul. *Freud and His Followers.* New York: New York University Press, 1985.

Samuels, Andrew. "Comment on 'Jung: A Racist' by Dalal." *British Journal of Psychotherapy* 4, no. 3 (1988).

Sherry, Jay. "Jung, the Jews, and Hitler." *Spring,* 1986.

Sklar, Dusty. *The Nazis and the Occult.* New York: Dorset Press, 1989.

Slochower, Harry. "Freud as Yaweh in Jung's *Answer to Job.*" *American Imago.* Spring 1981.

van der Post, Laurens. *Jung and the Story of Our Time.* New York: Pantheon Books, 1975.

Webb, James, *The Occult Establishment.* Glasgow: Richard Drew Publishing, 1981.

OTHER SIGNIFICANT WORKS

Bakan, David. *Sigmund Freud and the Jewish Mystical Tradition.* Princeton: Van Nostrand, 1958.

Cocks, Geoffrey. "C. G. Jung and German Psychotherapy, 1933–1940: A Research Note." *Spring,* 1979.

Diamond, Stanley. "Jung contra Freud: What It Means to Be Funny." In Karin Barnaby and Pellegrino D'Acierno, eds., *C. G. Jung and the Humanities: Toward a Hermeneutics of Culture.* Princeton, N.J.: Princeton University Press, 1990, pp. 67–75.

Jones, Ernest. "The Psychology of the Jewish Question." *Miscellaneous Essays,* vol. 1. London: Hogarth, 1951.

Klein, Dennis B. *Jewish Origins of the Psychoanalytic Movement.* New York: Praeger, 1981.

Lowenstein, Rudolph M. *Christians and Jews: A Psychoanalytic Study.* New York: International Universities Press, 1952.

Robert, Marthe. *From Oedipus to Moses: Freud's Jewish Identity.* Translated by Ralph Manheim. Garden City, N.J.: Anchor, 1976.

Wylie, Philip, and Frederic Wertham. "What about Dr. Jung?" *Saturday Review,* July 30, 1949.

Credits

The editors thank the following publishers for permission to reprint material copyrighted or controlled by them.

Human Sciences Press for "Carl Gustav Jung—Defender of Freud and the Jews" by Ernest Harms from *Psychiatric Quarterly*, April 1946, and for "Carl Gustav Jung and the Jews: The Real Story" by James Kirsch from the *Journal of Psychology and Judaism* 6, no. 2 (Spring-Summer 1982).

Princeton University Press and Routledge for excerpts from the *Collected Works of C. G. Jung*, trans. R. F. C. Hull, Bollingen Series XX: vol. 7, *Two Essays on Analytical Psychology*, copyright 1953, 1966 by Princeton University Press; vol. 10, *Civilization in Transition*, copyright 1964, 1970 by Princeton University Press; vol. 18, *The Symbolic Life*, copyright 1950, 1953, 1955, 1958, 1959, 1963, 1968, 1969, 1970, 1973, 1976 by Princeton University Press; and for excerpts from *C. G. Jung Speaking: Interviews and Encounters*, ed. William McGuire and R. F. C. Hull, Bollingen Series XCVII, copyright 1977 by Princeton University Press. Reprinted by permission of Princeton University Press and Routledge.

Alfred A. Knopf, Inc., for excerpts from *Moses and Monotheism* by Sigmund Freud, translated by Katherine Jones, copyright 1939 by Alfred A. Knopf, Inc., and renewed 1967 by Ernst L. Freud and Anna Freud. Reprinted by permission of the publisher.

Pantheon Books, Inc., and HarperCollins Publishers for excerpts from *Memories, Dreams, Reflections* by C. G. Jung, recorded and edited by Aniela Jaffé, translated by Richard and Clara Winston, translation copyright 1961, 1962, 1963 by Random House, Inc. Reprinted by permission of Pantheon Books, a division of Random House, Inc., and of HarperCollins Publishers Limited.

Jason Aronson, Inc., and Mark Paterson and Associates for excerpts